D0986818

THE OPERAS OF
CHARLES GOUNOD

THE OPERAS OF

Charles Gounod

STEVEN HUEBNER

Clarendon Press · Oxford

1990

Oxford University Press, Walton Street, Oxford OX2 6DP

Oxford New York Toronto
Delhi Bombay Calcutta Madras Karachi
Petaling Jaya Singapore Hong Kong Tokyo
Nairobi Dar es Salaam Cape Town
Melbourne Auckland
and associated companies in
Berlin Ibadan

Oxford is a trade mark of Oxford University Press

Published in the United States
by Oxford University Press, New York

British Library Cataloguing in Publication Data
Huebner, Steven
The operas of Charles Gounod.
1. Opera in French. Gounod, Charles, 1818–1893
I. Title
782.1'092'4
ISBN 0–19–315329–7

Library of Congress Cataloging in Publication Data
Huebner, Steven.
The operas of Charles Gounod/Steven Huebner.
Includes bibliographical references.
1. Gounod, Charles, 1818–1893. Operas.
2. Opera—France—19th century. I. Title.
ML410.G7H8   1990
782.1'092—dc20   89–35988   CIP MN
ISBN 0–19–315329–7

Typeset by Pentacor Limited,
High Wycombe, Bucks
Printed in Great Britain by
St Edmundsbury Press, Bury St. Edmunds, Suffolk

In memory of my father
Eric Paul Günther Huebner (1922–86)

PREFACE

'GOUNOD's work is spoken of by some with the familiarity which is often the precursor of contempt,' wrote the critic Arthur Hervey in 1903. It is something of an understatement to suggest that the pendulum has not reversed course since that observation was made. *Faust* and *Roméo et Juliette* still hold the stage internationally but have ceased to occupy the leading position in the repertoire they once had. *Mireille* and *Philémon et Baucis* are heard far less frequently in France today than they were one hundred years ago. Several of Gounod's less successful operas have never been honoured with respectful revivals, even as curiosities. Nor has Gounod benefited from the post-war efflorescence of musical scholarship. The few biographies that have appeared have mainly recycled old information rather than exposed new material. His cause has also not been helped by the fact that his immediate musical progeny, figures such as Massenet and Delibes, have fared poorly in the hands of musicologists. Many musicians and scholars alike see Gounod only as the composer of a certain maudlin counterpoint to a Well-tempered Clavier prelude, of a movement from a mass exhaling (in Ernest Newman's words) 'catholicisme sucré', or of tunes from *Faust*— perhaps the Soldiers' Chorus now become banal, or the Jewel Song, Gretchen scandalously trivialized.

This book does not make extravagant claims that Gounod should be restored to the pantheon of first-rate opera composers or that most of his operatic failures at the box-office by and large deserve a fate better than that which they received. But it does seek gently to nudge the pendulum in the other direction. The critic cannot ignore the sheer musico-dramatic effectiveness of certain scenes in *Faust* or the comic verve of *Le Médecin malgré lui*. The historian must acknowledge the prodigious number of performances that some of Gounod's works have received and the host of French composers who alluded to his importance in the evolution of French music. With good reason Maurice Ravel remarked in 1922 that 'both Fauré and Chabrier . . . used the work of this master as a point of departure. At their sides, Bizet, Lalo, Saint-Saëns, Massenet, followed by Claude Debussy, participated in varying degrees in the salubrious influence of the composer of *Mireille*.' Any attempt to understand Gounod's influence as an opera composer must be preceded by a study of the works themselves against their biographical, genetic, and musical backgrounds; the three parts of this study address each of these issues in succession. The book as a whole not only attempts a critical understanding of the success of *Faust* and

Roméo et Juliette, but also seeks to come to grips with the often no-less-stimulating question of why so many of Gounod's works for the stage never achieved popularity.

My thanks for assistance in the realization of this project go to the staff of the Bibliothèque de l'Opéra and the Département de la Musique of the Bibliothèque Nationale for responding to many unusual requests, to my friend and colleague Professor William Caplin for a critical reading of portions of the typescript, to Kathy McKinley for the preparation of the musical examples, to the Faculty of Graduate Studies and Research of McGill University for two timely grants that helped underwrite research costs, to the personnel of Oxford University Press for invaluable editorial input, and, in a larger sense, to the dedicatee of this book for having taught me by example the value of perseverance with good humour.

S. H.

McGill University
Montreal, Canada
December 1989

CONTENTS

LIST OF PLATES

Between pages 150 and 151

Introduction: Gounod's Operatic World

ON 2 December 1851, less than eight months after the operatic début of a relatively unknown composer named Charles François Gounod, President Louis Napoleon staged a *coup d'état* in which he overturned the elected National Assembly of the Second Republic and greatly enhanced the power of his office. The symbolism surrounding the date was lost to none—2 December was the anniversary of the First Napoleon's coronation in 1804—and, just as his great forebear had argued for consolidation of the gains of 1789 through the creation of an empire, so too did Louis Napoleon hold high the torch of 1848. A rekindling of the Bonaparte mystique brought massive popular support in a referendum to ratify Louis Napoleon's initiative. Promulgation of a new constitution, that of the Second Empire, did not follow far behind.

The new imperial regime fared poorly in the hands of historians for many decades after its fall in 1870. Louis Napoleon was no friend of republicans, and, not surprisingly, the indictments rendered against him even before the Second Empire—Adolphe Thiers's 'C'est un crétin' and Victor Hugo's 'Napoléon le petit' are among the more notorious—proved remarkably adhesive among writers of the subsequent Third Republic. Attacks upon the Empire's amalgam of dictatorial rule and phantom democracy, its rigid censorship, and its promotion of socially and intellectually undistinguished individuals figured prominently in later assessments, as did the Emperor's own lack of a traditional humanistic education and even his voracious sexual appetite. Echoes of this historiographical tradition seem to resonate among the general music-loving public today: the composer most readily associated with the Second Empire is not a purveyor of high art such as Gounod, Berlioz, or Bizet, but a master of parody and a veritable court jester, Jacques Offenbach.[1] The great success of *opéras bouffes* such as *Orphée aux enfers* and *La Belle Hélène* in their day was founded in good measure upon gibes at the contemporary social and political order, and that spirit of satire has also proven infectious among later generations.

Revisionist histories produced in recent decades have put Louis

---

[1] The characterization of Offenbach as 'court jester' comes from Alexander Faris, *Jacques Offenbach* (New York, 1981), 140; the author defends the position that Offenbach and his librettists were not critics of the regime bent on sowing the seeds of revolution among their audiences.

Napoleon and the Second Empire in a much more favourable light. The place of the libertine and inarticulate schemer has been taken by a genuinely kind-hearted individual and consummate politician who skilfully fostered an environment favourable to economic modernization. Innovations in the French banking system made available millions of francs from small investors to fund the growth of heavy industry and railways. Newly available capital also financed urban development projects, the most elaborate of which naturally took place in Paris. Long before he assumed the throne, Louis Napoleon had dreamed of making Paris the most resplendent jewel in an imperial crown, and shortly after becoming Emperor he set the Prefect of the city, Baron Georges Haussmann, to the task. Construction proceeded at a frantic pace: old neighbourhoods were levelled before the unfurling of boulevards, a vast innovative sewer system introduced an unprecedented level of hygiene to the city, and building consortia erected elegant restaurants, cafés, department stores, and apartment houses along the new thoroughfares. Fed by a growing network of railway lines and by a burgeoning leisure industry, as well as by the prestige attendant upon international exhibitions in 1855 and 1867, a refurbished Paris played host to more tourists from the provinces and abroad than ever before in its history. Offenbach's music may again be invoked in this more positive picture of the Second Empire: it contributed in no small part to a rapidly growing aura of *gaieté*, and to an image of Paris as the capital of mirth and pleasure, one that has persisted to this day in the popular imagination.

Of course, musically speaking, Louis Napoleon's Empire was not all Offenbach. Emerging from the smoke on the train platform among dozens of other tourists at the beginning of Offenbach's own *La Vie parisienne*, the Swedish Baroness de Grondremarck declares her intention to hear the great Adelina Patti in *Don Pasquale*. In this she was like most distinguished foreign visitors to the capital, who were drawn above all to the Théâtre-Italien and the Opéra. Italian opera performed in its original language was something of a cultural common denominator among upper classes in all corners of Europe (an English correspondent to the *Illustrated London News* remarked about one evening at the Théâtre-Italien that 'the hall presented the appearance of a congress of all nations: English, Spanish, Russian, and even Turkish were to be heard on all sides'),[2] and such was the Opéra's reputation for scenic extravagance that a performance there could not be missed. If those two houses were sold out, boxes might be had at the Opéra-Comique, Théâtre-Lyrique, and, after 1855, at Offenbach's Bouffes-Parisiens. In short, there were five lyric theatre companies in a city with a

---

[2] 'Foreign and Colonial News', *Illustrated London News*, 18 Oct. 1851.

population that fell slightly shy of two million by the end of the Second Empire. This is not to mention the indirect competition for opera from dozens of establishments that presented spoken drama. With artists' fees on the rise and a well-established tradition among some theatres for one-upmanship in stage paraphernalia, the stakes for impresarios were high. Small wonder that the editor of *Le Figaro* noted in 1854 that 'the theatre business today is febrile and mad: unbridled competition has pushed that industry along the dangerous path where even success can no longer assure a fortune and failure brings certain ruin'.[3] Each lyric theatre tried to carve out its own territory.

Contemporary testimony suggests consistently that the Théâtre-Italien was frequented by a more devoted and musically sophisticated clientele than the other houses. We have it on the word of the novelist Frédéric Soulié, for example, that, whereas the Opéra merely appealed to taste and fashion, the Théâtre-Italien was a real 'need and passion'.[4] Though it was also perennially the most expensive house to attend, it spent comparatively little on décor; according to our English correspondent, 'the French Opéra speaks to two senses, that of hearing and that of sight, while the Italian opera addresses itself only to that of hearing'.[5] Despite this limitation, the Théâtre-Italien did not enjoy greater financial stability than the other opera houses, in part because it received a much smaller annual subsidy from the government than the Opéra and the Opéra-Comique. The apogee of its success as a business and artistic enterprise actually occurred before our period, in the 1820s and 1830s; immediately after the 1848 revolution a Republican government hostile to the elitist character of the house (and cognizant of the fact that there was no political gain to be had from the type of work performed there) withdrew the theatre's subsidy, several stars on the roster declined to renew their contracts, and the directorship of the company passed through several hands within two years. (The subsidy was reinstated at the beginning of the Second Empire only to be withdrawn again in 1863.) The company never completely regained its former balance and in 1855 the critic Bénédict Jouvin even pronounced the verdict that 'the Théâtre-Italien in France is dying of old-age'.[6] His voice was far from isolated among those who nostalgically remembered the glory days of Rossini and evenings when the stage was graced with the presence of Garcia, Pellegrini, Malibran, Rubini, Tamburini, and Lablache. That the administration of the theatre during the Second Empire had a falling out with Verdi certainly did not help matters.

[3] Auguste Villenot, 'Chronique parisienne', *Le Figaro*, 2 Apr. 1854.
[4] Frédéric Soulié, *Deux séjours: Province et Paris* (Brussels, 1836), 225.
[5] 'Foreign and Colonial News', *Illustrated London News*, 3 Dec. 1853.
[6] 'Le Théâtre-Italien', *Le Figaro*, 16 Sept. 1855.

Angered because he had not received expected performance royalties from the Théâtre-Italien, the Italian composer petitioned French courts in 1856 to prevent Parisian performances of *Rigoletto*, *La traviata*, and *Il trovatore*.[7] His legal manœuvrings were unsuccessful, but Verdi soon did strike a blow to the Théâtre-Italien by contracting with the Opéra for a French language production of *Il trovatore*, a work which up to that time had done well at the Théâtre-Italien. Moreover, with relaxation of theatre monopolies in the 1860s, the Théâtre-Lyrique began regularly to pillage the stock of the Théâtre-Italien. None the less, Jouvin's remark was premature. The Théâtre-Italien survived in one form or another until 1913, continuing to provide a meeting-ground for foreigners and a venue for French composers to maintain direct contact with developments south of the Alps.

By far the most conspicuous of the companies in Second Empire Paris was the Opéra, and this despite a most inconspicuous location on a small side street, the rue Le Peletier, instead of its current position as a nexus for Haussmann's major boulevards. Its visibility was conditioned by historical and political circumstances: the Opéra was the oldest operatic institution in the country, with an unbroken line of performances stretching back to 1673, and over the years was mandated more-or-less explicitly to fulfil a role as a reflector for French *grandeur* and *savoir-faire*. To this end it received far larger government subsidies than other opera houses, during the Second Empire almost four times the amount apportioned to the Opéra-Comique and eight times that given to the Théâtre-Italien and Théâtre-Lyrique. There can be no doubt that the artistic directorship of the Opéra planned the repertoire with some cognizance of the company's official function. The Second Empire was a particularly sensitive time, since Louis Napoleon was perceived by the aristocratic establishment in France and abroad as an upstart—the Russian Tsar, for example, preferred to acknowledge him as 'mon ami' rather than as 'mon frère'[8]—and his court as somewhat short on the elegance befitting a French monarch. The Opéra could contribute much-needed prestige to the regime, not only by upholding a tradition of elaborate productions but also by introducing influential new works. Yet there was also the balance sheet to consider, since, despite subsidies, over half of the company's revenue was derived from subscriptions and ticket sales. The dictates of profit and artistic leadership did not always make comfortable bedfellows, and the record of reconciling the two during the Empire was distinctly inferior to that of the previous twenty years.

[7] Frank Walker, *The Man Verdi* (London, 1962), 281.
[8] Jasper Ridley, *Napoléon III and Eugénie* (New York, 1979), 357.

Impulse for artistic innovation at the Opéra faced major obstacles—from the Press, from audiences, from individuals within the company itself. Of course composers faced similar hurdles at other Parisian houses, but production problems seem almost invariably to have been greatly magnified at the Opéra. Its personnel could be particularly fractious and unwilling to submit to the instructions of a composer or, for that matter, even of a director. Writing to Camille Du Locle in 1869, two years after the failure of *Don Carlos* at that house, Verdi complained about the division of the company into individual fiefdoms, with each defending its own territory to the detriment of an organic, unified operatic whole.[9] The significant grand opera successes of the past were merely 'mosaics' in which 'patchwork and adjustments' were felt at all times. There was an overabundance of opinions at the Opéra; everyone had something to say: 'in the foyer [rehearsal area] of the Opéra after four chords they whisper all over the place 'Olà, ce n'est pas bon . . . c'est commun . . . ce n'est pas de bon goût . . . ça n'ira pas à Paris!' The *mise-en-scène* department, the *corp de ballet*, the singers, the conductor, the orchestra players, all extracted their dues from the composer and librettist, including a figure such as Verdi, who customarily exercised great authority in productions of his work. Even then success could not be taken for granted: lack of complete co-operation from some members of the roster contributed to the sinking of *Don Carlos*.[10] As may well be guessed, the Opéra's constituent branches were motivated more often by short-sighted vainglory combined with adherence to tradition and personal assessment of what was suitable for France's *première scène lyrique* than by a willingness to embrace the new and untried.

The critical Press was vociferous and enormous—during the Second Empire there were between twenty and twenty-five newspapers in Paris that regularly featured music reviews. The Opéra drew far more attention than other houses. Like members of the company itself, many reviewers formed very definite ideas about how the *première scène lyrique* should be run and what it should produce. For example, *Don Carlos* was attacked by some in the Press who felt that, as a matter of national pride, it was inappropriate for the Opéra to mount a work of a foreigner during the Exhibition of 1867.[11] In an era of strict Press censorship, the political opposition could also engage in indirect

[9] Letter of 8 Dec. 1869, in Hans Busch, *Verdi's Aida: The History of the Opera in Letters and Documents* (Minneapolis, 1978), 4–5.
[10] U. Günther, 'La Genèse de Don Carlos de Giuseppe Verdi', *Revue de musicologie*, 60 (1974), 156–7.
[11] Geneviève Chinn, 'The Académie Impériale de Musique: A Study of its Administration and Repertory from 1862 to 1870', Ph.D. thesis (Columbia, 1969), fo. 123.

needling of the regime by finding fault with one of its most visible institutions. Wagner's *Tannhäuser* proved to be an especially inviting target, since the decree to stage it came directly from the Emperor in 1860. It was attacked by papers on both the political Left and Right— the latter was plentifully represented at performances by members of the infamous Jockey Club, toting whistles to disrupt the performances— and the ensuing withdrawal of the work after only three evenings in March 1861 remains one of the most celebrated fiascos in operatic history.[12] A new opera also faced evaluation on purely aesthetic criteria. Many in the critical establishment drew these largely from the grand operas of Meyerbeer: *Robert le diable* (1831), *Les Huguenots* (1836), *Le Prophète* (1849), and the posthumous *L'Africaine* (1865) were considered by many to combine the epitome of 'ampleur de style' and 'science' with accessibility. 'The works of Meyerbeer are in no way inferior to those of Robert Schumann and Richard Wagner,' wrote the critic Caignard in 1864; 'they even have a certain advantage because they are better understood by the public and give it more pleasure.'[13] Such a critical position was taken as seriously during the Second Empire as it is readily dismissed today. Quite clearly any progressive musical language faced an uphill struggle at the Opéra: whereas Meyerbeer stood near the forefront of operatic innovation during the Orléanist regime, he was a fundamentally conservative figure during the Second Empire.

But principle could easily give way to other considerations in music criticism of the period. Extramusical matters such as business interests, ties of friendship, and outright bribes played an important role in shaping the character of many articles. Since he was Verdi's principal French agent, the publisher Escudier could be expected to run a highly favourable review of *Don Carlos* in *La France musicale*, the weekly paper put out by his firm, and a highly disparaging one of the chief competition for that opera during its first run, Gounod's *Roméo et Juliette* at the Théâtre-Lyrique. Berlioz privately dismissed the music of Gounod's *La Reine de Saba* after it was premièred at the Opéra in 1862, but dwelt almost exclusively on its redeeming features in his published review, largely because, one may suppose, Gounod was his friend. Meyerbeer seems regularly to have bought the support of certain journalists.[14] The historian Theodore Zeldin has pointed out that the

[12] For an account that assesses the political implications of the *Tannhäuser* production, see Jane Fulcher, *The Nation's Image: French Grand Opera as Politics and Politicized Art* (Cambridge, 1987), 189–95.

[13] 'Chronique musicale', *Le Courrier artistique*, 13 Mar. 1864, cited by Marie-Hélène Coudroy, 'La Critique parisienne et le Grand Opéra Meyerbeerien', *Revue internationale de la musique française*, 17 (1985), 40.

[14] Heinz Becker, 'Meyerbeer', *The New Grove*, xii. 253.

Chronique des théâtres and *Nouvelles* sections in the various newspapers were not independent gossip columns, but were usually paid for by theatres or individuals.[15] Furthermore, he documents that ostensibly objective reporting in articles was often, in fact, subsidized by an interested party, and that a sizeable percentage of the news content of a newspaper was really hidden advertising. Villemessant, the editor of *Le Figaro* during the Second Empire, was said by contemporaries to have been satisfied only when every line of an issue had been paid for. The extent to which this went on in music criticism has yet to be assessed. While some contemporary opinions about composers such as Verdi, Wagner, and Gounod will not lose interest as sources of information about musical attitudes and prejudices, other evaluations risk being unmasked as camouflage for motives unconnected to aesthetic positions.

The audience at the Opéra was just as distinguished as that which attended the Théâtre-Italien. Louis Véron boasted in his *Mémoires d'un bourgeois de Paris* of having opened the doors of the Opéra to the bourgeoisie during his tenure as director from 1831 to 1835. That was certainly true, but the corollary implied by Véron—that the aristocracy abandoned the house following a bourgeois onslaught—is not: analysis of contemporary administrative documents from the 1830s as well as from the 1860s shows that one-third of the subscribers were titled.[16] Aristocratic families were not repelled by sitting in boxes adjacent to those occupied by opera-goers who were not ennobled, and the presence of many titled subscribers supplied an atmosphere of prestige that proved alluring to members of the *haute bourgeoisie*. Two threads—the *embourgeoisement* of the aristocracy and the 'aristocratization' of the *haute bourgeoisie*—were inexorably intertwined in nineteenth-century France—indeed historians have come to speak of a country managed by an 'alliance of élites'[17]—and the Opéra was one of the many forums where the two social classes mingled freely. Attendance at the Opéra was even more of a social act than it is today: during Second Empire performances darkness did not descend upon the audience to cover those assembled in a veil of egalitarian anonymity in the face of Art.

The number of names registered on annual subscription lists in this period never exceeds 250, a seemingly small figure when one considers that the house had a capacity of more than 1,700. Many subscribers, however, rented complete boxes, and the most costly ones at that; as a

---

[15] Theodore Zeldin, *France 1848–1945: Taste and Corruption* (Oxford, 1980), 163 ff.
[16] Steven Huebner, 'Opera Audiences in Paris, 1830–1870', *Music and Letters*, 70 (1989) 208.
[17] Among the most influential exponents of this view is René Rémond in *Les Droites en France* (3rd edn. Paris, 1982).

result, between 30 per cent and 40 per cent of the annual revenue of the Opéra during the Second Empire came from subscriptions. Though few in number, the *abonnés* were a powerful lot, who regularly made their views known to the administration about operatic matters and even expected certain favours such as the privilege of attending dress rehearsals. Another of the perquisites attached to the more expensive subscriptions was unhindered access to the backstage area during rehearsals and performances. The *foyer de danse* was a popular destination among male *abonnés* and it was not uncommon for many of the pretty young ballerinas to have important protectors.[18] The secretary to Alphonse Royer, director from 1856 to 1862, noted in his memoirs that this emboldened some performers in their relationship with the administration, thereby exacerbating the centrifugal tendencies noted by Verdi: dissatisfied with the role assigned to her, a member of the ballet chorus is said to have responded on one occasion to her dance master, 'I am here because of the will of M. *** and if my salary is only 4,000 francs it is because I have been discreet; but I will only perform in works that please me and when it pleases me.'[19] An excessive number of people wandering through the backstage area during intermissions could also seriously impede the course of a production; in 1859 Achille Fould, the minister under whose jurisdiction the Opéra then fell, advised Royer to reduce the number of *abonnés* with backstage passes in order to accelerate set changes.[20] From a composer's point of view there was more than audience comfort at stake: long intermissions often had a direct effect on the music itself, for, if the evening were too long, scissors were almost inevitably applied to the score.

The catalogue of inefficiencies at the Opéra may be extended still further. Whereas at the Théâtre-Lyrique in this period conductors worked from a full score, at the Opéra until the mid-1860s they continued to direct from a short score called the 'violon principal'.[21] (A full score was produced by the Opéra's copy department for each work, but only after the première and merely for archival purposes.) Berlioz once noted that the use of such short scores imposed 'an unnecessary effort of memory upon the conductor',[22] and they surely rendered rehearsals more laborious than they need have been. The *corps de ballet*

---

[18] Nestor Roqueplan, *Regain: La Vie parisienne* (Paris, 1853), 86.

[19] Nérée Desarbres, *Sept ans à l'Opéra* (Paris, 1864), 37.

[20] Letter from Fould to Royer, 10 Jan. 1859, Archives Nationales (henceforth AN) AJ[13] 451.

[21] The main proof for this assertion comes from the fact that only the full scores produced by Opéra copyists after 1865 show signs of performance use in the form of conductor's cues. To judge from Gounod's extant operatic manuscripts, conductors at the Théâtre-Lyrique used the composer's autograph for early performances.

[22] Hector Berlioz, *Le Chef d'orchestre: Théorie de son art* (Paris, 1856), 37.

rehearsed not to a piano reduction of the composer's score but rather to, in Gounod's words, 'a monstrous reduction for two violins'.[23]

At an entirely different level, the very relationship of the Opéra with the government was especially cumbersome during much of the Empire. In 1854 the house reverted back to direct state control after nearly a quarter of a century of management by a private entrepreneur; only under government administration, it was reasoned in a report commissioned that year by the Emperor, could the Opéra maintain sufficiently high artistic standards and offer a varied repertoire including more revivals of masterpieces from the past.[24] The *directeur-entrepreneur* of the Opéra became a mere state functionary with an annual salary of 25,000 francs. Practically speaking, this reorganization made administration of the house extremely unwieldy. No decision taken by the director was immune from discussion in the forum of the *Commission supérieure* set up to oversee the Opéra, nor from scrutiny by the responsible minister, first Achille Fould, succeeded, in 1860, by an illegitimate son of the First Napoleon, Count Walewski. These ministers followed the operations down to the most picayune level, complaining when they were not consulted about the scheduling of operas or singers and penning angry memoranda about minor mishaps on stage during performances. But the new administrative apparatus did not produce the anticipated major artistic and commercial successes, and Emile Perrin, director from 1862 to 1870, was reinstated as a *directeur-entrepreneur* in 1866, a decision also consonant with the policies of *laissez-faire* economic liberalism during the late Second Empire. The government continued to pour ever larger annual subsidies into the house. As a result, though day-to-day operations could be conducted without bureaucratic meddling, Perrin was still accountable to a government committee. Moreover, the office of the censor usually furnished its own share of directives after a libretto had been submitted to it for approval during the month before a première performance.

In a letter of 27 September 1854 to director Roqueplan, Achille Fould noted with obvious annoyance that the Opéra relied heavily upon a rotation of 'only five or six' works.[25] That was a slight underestimation: at the time he wrote, the core repertoire actually consisted of eight works—the first three Meyerbeer grand operas, Halévy's *La Juive*, Donizetti's *La Favorite* and *Lucie de Lammermoor*, Auber's *La Muette de Portici*, and Rossini's *Guillaume Tell* (in a grossly emasculated

[23] Letter to Bizet, n.d. [1862], in Arthur Pougin, 'Gounod écrivain', *Rivista musicale italiana*, 19 (1912), 643–4.
[24] Jean Gourret, *Ces hommes qui ont fait l'Opéra* (Paris, 1984), 133–4; and 'Rapport de la Commission chargée d'examiner la situation de l'Opéra', *Le Moniteur universel*, 2 July 1854.
[25] AN AJ[13] 451.

version). The first six were the principal successes of the Orléanist regime, the last two date from the final years of the Restoration. All had achieved 'classical' status by the Second Empire. In short, new works competed at the box office with operas that were sanctioned by years of success, and of which the public showed no signs of tiring. The number of performances that regular subscribers attended of *Robert le diable* or *La Juive* in their lifetimes must dwarf the number of *Traviatas* and *Bohèmes* consumed by veteran opera-goers today. Sheer ubiquity must have lent a highly ritualized aspect to renditions of the famous Meyerbeer and Halévy works, with their familiar scenes, gestures, and symbols that formed a quasi-ceremonial focal point of social life for the Opéra's regular public. To break the force of social habit would have been a daunting prospect for any new work, even in the best of production circumstances! Of course, the enormous obstacle course facing works brought into rehearsal at the Opéra made a triumph that much more difficult to attain. And, as it turned out, there was no discernible difference in the number of barriers which lay, on the one hand, before operas that posterity has adjudged as artistically superior (Verdi's *Les Vêpres siciliennes* and *Don Carlos*, or Wagner's *Tannhäuser*) and, on the other, before those that are not likely to sustain prolonged revival today (Gounod's *La Nonne sanglante* and *La Reine de Saba*, Halévy's *La Magicienne*, or Mermet's *Roland à Roncevaux*). Despite the efforts of a succession of directors, few works premièred at the Opéra during the Second Empire had a life span longer than four years on its stage and most did not even last that long. The few bright spots in the new repertoire did not always provide evidence of real vitality. The success of Meyerbeer's *L'Africaine* in 1865 was predictable, and Verdi's *Le Trouvère* (1857) and Gounod's *Faust* (1869), both very popular, arrived as proven money-makers from other stages. Apart from *L'Africaine*, the distinction of greatest longevity among the homegrown works premièred at the Opéra in this period falls to Ambroise Thomas's *Hamlet* (1868).

The Opéra-Comique was not encumbered by the bureaucracy and political sensitivities associated with the Opéra. Nor was it surrounded by the Opéra's legacy of *grandeur*; having evolved from performances by troupes of ambulant actors on the fairgrounds of Paris at the beginning of the eighteenth century, the roots of the Opéra-Comique were far more modest. Now by the nineteenth century it had become a full-fledged member of the operatic establishment with an annual subsidy of its own—and a reluctance to programme works by young composers, to judge from persistent calls for a third French-language house where untried composers could exercise their craft. But the origins of the company as a purveyor of *divertissement* pure and simple did leave a mark on the ambience of the house. 'We laughed, heard some pretty contredanse and waltz music, and our eyes were charmed; what more could one ask for?' wondered one none-too-demanding journalist after an evening at the Opéra-Comique during the Orléanist period.[26] Attendance there was a less stuffy affair than at the Opéra and Théâtre-Italien. Whereas full evening dress was *de rigueur* at those houses, it was only required on state occasions at the Opéra-Comique.[27] Statistically, a performance at the Opéra-Comique was less of an event than one at the other two houses: both the Opéra and the Théâtre-Italien opened their doors only three times a week (the latter only from November to April) while the Opéra-Comique staged performances on every night of the year barring exceptional *relâches*. Prices were significantly lower at the Opéra-Comique than at the Opéra, and the fact that socially less-elevated individuals and families could afford to attend regularly must have had some effect on the atmosphere in the house. But the Opéra-Comique was not the exclusive enclave of the *petite bourgeoisie* that it has often been held to be by historians.[28] Subscription records from the season of 1846–7 show that close to one-fifth of the subscribers had noble titles; moreover, many of those who took out Opéra subscriptions that year were also *abonnés* at the Opéra-Comique. The absolute figures actually show that more aristocrats subscribed at the Opéra-Comique than at the Opéra (there were, however, a greater number of subscribers in total at the former). Such statistics are confirmed on many occasions by contemporaries; Léon Escudier, for example, noted after the première of Ambroise Thomas's *Raymond* that: 'The announcement of a new production at the Opéra-Comique is now more than ever the kind of artistic convocation which élite elements among the Parisian public cannot allow themselves to miss.'[29] Moreover, the *Seconde Salle Favart*, in which the company resided from 1840 to 1887, was an especially well-appointed theatre. Alone among the opera houses of Paris it could boast the availability of boxes with small *salons* to which their occupants could retire at any time during the performance; contemporary publicity for the house also made a point of noting that 'a bell-rope in each *salon* will assure that people do not need to disturb themselves to procure refreshments that are supplied by one of the best *cafés* in Paris'.[30]

[26] Cited by Patrick Barbier, *La Vie quotidienne à l'Opéra au temps de Rossini et de Balzac* (Paris, 1987), 81.
[27] According to the anonymous correspondent who supplied 'Foreign and Colonial News' to the *Illustrated London News*, 9 July 1853.
[28] Huebner, 'Opera Audiences in Paris', p. 216.
[29] *La France musicale*, 8 June 1851.
[30] Cited in Emile Genest, *L'Opéra-Comique connu et inconnu* (Paris, 1925), 160–1.

Unlike the Opéra during most years of the Second Empire—and despite ferocious competition from the newly created Théâtre-Lyrique—the Opéra-Comique was a profitable enterprise, especially under the energetic leadership of Emile Perrin from 1848 to 1857 (before his tenure at the Opéra) and the dual directorship of Adolphe de Leuven and Eugène Ritt from 1862 to 1870. The most successful new works of the period were not written by the *opéra-comique* composers popular during the Orléanist years. Though he remained active as a composer, Daniel-Esprit Auber was never able to repeat his great triumphs of the two decades preceding the Second Empire, works such as *Fra Diavolo*, *Le Domino noir*, *Les Diamants de la couronne*, and *Haydée* that continued to form pillars of the Opéra-Comique repertoire until the turn of the century. Adolphe Adam died in 1856 and Jacques-Frommental Halévy in 1862; neither produced a longstanding success in the last years of his life. Their place was taken by Ambroise Thomas, whose fortunes experienced a turn for the better after a lukewarm career during the Orléanist period. His *Le Caïd* (1849) and *Le Songe d'une nuit d'été* (1850) both did well and *Mignon* (1866) took more quickly than any previous *opéra comique*: it was performed no less than 131 times during its first year on the stage. Victor Massé and Félicien David also left a significant mark on the repertoire, the former with *Galathée* (1852) and *Les Noces de Jeannette* (1853), the latter with *Lalla-Roukh* (1862). One of the company's great repertorial coups was to attract Meyerbeer to write for it; both *L'Étoile du nord* (1854) and *Le Pardon de Ploërmel* (1859) were spectacular successes that soon made the rounds of major opera houses all over Europe. And, unlike the Opéra, where works written before the Rossini revolution of the 1820s lay by and large moribund, the Opéra-Comique continued to achieve a following with eighteenth-century classics such as Grétry's *L'Épreuve villageoise* and Monsigny's *Le Déserteur*.

The name of the company and the genre it performed were historically synonymous. Though *opéra comique* was traditionally perceived as different from opera in a number of respects, distinctions between what was appropriate to the Opéra-Comique and to the Opéra, frequently the object of debate in the history of French lyric theatre, became increasingly blurred after mid-century. Even the most obvious long-standing difference between the repertoires of both houses—in *opéra comique* the interstices between musical numbers are filled with spoken dialogue (*parlé*), whereas numbers in opera are separated by recitative—became obliterated on a few occasions, though only after the Second Empire: *parlé* never surfaced at the Opéra, but in 1873 Gounod's *Roméo et Juliette* became the first production without spoken dialogue at the Opéra-Comique. Massenet's *Werther* and *La Navaraisse*, Bruneau's *L'Attaque du moulin* as well as Bizet's *Les Pêcheurs de perles*, all works without *parlé*, followed before the turn of the century (none of these, however, was actually called an *opéra comique* by its composer).

A complete evening of entertainment at the Opéra-Comique traditionally consisted of a work in three acts or a pair of works in one or two acts. The norm for the repertoire of 'grand opera', developed after Auber's *La Muette de Portici*, was four or five acts. But there was not always a difference of size between works performed at each house. Ministerial instructions given to Véron in 1833 specified that he had to produce, not only one new 'grand opéra en quatre ou cinq actes' every year, but also a second opera in two or three acts, or two operas in one act.[31] A substantial number of these smaller pieces were performed at the Opéra during the course of the century. Ballet, however, was *de rigueur* at the Opéra but not at the Opéra-Comique. If one of the smaller operas—Rossini's two-act *Le Comte Ory* (1828) or Auber's two-act *Le Philtre* (1831), for example—did not contain an extended ballet, it was usually combined with a separate one- or two-act ballet to fill out the evening at the Opéra. Magnificent sets, massed choral tableaux, and impressive scenic coups were important ingredients of four- and five-act grand operas, whereas light *opéras comiques* such as Auber's *Fra Diavolo* generally did not call for this kind of display. Nevertheless, spectacle does not figure prominently in some of the smaller operas such as Thomas's *Le Guerillero* (1842) or Gounod's *Sapho* (1851), and the critic and impresario Castil-Blaze once held up Donizetti's popular *La Favorite* and *Lucie de Lammermoor* to justify his position that a sumptuous *mise-en-scène* was not necessary for an Opéra success.[32] In contrast, Meyerbeer's *Le Pardon de Ploërmel* was lavishly produced at the Opéra-Comique in 1859, complete with a real waterfall and drawbridge. Reviewing the Opéra-Comique première of David's *Lalla-Roukh*, critic Johannès Weber noted that the 'costumes and decorations are worthy of the Opéra'.[33] In the last of a series of articles on the history of *opéra comique*, Léon Ménau noted in 1861 that 'in recent years the Opéra-Comique has become a branch of the Opéra ... By copying the Opéra, the theatre of Favart and Sedaine has felt it necessary to place so much importance upon the *mise-en-scène* that most recent *opéras comiques* can no longer be performed in the provinces.'[34] In short, the Opéra did not stage only scenically elaborate works in this

[31] Alphonse Royer, *Histoire de l'Opéra* (Paris, 1875), 191.

[32] Castil-Blaze, *Théâtres-lyriques de Paris: l'Académie Impériale de Musique de 1645 à 1855* (Paris, 1855), ii. 270.

[33] Review of *Lalla-Roukh*, *Le Temps*, 20 May 1862.

[34] 'Histoire de l'Opéra-Comique', *Le Ménestrel*, 14 Apr. 1861.

period and the Opéra-Comique repertoire was not completely devoid of spectacle.

There were some differences between voice types employed at both theatres. Works in four or five acts at the Opéra usually feature two prominent female roles: a florid one—Eudoxie in *La Juive* and Marguerite in *Les Huguenots* for example—shares the stage with a more dramatic *soprano falcon*, such as Rachel and Valentine in both of these operas (the latter type was named after Cornélie Falcon, creator of both Rachel and Valentine and a noted Alice in *Robert le diable*). In *opéra comique* the most important female voice is the *chanteuse à roulades*, a light coloratura role that usually dominates the score to a far greater degree than either of the females in grand opera. The late-eighteenth-century Opéra-Comique star Louise Dugazon bequeathed her name to the second female in *opéra comique*; the *dugazon* part was taken by a performer who could act well but whose voice was not developed enough to execute *chanteuse à roulades* or dramatic roles. Such a part almost never includes extensive coloratura or *grands airs* in two movements and is usually allotted only one *romance* or set of *couplets* in addition to participation in ensembles. Often the *dugazon* is a trouser role, as with Siébel in *Faust* and Stéphano in *Roméo et Juliette*. These stem from an entirely different tradition from that of the page boys Urbain in *Les Huguenots* and Oscar in Auber's *Gustave III*, which are both small florid roles performed by female singers who also often took major parts. But the *dugazon* was not completely unknown at the Opéra: in the first edition of *La Reine de Saba* Adoniram's apprentice Benoni is listed as this voice type. The main *opéra-comique* male roles, the *ténor léger* and *basse chantante*, continued to demand florid singing until mid-century, and high notes in the former were taken with light head tone throughout the Second Empire. Taste at the Opéra took a different turn well before this. After 1837, the year tenor Gilbert Duprez emitted a high C with full chest voice to great acclaim in *Guillaume Tell*, the *fort-ténor* part containing high notes marked fortissimo became the norm at the Opéra. This practice eventually intruded upon the indigenous customs of the Opéra-Comique: the first 'ut de poitrine' there was sung by Adolphe Duchesne at the thousandth performance of Hérold's *Le Pré aux clercs* in 1871, and subsequently Opéra-Comique tenors such as Alexandre Talazac abandoned head tone almost completely.

Consistent differences in degrees of seriousness between works performed at the Opéra and those performed at the Opéra-Comique are impossible to establish. Though many tragic historical grand operas in four or five acts were written after 1830, not all operas featured serious subject-matter. Works such as Rossini's *Le Comte Ory* or Auber's *Le Philtre* and *Zerline* (1851) belong to a small canon of comic operas. In 1858 Auber's light-hearted *opéra comique Le Cheval de bronze* was translated to the Opéra stage, augmented with recitatives and a ballet. *Robert le diable* was commissioned by the director of the Opéra-Comique in 1827. Meyerbeer and his librettist Eugène Scribe came to the decision that their work was too large for that venue and reworked it for performance at the Opéra in 1831. The original *lieto fine* was retained for the Opéra production and, though the *buffo basse-chantante* role of Raimbaut was reduced and the visual element expanded, the devil Bertram kept most of the comic posturing initially planned for him; moreover the episodes for the soprano–tenor pair, Isabelle and Robert, were transferred unchanged from the Opéra-Comique plans to the Opéra version. Some grand operas, such as Halévy's *La Juive* and *La Reine de Chypre* (1841), are uniformly sombre and contain no comic relief. In *Le Prophète*, however, material for a *trio bouffe* is provided by an episode in which Oberthal, tongue in cheek, swears to abide by the beliefs of his mortal enemies, the Anabaptists, in order to gain entry into the town of Münster. And lively comic repartee is produced in the first act of *Les Huguenots* when the debonair Catholic nobleman, de Nevers, hurries to make the acquaintance of an unknown female visitor despite having formally renounced such escapades a few moments before. Other light episodes in *Le Prophète* and *Les Huguenots* may be readily cited, though both of these works have a tragic denouement. Examples of grand operas with a happy ending include Halévy's *Charles VI* (1843) and Auber's *L'Enfant prodigue* (1850).

That a work was predominantly serious did not preclude its designation as an *opéra comique*. As part of a campaign to familiarize Parisian audiences with his own Bouffes–Parisiens, and to invoke history to justify its frothy repertoire of operettas, Jacques Offenbach contributed an extended outline of the history of the Opéra-Comique to several newspapers in the summer of 1856.[35] He maintained that, although light works in what he believed to be the tried and true tradition of *opéra comique* were still occasionally being produced, the genre had become dominated by 'lugubrious effects' in recent decades. He pointed his finger at Hérold as the main culprit, arguing that, since the appearance of *Zampa* (1831) and *Le Pré aux clercs* (1832), 'the gracious and light genre of the early days almost disappeared to make room for large works'. *Zampa* does indeed place emphasis on the supernatural and clearly recalls *Don Giovanni* with a conclusion

---

[35] 'Histoire de l'Opéra-Comique', *Le Figaro*, 17 July 1856.

showing the villain dragged to hell by a statue of the girl he has wronged. Adolphe Nourrit is even said to have advocated performance of this work at the Opéra in the 1830s.[36] Many years later the critic Chadeuil observed that, 'if one were to remove the small amount of spoken dialogue, add an act, some recitatives, and one or two choruses, the work would be worthy of a place in the repertoire of our first lyric stage'.[37] *Scribe's libretto for the unsuccessful opéra comique, Lambert Simnel* (1843; music by Monpou and Adam), bears many points of resemblance to his later grand opera *Le Prophète.* Historical opera filled with political intrigue gained an additional foothold at the Opéra-Comique with works such as *Quentin Durward* (1858) by the Belgian composer François Gevaert and Meyerbeer's *L'Étoile du Nord*; *Quentin Durward* revolves around the attempt of the French king Louis XI to prevent an undesirable marriage alliance, and the central figure in *L'Étoile du Nord* is Czar Peter the Great. Although the majority of *operás comiques* produced during the Second Empire had happy endings, the ultimate demise of the hero or heroine was also not unknown. In 1856 Manon Lescaut expired in the arms of Chevalier Des Grieux in Auber's *opéra comique* based loosely upon the Prévost novel; earlier in the work the Chevalier had run through the Marquis d'Herigny with his sword. The protagonist in *Marco Spada* (1852) dies in a duel at the final curtain. 'Is not a serious *opéra comique* just a grand opera with spoken dialogue instead of recitatives?' asked Gustave Chadeuil in 1862.[38] Offenbach would undoubtedly have answered in the affirmative, but he overstated his case by claiming that light-hearted *opéra comique* had almost disappeared; among the most popular works of the period were such frivolities as *Fra Diavolo* and, to cite a work still in the international repertoire today, Donizetti's *La Fille du régiment.* In a study of *opéra comique* that appeared in 1865, A. Thurner offered perhaps the most satisfying succinct definition possible: '*Opéra comique* is neither a mixed genre, nor a bastardized genre but rather responds to a true sentiment of human nature: it is comedy that is lyric, cheerful, mischievous, sometimes tender and crossed by clouds of passion. Real buffoonery and clowning about have never characterized the French spirit.'[39]

Although of far more recent vintage than the Théâtre-Italien, Opéra, and Opéra-Comique, the Théâtre-Lyrique played a role in Second Empire operatic culture equally as important as the more established houses. Founded by the composer Adolphe Adam as the Opéra-National in 1847 and renamed in 1852, the Théâtre-Lyrique was

---

[36] This was reported by Jouvin in a review of a revival of *Zampa* at the Opéra-Comique in 1856 (*Le Figaro*, 4 Sept. 1856).

[37] Review of *Zampa*, *Le Siècle*, 9 Sept. 1856.

[38] In a review of Gounod's *La Reine de Saba*, *Le Siècle*, 4 Mar. 1862.

[39] A. Thurner, *Les Transformations de l'Opéra-Comique* (Paris, 1865), 263.

launched upon radiant ideals of bringing opera to the masses. Prices there were much lower than at the other houses and it was situated between the Porte Saint-Martin and the Bastille, that is, at a distance great enough from the Opéra and Opéra-Comique to avoid competition with them and in the heart of a district with many working-class inhabitants.[40] In an article on the new house that appeared in September 1853, Berlioz wrote disparagingly about an audience of 'poor dilettante workers' from the Bastille area and surrounding neighbourhoods who were frustrated by frequent and unexpected closings of 'their' opera house.[41] Nor did he have kind words for the level of performance at the Théâtre-Lyrique at that time, referring to it on one occasion in a letter as 'the gutter where all the donkeys of Paris defecate'.[42]

All that was to change with the ascension of Léon Carvalho to the directorship of the house in 1856. Under his stewardship the theatre's reputation was enhanced to the point where it was compared favourably to the Opéra and Opéra-Comique. When the article of September 1853 was reprinted in the anthology *Les Grotesques de la musique* in 1859, Berlioz added a footnote to his earlier negative remarks about the audience at the Théâtre-Lyrique: 'It is evident that I am not writing contemporary history here. Everything has changed in the direction of this theatre as well as in the comportment of its *habitués*.' Born in Mauritius in 1825, Carvalho made his way to Paris at an early age to forge a career as a singer. He was not very successful, filling only minor roles at the Opéra-Comique from 1847 to 1855, but his profession did permit him to become acquainted with a soprano who was doing considerably better, Marie Miolan. Professional association evolved into marriage in 1853. This was of some importance to Carvalho's future vocation as director of the Théâtre-Lyrique, since the star attraction of the house was also his wife. But beyond this advantage, Carvalho was shrewd in his choice of repertoire, mounting popular revivals of operas by Mozart, Gluck, and Beethoven, commissioning translations of Verdi's work, and launching the career of Georges Bizet. He also mounted the only French operas from the period (with the exception of Verdi's *Les Vêpres siciliennes* and *Don Carlos*) to have endured in the twentieth-century repertoire—Bizet's *Les Pêcheurs de perles*, and Berlioz's *Les Troyens*, as well as Gounod's three most famous works for the stage: *Faust*, *Mireille*, and *Roméo et Juliette*.

[40] Huebner, 'Opera Audiences in Paris', 222.

[41] Hector Berlioz, 'Les Dilettanti en blouse et la musique serieuse', first published in *Journal des débats*, 6 Sept. 1853, and repr. in *Les Grotesques de la musique*, ed. Léon Guichard (Paris, 1969), 113–16.

[42] Letter of 8 Feb. 1853, in *New Letters of Berlioz, 1830–1868*, trans. and ed. Jacques Barzun (New York, 1954), 102. See also the very fine study on the history of the Théâtre-Lyrique by T. J. Walsh, *Second Empire Opera* (London, 1981), 17.

PART ONE

Chronicle

1. *From the Seminary to the Stage*

THROUGHOUT the nineteenth century, until the creation of the *Société nationale* and the rise to prominence of concert organizations after 1870, the primary way for a young French composer to make a name for himself was by composing operas. The path to the theatre was lined with signposts. Study at the Conservatoire was followed by entry into the competition for the *Prix de Rome*. The first prize often came only after several attempts; it entitled the winner to a state-subsidized two-year period of leisurely study at the French Academy in Rome and an additional year in Vienna. After returning to Paris, most laureates sought to make a début on the stage. The supply of talent was greater than the demand; occasions were rare when an impresario would risk a commission on an unknown.

The institution of the *Prix de Rome*, as durable as it proved to be, was not without detractors. Long hours of luxuriating in the shadow of the Colosseum with great literature were not immediately relevant to the practical requirements of the opera composer. Berlioz, for one, acknowledged certain salubrious effects of direct exposure to the classical heritage but thought that the sojourn in Rome was quite useless for the purely musical training of young composers.[1] Descriptions of evenings at Roman opera houses supplied in his memoirs suggest insufferable performing standards for one accustomed to Parisian operatic seasons. Equating the prescribed two-year stay with enforced exile from musical civilization, Berlioz had his period of tenure shortened by several months in 1831.

Gounod's reminiscences about performances in Roman theatres during his stay at the French Academy from 1840 to 1842 were scarcely more favourable.[2] Nevertheless, he became a staunch supporter of the *Prix de Rome* institution—and a more prolific opera composer than Berlioz. Some explanation for Gounod's position surely lies in his contact with Ingres, then director of the French Academy. Intolerant and distant to some, Ingres seems to have shown an unusual degree of solicitude for the young composer. 'Drawing is the probity of Art' was

---

[1] Hector Berlioz, *The Memoirs of Hector Berlioz, 1830–1868*, trans. and ed. David Cairns (London, 1970), 169.

[2] Charles Gounod, *Mémoires d'un artiste* (Paris, 1896), 109.

the famous dictum of the painter and beneath this lay a deep-seated veneration of the Beautiful, a commitment to the principle that beauty for beauty's sake, embodied in the balance and harmony of classical or classicizing art, should be the guiding light for the artist. Nothing could have been further from the fundamentally romantic temperament of a Berlioz, but these aesthetic tenets did strike a responsive chord in the young Gounod. The notion that spiritual nourishment and the acquisition of craft are inseparable in the training of a real artist surfaces frequently in Gounod's correspondence and published writings. 'As if one cannot be an able practitioner and a vulgar artist [at the same time]!' Gounod fulminated late in life in an article on the French Academy; impregnation with immutable laws of beauty inherent in classical and Renaissance Italian art distinguished the artist from the artisan, the sublime from the commonplace.[3] Over thirty years before, Gounod rhapsodized about the splendours of Italy to his friend Jules Richomme:

I have always thought that a tour of Italy is a necessary complement to the studies of an artist, in whatever field he may be; for, in effect, art is but a single phenomenon, the many manifestations of which are different languages ... there is an undeniable and substantial profit to be gained by the poet and musician in beholding beautiful pictures, beautiful buildings, or a beautiful country.[4]

Gounod's own memoirs—significantly entitled *Mémoires d'un artiste*— attest to his fondness for the city of 'mysterious inducements and incomparable peace'.[5] It was an attachment that caused him to prolong his stay five months over the normal two-year limit.

Gounod fell under other influences in Rome. When he arrived, the well-known Catholic liberal Henri Lacordaire had recently completed his Dominican novitiate. Lacordaire would go on to restore the Dominican order on French soil, possessed by the belief that the most effective means to teach social consciousness in the French church was through a re-establishment of religious orders dismantled during the Revolution. Gounod was among the many who succumbed to his charisma. In Rome he soon joined an association of artists led by Lacordaire, the 'Confrérie de Saint-Jean L'Évangéliste', which was dedicated to the regeneration through sacred art of a world soiled by materialism. To judge by a letter he received from his mother, Gounod was soon prepared to go much further than membership in a voluntary lay association:

---

[3] Charles Gounod, 'L'Académie de France à Rome', in ibid., 304–5.
[4] Letter to Jules Richomme, 7 Oct. 1846, in Pougin, 'Gounod écrivain' (1912), 260.
[5] Gounod, *Mémoires*, p. 125.

I know that Monsieur Lacordaire is a man of great talent and learning. But I have to tell you my fears about the influence that he seeks to exercise over young people . . . Unless you have decided in your head and in your heart to become a Dominican (which I really do not think suits your passionate nature), be on guard and declare yourself explicitly an artist with religious sentiment and not a friar with many skills . . . [6]

Mother knew her son well. For the moment he backed away from the cloth, but tension between the *bon vivant* and the ascetic would remain an integral part of his character.

Gounod, none the less, continued to be preoccupied by the role of art in a Christian society and did not contemptuously dismiss all music-making in Rome. He found refuge from operatic abominations in performances of Palestrina's music at the Sistine Chapel. Where Berlioz detected only 'formulas and conundrums', Gounod heard works of enormous impact that were musical analogues to the great Michelangelo frescos. Both displayed 'the same simplicity, the same humility in the use of resources, the same absence of preoccupation with effect, the same disdain for seduction'.[7] According to Gounod, surface sensationalism in sacred music could, in the final analysis, only be transient; Palestrina's greatest attribute was that he resisted the temptations of mundane artifice in order to induce a profound spiritual experience within the listener.

That classical restraint and sobriety of expression could serve the higher purpose of an artist whose gaze was fixed inalterably upon God was a revelation of some import for Gounod's career. He soon attempted an *a cappella* mass in the style of Palestrina, which, along with his more up-to-date Requiem, was performed in Vienna during his final year of financial support. Most unusually for an alumnus of the French Academy, Gounod showed no inclination to look to the theatre for his future livelihood. Even before he left Vienna, he confided to a friend and benefactor that he would dedicate himself to rejuvenating French sacred music.[8] True to his word, in 1843 he took up a post as music director of the Missions Étrangères church in Paris. The performing forces were limited—two basses, a tenor, a boy soprano, and a decrepit organ—and the salary of 1,200 francs per annum was scarcely more than that of a last chair player at the Opéra-Comique. But Gounod was free to write according to his artistic conscience; much to the dismay of his parishioners, at least at the outset, counterpoint à la

---

[6] This undated letter is cited by Jacques and Jean de Lassus Saint-Geniès, *Gounod et son temps* (Paris, 1963), 33.

[7] Gounod, *Mémoires*, p. 101.

[8] Letter to the Marquis de Pastoret, 25 Mar. 1843, in 'Charles Gounod—Lettres de Jeunesse', *Revue bleue*, 49 (1911), 10.

Palestrina became regular fare at Sunday services. For nearly five years he remained on the periphery of Parisian musical life; newspapers rarely mentioned his name and his works never appeared on concert programmes. Gounod found the view from his spiritual ivory tower disquieting: 'Today art is a means rather than a real end in itself,' he complained in 1846; 'people work to make a fortune or a name, rather than to create a beautiful thing; everyone is enlisted under the flag of self-interest and with this multitude of individual proclivities it is hard to know where things are going'.[9] Such observations do not give the impression of one who could be comfortable in the materialistic world of opera.

Gounod withdrew even further before abruptly changing course. Understandably, documentation about the years at the Missions Étrangères church is scarce. There was continued concern for spiritual questions, absorption in biblical studies, and fascination with the fiery oratory of Père Lacordaire from the pulpit of Notre-Dame. Perhaps of greater significance was the ordination, in 1845, of Gounod's close friend Charles Gay, himself a musician in his youth. In the preceding year Gounod alluded once again to his own vocation for the priesthood.[10] He eventually pursued these convictions by enrolling formally at the Seminary of Saint-Sulpice in October 1847. Nor did the vacillations end there. Within a few months Gounod suddenly dropped that course of study: 'As soon as there is questioning, the question is resolved,'[11] the composer was to write many years afterwards in reference to his abandonment of formal theological training. According to Louise Héritte, daughter of the mezzo-soprano Pauline Viardot, the decision was not made without worldly enticement.[12] Héritte claimed that the unexpected and attractive prospect of providing a work for her mother to perform at the Opéra was enough to shift the balance irrevocably away from the seminary, and that Pauline Viardot, in obtaining a commission for him, had rescued the future composer of *Faust* from oblivion in the priesthood. Nevertheless, Gounod himself placed the first relevant meeting with Pauline Viardot after her sensational creation of the role of Fidès in Meyerbeer's *Le Prophète* (16 April 1849), and maintained that he had resigned from the post at the Missions Étrangères in order to seek his fortune in the world of opera at the outbreak of the Revolution in February 1848.[13] Perhaps it was the Revolution itself that ignited the more extrovert side of his temperament. With very few public performances to his credit, a background

[9] Letter to Jules Richomme, 5 Nov. 1846, in Pougin, 'Gounod écrivain' (1912), 263.
[10] Letter to the Baron de Vendeuvre, 27 Sept. 1844, in *La Revue musicale*, 16 (1935), 111.
[11] Letter to Ernest Legouvé, n.d. (late 1860s from contents), private collection.
[12] Louis Héritte de la Tour, *Mémoires de Louise Héritte-Viardot* (Paris, 1922), 88.
[13] Gounod, *Mémoires*, pp. 174–5.

almost exclusively confined to sacred music, and no guardian angel, Gounod admitted that an operatic career at that juncture represented an even greater challenge than it would have done to most young French composers.

The years of contemplation had not erased the picture that Fanny Mendelssohn had drawn years earlier in Rome of a highly demonstrative man prone to effusive outpourings of emotion over even commonplace events.[14] He was also handsome—contemporary portraits show delicately chiselled features and penetrating eyes (see the portrait by Jules-Léopold Boilly, plate 1)—well read, and ostensibly high-minded. Gounod was soon plying his considerable charms on the Parisian social circuit. According to Saint-Saëns, Gounod frequented the house of a prominent Parisian doctor 'to which he was drawn by a clique of beautiful women, patients of the doctor and fervent admirers of the musician'.[15] He seems to have regaled those assembled at the soirées with portions of an *opéra comique*, now lost, that he was writing in collaboration with a member of the doctor's family. That project never saw the boards, probably because Gounod soon could set his sights much higher. A mutual friend arranged an interview with Pauline Viardot after the *Le Prophète* triumph. Gounod's talent and suave personality impressed her immediately, no mean accomplishment considering both her own musical pedigree as a sister of the great soprano Maria Malibran and her connection with the brightest cultural luminaries of her age. By the beginning of 1850 Pauline Viardot was describing her find to George Sand as the great hope for French music. Sand was left reeling by her friend's enthusiasm: 'I am racking my brains to guess whom the genius you have announced to me will resemble. Will he proceed from the ancients or from the moderns? Will he make me forget Mozart?'[16] Good-humoured hyperbole aside, a young composer who spouted well-turned phrases about the higher mission of the artist was a welcome relief from the all-too-venal Meyerbeer. For Pauline, the role of Fidès was starting to wear thin.[17] And there can be little doubt that Gounod soon enjoyed a close personal rapport with the Viardot family and its circle of friends, including the Russian writer Ivan Turgenev; on 2 April, just a few hours after she had set off on a tour with her husband Louis, Gounod and Turgenev even collaborated to write a letter to her containing news of family members left behind.[18]

[14] Sebastian Hensel, *Die Familie Mendelssohn* (Berlin, 1880), ii. 118.

[15] Camille Saint-Saëns, 'Charles Gounod', in *Portraits et souvenirs* (Paris, 1899), 55–6.

[16] Letter to Pauline Viardot, 23 Feb. 1850, in George Sand, *Correspondance*, ed. Georges Lubin (Paris, 1972), ix. 462.

[17] Letter to George Sand, 26 May 1849, in *Lettres inédites de George Sand et de Pauline Viardot, 1839–1849*, ed. Thérèse Marix-Spire (Paris, 1959), 281.

[18] Letter to Pauline Viardot, 2–3 Apr. 1850, summarized in *Catalogue: Vente du vendredi 22 novembre 1968, Hôtel Drouot*, lot 78.

2. *Early* Succès d'estimes

IN January or February 1850 Pauline Viardot agreed, or perhaps even volunteered, to sing the lead role in an opera written by Gounod. The playwright Emile Augier, another friend of the Viardots, was approached to supply a libretto. In view of Pauline's well-documented interest in Greek literature and Gounod's own infatuation with the classical heritage, he was a natural choice. Augier, along with François Ponsard, was spearheading a movement to eliminate some of the excesses of Romantic drama and to reinstate the ancients in the French spoken theatre. With the early triumphs of *La Cigue* (1844) and *Gabrielle* (1849) behind him, Augier was more familiar to Parisian audiences than Gounod, but also a newcomer to opera. The legend of the poet Sappho and her love for the handsome Phaon was settled upon for the plot; it was suitably lofty and would, of course, supply a title role for Pauline.

The mezzo is said by her daughter to have made the commissioning of a work by Gounod and Augier a condition for the renewal of her Opéra contract for the 1850–1 winter season.[1] Even if it only took a recommendation on her part, as Gounod writes in his *Mémoires*, the prospect must have been an unsavoury financial proposition for the then director of the Opéra, Nestor Roqueplan. To diminish the risk, it was in the director's best interest first to engage the unknown composer and untried librettist for a short work that could be used as a curtain-raiser to some established, profitable ballet. The contract, signed by Gounod, Augier, and Roqueplan on 1 April 1850, called for the two-act opera to be delivered by 30 September following and for performances to take place no later than 1 April 1851.[2] In the end, however, *Sapho* was much longer than first anticipated and could occupy an entire evening on its own.

It was an extraordinary stroke of good fortune that Gounod's operatic début was to take place on the most prestigious stage in Paris. The Opéra had a perennial appetite for works by Meyerbeer, Halévy, and later Verdi, but its open-door policy regarding repertorial decisions did not extend beyond them. Many established French composers had to

---

[1] Héritte de la Tour, *Mémoires*, p. 88.

[2] A copy of the contract is at AN F²¹ 1069. The date of the contract is mistakenly given as 3 Apr. 1850 in Gounod's *Mémoires*, p. 182.

wait years for an entry. Both Adolphe Adam and Antoine Louis Clapisson had scored many triumphs at the Opéra-Comique and each had passed his fortieth birthday before the Opéra would invest in him, unsuccessfully in both cases. Ambroise Thomas graduated to the two-act Scribe opera libretto *Le Conte de Carmagnola* (1841) when he was only thirty (after five *opéras comiques*), but, following the failure of this work and *Le Guerillero* in 1842, he had to achieve a distinguished career at the Opéra-Comique before coming to the Opéra again with *Hamlet* in 1868. Victor Massé, a contemporary of Gounod, received his first performance at the Opéra (*Le Mule de Pedro*, 1863) many years after *Galathée* and *Les Noces de Jeannette* had become entrenched in the Opéra-Comique repertoire. The playbills on rue Le Peletier never did display the names François Bazin, Albert Grisar, and Henri Reber, whose music is now forgotten but was also popular at the Opéra-Comique during the Second Empire. That Nestor Roqueplan agreed to a commission for a composer whose greatest public successes had taken place in Vienna over seven years before with a mass and a requiem is as great a tribute as any to the prestige of Pauline Viardot after *Le Prophète*.

The singer's support went beyond the purely professional. A few days after the contract was signed, Gounod's brother Urbain suddenly died. The emotional trauma and legal formalities could not have come at a worse time in view of the close deadline for the completion of the opera. From Berlin the Viardots immediately extended assistance on several fronts. Louis offered money, presumably to help cover funeral and legal expenses.[3] Pauline threw open the doors of the family house at Courtavenel to Gounod and his mother, from whom he was virtually inseparable even at the best of times. He accepted Pauline's reasoning that the tranquillity of the country would enable him to resume work on *Sapho*; by the beginning of May mother and son were comfortably ensconced at the Viardot estate. Pauline also urged Ivan Turgenev to postpone a planned return to his homeland in order to comfort Gounod.[4] Turgenev agreed, out of genuine affection for the composer mixed generously with devotion to the singer herself. Gounod had burst into his life within a year of the probable consummation of his liaison with Pauline.[5] Turgenev became the odd man (excluding the hapless

[3] Letter from Gounod to Pauline Viardot, 14 Apr. 1850, BN MSS nouvelles acquisitions françaises (hereafter n.a.f.) 16272, fo. 191, and letter from Turgenev to Pauline Viardot, 10–13 Apr. 1850, in Ivan Turgenev, *Nouvelle correspondance inédite*, ed. Alexandre Zviguilsky (Paris, 1971–2), i. 32–6.

[4] Letter from Gounod to Pauline Viardot, 8 May 1850, BN MSS n.a.f. 16272, fo. 193 and letter from Turgenev to Pauline Viardot, 10–13 Apr. 1850, in Turgenev, *Nouvelle correspondance inédite*, i. 32–6.

[5] Leonard Schapiro, *Turgenev: His Life and Times* (Oxford, 1978), 70 ff.

Louis) in a delicate triangle with Gounod, a rival to whose charm he himself had partially succumbed. Both awaited anxiously at Courtavenel for separate letters from Pauline containing reports of her triumphs in Germany. (Gounod's were always longer than his, Turgenev grumbled.) There were lighter moments too. One evening they amused themselves by following her imagined progress through *Le Prophète* step by step, drawing in their breaths at each 'Ah! mon fils!', applauding wildly, and throwing flowers at the end.[6]

Turgenev was Gounod's 'great and only tribunal' during the first weeks of work on *Sapho*, although Pauline was kept informed by both composer and writer of every step in the genesis of the project.[7] One of Turgenev's letters to the singer contains an assessment, perhaps the earliest, of Gounod, the opera composer:

What Gounod lacks somewhat is a brilliant and popular side. His music is like a temple: it is not open to all. I also believe that from his first appearance he will have enthusiastic admirers and great prestige as a musician with the general public; but fickle popularity, of the sort that stirs and leaps like a Bacchante, will never throw its arms around his neck. I even think that he will always hold it in disdain. His melancholy, so original in its simplicity and to which in the end one becomes so attached, does not have striking features that leave a mark upon the listener; he does not prick or arouse the listener—he does not titillate him. He possesses a wide range of colours on his palette but everything he writes— even a drinking song such as 'Trinquons'—bears a lofty stamp. He idealizes everything he touches but in so doing he leaves the crowd behind. Yet among that mass of talented composers who are witty in a vulgar sort of way, intelligible not because of their clarity but because of their triviality, the appearance of a musical personality such as Gounod's is so rare that one cannot welcome him heartily enough. We spoke about these matters this morning. He knows himself as well as any man knows himself. I also do not think that he has much of a comic streak; Goethe once said 'man ist am Ende . . . was man ist'.[8]

Turgenev was clearly prepared to overlook Gounod's shortcomings because of the composer's apparent artistic integrity (or was it out of devotion to Pauline?). But his observation that Gounod did not have the

---

[6] Letter from Turgenev to Pauline Viardot, 29 Apr. 1850, in Ivan Turgenev, *Lettres inédites de Turgenev à Pauline Viardot et à sa famille*, ed. Henri Grandjard and Alexandre Zviguilsky (Lausanne, 1972), 19–22.

[7] Unfortunately, two-thirds of the Viardot family archives are still in private hands and inaccessible. Evidently the Gounod correspondence was divided entirely at random among three branches of the Viardot family; only two of the many letters from the period of the opera's genesis in the spring and summer of 1850 fell into the collection of Mme Maupoil that was donated to the Bibliothèque Nationale in 1968. For a description of the Maupoil collection, see Roger Pierrot, 'Le Don Marcelle Maupoil à la Bibliothèque Nationale', in *Cahiers Ivan Tourguenev, Pauline Viardot, Maria Malibran*, iv (1980), 32–4.

[8] Letter to Pauline Viardot, 16 May 1850, in Turgenev, *Nouvelle correspondance inédite*, i. 41.

gift of comedy was premature; the *opéra comique, Le Médecin malgré lui*, would lay to rest all observations of that sort, although admittedly this was a side of Gounod's musical personality that surfaced all too rarely; and, contrary to Turgenev's prediction, some of Gounod's works would prove to be very popular indeed. Turgenev's view of Gounod's idealism was not depreciatory; rather he welcomed it—as did Pauline herself—as a breath of fresh air on the French musical scene. Yet his views were also prophetic of those held by music critics hostile to the composer throughout his operatic career. In the world of the theatre, the qualities that Turgenev noted might assume a negative edge: disdain for popularity and disregard for paying audiences and critics could, after all, readily be seen as two sides of the same coin.

Despite the apparent pleasure he derived from witnessing the birth of Gounod's opera, Turgenev could not delay his return to Russia indefinitely. His literary career required personal attention at home and hope for fulfilment with Pauline was now too remote to keep him from these concerns. 'I do not wish to grieve you more by speaking about the sorrow I feel in parting from you,' Gounod wrote to Turgenev at the end of June, shortly after the writer had left Courtavenel. 'I have only one wish, perhaps two,' he continued; 'the first is that you do not forget me, the second is that I always know where you are, what is happening to you, and how to contact you.'[9] Words such as these from the pen of a favoured rival have a distinctly patronizing flavour. But Turgenev evidently took comfort in the knowledge that he was missed. 'Gounod has a heart of gold,' he remarked to Pauline in reference to the letter.[10] But his attitude towards Gounod cooled after he sided with the singer in a great quarrel that erupted between the Viardots and Gounod in 1852. Later in life Turgenev would have few favourable things to say about him. 'I dislike the man more than ever,' he reported to Pauline shortly after the *Mireille* première in 1864. 'He is surrounded by a shell as resistant to the truth as that which surrounds kings. And then there is also the ooze of the erotic priest that bubbles to the surface . . . I cannot stomach it!'[11]

Pauline Viardot's engagements in the summer of 1850 took her from German to English stages. The Viardots were able to hear at least some of Gounod's music for *Sapho* during that time. Both stopped at Courtavenel for a week or so at the beginning of June, and Louis returned for a few days in August. By the time that Pauline had fulfilled all of her summer contracts, the opera had been completely drafted.

---

[9] Letter of 22 June 1850, BN MSS n.a.f. 16275, fos. 238–9.
[10] Letter of 24 June 1850, in Turgenev, *Nouvelle correspondance inédite*, i. 44–6.
[11] Letter of 31 Mar. 1864, in ibid. i. 120–2.

Pauline's approval was vital to Gounod. His *Mémoires* relate that she expressed unqualified satisfaction with the work when he crooned the vocal parts for her in early September; within a few days she knew the opera well enough to play it at the piano by memory. But work on *Sapho* was much more of a collective effort than Gounod ever acknowledged. Louis was already dispensing advice in August to assure the predominance of his wife's role.[12] Pauline's letters to Turgenev reveal that she too suggested a number of revisions after her return; these included use of Gounod's earlier 'Chanson du pêcheur' for Sapho's final soliloquy 'Ô ma lyre immortelle', the only number from the work to achieve lasting fame.[13] Visitors to Courtavenel also hovered over the cradle. Tenor Gustave Roger, initially slated to sing the part of Phaon, made the trip from Paris and promptly declared that his role was not important enough.[14] Emile Augier was called upon to make changes to the poetry on location, and Henry Chorley, influential music critic for the *Athenaeum* in London and close friend of the Viardots, was also present for a few days. '[*Sapho*] feels that she is surrounded by grandmothers, godfathers, godmothers,' Gounod told Turgenev; 'until now we have only known her number by number, an arm here, a leg there; now she is starting to reveal more of herself to the intelligent and trustworthy observations of my dear entourage.'[15] A few weeks before Gounod had bemoaned his seemingly immature talent, so heavily dependent upon the suggestions of others.[16] Lack of maturity as a composer, however, may not have been at the root of his need for advice. This sort of reliance was to characterize the man throughout his operatic career.

Enlarged from the original two-act frame into three acts, *Sapho* went into rehearsal at the Opéra in the first week of February 1851. With the exception of Pauline Viardot, the cast included lesser lights on the Opéra roster: the young tenor Louis Gueymard in the role of Phaon, Brémond as his timorous companion Pythéas, and Poinsot as the courtesan Glycère. Production delays, endemic to the Opéra, pushed the work from a projected première on 15 March to 16 April. This did not bode well for *Sapho*, since Pauline was to take up foreign engagements at the end of May. The departure of a key player so early on might prove prejudicial to success. It was for this reason that Meyerbeer, always

---

[12]   Letter from Louis Viardot to Pauline Viardot, 2 Aug. 1850, private collection.

[13]   Letter from Pauline Viardot to Turgenev, 10–14 Sept. 1850, in Turgenev, *Nouvelle correspondance inédite*, i. 343–8. Also Julien Tiersot, 'Gounod's Letters', *Musical Quarterly*, 5 (1919), 46–7.

[14]   Letter from Gounod to Turgenev, 1 Oct. 1850, private collection.

[15]   Letter of 27 Oct. 1850, BN MSS n.a.f. 16275, fo. 240.

[16]   Letter to Turgenev, 1 Oct. 1850, private collection.

sure-footed in entrepreneurial matters, invariably sought assurances that an opening-night cast would be available for several months to launch a new opera.

The office of the censor produced further obstacles. It objected to certain numbers in *Sapho* on both moral and political grounds. A libretto submitted before the first performance to the authorities for verification contains many deletions of suggestive lines, with more suitable versions supplied in the margins.[17] Most of the changes were imposed to cover up the loose sexual mores of Augier's Greeks. To obfuscate the nature of an entente between Pythéas and Glycère which involved the exchange of sexual favours for a political document, Pythéas's 'prenez-moi pour amant' became 'traitez-moi tendrement'. The spicy hedonism of his quatrain in the same duet 'Oui, je comprends mignonne / Ton désir / Le mystère assaisonne / Le plaisir' was attenuated by revision as 'Oui, j'aime ton caprice / De candeur / Le mystère est complice / Du bonheur'. In spite of these and other modifications, the Pythéas—Glycère duet offended some members of the audience on opening night. Although the text had been expurgated, Brémond and Poinsot evidently played the scene in a suggestive manner. One reviewer noted that the number displayed 'excessive licence without precedent at the Opéra'.[18] Pauline later admitted that the execution was somewhat 'indélicat' but caustically reproached important subscribers for objecting to behaviour very much like their own.[19]

Blatant disregard for principles of law and order by one of the characters in the story ruffled sensitivities even further. Augier's Alcée originally did not mince words in Act I when exhorting his compatriots to overthrow the tyrant Pittacus: 'Tremblez tyrans forgeurs de chaines / ... Du sang qui coule dans nos veines / Monstres si longtemps engraissés.' A censors' report for *Sapho*, dated 12 April 1851, drew attention to this number as one that would have a 'dangerous effect' and even be 'an inducement to popular agitation'.[20] Nor were the censors impressed with Augier's deflation of the offending lines to 'Ô liberté déese austère / ... Mais de tes pas la vieille terre / Garde un souvenir immortel'. 'Although the modifications diminish the danger we feared, they do not eliminate it completely,' was the verdict rendered on the day before the première. The opera was authorized for only one night on condition that additional changes were made before the second performance. According to one critic, Théophile Gautier, sale of the

---

[17] AN AJ[13] 207.
[18] Review of *Sapho* by M. Bourges, *La Revue et gazette musicale de Paris*, 20 Apr. 1851.
[19] Letter to Turgenev, 27 Apr. 1851, in Turgenev, *Lettres inédites*, p. 396.
[20] AN F[21] 969.

libretto was prohibited on opening night,[21] but no source for the opera shows new corrections to Alcée's ode. It seems that the matter was dropped before the second performance, or that additional changes went unrecorded in the extant sources.

The incident is of greatest interest as an illustration of the paranoia of the upper-level bureaucracy in the French Second Republic before an imagined 'spectre rouge'. The triumph of the Radical Republicans in partial elections of May 1850 gave rise to fears of further gains on the Left in the projected elections of 1852. As a result, conservative bureaucrats, the ever malleable elements in a centralized pyramidic administrative machine responsible to President (soon to become Emperor) Louis Napoleon, stepped up their vigilance. Gautier, a confirmed Republican, scoffed at the censors' over-sensitivity in his review. But this was to underestimate what one historian has called the 'neurotic anxiety' of the forces of order in the days before the *coup d'état* of 2 December 1851.[22] The reviewer for the conservative daily *L'Union*, with clear reference to the bloody days of June 1848, was more supportive of the official line:

The performance of *Sapho* was almost disallowed. The Minister of the Interior did not approve of the part in which liberty and the death of tyrants are espoused. These kinds of exaggerations are out of fashion, and one should not expect to excite the public at the Opéra with redundant tirades. This kind of thing was effective in the days of *Muette* and *Guillaume Tell*. At that time, liberal fever was devouring the French nation. Today she has returned to wiser, more rational precepts. She has paid for her follies with the purest of her blood and the purest of her gold, and what she wants now is a stable regime. More astonishing than the susceptibilities of the Minister of the Interior are the illusions into which the director of the Opéra, whom we hold to be a capable and intelligent man, seems to have fallen. He is so unallied to the Republican cause that the victors of the day in 1848 wanted to take his privilege away. Being a reasonable individual, he had to resign himself to playing dead. He should know that his public has no greater taste for the Republic than he.[23]

Sapho did not draw well. Genuine ideological disenchantment and moral indignation of some members of the Opéra's regular public may have been minor contributing factors. Structural weaknesses in the opera were more significant. Critics complained about the slow pace of

---

[21]   Review of *Sapho*, *La Presse*, 22 Apr. 1851.

[22]   See P. A. Gagnon, *France since 1789* (New York, 1964), 149–56; John M. Merriman, *The Agony of the Republic: The Repression of the Left in Revolutionary France, 1848–1851* (New Haven, 1978); and Howard Machin, 'The Prefects and Political Repression, February 1848–December 1851', in Roger Price (ed.), *Revolution and Reaction in 1848 and the Second French Republic* (London, 1975), 286–302.

[23]   Theodore Anne, review of *Sapho*, *L'Union*, 21–2 Apr. 1851.

Augier's libretto as well as about Gounod's long declamatory sections, inexperience in scoring, and occasional awkward melodic writing. These were merely surface scars. Reviewers also acknowledged that the score contained genuinely novel and interesting features; many, including Berlioz, singled out the music of the third act as some of the finest written for the French stage in recent years. Indeed, few disagreed with the opinion of critic Pol Mercier that Gounod seemed to have a 'brilliant future'.[24] But a *succès d'estime* for the composer did not make for good box-office receipts. Survival at the Opéra was ultimately contingent upon the amount of money a work earned. Though Pauline wrote to Turgenev and George Sand of thunderous applause, nightly receipts for *Sapho* remained at the 4,000-franc level at a time when earnings of 8,000 or 9,000 francs were customary for standbys such as *Le Prophète* or *La Juive*.[25] Starting at the third performance on 23 April, a ballet by Edouard Deldevez was added so that the evening would close on a more festive note. This did little to improve attendance, and kept the audience in the theatre until 12.45 a.m.

The sixth and last performance with Pauline was on 12 May. In subsequent stagings of the work on 2 July and twice in December of the same year, Elisabeth Masson took up the lyre of the Greek poet. Gounod's own appraisal of this singer's talent was a lukewarm 'very passable'.[26] To judge by one reviewer's diplomatic refusal to compare Viardot and Masson, and another's outright assertion that the new interpretation left much to be desired, the already unpopular opera lost further ground.[27] It also became clear that *Sapho* had been treated with relative tolerance by the censors in April: the conspiracy element in the plot, including the entire role of Alcée, was suppressed for the December performances. In his successful consolidation of power after the coup of 2 December 1851, Louis Napoleon effectively silenced all remaining opposition in the political arena and in the Press; theatres were also subject to stiffer surveillance than before.

[24] Review of *Sapho*, *Le Théâtre*, 19 Apr. 1851.
[25] The figures are even worse than they first appear, when the total receipts are broken down between season subscribers and holders of tickets for single performances. When the Opéra calculated its earnings for any night, it accounted for season and half-season subscribers, whether they were present or not, by including in the total the amount each was paying in theory per performance. For the months of Apr. and May 1851 this sum hovered between 1,600 and 1,900 francs an evening. Hence the figure of ticket sales for a specific performance was more indicative of its popularity; an average of 2,000–2,500 francs for *Sapho* was dismal compared to the 6,000–7,000 francs that *Le Prophète* or *La Juive* regularly brought in from individual seat sales. The breakdown of attendance figures for this period is preserved at AN AJ[13] 181.
[26] Letter to Pauline Viardot, 29 June 1851, BN MSS n.a.f. 16272, fo. 198.
[27] 'Bulletin dramatique', *Le Ménestrel*, 21 Dec. 1851, and 'Nouvelles', *La Revue et gazette musicale de Paris*, 6 July 1851.

A single performance in London on 9 August fared even more poorly, despite the efforts of Henry Chorley. As early as May 1850 Gounod had entrusted Chorley with several autographs of sacred works that might serve for his London début.[28] Predictably, the *Athenaeum* ran a glowing appraisal of Gounod's abilities after these were performed at St Martin's Hall in January 1851. The way was paved for more performances of his music in London. Pauline Viardot's reputation across the Channel had also reached an apogee after her successful appearances as Fidès during summer seasons at Covent Garden. Even before the *Sapho* première in Paris, she was able to persuade impresario Fredrick Gye to include *Sapho* in her Covent Garden contract for 1851.[29] Gounod refurbished the opera with a new aria for Glycère and some ballet music to enliven the spectacle (both aria and ballet music are now lost),[30] but these efforts went largely unnoticed in the torrent of criticism from the London Press.

Gounod's faith in his opera was not completely eradicated. Neither was that of his younger admirers, such as Ernest Reyer and Georges Bizet, who continued to speak in glowing terms about *Sapho* well after they had established their own careers. Future Opéra directors were also receptive. A revival was arranged by Alphonse Royer in 1858 for which the quartet in Act I was rewritten and the original three acts were reduced to two, with concomitant excision of over half of the original music. The first performance was on 26 July with Reyer's ballet *Sacountala*. Summer was a difficult time for an opera to take hold and the revision received only passing notice from a few reviewers not on holiday. It ran for only ten performances. Gounod attempted to breathe new life into the work for yet another revival at the Opéra in 1884. Despite a recasting of much of the libretto and music, *Sapho* again met with an unenthusiastic response from audiences now acclimatized to the strains of Massenet. On this occasion even the composer's supporters saw in his tenacity something of 'the hard shell resistant to the truth' earlier detected by the unsympathetic Turgenev.

An operatic début at the Opéra gave Gounod a high profile on the French musical scene in 1851. His next project did not take long to materialize. On the very night of the *Sapho* première, François Ponsard, the well-known author of *Lucrèce*, asked him to provide choral pieces for a new five-act tragedy entitled *Ulysse*. By June 1851 Gounod was at work on the commission.[31] The going was harder than it had been with *Sapho*; Gounod's many letters to Pauline refer often to the painstaking

[28] Letter to Chorley, 9 May 1850, *Maggs Brothers Catalogue* no. 557 (1931), lot 289.

[29] A copy of the contract is at BN MSS n.a.f. 16271, fos. 13–14.

[30] Letter from Pauline Viardot to Turgenev, 29 June 1851, in Turgenev, *Lettres inédites*, pp. 310–15.

[31] Gounod, *Mémoires*, p. 190.

labour that Ponsard's excellent verse required. *Ulysse* was still far from complete at the end of the summer. By this time Gounod was downright disillusioned about it: 'I am still stretched out over my *Ulysse*, still difficult, still arduous work, and I think that I will not write incidental music for another tragedy for a long time to come.'[32] In a letter of 7 October 1851 to George Sand he was no less despondent and admitted frankly that his quest for a musical colour that effectively evoked an ancient setting was 'very tiring for the spirit'.[33]

Gounod's involvement with the new Ponsard play did not prevent him from casting about for a new operatic subject. In view of his apparent disenchantment with the ancients, it is not surprising that he looked elsewhere for material. The correspondence of May and June 1851 contains fleeting references to a five-act *Le Paria* with Augier and Hippolyte Leroy, but Augier soon withdrew from this project because he felt that a three-way division of the fee would leave him with too little.[34] In the same summer Gounod considered a libretto with a Spanish setting called *La Perle de Castille* with Félix Beudin and Édouard Foussier. This plan was also soon dropped, probably before a single note had been written. Another stillborn two-act scheme, highly reminiscent of elements from *Les Huguenots* and Halévy's *Charles VI*, centred upon a French conspiracy to dislodge English invaders from the stronghold of La Rochelle.[35]

Perhaps the most exciting prospect was a work with George Sand. Since their first meeting in February 1851 there had been talk of collaboration between the two. A commission for Gounod to provide incidental music based on Lully for Sand's play *Molière* fell through because of opposition by the theatre's conductor to the usurpation of his own habitual function as an arranger.[36] But later that year Gounod was given the opportunity to compose an instrumental piece for Sand's *Nello*.[37] In March 1851 Sand even planned to provide Gounod with a text for an opera set in her native Berry.[38] This must have been one of

[32]   Letter from Gounod to Pauline Viardot, 26 Aug. 1851, BN MSS n.a.f. 16272, fo. 205–6.

[33]   *Documents et autographes—Librairie C. Coulet et A. Faure 1968*, lot 1123.

[34]   Letters from Gounod to Pauline Viardot: 14 June 1851, BN MSS n.a.f. 16272, fos. 196–7; 'Mardi 20–10h', n.a.f. 16272, fos. 257–8 (the month is June 1851); 'Vendredi matin—8h1/2', n.a.f. 16272, fos. 261–2; 'Mercredi 3h', n.a.f. 16272, fo. 260.

[35]   Letter from Gounod to Pauline Viardot, 7 Feb. 1852, BN MSS n.a.f. 16272, fos. 207–9.

[36]   Letter from George Sand to Pauline Viardot, 15 Mar. 1851, in Sand, *Correspondance*, x. 146–8; letter from Sand to Pierre Bocage, 30 Mar. 1851, in ibid. x. 171–3; letter from Sand to Pauline Viardot, 4 Apr. 1851, in ibid. x. 186–7.

[37]   Letter from Sand to Gounod, 30 Oct. 1851, in ibid. x. 525; letter from Sand to Pierre-Jules Hetzel, 1 Nov. 1851, in ibid. x. 528–9. Gounod's music for *Nello* was never published. The autograph is in the Sand collection (no. 892) at the Bibliothèque Spoelberch de Lovenjoul, Chantilly.

[38]   Letter from Sand to Pauline Viardot, 16 Mar. 1851, in Sand, *Correspondance*, x. 146–8; letter from Gounod to Sand, 7 Oct. 1851, in *Documents et autographes—Librairie C. Coulet et A. Faure 1968*, lot no. 1123.

'our old projects' to which Gounod referred in a letter to her of 7 October 1851.[39] In response, Sand promised him a scenario, but at the beginning of 1852, referring specifically to the Berrichon project, she indicated that the libretto of their *paysannerie* would have to be postponed for three months while she wrote a volume of her memoirs.[40]

The delay, although slight, was long enough entirely to abort the project because a great rift developed between Gounod and the Viardot circle in May 1852. Sand sided wholly with Pauline in the affair. Whether Pauline Viardot and Gounod were ever lovers will perhaps never be determined with certainty. It is true that Gounod's side of the prolific correspondence between them in 1850 and the first months of 1851 frequently shows great affection: 'Je vous aime tendrement . . . Je vous embrasse comme je vous aime', went one undated note.[41] But coming from a man who in general was extremely demonstrative, even with near-strangers, such endearments do not necessarily mean that the liaison had progressed beyond the platonic.[42] It does appear that Gounod and Pauline grew apart after his last stay at Courtavenel in October 1851. Pauline discovered in late September that she was pregnant—not by Gounod nor by Turgenev, but by Louis—and during the subsequent period of withdrawal from professional obligations she turned inwards to her family.[43] Gounod, for his part, wrote to her less regularly; at the beginning of February he admitted that he was a frequent visitor at the household of Pierre Zimmermann, a retired counterpoint and piano professor at the Conservatoire.[44]

Events now moved more quickly than Pauline had thought possible. Before long she was confronted with the news of Gounod's impending marriage to one of the Zimmermann daughters. Gounod initially indicated that the marriage would be scheduled at the end of May 'unless the state of our dear Pauline (whose presence on that day is vital to me) obliges me to postpone it for several weeks'.[45] Space does not allow for a complete telling of the *dolorosa storia* about the ensuing

---

[39] Gounod also alluded to the project with Sand in two letters to her preserved at the Bibliothèque Historique de la Ville de Paris: 22 Oct. 1851, Fonds Sand, G 4150, and 6 Jan. 1852, Fonds Sand, G 4152.

[40] Letter from Sand to Gounod, 30 Oct. 1851, in Sand, *Correspondance*, x. 525; see also letter from Sand to Gounod, 10 Jan. 1852, in ibid. x. 637–40.

[41] Note marked 'Londres, mardi, minuit 1/4', private collection.

[42] On Gounod's exuberance, see Mina Curtiss, 'Gounod before Faust', *Musical Quarterly*, 38 (1952), 48–50.

[43] Patrick Waddington, 'Courtavenel: The History of an Artists' Nest and its Role in the Life of Turgenev', Ph.D. thesis (Cambridge, 1972), fos. 204 ff.

[44] Letter to Pauline Viardot, 7 Feb. 1852, BN MSS n.a.f. 16272, fos. 207–9.

[45] Letter to George Sand marked 'Mardi soir—11h', Bibliothèque Historique de la Ville de Paris, Fonds Sand, G 4156.

shipwreck of the friendship between Gounod and the Viardots.[46] Suffice it to say that the Viardots were *not* invited to the wedding and that Gounod intercepted and returned a wedding gift which Pauline sent to his bride, Anna. Calumnious rumours had leaked through to the Zimmermanns about Gounod's liaison with Pauline Viardot. Although he provided assurances to the family of the bride that his own conduct had been beyond reproach, Gounod thought it prudent to return the gift to the singer with what he felt was a convincing explanation. Suspicions about Pauline's alleged continuing passion for the composer, misguided as they were, must have been very alive in the Zimmermann family for Gounod to risk taking this action. According to the composer's own embarrassed account of the matter, he was caught between devotion to his new family and loyalty to his friends. Yet a courtesy visit to the Viardots arranged by a third-party conciliator as reparation for rejection of the wedding gift was never made, undoubtedly because suspicions continued to smoulder among the Zimmermanns; Anna could not be expected to call upon a woman whom she regarded as a rival. Unfortunately Gounod lacked the forcefulness, forever a weak point in his character, to quench these misrepresentations of Pauline's position.

On the professional front there were new opportunities for Gounod that would ensure his future livelihood without Viardot support. When the delicate issue surrounding the wedding gift arose in May and June 1852, it was much easier than it would have been in the preceding year for Gounod to risk offending and eventually alienating his benefactors. The scales may well have been tipped by his recent appointment to the directorship of an important amateur choral society, the Orphéon de la Ville de Paris. More important, Gounod signed a contract on 10 June— that is in the midst of the imbroglio with the Viardots—to set a five-act libretto by Eugène Scribe entitled *La Nonne sanglante*. This was a noteworthy accomplishment for a young ambitious composer, since the seven other composers who set Scribe behemoths for the Opéra had all been firmly established before they first collaborated with him on 'les cinq actes'.[47] Any commitment Gounod had to raising artistic standards on the French operatic stage was temporarily submerged by more practical thoughts.

Scribe's scenario for *La Nonne sanglante* was considered by a number of composers before Gounod. That it passed from hand to hand should not be understood as an indication of the sagacity and good taste of Gounod's predecessors in rejecting a subject that appears particularly

---

[46] The entire affair is recounted by Thérèse Marix-Spire in 'Gounod and his First Interpreter', *Musical Quarterly*, 31 (1945), 299–317.
[47] They were Cherubini, Meyerbeer, Auber, Halévy, Clapisson, Donizetti, and Verdi.

absurd today. Factors other than the estimated quality of the scenario
were responsible for its peregrination. It was in the hands of Berlioz for
almost ten years and certainly met the specifications for an opera that he
had given Scribe when they first considered collaboration in 1839: 'a
simple story of love, but of violent love, well highlighted by scenes of
terror featuring the movement of masses and set either in the Middle
Ages or in the last century'.[48] Scribe, however, was very slow to
complete the text. By July 1843 Berlioz was referring to it as 'that eternal
Nun which Scribe is not finishing'.[49] To compound his difficulties, the
Opéra joint directorship of Roqueplan and Duponchel looked with
wary eyes upon the prospect of a new Berlioz work. At the end of 1847
the directors did finally agree to stage Berlioz's La Nonne sanglante, but
from his standpoint the promise was a purposefully empty one, as the
attendant condition, that the opera be put into rehearsal immediately,
was impossible to meet. Not only was the libretto still unfinished, but his
conducting activities in England would also force him to draw out
completion of the music over a number of years. According to Berlioz,
Scribe was more than happy to have the libretto back.[50]

Shortly afterwards, the newspapers reported that Félicien David was
considering the work. Apparently Roqueplan and Duponchel had not
concocted the condition of rapid completion to discourage Berlioz
alone. The reason cited in the papers two weeks later for David's
rejection of the libretto was that he also felt that he was not being given
enough time to complete the score.[51] At the same time, Le Ménestrel
published a little anecdote, perhaps primarily as a specimen of
Meyerbeer-baiting, then a popular sport in the papers, which suggested
that the composer of Robert le diable himself had solicited Scribe's
collaborator Germain Delavigne for La Nonne sanglante. Delavigne is
supposed to have refused 'the great honour, replying maliciously to the
famous composer of Le Prophète and L'Africaine [these works had been
promised for years but remained unperformed] that "I am getting old
. . . and would like to see a staging of my work!" '[52]

There is concrete evidence of Verdi's involvement with the harrowing
text. A letter of 28 September 1848 from a high official in the Opéra
administration (probably Roqueplan himself) to Scribe urged the
librettist to finish his work because Verdi was calling for a rescission of
his contract with the Opéra to set La Nonne sanglante.[53] In an effort at

---

[48] Letter of 31 Aug. 1839, in Hector Berlioz, Correspondance générale, ed. Pierre Citron
(Paris, 1975–8), ii. 575.
[49] Letter to his sister, 12 July 1843, in ibid. iii. 105–7.
[50] Berlioz, Memoirs, pp. 546–52.
[51] 'Nouvelles', La Revue et gazette musicale de Paris, 30 Jan. 1848.
[52] 'Bulletin dramatique', Le Ménestrel, 23 Jan. 1848.
[53] Letter of 28 Sept. 1848, AN F^{21} 1069.

appeasement, Verdi was to be told that it would be ready by 15 November. The letter emphasized the great importance that the Opéra direction placed on the Verdi–Scribe combination, and how future plans would be disrupted by a failure of the agreement. Fail of course it did and Scribe did not finish the libretto until after Gounod had signed his contract. Newspaper reviews at the time of the première also associated the names of Auber, Clapisson, Halévy, and Grisar with the libretto, but no further information about their connection is known save for Berlioz's smug claim that Halévy and Grisar, as well as Verdi, had turned down the offer because they knew that Scribe had treated him so miserably.[54]

The project lay dormant for four years until Gounod signed his contract with Roqueplan in 1852.[55] According to the agreement, Scribe and Delavigne were to complete the libretto within three months. Gounod was to deliver the score to the Opéra by 1 December 1853. One may suppose that Roqueplan turned to Gounod because, after the *succès d'estime* of the *Sapho* music, he thought that Gounod would fare better with a more seasoned librettist. It was also advantageous for an Opéra director to keep new works by lesser known composers in reserve in the event that a work by one of the frontline composers—Halévy, Meyerbeer, or Auber—fell short of expectations. There was certainly no pressure on the Opéra to produce Gounod's work quickly; the contract left the administration free to give *La Nonne sanglante* as late as the season of 1856–7.

Despite his duties as director of the Orphéon, which involved the composition of smaller choral works as well as the direction of as many as four rehearsals each week, Gounod was able to meet the deadline stipulated in the contract. Meanwhile, the Roqueplan administration suffered a succession of box-office failures: Halévy's *Le Juif errant*,

[54] Berlioz, *Memoirs*, p. 551. Shortly before the first performance Berlioz informed Gounod, obviously in response to a belated apologetic query, that he felt no bitterness over the matter. It is interesting, and contrary to the impression left in the *Autobiographie*, that Gounod waited until shortly before the première to check with Berlioz, rather than doing so before he signed the contract. As Mina Curtiss has pointed out ('Gounod before Faust', p. 65), Gounod's tardy concern may have been prompted mainly by a desire to secure the support of the influential critic of the *Journal des débats* on the eve of the première.

[55] In the summer of 1851 a *scène dramatique* by Gounod for baritone, chorus, and orchestra entitled *Pierre l'ermite* (one of the principal characters in the opera *La Nonne sanglante*) was performed in London. This led Prod'homme and Dandelot to suspect that he may have known the libretto of *La Nonne sanglante* long before the contract was signed. Because the location of the manuscript for this unpublished work was unknown, verification of the hypothesis was then impossible. Fortunately an autograph reduction of *Pierre l'ermite* for piano four hands, purchased by the Swedish collector Rudolf Nydahl, now belongs to the Stiftelsen Musikkulturens Främjande in Stockholm. Enough of the text is present to certify that it is not related to the Scribe libretto. Even if this document did not survive, one would have to note the absence of any mention of a project with Scribe in the available correspondence with the Viardots.

Verdi's *Luisa Miller* in French translation, and *La Fronde* by Nieder-meyer all had short runs. As a result, *La Nonne sanglante* was put into rehearsal even before Gounod had completed the opera. For the first few months after the initial rehearsal in September 1853, however, the administration's efforts did seem tentative: a single chorus rehearsal here, sessions for individual soloists there, weeks of nothing. By February, the final cast had been selected, but rehearsals only proceeded on a regular basis in April in an unsuccessful attempt to stage the work before the summer.

    La Nonne sanglante finally appeared, after several additional post-ponements, on 18 October 1854. The music was well received by the Press and the opera was a moderate success with the public. Gounod overestimated the receipts at 7,000 to 8,000 francs a night in his *Autobiographie* but the actual figure of 6,000 to 6,500 francs, though not outstanding, was a respectable showing, and certainly better than that achieved by *Sapho*. Unfortunately for Gounod, these were turbulent times at the Opéra. In what proved to be more than an embarrassing incident for Roqueplan, the star soprano of the house, Sophie Cruvelli, collected her monthly paycheck one afternoon at the beginning of October and then promptly disappeared from view, failing to appear for her next scheduled performance as Valentine in *Les Huguenots* on the ninth of the month. She clearly felt no compunction to honour her contract, though Roqueplan had provided her with an unprecedented, and of course well advertised, salary of 100,000 francs for the season— a crafty publicity ploy to enhance her status in the eyes of the public. An even larger vein of mirth was mined from the affair. It was common knowledge in circles close to the imperial household that the Minister of the Imperial Household, Achille Fould, was infatuated with the soprano but had been repelled by her. Now, with highly compromising letters from the minister in her possession, she had fled with the young Baron Vigier. (Count Horace de Viel-Castel wryly noted in his diary that the newspapers had been effectively muzzled in their reports about this angle.)[56] Moreover, Verdi threatened to withdraw his new opera *Les Vêpres siciliennes* if the wayward soprano, for whom he had written the lead female role, did not reappear. The Opéra had been returned to direct state management in the summer after a regime of private entrepreneurship that had been put into effect since the days of Véron, but it had shown no sign of economic recovery. The disappearance of la Cruvelli was the last straw. Roqueplan was asked to resign on 6

[56] Entry for 26 Oct. 1854, *Mémoires du Comte Horace de Viel Castel sur le règne de Napoléon III* (Paris, 1883), 77–8.

November and François Crosnier, a former director of the Opéra-Comique, was immediately appointed his successor. The almost uninterrupted string of performances of *La Nonne sanglante* following the première may be attributable to the fact that the popular Cruvelli and her repertoire were not available to fill alternate nights. Some of the other principal female leads at the Opéra—Melanie Tedesco, Marietta Alboni, and Rosina Stoltz—were also absent because of foreign contracts.[57] The new director was as unfavourably disposed to *La Nonne sanglante* as Roqueplan had been favourable to it. According to Gounod, Crosnier frankly disclosed that, as long as he was in charge, he would not permit such 'rubbish' on the stage of the Opéra.[58]

The libretto, not the score, bore the brunt of hostilities. The Press unanimously lambasted it as a specimen *par excellence* of Scribe's declining abilities. 'Most definitely the opera libretto is in a state of decadence . . . the libretto of *La Nonne sanglante* is there to prove it,' wrote M. Bourges of *La Revue et gazette musicale de Paris*.[59] The government report of 1854 about the state of the Opéra may also have been in the forefront of Crosnier's mind.[60] Apart from its recommendation that the Opéra be returned to direct government control, the report had some candid observations about the nature of the repertoire. It argued that in the recent past the public had been swamped by the 'superficial attractions of noisy passions' and 'the charlatanism of forced expression; the new civil servant director's duty is to respect "the authority of good taste" over the seductions of easy entertainment'. Rather than bow consistently to audience demand, the director, with the security of the state's complete financial backing, was to enlighten his public by exposing it to higher forms of art. (Gluck revivals, it maintained, would be suitable vehicles to raise the collective level of taste.) Although too much emphasis on the classics engendered boredom, at the very least certain 'caprices of the hour' should be purged. The main target of these observations seems to have been Meyerbeer (though no names were mentioned), but in the sphere of the libretto it is probable that *La Nonne sanglante* was just the sort of facile product that the commissioners had in mind. To a greater extent than was usual with Scribe, the dramatic situations, some centring upon the appearance of a bleeding spectre within whom the flames of mortal love still flickered, were little more than sensational contrivances to titillate the audience. The eccentric Roqueplan, with his penchant for wearing

---

[57] See editorial by C. Desnoyer, *Le Siècle*, 14 Nov. 1854.
[58] Gounod, *Mémoires*, p. 195.
[59] Issue of 29 Oct. 1854.
[60] 'Rapport de la Commission chargée d'examiner la situation de l'Opéra', *Le Moniteur universel*, 2 July 1854.

red trousers and embroidered moccasins, would hardly have been one to quake before 'the authority of good taste'. But Crosnier may well have taken some of the report's proposals seriously in order to demonstrate a radical change of course at the start of his tenure.

On 17 November the eleventh and last performance of *La Nonne sanglante* was given; it has never been revived. Shortly before, Sophie Cruvelli had surfaced with Vigier in Germany and was persuaded to return to the rehearsals of Verdi's *Les Vêpres siciliennes* and perform-ances of *Les Huguenots*. Her escapade was not without a certain market value: earnings soared to around the 9,000-franc level for her first few appearances. *La Nonne sanglante* was not missed at the box office.

In both the *Autobiographie* and the *Mémoires* Gounod admitted utter incomprehension at the attitude of Crosnier, noting that 'directorial decisions . . . are sometimes motivated by underlying elements that are useless to attempt to discover'.[61] Scribe placed the blame for the failure of *La Nonne sanglante* squarely upon Gounod's shoulders. According to Gounod's *Autobiographie*, Scribe offered him a three-act *opéra comique* entitled *Le Livre d'or* immediately after the première of *La Nonne sanglante*, only to withdraw the proposal a short time later. Showing a curiously skewed view of his own œuvre, Scribe is supposed to have left the hapless composer with the remark that

For the moment I have had enough. And how! I gave you the most beautiful poem, the most dramatic, the most effective, that I have ever written, and now the *feuilletons* tear it to pieces. They scream out that I have passed my prime and that there is nothing left for me to do but retire! Very well; I will do so. So do not count on me.[62]

Crosnier's own assessment of the work as rubbish must have been made in reference to the libretto and not to the music; he thought highly enough of Gounod soon to offer him another five-act opera, *Ivan le terrible* to a libretto by Henri Trianon and François Hippolyte Leroy. By the summer of 1856 Gounod confessed to an unspecified correspondent that this project was taking up the limited amount of time he had at his disposal to compose.[63] It was first rumoured that the new Gounod work was scheduled for performance immediately after Biletta's *La Rose de Florence* (première on 10 November 1856). But the Opéra admini-stration was slow to start the production process, despite the prodding of papers such as *Le Figaro*. Crosnier fell from grace in 1856. The new

---

[61]   Gounod, *Mémoires*, p. 195.
[62]   *Autobiographie de Charles Gounod et articles sur la routine en matière d'art*, ed. Georgina Weldon (London, 1875), 24–5.
[63]   Letter of 20 Aug. 1856, BN Mus. Gounod lettre autographe signée (hereafter l.a.s.) 20.

director, Alphonse Royer, seems only to have taken interest in *Ivan le terrible* at the end of 1857, after Gounod had regaled him with a preliminary reading at the piano.[64] Yet Royer admitted a few months later, in a letter to Achille Fould, that *Ivan* would be 'impossible to present because the plot centres on a conspiracy against an emperor and empress of Russia'.[65]

Just why the libretto suddenly became impossible after it had been in Gounod's hands for over two years—and had been offered to him by Royer's predecessor—may be explained by contemporary political circumstances in France. On 14 January 1858, that is between Gounod's reading at the Opéra and Royer's letter to Fould, Napoleon and the Empress Eugénie narrowly escaped with their lives after a bomb planted by an Italian expatriate, Felice Orsini, exploded beneath the imperial carriage as the two were disembarking to attend a performance at the Opéra. Ironically, the programme that night, a benefit for the famous bass Eugène Massol, consisted entirely of excerpts drawn from works centring upon political conspiracy or regicide, the operas *Gustave III*, *La Muette de Portici*, and *Guillaume Tell*, as well as Schiller's *Maria Stuart*. As Alain Plessis, the historian, has noted, the assassination attempt forced Napoleon's top officials to realize how much the stability of the entire regime depended upon the Emperor's continued good health.[66] Repressive measures aimed at would-be dissidents, at first only half-heartedly endorsed by Napoleon himself, were quickly codified in a *Loi de sûreté générale*, promulgated on 27 February. In the *Ivan* libretto as set by Bizet, to whom it eventually passed in 1863, Czar Ivan ultimately survives to send the principal conspirator to the scaffold.[67] Even had Gounod's opera finished in this manner, the climate of political unrest in the work was inappropriate for France's first stage in the wake of the Orsini affair, particularly since the theatre was now under direct state management.

There may well have been substantial differences between the text that Bizet set and that which Gounod was offered. Changes were made to the libretto even while it was in Gounod's possession. In an undated letter to Prince Poniatowsky, composer of the successful four-act opera

---

[64] 'Nouvelles', *Le Figaro*, 15 Nov. 1857.
[65] Letter of 30 Apr. 1858, AN AJ[13] 443. See below, p. 48.
[66] Alain Plessis, *De la fête impériale au mur des fédérés, 1852–1871* (Paris, 1979), 192–3.
[67] On the Bizet work, see Leslie Wright, 'Bizet before Carmen', Ph.D. thesis (Princeton, 1981), and Winton Dean 'Bizet's Ivan IV', in Herbert van Thal (ed.), *Fanfare for Ernest Newman* (London, 1955), 55–85. Dean gives a complete plot summary and corrects the information supplied by J. G. Prod'homme and A. Dandelot in *Gounod: Sa vie et ses œuvres* (Paris, 1911), i. 177, that the Bizet libretto was written by Edouard Blau and Louis Gallet.

Pierre de Médicis (1860), Gounod mentioned that his librettists had just completely changed the book so as to render it unrecognizable to the censor.[68] He must have referred here to an unsuccessful attempt to save the project after the political events in early 1858. An autograph score of *Ivan le terrible* which was put up for sale at an auction in the early 1960s suggests that Gounod had made substantial progress with the work before it was dropped. The vocal parts were filled in throughout the document and some of the pages contained orchestration as well.[69] Although the score has since been destroyed, not all of the music from *Ivan le terrible* has disappeared. Gounod was persuaded to include a march chorus from the rejected work in another project that had taken shape: a setting of *Faust*. It became the Soldiers' Chorus, perhaps the most famous number in an opera that would secure Gounod's reputation world-wide.

[68] *Privat Catalogue*, no. 288 (1954), lot 382.
[69] *Manuscrits musicaux de Charles Gounod* (Catalogue of sale of Gounod autographs), Hôtel Drouot, 27 Nov. 1963, lot 31.

3. *Turn to the Théâtre-Lyrique*

GOUNOD'S interest in Goethe's *Faust* as a possible source for an opera was longstanding; the subject was bound to attract one who had frequently argued that French opera was sorely in need of greater artistic substance (*La Nonne sanglante* notwithstanding). The seed was planted at the French Academy in Rome, where Gounod familiarized himself with *Faust* in the French translation by Gérard de Nerval. According to the *Mémoires*, some musical motives for the 'Nuit de Walpurgis' came to him during a nocturnal excursion on the Isle of Capri; before long he had filled his copy of Nerval's translation 'with scattered notes of different ideas that I supposed would serve me when I would attempt to treat the subject as an opera'.[1] It is not surprising that, when Gounod emerged from the Missions Étrangères years, one of the first projects he embarked upon was a setting of Gretchen's scene in the church. The present location of this score is unknown, but a brief auction-catalogue description does suggest that the music of this isolated setting of an episode from Goethe's *Faust* is different from the corresponding scene in the opera.[2] In reporting Gounod's marriage to Anna Zimmermann in 1852, one newspaper in Germany noted that 'the fiancé is composing a *Faust*'.[3] One suspects here that the journalist relayed the composer's sounding-off about distant plans as a more immediate project than it actually was. Gounod did not have the libretto for *Faust* in his hands until 1856 and the extant letters to the Viardots of 1850–2, although filled with references to operatic projects, never hint at a setting of Goethe's work. It was only after the *La Nonne sanglante* fiasco that Gounod actually first met the principal players in the *Faust* project and indeed in his subsequent operatic career: the librettists Michel Carré and Jules Barbier, and the impresario Léon Carvalho.

Within a week after Gounod's death in 1893 contradictory accounts of the *Faust* genesis were published by Jules Barbier and Carvalho.[4]

---

[1] Gounod, *Mémoires*, p. 118.

[2] *Manuscrits musicaux de Charles Gounod*, Hôtel Drouot, 27 Nov. 1963, lot 9. It is noteworthy, however, that the catalogue's facsimile of the first page of the full score shows a piece in C minor with a contrapuntal organ prelude, both features of the scene in the opera.

[3] Prod'homme and Dandelot, *Gounod*, i. 187.

[4] Barbier's account appeared in an article entitled 'Souvenirs sur Gounod', *Le Journal*, 27 Oct. 1893; that of Carvalho appeared in Albert Montel, 'Souvenirs de M. L. Carvalho', Literary Supplement, *Le Figaro*, 28 Oct. 1893.

Each claimed the honour of having first suggested a *Faust* to the composer. Both acknowledged that Gounod had responded to their offer by exclaiming that the subject had been 'in his gut' (to use Carvalho's expression) for many years. Barbier's memories of his first dealings with Gounod centre upon the *Faust* project. During a chance meeting in the street shortly after they were introduced to one another, he impetuously proposed a *Faust* to Gounod, who eagerly seized the opportunity. But on this point Barbier's reminiscences are flawed. *Faust* was not the project that brought them to consider collaboration for the first time. In the spring of 1855 two friends of the composer, the singers Anatole and Hippolyte Lionnet, persuaded the publisher Heugel to distribute one of Gounod's *mélodies*.[5] Gounod was grateful enough to offer to write a short *opéra comique* for them. In response, the Lionnets directed Gounod to their good friends Barbier and Carré, who had recently started to make a mark as a libretto-writing team with *Galathée* and *Les Noces de Jeannette* for Victor Massé. The project for the Lionnets was abandoned when *Faust* became a reality.

Carvalho's account, published a day later than Barbier's, maintains that he himself suggested a *Faust* for the Théâtre-Lyrique to Gounod in December 1856. The discrepancy between both versions involves more than biographical minutiae. According to Barbier, Gounod and he first approached the Opéra administration with the plan, only to be rebuffed by the response that the subject lacked the necessary pomp for France's first stage; none the less, the implication is that the work was first envisaged with recitative instead of spoken dialogue and with a ballet, since both were performing conventions at the Opéra. The Barbier version has been given credence by many later writers (perhaps because of the self-congratulatory flatulence of Carvalho's article), in spite of a revised account published one year later in which Barbier showed cognizance of the Carvalho version by introducing modifications that took it into account: 'I think that in reality Carvalho and I proposed it [*Faust*] to him at the same time. He [Gounod] even said to Carvalho, who may perhaps claim priority, that "I've had this in my gut for ten years".'[6] In acknowledging this, Barbier naturally dropped his contention that the Opéra was the theatre first approached. Furthermore, Gounod's own *Mémoires* record that the Théâtre-Lyrique was the intended destination from the beginning.

Carvalho's recollections are suspect on another point. His story that Gounod had 'almost finished' the work by 27 February 1857, after

---

[5] The Lionnet account, supported by a contemporary letter from Gounod to them, appeared in *Le Gaulois*, 14 Dec. 1894.

[6] Jules Barbier, 'Trois millièmes', *La Vie théâtrale*, 5 Dec. 1894, 4–5.

having received the commission only the previous December, seems improbable Even allowing for Gounod's usual writing speed, and for the possibility that he may have sown some of the seeds in previous years, he could hardly have almost completed this long opera within two months, especially in view of his ongoing work with the Orphéon. On 27 February Carvalho told Gounod that, because the Théâtre de la Porte-Saint-Martin had recently announced plans for a sumptuous treatment of the Goethe tragedy, he would have to postpone the Théâtre-Lyrique *Faust* indefinitely.[7] Gounod's account of the project's chronology in his *Autobiographie* supports Carvalho's date for the postponement by placing it in the first months of 1857. But it is more believable on the question of how long the work actually took to write. Gounod notes that he had completed half of *Faust* in 'about one year' before the director broke the unhappy news to him.[8] This is supported by a contemporary interview with *Le Figaro* in which Gounod indicated that he had written two acts of *Faust* (that is, three acts of the opera as it is printed in all editions) before he had been obliged to drop it.[9]

Gounod responded to Carvalho's decision by protesting that the Théâtre-Lyrique did not need to fear competition, because 'the public that would go to see a large boulevard melodrama and that which comes to your theatre are completely different and have no influence upon each other'. In Gounod's brief account of the episode one senses a certain wounded pride that his artistic ideals had to give way to a crass boulevard showpiece.[10] What probably disturbed Carvalho more than competition for attendance was mere comparison with the Porte-Saint-Martin. Since the 1820s this theatre had catered to the taste for spectacle

---

[7] That *Faust* had been shelved by the end of Mar. 1857 is suggested by a letter from Gounod to Emile Augier, postmarked 27 Mar. 1857, in which Gounod refers to their collaboration on an unnamed opera scenario; this project was probably the result of Gounod's search for new operatic subjects after Carvalho's disappointing news of 27 Feb. 1857 about the *Faust* postponement. The project with Augier was soon abandoned. A facsimile of this letter is given as the frontispiece of Henri Liebrecht, *Théâtre de la Monnaie, 250e anniversaire* (Brussels, 1949).

[8] Gounod, *Autobiographie*, p. 27. In a letter of 20 Aug. 1856 to an unnamed correspondent, Gounod indicated that he was not available for an operatic collaboration because he was working on 'five acts' (*Ivan le terrible*) as well as 'a symphony promised for this winter, a requiem in progress . . . [and] an engagement for one act and for three acts with Barbier and Carré' (BN Mus. Gounod l.a.s. 20). There is little possibility that the 'five acts' could refer to *Faust* itself, for *Ivan le terrible* had been given to Gounod at the beginning of 1856. He would have mentioned this opera in a letter that outlined his current compositional obligations. If *Faust* pre-empts the 'five acts' designation in the letter, *Ivan le terrible* would not be accounted for. It also seems likely that the one-act piece listed is the little *opéra comique* that Gounod promised to the Lionnets. Because the immediate model for the *Faust* libretto was Carré's three-act play *Faust et Marguerite*, it is possible that at the earliest stages the opera was also planned in this shape.

[9] *Le Figaro*, 8 Oct. 1857.

[10] Gounod, *Autobiographie*, p. 27.

of a large portion of the theatre-going public—'l'opéra du peuple' it had been called.[11] Under the direction of Marc Fournier in the 1850s it turned out ever more colossal plays and *féeries*, ostentatious productions in which any semblance of plot was an excuse to provide a 'machine à grand spectacle'. The Théâtre-Lyrique was still viewed as something of an upstart operatic enterprise. Carvalho was particularly anxious to establish a high standard of performance and *mise-en-scène*, not only to secure prestigious standing for his house, but also to earn a coveted state subsidy. It would be difficult to negate the impression that, in producing *Faust*, the Théâtre-Lyrique was taking its cue from an 'opéra du peuple' success. Indeed, when Gounod offered *Faust* to the Opéra after Carvalho balked, Royer's objection to it, expressed in a letter to Achille Fould, was that *Faust* was about to appear at another theatre, *a priori* one of lower status. Carvalho's position was probably similar. After outlining the chances for a new work from either Verdi or Meyerbeer, Royer described his next most important priorities:

After these two great masters, the composers of talent heralded by public opinion and developed enough to be presented with honour at the Opéra are Messrs. Gounod, Félicien David, and Gevaert.

Gounod has two large works; one Yvan [*sic*] le Terrible is unfortunately impossible because of its premiss, a conspiracy against the lives of the emperor and empress of Russia; the other is a Faust, which I would not risk producing at this moment because the Théâtre de la Porte-Saint-Martin is giving a Faust drama within three months with a sumptuous *mise-en-scène*, and we would appear to be copying a secondary theatre. These obstacles are very annoying because it is Gounod whom I would have proposed to choose first as closest to the level of the masters.[12]

It is also possible that Royer, like Carvalho, was actually concerned about being scenically outshone by the Porte-Saint-Martin, a humiliation that would have been all too obvious because of the identical subject-matter. France's 'first stage' was supposed to be first in all areas, but the boulevard theatres, the Porte-Saint-Martin in particular, often matched the Académie in decorative opulence.

The situation was not entirely bleak for Gounod and his librettists. As consolation for the *Faust* disappointment, Carvalho soon proposed that they combine to adapt Molière's comedy *Le Médecin malgré lui* for the operatic stage. They set to work immediately. Since Molière's prose was used for all of the spoken dialogue, and the verse destined for musical setting was also based upon the original text, the libretto was produced

---

[11]   Marie-Antoinette Allévy, *La Mise-en-scène en France dans la première moitié du dix-neuvième siècle* (Paris, 1938), 55 ff.

[12]   Letter of 30 Apr. 1858, AN F²¹ 1069. Another copy is at AN AJ¹³ 443.

quickly. Gounod composed the score in roughly five months and it was ready to go into rehearsal when he suffered a severe nervous breakdown at the beginning of October 1857. A reading of *Ivan le terrible* at the Opéra in the second week of November notwithstanding, Gounod wrote to an unnamed correspondent on the nineteenth of the month that he could not resume work until the beginning of December.[13]

The staging of an *opéra comique* so closely based upon Molière was bound to lend the Théâtre-Lyrique the cachet of distinction that Carvalho craved. It also steered him into trouble with the authorities. At a time when each theatre in Paris had a legally entrenched monopoly over its repertoire, the Comédie-Française was quick to object to what it regarded as wanton plundering of its jurisdiction. Upon return to professional life, Gounod appealed directly to Achille Fould to save the project, writing that he had long sought a highly artistic subject for a quintessentially French *opéra bouffe* and that it seemed entirely natural to draw upon the work of France's comic genius for this purpose.[14] Gounod's personal petition, as well as the intervention of Princess Mathilde on his behalf—-in gratitude Gounod dedicated the work to her—finally drew reluctant approval from the government. In recommending acceptance to Fould, Camille Doucet, chief of the theatre division in the ministry, pointed out that there were few precedents and that, because the Théâtre-Lyrique did not receive government subsidy, leniency should be exercised on this occasion.[15] The various jurisdictions of French theatres ceased to be a matter for official control with the promulgation of a law on 6 January 1864 that permitted all theatres to perform any work that had fallen within the public domain.

Le Médecin malgré lui was first performed on 15 January 1858. This time the libretto was insulated from criticism, for to find fault with it was also to find fault with a seventeenth-century national treasure. The critics, on the whole, responded favourably to the music as well. Some of the acclaim must have warmed Gounod. 'Gounod has not merely achieved one of those facile victories sanctioned by the masses, but he has also succeeded from the standpoint of art,' wrote Jules Lovy of *Le Ménestrel*.[16] Many echoed Lovy's assessment that the composer was particularly skilled at adapting eighteenth-century gestures—the names of Lully and Grétry were frequently invoked—to a modern harmonic palette. Berlioz also expressed approval, but his concerns that the opera

---

[13] BN Mus. Gounod l.a.s. 104. See also letter to Jules Richomme, 19 Oct. 1857, *Revue hebdomadaire*, 2 Jan. 1909, 33.
[14] Letter of 1 Dec. 1857, AN F²¹ 1121.
[15] Doucet's memo is conserved in AN F²¹ 1121.
[16] Review of *Le Médecin malgré lui*, *Le Ménestrel*, 17 Jan. 1858.

might not be a financial success proved well founded. By March *Le Médecin malgré lui* faltered at the box office. Bizet, then in Italy as a *Prix de Rome* laureat, was stunned by this news; it was bound to be discomforting for a young composer enamoured of Gounod's style and eager to leave a mark of his own. 'This is discouraging, crazy, and revolting,' he wrote to his mother. 'If one cannot achieve success with music like that, then to hell and damnation with everything!'[17] When he actually saw the music two months later, he declared it 'the best thing that has been done in the comic vein since Grétry'.[18] Though the work was not completely abandoned by the Théâtre-Lyrique (it attained 142 performances by 1870), in later years it was only sporadically revived at the Opéra-Comique. To this day, the substance, if not the tone, of Bizet's outburst still rings true; of Gounod's less-successful operas, *Le Médecin malgré lui* is the one whose poor performance history is least reflective of intrinsic artistic merit.

Soon after the première of *Le Médecin malgré lui*, Gounod busied himself with the reworking of *Sapho* for the Opéra. 'This return to my operatic première, and one of my first pieces, flatters me in some way more than the opportunity to write a new work: it is a sign of retrospective esteem,' wrote Gounod to Emile Augier in March.[19] But, after both *Ivan le terrible* and *Faust* had been turned down by Royer, the *Sapho* revival was, at best, a consolation prize. Gounod's words sound suspiciously like those of one who is trying to put a good light on a disappointing situation. As it happened, his professional outlook rapidly improved. Marc Fournier of the Théâtre de la Porte-Saint-Martin decided to delay his *Faust* production until September 1858 and Carvalho changed his mind about Gounod's *Faust*, perhaps because he grew impatient waiting indefinitely for a rival initiative. One of the first indications in available documentation that Gounod had taken it up again is an aside to Bizet on 30 April that he was 'à cheval sur Faust'.[20] It had to share time with the rehearsals for the *Sapho* revival, in full swing by the third week of May; that 'retrospective esteem' was now less important than it had been in the previous months is suggested by Gounod's decision to forgo attendance at the *Sapho* première on 26 July in favour of concentrated work on *Faust* in Switzerland.

---

[17] Letter of 30 Mar. 1858, in Georges Bizet, *Lettres: Impressions de Rome, 1857–60*, ed. Louis Ganderax (Paris, 1907), 52. Many of the letters in this volume are incomplete; a copy of the book once owned by Bizet's biographer Mina Curtiss, with manuscript and typed additions of the missing portions, is at BN Mus. Rés. 2704. An unpublished section of this letter is cited here.

[18] Letter to his mother, 16 May 1858, in Bizet, *Lettres de Rome*, p. 61, at BN Mus. Rés. 2704.

[19] Letter of 26 Mar. 1858, Charavay in-house file of autographs.

[20] Pougin, 'Gounod écrivain' (1912), 279.

Gounod delayed most of the work on the final three acts of *Faust* (Acts IV and V as performed today) until the summer. Writing to Desirée Artot, the Sapho of 1858, on 18 July from Interlaken, he confessed: 'I have composed very little since my arrival; but I have written some of the vocal parts for the third act . . . on another front, I have been informed that once again there is a possibility, this time very serious, of Madame Carvalho's entry into the cast.'[21] Until then, Gounod had intended the role of Marguerite for Delphine Ugalde, a well-known *chanteuse à roulades* whose voice had none the less deteriorated since her brilliant creation of the title role in Massé's *Galathée* several years before (from his distant vantage-point Bizet termed the choice 'disastrous').[22] The casting problem must have been resolved by 15 August, when newspapers reported that Marie Miolan-Carvalho was to perform in *Faust*. Miolan-Carvalho's star was still on the rise, but to deal with any singer whose husband (or lover) was the director could not have been an enviable undertaking for any composer. During rehearsals at the Opéra for his *Dom Sébastien* over ten years before, Donizetti had quite literally been driven mad by Rosina Stoltz, mistress of director Léon Pillet. Gounod's cause was certainly helped by performances that propelled Miolan-Carvalho to international fame, but in the future her imperiousness would not always be advantageous to his work.

Only the 'Nuit de Walpurgis' tableau remained to be completed when Gounod returned to Paris at the beginning of September 1858.[23] While Gounod scrambled to finish the orchestration of *Faust*, rehearsals were launched with a view to a first performance by the end of the year. There were the usual mishaps and upheavals to delay the première until 19 March 1859. Following the practice of many other composers for the French stage, Gounod had written too long a work. Nearly one-third of the original score was cut during rehearsal. Some of the cuts were made at the behest of the Carvalhos, creating, as Léon Carvalho later remembered it, temporary friction between the parties. Bizet once again took up the cudgels for his mentor: 'I am enraged to see that Gounod is subjected to such ridiculous demands [of Madame Miolan-Carvalho],' he wrote at the end of 1858; unfortunately Bizet did not detail these.[24]

[21] *Documents and Autographs Limited*, Catalogue no. 4, Oct. 1965.
[22] Letter to his mother, dated Apr. 1858, in Bizet, *Lettres de Rome*, p. 54, at BN Mus. Rés. 2704.
[23] On 17 Aug. 1858 Gounod told his brother-in-law Édouard Dubufe that, after some weeks of poor production, his work on the opera was now finally going well. The third act was almost completely orchestrated and the prison tableau had been drafted; only the 'Nuit de Walpurgis' music was still quite incomplete. The letter is in the collection of Madame Serge Grandjean.
[24] Letter to Hector Gruyer, 31 Dec. 1858, in Bizet, *Lettres de Rome*, p. 61, at BN Mus. Rés. 2704.

The censors were disturbed by scenes that might adversely excite local church authorities or, worse, cause a diplomatic row with the Papal States. Siébel's recourse to holy water to revive a withered daisy in Act III ('Si je trempais mes doigts dans l'eau bénite') and the entire cathedral tableau were deemed hazardous. Gounod's contacts in the church served him well in this instance. The Papal Nuncio in Paris, a friend of the composer, appeased the censors by declaring that there was nothing objectionable in the work.[25]

Another serious problem arose when Hector Gruyer, the young tenor originally hired for the role of Faust, became hoarse during the final dress rehearsal at the end of February. Since Gruyer was a prize student of his father, Bizet had particularly high hopes for him. In truth, the role was ill-suited to his voice. Gounod admitted to Bizet in January that there were weak moments in his execution.[26] When Gruyer actually did perform the work at the Théâtre-Lyrique later that year, he was soon forced to withdraw because of hostile critical reception. Rather than wait for Gruyer to recover in February, Gounod and Carvalho thought it safer to proceed with another tenor for the première. Fortunately, a veteran from the Opéra-Comique roster, Joseph Barbot, was available. The first performance of *Faust* was delayed three weeks while he learnt the role. Bizet took the whole matter as a personal affront, erroneously believing that Gounod had abandoned Gruyer because of the nefarious influence of his wife Anna.[27] The Viardot affair must have been in the forefront of Bizet's mind when he wrote to his mother: 'Gounod is the least reliable man in the world when it comes to friendship . . . he is the most extraordinary musician we now have (excepting Rossini and Meyerbeer), which again proves that to be a great artist it is not necessary to be an honest man.'[28]

Gounod's opera faced formidable competition, as the opening nights of David's *Herculanum* at the Opéra and of Meyerbeer's *Le Pardon de Ploërmel* at the Opéra-Comique occurred within a few weeks of the *Faust* première. Bizet was sceptical about Gounod's prospects: 'Unfortunately my fears on the subject of *Faust* are mounting every day. It will not be a success. There are at the moment three champions in the arena: David at the Opéra, Meyerbeer at the Opéra-Comique, and Gounod at the Théâtre-Lyrique; there will be two losers and one of them will not be Meyerbeer.'[29] As it happened, Bizet was wrong; all three

[25] This anecdote is told by Carvalho in 'Souvenirs de M. L. Carvalho', Literary Supplement, *Le Figaro*, 28 Oct. 1893.

[26] Letter of 4 Jan. 1859, in Pougin, 'Gounod écrivain' (1912), 282–3.

[27] Michel Poupet, 'Gounod et Bizet', *L'Avant-scène*, 41 (1982), 115.

[28] Letter of 5 Mar. 1858, in Bizet, *Lettres de Rome*, p. 139, at BN Mus. Rés. 2704.

[29] Letter to his mother dated 'fin janvier 1859', in Bizet, *Lettres de Rome*, pp. 125–9.

works did well at the box office during their first runs. Gounod's opera, of course, went on to establish an international career and to eclipse both *Herculanum* and *Le Pardon de Ploërmel*.

Few of Gounod's works before *Faust* had been published: the Zimmermann family had financed a piano–vocal score of *La Nonne sanglante* (reduced by Bizet), Escudier had published the incidental music from *Ulysse*, and Colombier had brought out *Le Médecin malgré lui*. Even in the days after the *Faust* première, publishers were wary of Gounod's music. Colombier offered to buy the publication rights for 4,000 francs, the same sum he had paid for *Le Médecin malgré lui*, a much shorter work. His offer was declined. Neither Heugel nor Escudier would have anything to do with the new score. Finally, a small publisher of *salon* pieces named Antoine Choudens agreed to purchase the work for 10,000 francs (two-thirds to Gounod)—with no provision for royalties, according to the French custom.[30] This was a modest enough sum when one notes that Meyerbeer had sold the publication rights for *Le Prophète* for over four times this amount, and even more modest considering that *Faust* catapulted Choudens to prosperity. In view of Gounod's future well-known affiliation with Choudens—he was to publish his next five operas—the composer's remarks to Pauline Viardot in a letter of 10 June 1851 are amusing, and an indication of a certain self-confidence that would give way to more realistic considerations:

Yesterday I received a letter from M. Choudens the music dealer at 385 rue Saint-Honoré near rue Nationale, who tells me that several pieces from my charming opera [*Sapho*] are being requested with persistence. He asks me when it will be published, adding that it is regrettable that this has not already been done. What do you think of this? Should I talk to him and sound him out on the matter of an edition? This seems a rather unattractive house to give its name to the publication of a score.[31]

There can be no doubt that Choudens was an astute entrepreneur who was willing to take risks. In late 1859, for example, he brought out both *Sapho* and *La Nonne sanglante* in order to capitalize on the popularity of *Faust* by publishing Gounod's lesser known compositions. By arranging performances of *Faust* at provincial and foreign houses, Choudens also kept it afloat after it was dropped from the repertoire of the Théâtre-Lyrique in April 1860. That *Faust* temporarily disappeared from Paris seems to have been connected not with its popularity, but rather with Carvalho's relinquishing of the Théâtre-Lyrique directorship in 1860. For a mysterious reason—perhaps because Miolan-Carvalho

---

[30] The contract is reproduced in Prod'homme and Dandelot, *Gounod*, i. 225–6.
[31] Letter of 10 June 1851, BN MSS n.a.f. 16272, fos. 114–15.

was no longer available—Carvalho's successor, Charles Réty, did not stage the work during his two-year period of tenure. When Carvalho and his wife returned to the Théâtre-Lyrique at the end of 1862, *Faust* was reinstated. In the interim, Choudens set about to arrange performances at Strasburg, Rouen, and Bordeaux in April 1860, for the first time with recitatives in place of the original spoken dialogue. Spectacular successes on virtually all of the major German stages followed in the next eighteen months. Predictably, German critics attacked the libretto, but sensitivities about the desecration of a national literary monument were assuaged at the Dresden première (31 August 1861) by a rechristening of the work as *Margarete*, a title that has endured on German stages to this day.

Whereas Gounod was comforted for many years by the assumption that the conducting tours were organized by Choudens to fulfil a higher artistic mission, a cooling of relations between them in the early 1870s brought with it a new perspective: quite simply, it was good for business to have Gounod personally oversee early performances of the work. Noting that Verdi was customarily paid a small fortune to travel, Gounod decried the fact that only his expenses had been covered and that he had played the role of 'a billboard, a sidedrum with which Choudens could advertise his merchandise abroad'.[32] That Gounod could ever have thought otherwise bespeaks a remarkable degree of *naïveté* about the mechanics of the operatic world. Moreover, Choudens cannot be entirely faulted for failing to offer remuneration to the composer; the analogy to Verdi, which may have made sense to a Gounod who was famous in the 1870s, was hardly apt in reference to the relatively obscure figure of 1860.

Following this succession of appearances in Germany, Gounod oversaw rehearsals for the Italian-language première of *Faust* at La Scala in November 1862. A London production was slower to materialize, though the Chappell publishing firm acquired the English rights for the opera soon after its première. Since this investment was worthless without popular demand created by performances, the Chappell brothers offered to underwrite some of the costs for a staging at the Royal Italian Opera, Covent Garden. After two years of trying in vain to get Gounod's work on to the boards of that house, they found a more willing impresario in James Mapleson, manager of the rival Her Majesty's Theatre. In view of Gounod's slender reputation in England, Mapleson recognized that special precautions were in order. He scheduled the opera for four nights in succession and managed to give

---

[32] Gounod, *Autobiographie*, p. 30.

away all tickets for the first three nights, 'after a prodigious outlay in envelopes, and above all postage stamps', he later wrote in his memoirs.

When ... would-be purchasers were told that 'everything had gone' [he continued], they went away and repeated it to their friends, who, in their turn, came to see whether it was quite impossible to obtain seats for the first performance of an opera which was now beginning to be seriously talked about. As the day of production approached, the inquiries became more and more numerous.[33]

Mapleson had ignited public interest so effectively that *Faust* had little trouble taking hold at Her Majesty's Theatre in June 1863, in Italian, with Thérèse Titiens and Antonio Giuglini in the leading roles. Fredrick Gye of Covent Garden swallowed his error in judgement and launched rehearsals of his own before the month was out, scoring something of a coup by engaging Marie Miolan-Carvalho. His production, by all accounts more lavish than that of Mapleson, appeared on 2 July.

The spectacle of two rival houses competing for public interest with *Faust* was certainly one of the highlights of Gounod's career, but his memory of it was soured by attendant business misfortunes. According to a treaty between France and England, the scores of new works had to be registered in both countries within three months of a première in order for composers and librettists to draw money from performances in England over the next twenty-eight years. Although the vocal score was sent to Chappell on 13 June 1859, he did not register it in London until 22 June (the French première had taken place on 19 March, it will be recalled). Characteristically, Gounod was unaware of the possibility for English performing rights until this was drawn to his attention in June 1863 by an art dealer named Gambart, whom he promptly appointed as an agent to look after his affairs in England. Gounod initially reached an out-of-court settlement with Gye, granting him exclusive performing rights in the United Kingdom in exchange for 15,000 francs to be divided between the composer and his librettists, a sum far below the French standard. When Gye, in turn, attempted to extract a performing fee from Mapleson, the ensuing legal battle established that, because of the late registration, the English performing rights were not Gounod's to sell and that, consequently, any impresario was free to produce *Faust* without payment of this fee. Gounod eventually returned the money to Gye. Initiation to the rigours of the business world could be expensive indeed: Gounod once estimated that he and his librettists took a lifetime

[33] James Mapleson, *The Mapleson Memoirs, 1848–1888* (London, 1888), 67–72.

loss of 250,000 francs, the French norm of 5 per cent of box-office receipts, because of the delay.[34]

Faust may well have been the most frequently performed opera in London, indeed even internationally, during the last third of the century. Shaw, for one, complained in 1893 that the professional critic in London 'has to spend about ten years out of every twelve of his life listening to *Faust* . . . I am far from sure that my eyesight has not been damaged by protracted contemplation of the scarlet red coat and red limelight of Mephistopheles' (he went on to congratulate a current performer for changing the customary hue to an 'unexciting mouse colour').[35] Only *Aida* (1871) was performed more frequently at La Scala and La Fenice in this period. After its translation to the Opéra in Paris in 1869, the number of performances of *Faust* soon surpassed the record achieved by *Les Huguenots* (1836), the once seemingly indomitable frontrunner. By the end of the century *Faust* had also drawn a large number of detractors. Wagner once alluded to Gounod's 'real talent' but was repulsed by the surface sentimentality of *Faust*. It was a thesis that Ernest Newman would develop further in later years, lambasting the opera as 'a blend of the pantomime, the novelette, and the Christmas card' and finding few redeeming features in a work written by a composer who 'lacked the brains to grasp the austere philosophy of a subject of this kind'. 'I fear we all took it seriously at one time,' he continued, with the implication that, by the turn of the century, western civilization had outgrown this trifle.[36]

These kinds of acidic remarks about trivialization of Goethe's *Faust* are rare in early French and English assessments; the relationship of the opera to that play was simply not an issue for most of these reviewers. The few who did write that the work had not sounded the heights and depths of Goethe's model remained undistressed by this, noting, like the French critic Bénédict Jouvin, that 'the libretto follows the original work as closely as the dramatic taste of the audience for which it was destined allows'.[37] An anonymous reviewer of the production at Her Majesty's Theatre recognized that the 'book is a complete travesty on Goethe's celebrated poem' but went on to suggest that this was unimportant since it was ideally suited for musical elaboration—a critical stance that has much to recommend it still today.[38] More important is that virtually all

[34] For a more detailed account, see Gounod, *Autobiographie*, pp. 59 ff, as well as Mapleson, *Memoirs*, p. 72.

[35] George Bernard Shaw, *The Great Composers: Reviews and Bombardments*, ed. Louis Crompton (Berkeley, 1978), 285–6.

[36] Ernest Newman, 'Faust in Music', in *Musical Studies* (London, 1905), 75.

[37] Review of *Faust*, *Le Figaro*, 24 Mar. 1859.

[38] *The Standard*, 15 June 1863.

early reviewers did regard the musical substance of the piece as learned
and serious. Even Gounod's detractors treated *Faust* as 'a veritable
grand opera', in other words, as the highest form of operatic art.[39] In
part this was because the five-act layout and lavish sets ('equal to those
at the Opéra', remarked Escudier)[40] gave it the external appearance of
grand opera. For many, Gounod's style was too lofty. It was certainly
not understandable after a single hearing, noted one observer.[41] Others
complained outright that certain aspects of the music were incomprehensible. 'He sets at nought the time-honoured laws of musical art, and
indulges in (so-called) harmonies and modulations that would have
driven Mozart or Cimarosa crazy and are no small trial to the nerves
even at the present day,' wrote the reviewer for the *Illustrated London
News*.[42] The charge of unmelodiousness, the most difficult one to
fathom from today's perspective, was also levelled repeatedly; Berlioz
noted that even the melody of 'Salut, demeure chaste et pure' seemed to
have been incomprehensible to most attending the première.[43] The
polemical tone of some attacks induced Gounod's supporters to respond
in kind when defending his work. Ernest Reyer offered the following
endorsement in the pages of the *Courrier de Paris*:

Silence yourselves, bands of flies, because the chorus of admirers is advancing
and will drown out your monotonous buzz with its ringing voice. Gounod's
supporters are numerous, those who understand his talent and who admire him,
those who bow before the young master and dare to follow him to the lofty
regions which he inhabits. I join them to proclaim the success of *Faust*, a success
of fine alloy that rests entirely with the merit of the work . . . [44]

Nor was a score of this nature entirely unexpected; after his spiritual
isolation in the 1840s, followed by a setting of a classical subject and a
literal adaptation of a Molière play, Gounod's reputation as one of the
most erudite composers in France was firmly secured by the appearance
of *Faust*.

[39] Paul Scudo, 'Chronique musicale', *La Revue des deux mondes*, 30 Mar. 1859.
[40] Review of *Faust*, *La France musicale*, 27 Mar. 1859.
[41] P. A. Fiorentino, review of *Faust*, *Le Constitutionel*, 21 Mar. 1859.
[42] Anonymous review, 11 July 1863.
[43] *Journal des débats*, 26 Mar. 1859.
[44] Reprinted in Ernest Reyer, *Quarante ans de musique* (Paris, n.d.), 249.

4. *An Unsteady Career*

In January 1859, while *Faust* was being rehearsed, Gounod and his librettists Barbier and Carré received a commission to write an *opéra comique* based on La Fontaine's poem *Philémon et Baucis*. It came from Édouard Bénazet, director of the summer theatre and casino at Baden-Baden, a popular holiday resort for the upper castes of European society. (Meyerbeer was a frequent visitor, taking the waters for a seemingly interminable succession of ailments.) Today Bénazet's principal claim to fame is, perhaps, the commissioning of Berlioz's delightful *Béatrice et Bénédict*, also composed for the summer theatre at Baden and first performed there in 1862.

In Paris, Carvalho soon got wind of Gounod's Baden commission. He was so eager to follow the box-office success of *Faust* with another Gounod work that he encouraged Bénazet and the composer to reroute *Philémon et Baucis* to the Théâtre-Lyrique. There was more than Carvalho's persuasive power behind the move from Baden to Paris. In June 1859 it was reported that 'the opera commissioned from Gounod by M. Bénazet for the present season [i.e. *Philémon et Baucis*] will not be performed at Baden until political circumstances permit'.[1] During these months Napoleon had finally delivered on his verbal promise to Cavour to help liberate Italy from Austrian domination. After a series of diplomatic machinations had goaded the Habsburg Empire into an attack on Piedmont in April 1859, Napoleon personally led his troops into battle on the side of the Italians. German opinion had been divided between support of the Italian nationalist cause and sympathetic identification with the Habsburg Empire, which, although Austria itself shared the same language and culture, was one of the great obstacles to German unification. But German sentiment rallied overwhelmingly against the Emperor's opportunistic meddling when he stepped into the fray. After French victories at Magenta (4 May) and Solferino (24 June) Napoleon looked prudently upon the mobilization of Prussian troops along the Rhine. Declaring that 'the war might assume proportions that are against the interests of France', he hastily concluded the armistice of Villa Franca with the young Franz-Joseph on 12 July. According to the music critic Gustave Chadeuil, the tense political situation between

[1] 'Nouvelles', *La Revue et gazette musicale de Paris*, 19 June 1859.

Germany and France during the summer of 1859 ultimately forced Gounod's new score 'back to its own land, where it would not be exposed to the heckling of the [German] confederacy'.[2] *Philémon et Baucis* was initially postponed from the summer season of 1859 to that of 1860 at Baden. Gounod was supposed to have composed first a *Don Quichotte* for the winter season of 1859–60 at the Théâtre-Lyrique. The idea of a *Philémon et Baucis* for that season probably only occurred to Carvalho after the Baden postponement, since the newspapers were still listing *Don Quichotte* for the new season in September 1859.

There was a certain timeliness to an operatic adaptation of La Fontaine's *Philémon et Baucis* for the Parisian stage. The long first run of Offenbach's *Orphée aux enfers* at the Bouffes-Parisiens was finally brought to an end in June 1859, due to the exhaustion of the cast more than anything else. Carvalho followed with a staging of Gluck's *Orphée* at the Théâtre-Lyrique in the autumn of 1859. It is possible that each of the principal new productions of that season at the Théâtre-Lyrique, *Orphée* and *Philémon et Baucis*, was an attempt to capitalize on the success of Offenbach's *opéra bouffe*. Parody can, after all, be a form of flattery, and what better time to resurrect one of the models for Offenbach's merriment than after it had been given contemporary relevance at the Bouffes-Parisiens. And it may be that Carvalho was eager to acquire *Philémon et Baucis* from Bénazet in order to reap benefits from the public's obvious taste for mythological comedy. At the same time, the Opéra-Comique was presenting a revival of Massé's *Galathée*. With a small cast of four characters, limited choral participation, and comic embellishment of the Pygmalion legend, this work was a clear forerunner of *Philémon et Baucis*.

Despite the currency of its subject-matter, Gounod's *opéra comique* did not succeed at its first appearance. It survived for only thirteen performances after its première on 18 February 1860. The disappointment must have been all the greater for Carvalho, since he had invested in a lavish production, easily prevailing upon Gounod to expand considerably the scope of the work first envisaged for Baden. Gounod compensated Édouard Bénazet for the loss of *Philémon et Baucis* with *La Colombe*, another *opéra comique* based on a La Fontaine model. Indeed, with only two acts and four soloists, *La Colombe* is the kind of work *Philémon et Baucis* was first intended to be, 'just a bagatelle in the composer's operatic œuvre, but an exquisite one', wrote Bénédict Jouvin of *Le Figaro*.[3] It did well during a run of four performances at Baden in

[2] Review of *Philémon et Baucis*, *Le Siècle*, 28 Feb. 1860.
[3] Review of the 1866 production of *La Colombe* at the Opéra-Comique in *Le Figaro*, 14 June 1866.

August 1860 and would serve Gounod again a few years later. Following the demise of *Mireille*, Gounod actively considered a début at the Opéra-Comique with an important new work: projects based on Molière's *Amphytrion* and the Scribe-Legouvé comedy *Les Contes de la Reine de Navarre* surfaced at the time, but in the end the demands of *Roméo et Juliette* forced Gounod to abandon these plans. Because *La Colombe* had appealed to holidaymakers at Baden and had already been published in vocal score, Gounod offered director de Leuven a slightly revised version of the work for the 1865–6 season at the Opéra-Comique. It was performed there in June 1866 with only moderate success and soon disappeared from the repertoire.

By April 1860 the large debt Carvalho had incurred in the recent sumptuous productions of Gluck's *Orphée*, *Philémon et Baucis*, and, especially, *Faust* proved unmanageable. On the first day of the month he resigned his post as director of the Théâtre-Lyrique and set off with his wife for a series of foreign engagements to reap profits from their principal remaining financial asset: her voice. Carvalho left his amiable but colourless successor Charles Réty with rehearsals of *Fidelio* in full swing and, if one is to believe the *feuilletonists*, plans for a new opera by Gounod entitled *La Reine Balkis*.[4] The Beethoven opera, furnished with additional dialogue by Barbier and Carré and transplanted to the seamy political environment of late-fifteenth-century Milan, was staged unsuccessfully at the beginning of May, with Pauline Viardot in the role of Leonora, renamed Isabella, Duchess of Aragon. Réty operated on a more limited budget than his adventurous predecessor. It may have been out of reluctance to commit himself to a costly *mise-en-scène* for a five-act opera featuring, among other sensationalistic trappings, an exploding furnace and streams of molten metal, that he did not pursue the new Gounod work, which eventually became *La Reine de Saba*. In August 1860 Gounod reported to Bizet from Baden-Baden that, after the performances of *La Colombe*, he intended to set to work in earnest on a large opera in five acts. He could only have been referring to *La Reine de Saba* and reports in *Le Figaro* still associated it with the Théâtre-Lyrique.[5]

Gounod soon decided to turn to the Opéra with his new work. It was high time to try his hand again on that stage; one writer had even

---

[4] On the change of directors at the Théâtre-Lyrique, see Walsh, *Second Empire Opera*, pp. 123 ff. The 'A travers les théâtres' column in *Le Figaro*, 8 Apr. 1860, noted that the Théâtre-Lyrique had announced a *Le Roi* [sic] *Balkis* by Gounod. *La Revue et gazette musicale de Paris*, 8 Apr. 1860, wrote that 'Après le Fidelio de Beethoven, le Théâtre-Lyrique doit monter un opéra à grand spectacle de M. Gounod: La Reine Balkis'.

[5] Letter to Bizet, 7 Aug. 1860, in Pougin, 'Gounod écrivain' (1912), 638–9. See also *Le Figaro*, 30 Aug. 1860.

recently criticized him for wasting his energies on 'opéras de salon'.[6] Furthermore, Gounod had resigned his post at the Orphéon, so a success at the Opéra, with its generous royalty plan, would have provided a new source of income. Alphonse Royer was still willing to mount a work by Gounod. Although *Faust* had proved at last that the composer could write a major work that drew audiences, the letter from Royer to Achille Fould cited above in connection with the postponement of *Faust* at the Théâtre-Lyrique in 1857–8 shows that even before this achievement the Opéra director was prepared to invest in Gounod as one of a triumvirate of promising young composers that included David and Gevaert. Another report from Royer, which may be dated January or February 1861 from its contents, reveals that his strategy for the repertoire had changed little in three years. David's *Herculanum* had been given with some success in 1859, which left Gounod and Gevaert to be heard. But if Meyerbeer chose to rouse *L'Africaine* from its apparently permanent state of hibernation (Royer was still waiting with bated breath for this to happen), Gounod's new opera would necessarily have to be postponed:

Gounod is asking for seven months to complete his score for La Reine de Saba. He could be ready to give it to the copy department by August 1 1861 . . . If he holds to his word we could start rehearsals on September 1. But the first two weeks of October have been chosen by Meyerbeer for the first rehearsals of L'Africaine, which the great master told me personally he was ready to give to the Opéra. Therefore we cannot commit ourselves in advance to put Gounod into rehearsal in September if Meyerbeer produces L'Africaine. Gounod's turn would then be fixed contractually for next year, and before Meyerbeer we will have given an opera by Gevaert, which will be ready to go into rehearsal on the day after the Tannhäuser première, and will make its public appearance by October 15 . . . [7]

Shortly after the *Tannhäuser* débâcle in March 1861, Royer also made a commitment to stage Berlioz's *Les Troyens*. Although glad to have at last received a positive response from the Opéra, Berlioz quite understandably was annoyed by the director's priorities. In a letter to his son dated 2 June 1861 he noted that Gounod had been given precedence over both Gevaert and himself, even though he was ready to 'go into rehearsal tomorrow while Gounod cannot be performed until March 1862 at the earliest'.[8] Unfortunately for Berlioz, Royer reaffirmed his old strategy in a memo to his secretary on 8 June, stressing that the operas by Gounod, Meyerbeer, and Gevaert were to take precedence

---

[6] The critique came from Emile Perrin, in 'A Propos de l'Opéra', *Le Figaro*, 30 Aug. 1860.

[7] AN AJ[13] 443.

[8] Letter to Louis Berlioz, 2 June 1861, in *Correspondance inédite de Hector Berlioz, 1819–1868*, ed. D. Bernard (Paris, 1879), 282.

over *Les Troyens*. He went on to note that, because of this, Berlioz would probably have to wait at least three years to see a production of his work.[9] By the beginning of 1861 Gounod, for his part, was definitely working on *La Reine de Saba* with an eye to the Opéra and the daunting prospect of furnishing the next major opera for this house after the Paris première of *Tannhäuser*. With his customary punctuality he delivered the complete score in the autumn of the same year.[10]

As with *Faust*, the opera that Gounod had composed was much too long for a single evening. The score was considerably reduced during the rehearsal period. Now by 1861 Gounod enjoyed a certain amount of official favour; in his role as *fonctionnaire* with the Orphéon he had produced an assortment of tub-thumping choruses to celebrate the Empire and, more recently, had even received an invitation to visit the court at Compiègne, a widely coveted token of imperial favour. This was advantageous to him at the state-run Opéra in a way it could not have been at a private enterprise such as the Théâtre-Lyrique. Just how far he went in attempting to use his influence to veto cuts he opposed may never be known, but it is clear that he managed to stipulate some conditions for the rehearsal and performance of *La Reine de Saba*. When Pierre Dietsch, the conductor of the orchestra, balked at some of the composer's suggestions, Gounod appealed successfully to the Minister of State, Count Walewski, to encourage a more co-operative attitude.[11] The future of Gounod's opera was certainly not promising under the stewardship of the notoriously incompetent Dietsch, whose principal claim to fame today rests in his entanglements with prominent composers of his day. The year before, Dietsch had completely mishandled *Tannhäuser*, while, in Gounod's own words, the helpless Wagner 'writhed like a raging lion in the director's box'.[12] And in 1863 Verdi disassociated himself from a revival of *Les Vêpres siciliennes* because Dietsch showed no inclination to discipline unruly players in his string section.[13] Soon after that incident he was replaced.

A letter from the office of Walewski to Royer, dated 5 February 1862, shows that Gounod set additional terms by dealing directly with the minister:

    [9] Memo of 8 June 1861, AN F²¹ 1069.

    [10] As early as 21 Apr. 1861 *Le Figaro* reported that 'Gounod a livré à l'Académie impériale de musique trois actes de son grand opéra la Reine de Saba, puis il s'est retiré à la campagne pour composer les deux derniers'. On 1 Aug. 1861 Gounod wrote to an unnamed correspondent: 'J'ai travaillé comme un galérien depuis plusieurs mois. J'ai livré hier à la copie, le quatrième acte de mon opéra et j'emporte la cinquième que j'éspère bien avoir fini à mon retour' (extract of letter cited in *Catalogue V. Degrange*, Apr. 1979, lot. 1092).

    [11] Prod'homme and Dandelot, *Gounod*, ii. 27.

    [12] Gounod, *Autobiographie*, p. 101.

    [13] For a fuller account of this episode, see Marcello Conati, *Interviews and Encounters with Verdi* (London, 1984), 40–3.

Gounod saw the minister this morning and obtained his consent; more partial rehearsals will precede the final dress rehearsal and will ensure a more perfect performance. The minister will, therefore, not go to the Opéra tomorrow, and will determine at a later date the day on which he will judge the new work himself. But what the minister specifically wants understood, in accordance with the wishes of the composer, is that for all rehearsals preceding the final dress rehearsal the hall shall remain empty and the doors only open to people who accompany Gounod.[14]

A few days later, Gounod told a friend that he had temporarily post-poned the full rehearsals with orchestra and soloists because he was not satisfied with the progress of the opera and wished to do more work on details before putting it together. In the interest of maintaining frankness with his singers, and at the same time protecting their reputations, he did not want witnesses to the rehearsals.[15]

It seems that a final dress rehearsal, or *répétition générale*, never took place in the accepted sense of the word. A letter from the minister's office to Royer sixteen days later set Friday, 28 February, as the day for the first performance and the preceding Tuesday for a final rehearsal: 'As for the final dress rehearsal, it will take place on Tuesday, but without orchestra and as Gounod has proposed. In short, it will be a last rehearsal rather than a full *répétition générale*.'[16] The proposal was that, again, the hall remain closed, even on an occasion when hundreds of people, including representatives of the Press, were customarily admit-ted. This much can be ascertained by a complaint of the critic and publisher Heugel that the usual final *répétition générale* had not been held, and that reviewers had heard the work for the first time on the evening of the première.[17] In this way, Heugel argued, the composer's fortunes had been severely damaged because critics had not received enough exposure to the new work to judge it adequately after a single performance. But Gounod never changed his position. Over twenty years later he would inveigh against the continuing practice of open *répétitions générales* in print:

I can only see numerous inconveniences in this [practice]. A major one is that it gives the listener an inaccurate impression of the work to which he has been admitted and which has a thousand chances to be executed inadequately by performers burdened with fatigue and careful to preserve their resources for the opening night. A second inconvenience is that it takes away from the authors, the performers, and the director—all those who co-operate to produce a

[14] AN AJ[13] 502.
[15] Letter of 9 Feb. 1862, *Charavay Catalogue* no. 808, Apr. 1962.
[16] Letter of 21 Feb. 1862, AN AJ[13] 502.
[17] Review of *La Reine de Saba*, *Le Ménestrel*, 2 Mar. 1862.

theatrical work—the last session that is available to exchange their reciprocal observations and to assure that all is in order.[18]

References to rehearsals for *La Reine de Saba* in the newspapers after October 1861 are surprisingly scarce for an opera of these dimensions. To judge by Gounod's desire to proceed with closed rehearsals, the lack of advance notice was due to the composer's reluctance to volunteer information to the rumour mill of the papers. Gounod's approach in this area differed radically from that of a composer like Meyerbeer, who had, as Verdi once noted, a well-refined ability 'to bring a success to the boil six months before the event in the cauldrons of the Press, and thereby time the explosion of interest precisely for the first night'.[19] Gounod never sought to develop this kind of rapport with the Press. There was also the recent example of *Tannhäuser*, which had been heralded by advance publicity of an entirely different sort from the accolades that prepared Meyerbeer operas. It was perhaps to avoid damage to the fortunes of his new work by unfavourable reports *avant l'heure* in certain critical quarters which were hostile—Blaze de Bury, Scudo, or Azevedo, for example—that Gounod took measures to ensure limited access before the première.

Gounod's insistence upon closed rehearsals brought accusations of arrogance and aloofness from some writers of the time. Such criticisms were re-enforced when it was learned that the piano–vocal score of *La Reine de Saba* had been engraved before the première. 'He affixed his supreme stamp, the fatal seal, before the first performance. Vanity of vanities! So much pride to end only in disaster!' wrote Pier Fiorentino.[20] Even Meyerbeer and Halévy waited until a few weeks after the première to proceed with engraving. So early a release was still unusual in France. In retrospect, this gives the impression of having been a step on the road to the assertion by French composers of the inviolability of their creations, a notion that attained its logical conclusion when the mature Massenet appeared at the *first* rehearsal of a new work with a printed vocal score. But, given the number of changes made during rehearsals for *La Reine de Saba*, it is probable that early engraving was the idea of Choudens, a new marketing technique to boost interest in an opera by making it available for sale immediately after the première. The scores of *Mireille* and *Roméo et Juliette* were to appear even sooner after the first

[18] Gounod, 'Considérations sur le théâtre contemporain', in Édouard Noel and Edmond Stoullig (eds.), *Les Annales du théâtre et de la musique*, 11 (1885), pp. xx–xxii.

[19] Julian Budden, *The Operas of Verdi* (New York, 1973–81), ii. 179. Verdi was in fact citing a recent observation of Dumas; the composer's remark was in reference to the première of Meyerbeer's *L'Étoile du nord*.

[20] P. A. Fiorentino, *Comédies et comédiens* (Paris, 1866), ii. 217.

performance than that of *La Reine de Saba*; preparing the score for immediate sale came to take precedence over changing the plates so that the first edition would be an accurate reflection of the first performance.

To certain critics such strategies seemed to rise from the murky pool of *wagnérisme*. Rumours of Gounod's friendly association with Wagner emerged even before the rehearsals for *La Reine de Saba*. There is no evidence, however, that Gounod and Wagner were particularly close during Wagner's stay in Paris from 1859 to 1861, although both frequented the *salon* of Princess Mathilde. At most, Gounod showed respect for Wagner's musical judgement during this period. In a request for complimentary tickets to enable Wagner to attend *Faust* during its first run, Gounod wrote that his 'support and even criticism are of the kind that is sought after and I would be very disappointed if the performances were to end before he could become acquainted with my work'.[21] On another occasion shortly before, Gounod remarked that *Tannhäuser* might succeed on the Parisian stage but that the public, with its deeply ingrained tastes, would not find enough musical numbers in the work.[22] Gounod insisted later in life that he had never pretended that 'Wagner was a sun without spots'[23] and consistently denied having been influenced by him. When the English critic J. W. Davison warned him to avoid the Wagnerian bug in 1874, Gounod half-jokingly expressed alarm that he appeared to show symptoms of this ailment, promising that, if this were confirmed, he would seek the services of a doctor 'pour me Wag—ciner!'[24] Ironically, later in the century Gounod's independence from Wagner's style was seen as his strongest suit in many quarters. Even Debussy, hardly an enthusiastic proponent of Gounod's work, congratulated him for having so successfully escaped the 'domineering genius' of Wagner and concluded that, because of this, 'Gounod, with all his shortcomings, is necessary'.[25] But in the early 1860s anti-Wagnerian critics such as Jouvin of *Le Figaro* and Azevedo of *L'Opinion nationale* repeatedly described Gounod as a fanatical *wagnérien*. Although he had not been present at the rehearsals for *La Reine de Saba*, Pier Fiorentino declared authoritatively that Gounod's behaviour even outdid Wagner's histrionics while *Tannhäuser* was being prepared:

After Sapho, a succès d'estime, and after the Nonne, a bloody failure, he comes

[21] Pougin, 'Gounod écrivain' (1912), 637.

[22] Letter to Jules Barbier, cited in Barbier, 'Trois millièmes', *La Vie théâtrale*, 5 Dec. 1894, 7.

[23] Gounod, *Autobiographie*, p. 17.

[24] Letter from Gounod to J. W. Davison, 19 May 1874, in Henry Davison (ed.), *From Mendelssohn to Wagner, Being the Memoirs of J. W. Davison* (London, 1912), 311.

[25] In 'A propos de Charles Gounod', *Musica*, 46 (1906), 99, reprinted in *Monsieur Croche et autres écrits* (Paris, 1971), 192–4.

back to the great stage of Rossini and Meyerbeer. Do you think that he is diffident, that he trembles and pales in the face of his own work? Assuredly M. Wagner is not modest, but his friend has surpassed him. He was seen hurling himself into the arena with fiery impatience, rushing about, losing his breath, and singing his music everywhere like ancient rhapsodies . . . [26]

Gounod himself remarked to Halévy in a level-headed assessment of the opera's fate that certain reviewers displayed traces of wilful hostility, implying that the attacks were directed beyond a single fiasco. [27]

A substantial number of French critics throughout the Second Empire judged Gounod's music to be learned and inaccessible. After the *Tannhäuser* performances in 1861, the epithet *wagnérien* entered the active vocabulary of French critics to describe innovative works, and *La Reine de Saba* was probably the first French opera so designated. The term would be used with similar lack of discrimination with reference to new French works until the end of the century. Many critics without an axe to grind complained that there were not enough recognizable forms in *La Reine de Saba*. 'Gounod's opera is a vast physiognomy of vapourous and fleeting contours' was the characteristic observation of Paul Smith of *La Revue et gazette musicale de Paris*. [28] In addition, the libretto, based on a story by Gérard de Nerval, was received even more unfavourably by the Press than some of Scribe's less fortunate products. *La Reine de Saba* ran for only fifteen performances at the Opéra in 1862.

Such was the reputation of *Faust* in Germany and Belgium that the ducal court at Darmstadt and the Théâtre de la Monnaie in Brussels still invested in their own productions of the new Gounod work. The opera was greeted with enthusiasm at both centres in the season of 1862–3 and went on to earn a niche in the repertoire of the Théâtre de la Monnaie. Two years later there was also an attempt to acquaint the English public with *La Reine de Saba* in concert performances at the Crystal Palace. For this occasion Gounod authorized a secularization of the libretto to accord with local taste: 'Like Rossini and some other composers, M. Gounod has been guilty of what we in England consider the monstrosity of a sacred opera,' noted the reviewer for the *Musical Standard*. [29] (Saint-Saëns would encounter similar obstacles with *Samson et Dalila* years later.) Rechristened *Irene* and transplanted to Turkey, Gounod's work was none the less poorly received, largely because, according to the same observer, 'the new libretto is so lamentable a piece

---

[26] Fiorentino, *Comédies et comédiens*, ii. 217.
[27] Letter of 8 Mar. 1862, in Pougin, 'Gounod écrivain' (1912), 644–5.
[28] Review of *La Reine de Saba*, 9 Mar. 1862.
[29] Review in the *Musical Standard*, 26 Aug. 1865, 63.

of work and the transformation of an opera into a dramatic cantata [is] a process so thoroughly emasculating'. On 27 November 1900 a short-lived enterprise named the Théâtre-Populaire revived *La Reine de Saba* in Paris, with no success. The opera does not appear to have been staged again until performances at Toulouse's Capitol theatre in 1962.

To his close friends Gounod did not make a secret of his disillusion-ment after the poor reception given to *La Reine de Saba* by Opéra audiences and the severe blows meted out in the Press. The current of bitterness ran close to the surface, even in a letter as diplomatic and composed as the one that Gounod penned to Fromental Halévy just a week after the première: 'Like any other composer, naturally I wish to succeed, but even more, I have a desire to perfect myself; and I think that this preference is praiseworthy because the greatest momentary success of a work is not always an infallible sign of its equivalent worth.'[30] It is difficult to escape the impression that with such pronouncements Gounod was, more than anything else, attempting to sustain his own morale in the difficult days following the première.

A holiday was certainly in order and at the end of the month the composer and his family made a trip to Italy. By May, objective analysis of the failure had degenerated to despondency: 'I am forgetting music, learning the guitar, and drawing,' he wrote to Choudens. 'I do not know where I will find within myself that which is needed to create an opera when the time comes to write one; perhaps it will come to me . . . there are those, on the other hand, who say that it has never come to me.'[31] News of the success of Félicien David's *Lalla-Roukh* the next month only deepened the wound: 'Tell Carré that I congratulate him this time for having fallen into hands that do not have the misfortune, as mine do, of assassinating everything they touch. If he had given *La Reine de Saba* to Meyerbeer, the libretto and the music would have been judged excellent, and both would have had the greatest triumph.'[32] The stark fact that healthy relations with Press and public could secure a following was annoying to one whose personality and artistic inclinations did not lean in that direction. After the experience of *La Reine de Saba* the value of salesmanship may have been all too clear to Gounod, but in the mid- and late 1860s his friends and business associates, most often Choudens and Carvalho, were more aggressive promoters of his work than the composer himself.

Gounod was contemplating new operatic subjects in spite of his bouts

---

[30] Letter of 8 Mar. 1862, in Pougin, 'Gounod écrivain' (1912), 644–5.
[31] Letter to Choudens, 25 May 1862, in ibid. 646.
[32] Letter to Choudens, 27 June 1862, cited in Camille Bellaigue, *Gounod* (Paris, 1910), 95.

of depression. The names Mignon and Mireille appear in a letter of 27 June 1862 to Choudens.[33] It is perhaps not fortuitous that Gounod turned once again to female tragic figures. After the failures of *Philémon et Baucis* and *La Reine de Saba* in Paris, and in view of the success of *Faust*, he may have felt that they had the greatest potential for public appeal. Emile Perrin, then director of the Opéra-Comique, evidently had approached Gounod with a *Mignon* project based on Goethe in May or June. Gounod insisted upon Madame Miolan-Carvalho for the lead role in his next opera, but it was unclear during the summer whether she would be available. As it turned out, Léon Carvalho took charge of the Théâtre-Lyrique once again in the autumn, which meant that his wife could not appear in the rival Opéra-Comique's *Mignon* production. *Mignon* was the first of two projects—the other was *Françoise de Rimini*—which Gounod seems once to have thought about seriously but which were eventually set by Ambroise Thomas. Although Thomas's Goethe opera was premièred a few years after *Faust*, and *Hamlet* followed *Roméo et Juliette* by a year, a view of Thomas as a canny exploiter of ground popularized by Gounod is not justified. *Mignon* was not the fruit of his own initiative, but was offered to him by the Opéra-Comique, which had laid claim to the subject as early as 1862, and a letter of 1863 from the director of the Opéra to the Ministry of State shows that Thomas had nearly finished *Hamlet* long before *Roméo et Juliette* was even conceived.[34]

Gounod's assertion in the letter of 27 June 1862 that, if the Goethe plan fell through, 'we will have to return to Mireille' implies that he considered *Mireille* even before Perrin proposed a *Mignon*. A letter dated 17 January 1862 from the Provençal poet of *Mirèio/Mireille*, Frédéric Mistral, to an unknown correspondent suggests that Gounod may have looked to Provence for the setting of his next opera even before the February première of *La Reine de Saba*: 'It may well be that in the interval, as burdened as I am, I will be obliged to refuse the offer of a famous composer who wants to turn Mireille into an opera.'[35] Although the identity of the composer is not revealed, Gounod seems the most likely candidate. By 10 November 1862, slightly over a month after Carvalho had been reinstalled as director of the Théâtre-Lyrique, Gounod could state unequivocally that his new opera for this theatre would be *Mireille*.[36]

---

[33] Cited partially by Prod'homme and Dandelot, *Gounod* ii. 44.

[34] AN AJ[13] 444.

[35] I am indebted to N. Berne on the staff of the Bibliothèque Méjanes, Aix-en-Provence, for indicating the presence of the letter in this collection.

[36] Letter to Mme Augé de Lassus, 10 Nov. 1862, in Pougin, 'Gounod écrivain' (1912), 649.

The playwright Ernest Legouvé, a mutual friend of Gounod and Mistral, paved the way for a meeting of the men. The Provençal poet readily consented to an adaptation of his recently published epic poem for the operatic stage by Michel Carré.[37] The contract signed with Choudens stipulated that Mistral was to receive half of the librettist revenues from performances and sale of the five-act score and libretto; his name was also to be given prominent billing on scores and posters.[38] That the author of the proximate literary source for a libretto had such a large financial stake in the opera was most unusual. This more than anything else may have persuaded Barbier and Carré to abandon partnership on this occasion, since they probably felt that three-way division of the librettists' revenues was not sufficient remuneration for the work each put into a collaboration.

On 16 February 1863 Gounod wrote to his childhood friend Mme Augé de Lassus that he had been engaged to conduct eight fragments from *La Reine de Saba* at a concert in Lyons and that he might use the occasion to undertake a pilgrimage to the Saintes-Maries in Provence.[39] His resolve to visit the land of Mireille was strengthened by an outright invitation to 'come to Arles, to Avignon, to Saint-Rémy' from Mistral himself.[40] Gounod had initially envisaged a stay of only a few days in Provence, after which he planned to proceed to Nemi, a town near Rome. He hoped to find there the necessary tranquillity to compose his new opera. Although the 'Chanson de Magali', which may have been the first music for the opera that he wrote, had already been composed by this time, Gounod found it just as difficult as he had during the composition of *Faust* to give his attention to a major project amidst the social pressures and general frenzy of Paris. So impressed was he with Mistral the man and with the relaxed pace of Provençal life—Italy in France he called it—that he remained in the Midi until the end of May.

Not only did the poet serve as a tour guide for Gounod—the composer actually visited the site of each tableau in his opera—but Mistral also followed the progress of the work. Gounod even considered taking up temporary residence in Mistral's house at Maillane but in the end settled in nearby Saint-Rémy. It is significant that the author of the proximate literary source for *Mireille* was actually in contact with Gounod while the score was being drafted. He could, if the occasion arose, make certain that the substance of his work was not violated. Mistral's suggestion to include a *chœur des moissonneurs*, not part of

[37] Letter from Gounod to Ernest Legouvé, 26 Mar. 1863, in ibid. 653.
[38] A copy of the contract is in the Choudens archives.
[39] Pougin, 'Gounod écrivain' (1912), 650.
[40] Ibid. 657.

the original prose scenario, was readily taken up by Gounod.[41] There is even some evidence of contrasting views on other issues. 'Between us, and us alone, I must confess that, until now, Mistral has been uncompromising on the denouement of Mireille,' Gounod wrote to Choudens in May 1863.[42] One can guess that Mistral was insisting upon a tragic denouement for the opera, in accordance with the poem, despite dissenting opinions. (The opera remained faithful to the original conclusion at the première but not at some revivals.)

Gounod found inspiration in the Provençal countryside. Notebook in hand, he set off each morning to work on the project, recording daily events in a travel diary. 'The weather is superb,' reads the entry for 30 March. 'I have found my chorus [the 'chœur des moissonneurs' in Act IV]. What virtue there is in the sun . . . it shines through these two phrases. At noon I leave for the valley of Saint-Clerc. Adorable silence; the shadows of pines. Thousands of violets . . . I stay there three hours, dreaming, listening to the sound of insects, working.'[43] The score advanced rapidly. 'The motifs came to me like fluttering butterflies; I had but to extend my arm to catch them,' Gounod later told an interviewer.[44] By the time he returned to Paris at the end of May, Gounod had drafted much of the opera in short score.[45] The task of orchestration was slowed during the summer because of the trip to England for the Covent Garden première of *Faust* and a subsequent recurrence of the nervous disorder that had plagued him at various intervals in the earlier part of his career. He even expressed fear that he would not have his first two acts finished by the deadline of 15 August set by Carvalho.[46] It was only at the beginning of November that Gounod could announce that he was about to complete the new opera. The pressures from this work may account for a relapse into illness that occurred in December.

Rehearsals at the Théâtre-Lyrique had started by that time. During a visit to Gounod in April 1863, Madame Miolan-Carvalho admonished him to be 'brilliant, brilliant, brilliant'. This by itself did not augur well for the future of his carefully cultivated plans, but an additional message from her husband warning Gounod to be even more brilliant virtually guaranteed massive upheavals within the walls of the Théâtre-Lyrique.

---

[41] Letter from Gounod to Choudens, 27 Mar. 1863, cited by Martial Ténéo, 'Le Centenaire de Charles Gounod', *La Grande Revue*, 96 (1918), 596.

[42] Letter of 27 May 1863, in ibid. 599.

[43] Cited in a commemorative issue for Gounod of *Les Annales*, 7 (Sept. 1913), 205–6.

[44] Cited in Prod'homme and Dandelot, *Gounod*, ii. 55.

[45] See undated letter to Bizet, BN MSS. n.a.f. 14346, no. 39.

[46] See letter to Madame Desvallières, 2 Aug. 1863, in Pougin, 'Gounod écrivain' (1912), 657.

The rehearsals lived up to these bad omens. At one point the relationship between Gounod and the Carvalhos became so strained that communication between them was reduced to an exchange of notarized letters. A reconciliation was eventually worked out and, as usual, it seems that Gounod did most of the compromising: the final score contained far more coloratura writing to display Madame Miolan-Carvalho's virtuosity than he had first intended. There were also problems with tenor François Morini. Gounod had not raised objections to the possible casting of Morini as Faust for the Covent Garden première of that opera in 1863 (though his first choice had been Tamberlick) and the tenor had acquitted himself satisfactorily in the role of Nadir during the first run of Bizet's *Les Pêcheurs de Perles*. But he proved incapable of sustaining the role of Vincent in *Mireille*. Even his only solo number in the opera, the Act V *cavatine* 'Anges du paradis', had to be sacrificed in the whittling down of his part. By opening night he participated only in a duet with Mireille in Act I and in the finales of Acts II and V.[47] Saint-Saëns later recalled that the work which appeared at the première on 19 March 1864 was considerably different from the one that Gounod had played for an intimate gathering of friends the previous autumn.[48]

The first performance of *Mireille*, five years to the day later than the *Faust* première, did not duplicate the triumph of the earlier work. In spite of last-ditch efforts to rearrange some of the scenes after opening night, it could not be rescued. The upheavals in the opera before and during its first run were only the beginning of its turbulent history. *Faust* had been received so well at Her Majesty's Theatre in the summer of 1863 that Mapleson agreed to stage the new Gounod work as soon as possible. *Mireille* was given there in Italian on 5 July 1864, with recitatives composed for this production and a new happy ending. These changes did not improve the work's standing with the public. Nor was Carvalho's attempt in December 1863 to revive *Mireille* in three-act form, and with additional changes, very popular. It was, however, received a good deal more favourably by the Press than it had been in March. Arthur Pougin, for example, had dismissed *Mireille* as 'colourless, weak, and of little significance' at its first appearance.[49] In December, he predicted that in its new form *Mireille* would be blessed with a long series of performances.[50] The opera did not last beyond fifteen evenings on this occasion, but ultimately Pougin was correct in

[47] See review of *Mireille* by Johannès Weber, *Le Temps*, 5 Apr. 1864.
[48] Saint-Saëns, *Portraits et souvenirs*, pp. 92–3.
[49] Review of *Mireille*, *Le Théâtre*, 28 Mar. 1864.
[50] *Le Théâtre*, 18 Dec. 1864.

his prediction of success. When it was resurrected at the Opéra-Comique in 1889 in a form close to that performed at the Théâtre-Lyrique in December 1864, the opera finally drew a favourable response from audiences. It became one of the most popular pieces in the repertoire of the Opéra-Comique (surpassed only by *Carmen*, *Manon*, *Mignon*, and *Lakmé*) until its closing in 1972. In 1939 the Opéra-Comique returned to a five-act version which, though billed as Gounod's original score, still contained discrepancies from the work that was rehearsed at the Théâtre-Lyrique in early 1864.

5. *Parisian Triumph At Last*

ALTHOUGH *Mireille* had been Gounod's third Parisian failure in succession, his name was not about to fall into oblivion; remarkably, he maintained his status in the forum of critical opinion as an important, perhaps the most important, French composer of the mid-1860s. The most compelling testimony of this is that his work and personality could still induce vituperative attacks of the kind that implied he was actually a menace to French music. A study of the composer by J. Debillemont that appeared shortly after the first set of performances of *Mireille* furnishes a compendium of contemporary objections to Gounod—accusations of rampant eclecticism with which he had been tagged since *Sapho*, of lack of dramatic fibre, and of obnoxious trumpeting of a coterie that 'elevated the shortcomings of the composer to artistic principles'.[1]

In 1866 Léon Escudier published an even more devastating attack on Gounod cast in the form of a dialogue between a German music-lover and a loquacious Frenchman named Raoul Ordinaire.[2] In response to the devotee's string of questions about the Gounod phenomenon, M. Ordinaire dismantles each of the composer's operas, all the while shaking his head over the sorry fate of a culture that has been reduced to holding an inconsistent, lifeless talent in such high esteem. Escudier had been enthusiastic enough about Gounod's capabilities to bring out the score of *Ulysse* in 1852 and had given a positive review to *Le Médecin malgré lui*. But he suddenly developed numerous reservations about *Faust*, and for the operas after *Faust* the Escudier paper, *La France musicale*, was unrelenting in its condemnation. The success of Choudens as a publisher after *Faust* was probably behind the poor reception given these works by Escudier's publication, an effort to discredit a rival firm's principal composer.

Contrary to his state of total dejection following the failure of *La Reine de Saba*, Gounod actively considered new projects shortly after the first run of *Mireille*, despite its poor reception. In April or May 1864 Barbier approached him with a proposal based on Schiller's *Die*

---

[1] 'Charles Gounod—Étude', *Nouvelle Revue de Paris*, 2 (1864), 559–68.
[2] 'Les Opéras de M. Gounod', *L'Art musical*, 14 June 1866, 219–21.

Verschwörung des Fiesko to which Gounod was favourably disposed, urging the librettist to get down to work as soon as possible. Perhaps in recognition of past weaknesses in his dramatic compositions, Gounod, sounding very much like Verdi, advised 'let us not lose sight of momentum, let us be tight and rapid—a maximum of four acts'.[3] Gounod's friend Ernest Legouvé also pressed him for a collaboration. In a letter of June 1864 the composer informed the playwright that Barbier was not interested in working with Legouvé on an adaptation of Corneille's *Le Cid*: 'He has renounced any kind of collaboration and only wants to work either for himself, or for a musician, alone, absolutely alone'—a vow that Barbier would of course break by writing *Roméo et Juliette* with Carré in 1865.[4] Gounod went on to write that, in any case, he would be unable to attend to an opera drawn from *Le Cid* in the near future, for reasons that he would divulge upon his return to Paris. He also mentioned a proposal to provide incidental music for one of Legouvé's plays. This project must have been *Les Deux Reines de France*, which Gounod embarked upon seriously in August 1864 in spite of his reservation about the possibility that adequate vocal, instrumental, and dramatic personnel could be assembled in one theatre.[5] The Schiller opera does not surface in the correspondence again, and Gounod busied himself with the considerable incidental music for Legouvé and the revisions of *Mireille* until the end of the year. Under new legislation proclaiming the 'liberty of theatres' that was promulgated in January 1864, monopolies were lifted so that all theatres could perform any genre of stage entertainment—opera, *opéra comique*, spoken plays, *féeries*, or farces—without restriction. Carvalho agreed to stage *Les Deux Reines*. The prospect of a solid musical performance at the Théâtre-Lyrique, as opposed to a more risky situation at the Comédie Française, where musicians would have to be hired, must have persuaded Gounod to lift his previous objections.

Once again, contemporary political circumstances succeeded in impeding the performance of a Gounod stage work. The play was centred on King Philippe Auguste's imprisonment of his wife, the Danish princess Ingeborge, so that he could pursue an extra-marital affair, and Philippe's subsequent imbroglio with Pope Innocent III, who forced him

---

[3] Letter of 9 June 1864, in Pougin, 'Gounod écrivain' (1912), 659. The Barbier papers at the Bibliothèque de l'Opéra contain sketches, prose scenarios, and a complete manuscript copy of *Fièsque* (in five acts however) by an anonymous copyist at the Leduc firm of *copies dramatiques*. Red crayon deletions throughout the manuscript indicate cuts, suggesting that Barbier and Gounod went through the whole libretto with a view to tightening the action.

[4] Letter of 12 June 1864, in Pougin, 'Gounod écrivain' (1912), 273. There are gaps in the published version and the letter is curiously misdated to 1856; the autograph is in a private collection.

[5] Letter to Legouvé, 12 June 1864, private collection.

to restore the crown to Ingeborge by levying a papal interdict on his kingdom. After Louis Napoleon's Italian campaign, conservative Catholics attacked the imperial regime for its destabilizing interventionist policies that threatened the security of the Papal States. In response, the government closed the staunchly conservative Catholic daily *L'Univers* and clamped down upon religious orders. Whereas the immediate purpose of Pius IX's encyclical *Quanta cura* (8 December 1864) was to attack liberal French Catholic support of the equality of all sects before the law, Napoleon quite correctly perceived that the broader aim was to discredit the imperial regime. Decrying papal intervention in the affairs of state, the Emperor forbade its publication in France. In the censors' report for *Les Deux Reines de France*, dated 21 January 1865, the authorities recognized that, although at any other time the play would have been innocuous, it could not be performed because of current tensions.[6] Shortly before the scheduled première, Gounod himself expressed misgivings because the seasoned baritone Meillet had suddenly left the cast and because Bizet, who, one may guess, was to have arranged the piano–vocal score, had fallen sick. In a letter of 14 January 1865 Gounod suggested that the opening night be postponed.[7] The censors' verdict resulted in a much longer delay than anticipated by the composer; *Les Deux Reines de France* had to wait until 1872 to receive its first public performance, at the Théâtre Ventadour.

By the end of 1864 other projects simmered in Gounod's mind. In a short note to Pauline Viardot, dated 17 December, he wrote that he was finishing *Les Deux Reines*, starting an *Amphytrion*, a mythological comedy based on Molière's play of the same name, and thinking about a *Roméo et Juliette*.[8] The letter of 14 January 1865 implies that Legouvé himself was to be the librettist for *Amphytrion*—'in any case, we shall still dine together over *Amphytrion* on Wednesday or Thursday' the composer had added in a brief postscript. By the middle of March this project had been abandoned. In its place Gounod and de Leuven, the director of the Opéra-Comique, agreed to an adaptation of the comedy by Scribe and Legouvé entitled *Les Contes de la Reine de Navarre*. Gounod actively considered this new project and made musical sketches in the margins of the libretto that Legouvé produced.[9] The plan, however, was to give way to Gounod's total preoccupation with *Roméo et Juliette* for the Théâtre-Lyrique. In a letter of 2 May 1865 the composer told the playwright in the most graceful terms that his work

[6] AN F²¹ 991.
[7] Private collection.
[8] BN MSS n.a.f. 16272, fo. 214.
[9] Letter to Legouvé, 2 May 1865, in Pougin, 'Gounod écrivain' (1912), 663.

on the Barbier and Carré libretto was going so well that he had to devote himself solely to it so as not to lose the thread of inspiration.

Gounod had found the atmosphere of Provence so congenial for work on *Mireille* that, when he was ready to go into confinement, as he called it, with *Roméo et Juliette*, in April 1865, he returned to the Midi. This time he installed himself at Saint-Raphaël by the sea. The many letters to Choudens and Anna reveal that in a little over a month he had sketched most of the numbers in the opera. From these short jottings he proceeded to a short-score draft of the entire work—his usual working method—and made good progress with this after he returned to Paris in the middle of May.[10] Just when he set out to orchestrate *Roméo et Juliette* is unknown, but it is clear that progress with the opera was soon greatly slowed. The explosion of creative energy in Provence and shortly thereafter was, as in the past, followed by nervous fatigue and depression. The second half of 1865 remains today, as it was for Prod'homme and Dandelot, a period of his life about which little is known, almost certainly the result of withdrawal from public life due to illness. Though he could see far enough ahead to sell the publication rights of *Roméo et Juliette* to Choudens at the beginning of 1866, Gounod nursed serious doubts about his future as an opera composer. When Henri Meilhac suggested a collaboration in March of that year, he responded that *Roméo et Juliette* would be his last work for the stage.[11]

The work was finally ready for rehearsal in August 1866 after Gounod had recast his original rendition of the wedding tableau in Act IV.[12] Ever reluctant to plunge into business matters, the following month he gave Carvalho a free hand to start arrangements for a production of *Roméo et Juliette*. Naturally Madame Miolan-Carvalho would take Juliette and bass Cazaux, the Théâtre-Lyrique's current Méphistophélès, the role of Frère Laurent. The part of Roméo proved more controversial. Both Carvalho and Choudens pressed the directors of the Opéra-Comique with a large sum of money to release the sensational young tenor Victor Capoul for the *Roméo et Juliette* production. Referring to Capoul's own willingness to take the role, Choudens told Gounod that the engagement was a *fait accompli*, needing only his final approval. But as much as a month later the *feuilletonistes* expressed doubt that conditions would allow Capoul to

---

[10] This draft is currently at the Bibliothèque de l'Opéra, Rés. 650 (1). On the first and last pages of the Act I duet, as well as on the page bearing an excised duet for Juliette and Gertrude in the same act, Gounod pencilled in the date 'Buc, 12 juillet 65'.

[11] This letter to Meilhac is cited in Curtiss, 'Gounod before Faust', pp. 159–60; it came up for sale on 14 Feb. 1985 at the Hôtel Drouot.

[12] Letter from Gounod to Choudens, 3 Aug. 1866, Bibliothèque de l'Opéra (hereafter BO) Gounod l.a.s. 37.

cross over to the Théâtre-Lyrique.[13] Clearly, Gounod had been poorly informed about the resistance that had arisen in Paris to Capoul's engagement; on 28 September, writing from Villerville in Normandy, he expressed surprise that the affair had not been concluded.[14] Not only did de Leuven and Ritt refuse to abrogate Capoul's contract and were thoroughly annoyed at the persistence of the Théâtre-Lyrique, but the artists at the Théâtre-Lyrique were also indignant over the prospect that their veteran tenor Michot would be shunted aside in favour of a young star. Gounod's delegation of authority in business arrangements did not always serve him well: ironically enough, in this instance he was seen as the villain. When the composer returned to Paris, he wasted little time in mollifying the concerned parties by withholding his support of Capoul's engagement in favour of Michot.[15]

In the letter of 28 September Gounod also expressed irritation that Choudens had not started to engrave the vocal score; what had been an unusual procedure just a few years before was now taken for granted by the composer.[16] After losing English performing rights for *Faust* because the score was registered late, Gounod was anxious to have his work appear in print well before deadlines provided by international agreements. Choudens set to work soon, but once again early engraving did not preclude the usual sacrificial offerings to the Carvalhos, including the addition to Juliette's role of coloratura passagework. The last days of preparation in April were even more hectic than usual. In his reminiscences Carvalho recalled that the final dress rehearsal was a disaster. Gounod himself, in a letter to Legouvé written about one week before the première, complained that rehearsals were going badly: Juliette was tired, conductor Deloffre sick, and the whole opera was still not being interpreted with the right expression.[17] In addition, Gounod noted that, as it stood, his score was producing three and a half hours of music. With one and a quarter hours of intermission, that made for an evening of four and three-quarter hours; new cuts would have to be introduced because, even with an early 7.30 start, the opera would not finish by midnight. As one Italian correspondent noted, shows could not extend much beyond this hour, since the last trains to the suburbs and outlying districts were at 12.45 a.m. 'Nor can the curtain go up any earlier since no one wants to make opera-goers hurry their dinner.'[18] There was no question of diminishing the length of intermissions, since

[13] See 'Semaine théâtrale', *Le Ménestrel*, 14 Oct. 1866.
[14] BO Gounod l.a.s. 18.
[15] Prod'homme and Dandelot, *Gounod*, ii. 80–1.
[16] BO Gounod l.a.s. 18.
[17] Pougin, 'Gounod écrivain' (1912), 666.
[18] Budden, *The Operas of Verdi*, iii. 24–5.

the time was needed to effect set changes. Gounod lamented that he no longer knew how to apply 'the hatchet'.

Like *Faust*, *Roméo et Juliette* emerged in the company of important new productions at rival theatres. Verdi's *Don Carlos* was premièred at the Opéra on 11 March, Offenbach's *La Grande Duchesse de Gerolstein* followed on 12 April at the Théâtre des Variétés, and Gounod's opera finally appeared on 27 April. All three companies hoped to reap benefits from the large *Exposition universelle* officially inaugurated by the Emperor on 1 April. A celebration not only of technological progress and cultural diversity the world over, but also of Haussmann's Paris and the achievements of the Second Empire, the Exhibition drew thousands of visitors from the provinces and abroad. Although Verdi's opera received an icy reception from many Parisian *cognescenti*, Bizet's prediction on the night of the première that 'the Exhibition will perhaps prolong the agony' proved accurate.[19] The last French language performance of *Don Carlos* before it became part of the Italian canon was given in November, when the clientele was once again reduced to *habitués* of Parisian theatres. The Offenbach work, on the other hand, did well, and, despite the pre-performance jitters, *Roméo et Juliette* was a spectacular success, drawing full houses for many consecutive nights after the première. Escudier outdid himself in hostility, publishing his own vitriolic review as well as an anthology of negative comments about Gounod's opera meticulously culled from reviews by colleagues in the Press 'as objective as we are'.[20] His task could not have been easy, since a large majority of reviews concurred that Gounod had produced a worthy successor to *Faust*, though most recognized the continuing pre-eminence of the earlier work.

Roméo et Juliette began a rapid conquest of foreign stages at Covent Garden on 11 July 1867; before the end of the year it was seen at major houses in Germany and Belgium. Gounod's supporters could at last derive some satisfaction from the sanctioning of genius by a *coup de foudre* success. It was the highwater mark of his career, a time when, in the words of Saint-Saëns, 'all women sang his melodies, all young composers [in France] imitated his style'.[21] *Roméo et Juliette* secured his reputation to such an extent that, when Auguste Mariette set out two years later to commission a composer for the work that would inaugurate a new opera house in Cairo, he named Gounod as a principal candidate, along with Verdi and Wagner.[22]

[19] Günther, 'La Genèse de Don Carlos', p. 155.
[20] *L'Art musical*, 9 May 1867.
[21] Saint-Saëns, *Portraits et souvenirs*, p. 91.
[22] Letter from Mariette to Camille Du Locle, 28 Apr. 1870, cited in Busch, *Verdi's Aida*, p. 17.

Not surprisingly, Gounod once again developed enthusiasm for operatic composition, but the good fortune of *Roméo et Juliette* only partially explains this renewed vigour. Around the time of the première, an important friendship blossomed between Gounod and a young female sculptor, the Duchess Castiglione Colonna, who, wishing to be evaluated on her own merits rather than family background, took the pseudonym of Marcello. Her beauty, talent, and social standing inspired reverence from many prominent artistic and literary figures in Second Empire Paris. 'If I were twenty I would send you verses in homage. But I am in the age of dry leaves, which now fall at your feet. Please accept them,' was Lamartine's wistful tribute.[23] For Gounod she was more than a fellow artist; she was a soulmate in speculative forays among higher spheres of art and beauty, a source of intellectual companionship to fill a void in his existence with the more earthbound Anna. Gounod reassured the duchess in one letter that their bond was inviolable since artists communicated to one another through their works in a secret language spoken only by members of an inner sanctum: 'Only to us, to artists, that discourse, the charm and peace of which cannot be troubled nor disrupted by the obtrusive clamour of quarrelling.'[24] This view of an Olympian community that transcended petty philistinism owes much to German musical Romanticism of a few decades before. Gounod struck a different path, however, by interpreting the communication of artistic vision as a fundamentally Christian act, one in which the artist is rendered 'richer by giving than receiving … He who knows this understands life, faith, and love!'[25] It was a characteristically spiritual twist that met with favourable response from the duchess.

Marcello's side of the exchange was to introduce Gounod to Dante, whose works the composer ecstatically embraced. Soon after the *Roméo et Juliette* première he made plans for an opera based on the Francesca da Rimini episode from the *Inferno*. The autobiographical reverberations in the subject are unmistakable: left in seclusion to read about the love of Lancelot and Guinevere, Francesca and Paolo fall helplessly into adultery. Dante's poetry, it seems, had a similar effect upon Gounod: 'Here I am now, immersed in your, in *our* beloved Dante! Dante, who, with you, introduces me to Francesca! Dante by means of whom I will be able, from this moment, to call upon you at all hours of the day and night.'[26] But his efforts to push the friendship beyond the platonic in the

---

[23] Cited in Comtesse d'Alcantara, *Marcello: Sa vie, son œuvre, sa pensée, et ses amis* (Geneva, 1961), 197.

[24] Ibid. 102. The date of this letter is not given. The relationship between Gounod and Marcello has never been mentioned by the composer's biographers. D'Alcantara's book draws heavily upon unpublished, and currently unavailable, correspondence between the two.

[25] Ibid.

[26] Ibid. 103. The date of this letter is not cited.

spring of 1867 were gently rebuffed by the duchess, and the trial for his own conscience was played out in the shaping of the libretto. Gounod tore up his first ending, in which Francesca and Paolo were seen joining the company of Beatrice in Paradise, replacing it with one in which, as in Dante, they were condemned to the nether regions. 'When I saw myself grappling with paradise at the threshold of adultery, my courage failed me,' he later explained.[27] At the end of 1867 he succumbed once again to depression, this time even more severe than usual. The opera was put aside soon afterwards. He continued to correspond with Marcello for the next three years, and the explanation for the renewed bout of lethargy undoubtedly lies buried in these letters, largely inaccessible at present. One can only guess that an entwinement of guilt, unrequited love, and a drying up of inspiration for the Francesca project strangled his entire creative impulse. In May 1868 Gounod informed another correspondent that he would no longer write operas.[28]

Unexpected professional problems also arose in this period. Because *Roméo et Juliette* appeared more than twice a week at the Théâtre-Lyrique in 1867, its future with the Parisian public seemed as secure as that of *Faust*. But performances of both operas were suddenly brought to a halt in the next year. At the beginning of 1868 Carvalho had his privilege extended to include the management of another newly created house, the Théâtre de la Renaissance, to which he hoped to transfer the Théâtre-Lyrique's major productions while keeping his first theatre for the works of younger, untried composers. The undertaking proved too ambitious and in May both enterprises collapsed.[29] Sensing impending disaster, Carvalho had secured a verbal agreement from Gounod before the bankruptcy not to seek a new production for his operas until 1 September 1868, thereby leaving himself some time to reopen without losing his chief money-makers. But this precaution did not deter other directors from making advances. Soon after Carvalho went out of business, Emile Perrin was on Gounod's doorstep with a request for permission to stage both *Faust* and *Roméo et Juliette* at the Opéra.[30] Swift action was necessary, since Perrin had set his sights upon a production of *Faust* that winter to revive his own declining fortunes and Gounod would need time to compose the necessary balletic insertion

---

[27] Ibid. 103. The date of this letter is not cited. The librettists for the project are not mentioned in the available correspondence, though one may suppose that they were Barbier and Carré since they were credited with the libretto for Thomas's later opera on the same subject.

[28] Letter to A. Lavignac, 28 May 1868, in Pougin, 'Gounod écrivain' (1912), 669.

[29] Walsh, *Second Empire Opera*, pp. 237–9.

[30] Gounod describes Perrin's visits in a letter of 6 July 1868 to Jules Barbier; a photocopy of this letter is at the Bibliothèque de la Société des Auteurs et Compositeurs Dramatiques (SACD), Paris.

before that. Barbier and Carré, who had not been party to the composer's verbal agreement with Carvalho, assured Gounod that there were no legal obstacles and urged him to consent.[31] The composer resisted for several weeks, a measure of his own highly scrupulous nature, but at the end of July finally capitulated. Carvalho was none the less still able to extract some money from *Faust* later that year. Claiming that the opera was his property because the Théâtre de la Renaissance was about to open its doors once again, he threatened to sue Perrin, Gounod, Barbier, and Carré for robbing him of his chief artistic asset. Rather than submit to a long delay of his own production while the case was argued in court, Perrin agreed to pay Carvalho 20,000 francs in damages and to sponsor a benefit performance for Madame Miolan-Carvalho at the Opéra.[32] Despite this infusion of much-needed capital, and sensationalistic rumours planted in the Press that Wagner's *Lohengrin* would be among the first offerings of the rejuvenated house, Carvalho was unable to reopen.

Gounod took only half-hearted interest in the new production of *Faust*. He was still reeling from nervous depression; cajoling from his colleagues to act against his wishes did little to help him regain his balance. The prospect of supplying a ballet proved so daunting that he even attempted to delegate the task to Saint-Saëns.[33] It was, of course, patently absurd to expect the Opéra administration to accept that solution. Gounod set about composing the ballet himself in the autumn of 1868 but still could not muster much enthusiasm for his work; debilitating 'mental fatigue', as he called it, kept him from progressing with the score at his usual pace.[34]

As in the past it was to Italy that Gounod looked for spiritual balm, choosing to forgo the *Faust* rehearsals at the Opéra for a trip to Rome. In December he surrendered himself to the maternal embrace of the city that had so stimulated him almost thirty years before:

It seems that Rome is saying: 'Be silent and listen to me.' This slow fermentation, which, on the one hand, arouses our impatience and our feverish zeal, is, on the other hand, healthy because it forces us to look inward to the depth of ourselves and permits us to settle into that interior and exterior peace without which there can only be restless and fleeting works of art.[35]

As in the letters to Richomme of 1846, there were imprecations against

---

[31] Letter from Barbier to Gounod, 1 July 1868, in Prod'homme and Dandelot, *Gounod*, ii. 99–100.

[32] Ibid. ii. 101.

[33] Saint-Saëns, *Portraits et souvenirs*, p. 87.

[34] Gounod describes his difficulties in a note to Perrin, 23 Oct. 1868, Bibliothèque de la SACD.

[35] Diary entry cited (without date) by Bellaigue, *Gounod*, p. 138.

those who ignored the spirit of altruism communicated by classical culture. Gounod listened, meditated, and soon gained the strength to take up new projects, to defend *le beau, le bien, et le vrai* with his own work. An oratorio based on the martyrdom of St Cecilia, the scenario of which he had taken with him to Rome, was replaced on his work table by *Rédemption*. Gounod even showed some concern for the future of the *Francesca* libretto.[36] Rome must have also provided the inspiration for *Polyeucte*, his next opera, though he only began to lay the groundwork in the summer of 1869. Indeed, the *Polyeucte* project was in some respects a descendant of the St Cecilia oratorio. Gounod cooled towards the St Cecilia project largely because he felt that the libretto had become too operatic for the genre of oratorio; it was 'opera without theatre', he wrote to his collaborator, the Marquis de Ségur.[37] Whereas *Rédemption* provided material for a succession of frescos that Gounod described in the same letter as more appropriate for oratorio, he was to see Corneille's *Polyeucte* as a viable foundation for a *real* opera based upon the struggles of early Christian martyrs; it even afforded an opportunity to set a grand baptismal scene, just as initially projected for the oratorio. Corneille's play also includes the encounter of a woman with a former lover after she is married to another, like the Francesca da Rimini episode in the *Inferno*. In view of his difficulties with the theme of adultery in the Francesca project, one may suppose that Gounod took comfort in the fact that Corneille's characters resist temptation.

Meanwhile *Faust* was given at the Opéra on 3 March 1869 before a glittering array of Second Empire notables. There were remarks in certain quarters that it was simply not 'grand' enough, that Gounod did not have 'enough breath to fill the great stage over which hover the ghosts of Rossini, Meyerbeer, and Halévy'.[38] No doubt such assessments were caused as much by status consciousness as by purely musical considerations. Affluent subscribers could not help noticing that, after perennial failures with its own new productions, the Opéra had turned to a work that had thrived at a theatre that was artistically and socially inferior. It was even reported that Gounod himself was not immune from the mystique. Returning to Paris during the last days of rehearsal, the composer recommended slower tempos at many places 'to increase the solemnity of the work', according to the reviewer Gustave Bertrand.[39] Doubtless *Faust* would have become a favourite at its new location without these precautions. The production was so popular that

[36] Letter to Barbier, of 8 Feb. 1869, in Prod'homme and Dandelot, *Gounod*, ii. 106–7.

[37] Letter to de Ségur, 21 Dec. 1868. The correspondence (14 letters) between Gounod and de Ségur about this project is preserved at BN MSS n.a.f. 22832.

[38] Hippolyte Prévost, review of *Faust*, *La France*, 5 Mar. 1869.

[39] Review of *Faust*, *Feuilleton du nord*, 8 Mar. 1869.

it even generated a succession of parodies—noteworthy for a work that was ten years old—including *Le Petit Faust* by Hervé at the Théâtre des Folies Dramatiques on 23 April. Prussian hegemony was one of the most topical issues of the day and Hervé found that *Faust* offered a fine vehicle to mix operatic parody with barbs directed at France's neighbours across the Rhine. In *Trio du Vaterland* Faust and Marguerite find the strongest emotional bond between them to be their German heritage; earlier Marguerite made her first appearance to the following verse:

> Fleur
> De candeur
> Je suis la petite
> Marguerite
> Mon cœur ne sais rien
> Ni le mal, ni le bien,
> Et les Salumands m'abbellent Gretchien

Such light-hearted quips must have returned to haunt the authors after the international developments of the following year.

6. *England and Afterwards*

By the time of the *Faust* première at the Opéra the future of *Roméo et Juliette* still remained to be settled. Much to the dismay of Perrin, Gounod and his collaborators soon extracted an agreement from the administration of the Opéra-Comique to produce the work sometime between 1869 and 1871. Perrin urged Gounod to reconsider but the composer would not deal with him personally over the matter, declaring with his usual moral rectitude that, because his word had been given to one party, he could not actively court another. None the less, negotiations between the Opéra and Opéra-Comique took place without Gounod, and by the middle of 1870 *Roméo et Juliette* had changed hands.

Gounod appeared on the verge of establishing the type of pre-eminence at the Opéra previously enjoyed by Meyerbeer, or so it must have seemed to contemporaries. Not only did Perrin guarantee to stage *Roméo et Juliette* in the season of 1870–1, but he also agreed to produce *Polyeucte* the following winter. These plans were unravelled by political circumstances. In the summer of 1870 the French were manœuvred into war by Bismarck, the imperial armies were routed at Woerth and Gravelotte-Saint-Privat, and, finally, the Emperor himself was taken prisoner at the small town of Sedan on 2 September. After the ignominious demise of the Second Empire, a Government of National Defence forestalled the surrender of the French until the end of January. Even at that stage France had not yet endured the worst of *l'année terrible*. In March 1871 local authority in Paris fell to the Left. Completely distrustful of the conservative national government installed at Versailles, the Parisian government, or Commune, openly declared autonomy from the jurisdiction of the Assembly; the suppression of this revolt in street-to-street fighting in May 1871 became one of the bloodiest episodes in French history.

Resumption of cultural business was contingent upon the re-establishment of peace. Because Perrin had resigned from his position at the Opéra, *Roméo et Juliette* was once again left without a home. Gounod's letters of that summer reveal that he turned once again to Du Locle of the Opéra-Comique with *Roméo et Juliette*, but that Du Locle had to relinquish the project because his parallel negotiations with

Madame Miolan-Carvalho, without whom Gounod would apparently not consent to the opera's Parisian revival, had failed.[1] Gounod immediately offered the opera to Halanzier, the new director of the Opéra, who was also negotiating with the same singer.[2] By the middle of October this plan had failed as well and, in the end, *Roméo et Juliette* was taken up in January 1873 by the Opéra-Comique with Madame Miolan-Carvalho. *Roméo et Juliette* flourished there until it was finally transferred to the Opéra in 1888.

Though Gounod had drafted much of *Polyeucte* in short score by the end of 1869, performances of that opera were delayed much longer than a reprise of *Roméo et Juliette*. The fate of *Polyeucte* became inexorably bound with an episode in Gounod's life that attracted nearly as much attention when it happened as his music. Several of the earlier biographers, especially Prod'homme and Dandelot, avoided extensive description of the 'Weldon Affair', as it became known, perhaps out of deference to family members still alive or perhaps as an antidote to contemporary accounts that blew it out of perspective. Only a brief discussion is possible here; a fuller one based upon a complete exposition and interpretation of the related documents must await a new biography.

Fearing prolonged and bloody warfare before the capitulation of France, Gounod moved his family to England within a week of the Sedan débâcle. He suspended work on *Polyeucte*, partly to compose *Gallia*, a large choral elegy for his homeland, and partly out of financial necessity; a living was to be made from smaller compositions destined for the English household market.[3] Gounod made contacts easily: 'one could not approach him without being conquered by his grace and wit,' Paul Viardot, son of the singer, once remarked. In that respect he had changed little over the years. He was to Paul Viardot, just as he had been to Pauline, the 'king of charmers [who] sought to please for the sake of pleasing, to be liked, and this without hidden reasons or ulterior motives'.[4] Gounod found a ready vessel for his charms in Georgina Weldon, an amateur singer to whom he was introduced in March 1871. She had long been an admirer of his music, and, to believe her later account, the moment was thoroughly intoxicating; her overwrought metaphors betray a fanaticism that Gounod would come to regret:

I compare [the music of] Wagner to a brilliant sunny garden plot, where tulips

[1]   Letter to Halanzier, 31 July 1871, in Pougin, 'Gounod écrivain' (1912), 685.
[2]   Letter to Choudens, Sept. 1871, BO Gounod l.a.s. 55.
[3]   Letter from Gounod to Choudens, 17 May 1871, BO Gounod l.a.s. 42: 'Je n'ai pas fait une note de POLYEUCTE depuis neuf mois; il a fallu travailler pour vivre.'
[4]   P. Viardot, *Souvenirs d'un artiste* (Paris, 1910), 71.

and gaudy flowers with long branches and curious leaves bloomed, before which one stands and gazes bewildered by their beauty; but [the music of] Gounod appeared to me as a mossy dell in some wood, lit up by great rays of sunlight athwart the foliage—a dell where, in dreaming repose, hours might be spent upon which one sinks as on heaps of soft sweet-scented hay—a dell where lay encrusted precious stones—a dell, sparkling here and there with pebbles overlaid with soft moss, green as the lizard, yellow brown, pale blue green, hardy lichens—a dell where the young oak sapling would rear its head (an acorn having been dropped there by a fairy hand)—a dell where lay hidden dark grand spreading roots in the deep shade, violets, periwinkles, foxgloves, tangled ferns . . . When I began to teach in downright earnest, I resolved that my pupils should be the interpreters and apostles of this Messiah of the Gospel of New Music.[5]

Gounod at first welcomed the efforts of Georgina Weldon and her husband to promote his music in England. Yet iᴜ must surely have been easy to interpret the singer's unction as something more than professional commitment, and, not surprisingly, Anna Gounod looked askance at her husband's new friends. The situation soon came to a full boil. Anna returned home alone in May 1871, after order had been restored in the streets of Paris. A three-year period of estrangement followed, Anna persistently rejecting Gounod's demands that she receive the Weldons with courtesy. The separation was something of a re-enactment of the Viardot affair, only this time—one may guess that the strong will of Georgina Weldon herself was a persuasive factor—Gounod rested his case uneasily on the principle of loyalty to friends.[6] His fragile temperament cracked more than once under the strain.

Shortly after Anna's departure, the Weldons invited Gounod to room with them at Tavistock House in London, the former residence of Charles Dickens (as no biographer of Gounod fails to mention). By then they had come to exercise considerable influence over the composer. For example, when Gounod was offered the directorship of the Conservatoire following the death of Auber in June—he was obviously a prime candidate—Georgina was instrumental in persuading him to reverse his initial inclination to accept.[7] Though his refusal did arouse the ire of nationalists in the French Press, one can only applaud her perspicacity in

[5] Georgina Weldon, *My Orphanage and Gounod in England* (London, 1882), i. 36.

[6] Gounod gave a long explanation of his position in an important undated letter to Dr Emile Blanche now at the library of the Institut de France, Fonds Blanche, fos. 173–6: 'J'ai deux sortes de devoirs à concilier—mon foyer et mes amis—Jusqu'à présent j'ai épuisé en vains efforts le désir et le besoin de cette conciliation . . . J'ai enduré le plus pénible des chagrins en voyant la porte de ma maison fermée aux meilleurs et aux plus dévoués de mes amis: supporter qu'on leur fasse injure c'est la leur faire moi-même: Je ne *dois* pas, je ne *veux* pas, et je ne *peux plus* accepter qu'il soit ainsi.'

[7] Weldon, *My Orphanage*, i. 53.

this matter: Gounod's personality was ill-suited to the daily demands of an administrative post.

Georgina was also his confidante in business affairs. At this time the principle of royalty payments to authors and composers was common in the English music publishing industry. Gounod had become accustomed to receiving royalties for performances of his works in France and even in some cases abroad; that he could also draw income from a work according to a formula based upon sales of the score was something of a revelation to him when he settled in England. Even before he met the Weldons he had reached royalty agreements with English publishers for his new compositions, though some of these contracts, notably with Littleton, were not fully honoured, or at least so Gounod felt. Georgina Weldon took up Gounod's defence against Littleton and, more important, urged him to introduce royalty clauses into contracts with his French publisher. Choudens refused, arguing that market conditions in France prevented music publishers there from paying royalties to composers. A protracted epistolary duel between the parties ensued.[8] The situation was further aggravated by Choudens's insinuations that English publishers could afford to offer royalties only because they were unscrupulous in their business dealings. An affront to Georgina's national pride had been added to abuse of her artistic idol; the influence of the singer is not difficult to discern in Gounod's uncharacteristically pugnacious side of the correspondence. In May 1872 Gounod served notice to Choudens that he had found a new French publisher, Achille Lemoine, who, 'unlike you, does not believe that he is *disgracing* his firm by dealing with me on the basis of the royalty system'.[9]

Georgina Weldon continued to harbour resentment against Choudens; the rancorous streak in her character had significant ramifications for Gounod's professional life. In the wake of his successful production of *Roméo et Juliette* at the Opéra-Comique, Camille Du Locle informed Gounod early in 1874 that he also intended to stage *Mireille*. To undertake the project Du Locle had to rent the full score and parts from Choudens. Though the failure of *Mireille* ten years before had been one of the major disappointments in his career, Gounod decided, almost certainly with prodding from Georgina, that this time it would be preferable to keep the opera out of circulation rather than to have Choudens profit from its revival. Gounod asked Du Locle to forgo *Mireille* and offered him a new work in its place, an *opéra comique* based on Molière's *George Dandin*. He had already drafted several numbers of this score when he learned two months later that Du Locle planned to proceed with *Mireille* against his wishes. In a letter to Du Locle of 26 March the composer did reluctantly withdraw his veto, but caustically added that the Opéra-Comique should forget about *George Dandin*.[10] He soon put it aside. After loss of the initial impetus to write the work, Gounod never returned to it. The incident with Du Locle betrays a degree of spite that was fundamentally foreign to Gounod's character. It is all the more regrettable because *George Dandin* promised to be a landmark in the French repertoire, a setting of Molière's original prose instead of a versified adaptation, more than fifteen years before operas with prose librettos were composed by Bruneau and Debussy.

Claims of altruism are sprinkled liberally throughout Georgina's reminiscences of her association with Gounod. Keeping the shrine was evidently a full-time occupation: 'I lived to enable him to work; I cheered him up as much as I could . . . notwithstanding the time which failed me, the rest which I needed so much. I sometimes played at backgammon, double dummy, and cribbage with him for eight hours a day.'[11] One does not need to look very far beyond such accounts to see that she also had something to gain from the friendship. It is a stark fact that, at the time Georgina was introduced to Gounod, she had few professional engagements behind her and was scarcely known even in England. She had long wanted to establish a music school for orphans; certainly Gounod's name could lend prestige to this project as well as to a new vocal method that she had developed. Gounod also thought well enough of Georgina's abilities as a singer to arrange engagements for her in Paris (one cannot, of course, help wonder about how objective he was in his assessment). In October 1871 she sang the solo part in *Gallia* for the Société des Concerts du Conservatoire, to lukewarm critical response. Gounod sought more appearances for Georgina with that organization and also suggested her to Halanzier for the role of Pauline in *Polyeucte*. Halanzier agreed, and promised to give that work in 1872 or 1873.[12] A fire at the Opéra on rue Le Peletier in 1873 contributed to an initial postponement, since it severely curtailed the number of new works that Halanzier could afford to stage.

Another obstacle produced an additional delay. This time the stumbling block was Georgina's rage, ignited when Gounod abruptly

---

[10] Letter from Gounod to Du Locle, in Pougin, 'Gounod écrivain' (1913), 475. On the *Mireille–George Dandin* affair, see also letter from Georgina Weldon to Gounod's lawyer Delacourtie, 15 Mar. 1874, in Weldon, *Mon Orphelinat et Gounod en Angleterre* (London, 1875), iii. 140–1 (the French edition of *My Orphanage*), and letter from Gounod to Du Locle, 25 Mar. 1874, in the Gounod file, Bibliothèque de la SACD. The incomplete full score of *George Dandin* came up for sale as lot 37 at the Hôtel Drouot on 20 June 1977. The identity of the buyer is unknown.

[11] Weldon, *My Orphanage*, ii. 78.

[12] Letter from Gounod to Weldon, 3 Aug. 1871, in Weldon, *Mon Orphelinat*, iii. 9.

decided to return home in 1874. In the end, the strain of separation from family and native culture proved too difficult to bear. Barbs from some French journalists—'Gounod has long ceased to be what one might call a practising Frenchman,' wrote Jules Clarétie in 1872—were unpleasant enough;[13] Gounod's friends on the other side of the Channel, including Jules Barbier, had also made no secret of their distaste for his new *mode de vie*.[14] Striken with a nervous attack at the beginning of June while the Weldons were away, Gounod summoned his friends Gaston de Beaucourt and Dr Blanche to escort him back to France. At first Gounod had every intention of maintaining cordial relations with the Weldons, but from Georgina's perspective this was impossible: in the eyes of the world he seemed to be returning to the domestic fold after a dalliance with an English adventuress, an impression produced, according to Georgina, largely because he had not had the courage to wait for Anna to break down and join him in England.[15] Georgina cast herself as the martyr in the affair, a role that she might have rendered more convincingly had it not been for the vindictive side of her temperament. As it happened, Gounod had left many personal belongings behind at Tavistock House, including the draft and nearly completed full score of *Polyeucte*. When he asked Georgina to forward them to him in France, she adamantly insisted that he claim them in person. It is difficult to separate a point of principle from emotional considerations in the reaction that followed from Gounod's camp. To attach a condition to the recovery of personal possessions was offensive enough. The substance of that condition was probably both intolerable to Anna, with whom Gounod had been reconciled, and inadvisable from the medical point of view. The only alternative seemed to be legal proceedings, which were launched in late June 1874.[16] Georgina declared in turn that she would rather destroy *Polyeucte* than be pressured in that way.[17] It soon occurred to Gounod that he might never see his score again. In the summer he began to plumb the depths of his memory to set the music to paper a second time, a chore that took nearly a year to complete; the

[13] Claretie's article appeared in *L'Événement* in July 1872; it is cited by Weldon in *Mon Orphelinat*, iii. 82. Even a Gounod supporter such as the critic Henri Moreno had disapproving words for Gounod: 'Nous ne pensions pas sans amertume à [Gounod] qui semble s'en être allé chercher une autre patrie sur les bords de la brumeuse Tamise et jouer au nouvel Haendel chez nos voisins d'outre-Manche; et cela, au moment où la France a plus besoin que jamais de toutes ses gloires artistiques pour conserver au moins une suprématie, la plus enviable, celle de l'intelligence' (review of a reprise of *Le Médecin malgré lui*, *Le Ménestrel*, 26 May 1872).

[14] Letter from Gounod to Barbier, 13 Mar. 1872, in Weldon, *Mon Orphelinat*, iii. 72.

[15] A succinct review of Georgina's position appears in 'Le Procès Gounod-Weldon', an unsigned article published in *Le Figaro*, 11 May 1885.

[16] Prod'homme and Dandelot, *Gounod*, ii. 154.

[17] Ibid. ii. 155.

effort bespeaks both confidence in the work—later in life Gounod held it to be his best opera—and a deep personal commitment to its Christian theme. Defiance of Georgina Weldon may also have been a factor, but in this respect Gounod was to be outdone: not long after he had finished reconstructing *Polyeucte*, he received a package containing the original autograph along with his other missing belongings.[18]

Georgina was not about to let Gounod forget her. He could certainly not look at the original *Polyeucte* draft without being reminded of his former protectrix: before sending it back she had scrawled her name diagonally across each page with crayon.[19] She went on to launch a number of suits against him (none of them was successful), claiming, among other things, that Gounod had spread libellous rumours about her in the French Press and that he had broken a contract by suddenly denying her the role of Pauline. Gounod found an outlet for his irritation in his art. When he reworked the score of *Sapho* for the 1884 production at the Opéra, he found it easy to recast the role of Glycère, the villain in that work. 'Just imagine,' he would write to an unspecified correspondent, 'I have worked so hard on the characterization [of Glycère] that last night I had a dream about her model . . . who seemed horrible in all her satanic ugliness.'[20]

Bursts of enormous creative energy followed by periods of complete lassitude had formed an unending cycle in Gounod's earlier career. If one is to believe Georgina's reminiscences, the bouts of depression became even more frequent and acute during the London years, exacerbated, of course, by Gounod's struggle with his own conscience. Yet the Weldon episode seems also to have been something of a cathartic experience for the composer, a series of wrenching breakdowns to end all breakdowns. Extant documents suggest that Gounod emerged from the tempest on a stable course to assume the role of elder statesman of French music. Despite his characteristic grace and wit, and the fact that his operas were performed more often in the last third of the century than those of any other French composer, in the eyes of the critical establishment and the younger generation of French composers he never quite attained the Olympian position that a figure such as Verdi enjoyed in Italy. The lingering reverberations of the Weldon affair as well as a pronounced streak of eccentricity tempered that sort of adulation. Moreover (and the contrast to Verdi is still apropos here), Gounod's style was widely perceived to suffer from severe ossification after the

[18] The recopied version of *Polyeucte* is at the Stiftelsen Musikkulturens Främjande in Stockholm; the location of the original full score is unknown. It is probable, of course, that Gounod also did some recomposing in the process of rewriting the score.

[19] See Julian de Perthius, 'Gounod contre Weldon', *Le Figaro*, 13 Jan. 1886.

[20] Prod'homme and Dandelot, *Gounod*, ii. 200–1.

London period. It is noteworthy that his most significant innovations and only enduring successes on the stage came during years when he was a regular patient at Dr Blanche's mental clinic. Even the most partial admirer cannot help observe that greater personal equilibrium later in life was accompanied by a drying up of inspiration, though just how much the two phenomena were related, if at all, is open to speculation. It does seem certain, however, that personal stability produced great resilience to the failure of new works and a career in opera that continued longer than it should have done.

In the early 1870s Du Locle of the Opéra-Comique took the place of Carvalho as the standard bearer for the operas of Gounod in Paris. His audiences were not entirely hospitable. Both a staging of *Le Médecin malgré lui* in 1872 and the *Mireille* production two years later (with a return to a tragic denouement) were unsuccessful. But in 1876 *Philémon et Baucis*, reduced to two acts from the original three, joined *Roméo et Juliette* in the Opéra-Comique repertoire; it was given there regularly until the Second World War. The success of these two works, however, was not enough to extricate Du Locle from the severe financial difficulties that beset him after 1874. He does deserve the gratitude of posterity for having produced *Carmen* in 1875, but at the time this was not good for business. Though serious works were not unknown at the Opéra-Comique before this period, to many the repertoire seemed to be taking an excessively sombre turn. *Carmen* was the third major production in as many years (following *Roméo et Juliette* and *Mireille*) to have a tragic denouement, and this time the morality of the heroine herself was called into question. Bizet's opera received forty-eight performances in the first six months after its première, but the house was rarely full.[21]

In May 1876 Du Locle declared bankruptcy. If Gounod feared massive upheavals in repertorial policy, these must have been quickly assuaged by the appointment of Du Locle's successor, none other than Léon Carvalho. A fresh start for the Opéra-Comique was clearly in order and Carvalho brought his customary energy to the job: during the summer he held auditions for an entirely new troupe and refurbished the interior of the hall.[22] He realized as well that it would be important to make a mark with a major new production as soon as possible. Obviously hoping to duplicate the successes of the Théâtre-Lyrique years, Carvalho turned to Gounod sometime in the late summer or early autumn of 1876. From experience he also knew that Gounod could be counted on to respect deadlines and to compose quickly. His faith was

[21] See Mina Curtiss, *Bizet and his World* (New York, 1958), 388–409.
[22] 'Semaine théâtrale', *Le Ménestrel*, 27 Aug. 1876.

well placed: by the beginning of January a new work, *Cinq-Mars*, was ready for rehearsal.[23]

All was not a replay of the past. For the first time since *La Nonne sanglante* Gounod set a libretto by writers other than Barbier and Carré; the latter had died in 1872 and Gounod's relations with Barbier had cooled because of conflicting opinions about how to deal with Choudens over their previous collaborations. The scenario for *Cinq-Mars* was furnished by a certain Paul Poirson and the verse written by Louis Gallet, who would emerge as one of the most prominent librettists of *fin de siècle* French opera. Although by the end of the decade Gounod would effect a reconciliation with Choudens, that bridge still had not been mended. Léon Grus, a millionaire for whom music publishing was something of a hobby, paid Gounod 100,000 francs for the score, double what Gounod had earned from *Roméo et Juliette* a decade before.[24]

True to form, Carvalho poured a large amount of money into the production of *Cinq-Mars*. The critic Albert de Lasalle hoped that the lavish staging 'would erase the memory of the lamentable exhibitions that had been permitted in the last four or five years';[25] indeed the very novelty of a grand spectacle at the Opéra-Comique following a lean period may partly account for the strong start of *Cinq-Mars* after its première on 5 April 1877. The first appearance in ten years of a new opera by as prominent a figure as Gounod was bound to attract a flurry of attention. The composer was delighted to report to an acquaintance five days later that the first sixteen performances had already been sold out, though he attributed the initial success to a fine cast and the fact that the work was 'easy to understand'.[26]

Perhaps too easy, for the score rapidly wore thin. It is true that, with the exception of critics who were perennially hostile to Gounod, the majority of reviewers did manifest goodwill towards the composer and his score. But it is not hard to detect beneath these expressions of respect a certain disappointment that the music was not more memorable. 'If the score of *Cinq-Mars* does not add anything to the glory of Gounod, it does not diminish it either,' was the diplomatic remark of the reviewer for *La Comédie*.[27] Many attributed the result to the fact that the opera

---

[23] Rumours of Gounod's interest in this subject had surfaced as early as 1864. In Nov. of that year a correspondent for *Le Figaro* reported that he intended to write a *Cinq-Mars et de Thou* ('Petit Courrier de Théâtre', *Le Figaro*, 17 Nov. 1864).

[24] One would presume that there were additional provisions for royalty payments; unfortunately I have been unable to locate the contract between Grus and the team of Gounod, Poirson, and Gallet.

[25] Review of *Cinq-Mars*, *Le Monde illustré*, 14 Apr. 1877.

[26] Letter to Victor Schwab, 10 Apr. 1877, BN Mus. Gounod l.a.s. 122.

[27] Review of *Cinq-Mars* signed 'Lyonel', *La Comédie* (1877), no. 18.

was composed in a few weeks. The critical climate had also changed perceptibly during the previous decade. It is significant that now even conservative reviewers, though they still placed Gounod in Wagner's camp, did not complain that his style was impenetrable. Henri Blaze de Bury's assessment is revealing:

He flirts with *wagnérisme*, he systematically manipulates dissonances, delayed harmonic resolutions, and other chemical concoctions from the dispensary of *Tannhäuser* and *Lohengrin*; but this melody, this restless harmony, all of these devices soon become worn out if they are not invigorated by individual genius, and the moment arrives when the novelty of yesterday seems as outmoded, as old and withered as the Italian cadence.[28]

Clearly Gounod's idiom had been thoroughly assimilated. There was nothing objectionable about this in itself and supporters such as Ernest Reyer would protest that it was bad grace to reproach Gounod for continuing to write in a style that was a cornerstone of modern French music.[29] But others found it unpalatable that the progenitor himself was not participating in trends that he had helped to launch. There was also grumbling in certain quarters that the plot of the new opera, based upon a celebrated novel by Alfred de Vigny about a conspiracy to kill Cardinal Richelieu, was no less sombre than some of the recent fare at the Opéra-Comique. (Meyerbeer himself had at one time even considered the same subject as a plot for a grand opera.) Once the novelty of *Cinq-Mars* had evaporated, its days were numbered. Despite revisions that Gounod introduced at the request of the Italian publisher Lucca, *Cinq-Mars* did not find favour with Opéra-Comique audiences when it reappeared there after the summer break of 1877. Nor was it successful at La Scala the following January.

Gounod could distract himself from this failure by looking forward to a *Polyeucte* at the new (and present) home of the Opéra. Had it not been for the unpleasant rupture with the Weldons, this work might well have been the first new production on that stage. As it was, Halanzier made commitments to Auguste Mermet and Jules Massenet while Gounod tried to recover and then reconstruct his score. There was also the matter of finding a suitable singer for the role of Pauline now that Georgina's spell had worn off. Gounod at first encouraged Halanzier to hire Adelina Patti, who had yet to be heard at the Opéra, but then became enthralled with the voice of the Austrian singer Gabrielle Krauss when she made her début there as Donna Anna at the end of 1875; there was no more direct route to Gounod's heart than a successful performance of

[28] Review of *Cinq-Mars*, *La Revue des deux mondes*, 15 Apr. 1877.
[29] In his review of *Polyeucte*, *Journal des débats*, 15 Nov. 1878.

Mozart's music. La Krauss also had the kind of bearing and vocal versatility that reminded many of Pauline Viardot at the height of her powers; small wonder that she was Gounod's choice for the title role in the 1884 revival of *Sapho*, as well as for Pauline and for Hermosa in *Le Tribut de Zamora*.

Paris played host to yet another world exhibition in 1878 and *Polyeucte* (like *Roméo et Juliette* over a decade before) was planned as one of the major musical events of that year. But unlike *Roméo* it was unveiled in October, too late for visitors to prolong appreciably its run. Moreover, the benevolence extended by reviewers to *Cinq-Mars* had largely vanished. Not only had Massenet's *Le Roi de Lahore*, given at the Opéra the preceding year, served to throw Gounod's stagnation as composer into clear relief, but rumours also circulated even before the *Polyeucte* première that it was undramatic, much more like an oratorio than an opera. These fires were fed by the dissemination in the Press of Gounod's own manifesto about his new work:

To celebrate the new life that Christianity has spread among humanity, the unknown and irresistible powers that it has communicated first to individuals, and then, through them, to modern society, the triumph of those generations purified in the light of Faith and in the flames of divine Charity over the old pagan world, corrupted, corroded, and cankered to the marrow by the crass cult of material things; to show those souls recast in the image of Man–God, engulfing like a deluge the ruins of gods made in the image of all that is base in man: that is the philosophy that generated the choice of this subject and the composition of *Polyeucte*.[30]

Turgenev's erotic priest was not nearly so interesting as a modern-day apostle (a prolix, abstruse one at that). Now Parisian audiences did have a history of savouring religious tableaux, particularly when these rubbed shoulders with more sensuous scenes (they would become as much part of Massenet's stock-in-trade as they had been Gounod's in previous years), but in the opera house religion could only fall flat when it was not offset by convincing portrayal of emotion and character. Few disagreed with the verdict of Jacques Hermann that 'one cannot hear a single musical phrase in the opera without ... saying "this is by Gounod", but regardless of the character on stage one can never say: "This is the martyred Christian, this is the sublime spouse, this is the generous lover." '[31] *Polyeucte* ran for only twenty-nine performances. It was small comfort that Donizetti and Scribe had also been unsuccessful in 1840 with *Les Martyrs*, their adaptation of the same Corneille play.

[30] Cited by Adolphe Jullien, *Musiciens d'aujourd'hui* (Paris, 1892), 150.

[31] 'A propos du Polyeucte de M. Gounod', *Revue du monde musical et dramatique*, 14 Dec. 1878.

Gounod had, of course, known a succession of failures before. But the resurrection that accompanied *Roméo et Juliette* at the end of the Second Empire was not destined to be re-enacted with his next opera. Wheels for another project were already set in motion well before the first performance of *Polyeucte*. In the summer of 1877 Gounod, Gallet, and possibly Paul Poirson as well planned a work based on the lives of Abélard and Héloise.[32] *Maître Pierre* it was to be called, and Gounod promised that it would not merely be 'a series of love duets; rather it [will be] a personification, an embodiment of the highest philosophical and religious concepts'.[33] This was not good strategy, to judge from the fate of *Polyeucte*. Halanzier realized this even before the première of that work. Though by the summer of 1878 Gounod had written and orchestrated almost half of *Maître Pierre*, the director called him into his office to hear a reading of a more down-to-earth libretto initially intended for Verdi, *Le Tribut de Zamora* by Adolphe d'Ennery, author of the rival *Faust* in 1858, and Jules Brésil. Since a staging of *Maître Pierre* did not appear imminent, Gounod dropped that project (he would later organize the finished material into a *Suite dramatique en quatre parties*)[34] and took up the challenge of setting a tawdry bit of melodrama. And a formidable challenge it was, not only because of the inherent weaknesses in a plot that hinged upon the recovery of reason by a mad woman and her subsequent recognition of a long lost daughter—seen fifty times before on boulevard theatres said one reviewer[35]—but also because d'Ennery and Brésil were inexperienced as versifiers for opera. Their habit of changing accentuation patterns in the verse after the music had been composed was bound to be disconcerting for a composer as careful about text setting as Gounod.[36]

More than anything else, the spectacular success of Gabrielle Krauss kept the opera in the repertoire for almost fifty performances following its première on 1 April 1881. The score itself was roundly condemned by many as inferior even to *Polyeucte*. Frustrated nationalist sentiment, linked at the deepest level to the defeat of 1870, lay behind at least some of the expressions of annoyance with Gounod's work. Many critics clamoured for a figure whom they could endorse as the leader of French

[32] There are five letters about *Maître Pierre* written in Aug. and Sept. 1877 from Gounod to a 'Paul' (probably Paul Poirson) at BN Mus. Gounod l.a.s. 126–31.

[33] Gounod discussed the project in an interview with the famous critic Hanslick in 1878; this interview was reproduced by Adolphe Jullien in 'Un entretien de M. Gounod', *Revue du monde musical et dramatique*, 3 May 1879.

[34] The autograph full score of *Maître Pierre* is at BN Mus. MS. 14996.

[35] Édouard Noël and Edmond Stoullig (eds.), *Las Annales du théâtre et de la musique*, (Paris, 1881), 11.

[36] A series of letters about the project from Gounod to Brésil is at the Bibliothèque de la SACD.

opera; there was great disappointment that the most obvious candidate had fallen so short of the mark so many times. Critic Edmond Hippeau even advocated that France disown *Le Tribut de Zamora* completely: 'Gounod exposes us all to attacks, though he alone is the only one who merits them.'[37] Progressive reviewers—and it should be remembered that the voices of those who saw Wagnerian music drama as providing the standard for modernity were becoming more numerous in Paris— were also alarmed that now even the 'Italian school' (namely Verdi) seemed to be more forward-looking than Gounod. It is not hard to read between the lines of most reviews the recommendation to the composer that he give up opera composition.

Gounod would have done well to follow that advice to the letter. As it was, he persuaded the Opéra administration to undertake a new production of *Sapho* for Krauss in 1884, with considerable enlargement of the original score. That Gounod's last work for the stage was a reworking of his first is remarkable. A measure of this may be obtained by a comparison to Verdi or Wagner: revisions of *Oberto* or *Die Feen* late in their careers would have been inconceivable. The first *Sapho* is not as similar stylistically to *Faust* as are *Cinq-Mars* or *Polyeucte*, but, because Gounod wrote his first opera relatively late in life, after he had become technically accomplished, and because his style and approach to form and dramaturgy in opera evolved little after *Faust*, the distance travelled between 1851 and 1884 was relatively short. The *Sapho* revival was another disappointment. There were to be triumphs of old operas in subsequent years—*Roméo et Juliette* at the Opéra in 1888, *Mireille* (finally) at the Opéra-Comique in 1889—and successes with sacred works such as *Rédemption* and *Mors et vita*. But Gounod remained something of an anachronism, a shadow of the progressive figure he cut during the Second Empire.

---

[37] Review of *Le Tribut de Zamora* in *La Renaissance musicale*, 3 Apr. 1881.

PART TWO

The Operas

7. Faust

Faust and the French

During his first stay in Rome Gounod became intimately acquainted with Goethe's *Faust*. 'The work did not leave me; I carried it everywhere,' he later remembered.[1] The Sistine Chapel, Ingres, Palestrina, *Faust*—Gounod swallowed the entire heady mixture, inviting an assault against the bastion of classical art by more progressive forces. To revere *Faust* was, after all, to draw sustenance from the same well-spring as the Romantic thoroughbreds. The first encounter of Berlioz with Goethe's immortalization of the Faust legend seems to have been nothing short of a religious experience: 'Goethe's *Faust* ... made a strange and deep impression on me. The marvellous book fascinated me from the first. I could not put it down. I read it incessantly, at meals, at the theatre, in the street.'[2] We have it on the word of Théophile Gautier in his *Histoire du Romantisme* that *Faust* occupied a vital place in the curriculum of all French Romantics:

What a marvellous era! Walter Scott was in the full bloom of his success; we initiated ourselves to the mysteries of Goethe's *Faust* which embraces all, according to the maxim of Madame de Staël, and even something a bit more than that. We discovered Shakespeare ... and the poems of Lord Byron, the *Corsaire, Lara, Le Giaour, Manfred, Beppo, Don Juan*, came to us from an Orient that had not yet been made banal. How all of this was young, new, strangely tinted, of an intoxicating and overwhelming flavour![3]

The springboards for this enthusiasm were the first French translations of Goethe's Part I, two in 1823 by Louis de Sainte-Aulaire and Albert Stapfer—Delacroix supplied a famous series of seventeen lithographs for a reimpression of the latter—and a version by Gérard de Nerval that appeared in 1827. Even discounting the fact that he was only eighteen when he completed the translation, Nerval's is a fine achievement, and, as Goethe himself recognized, markedly superior to the work of his two precursors. It became the preferred version of Berlioz, Gounod, and many others of their generation.

Given the rich synthesis of styles and genres in Goethe's *Faust*—its 'Shakespearian' quality, to use a term of reference familiar to Berlioz

[1] Gounod, *Mémoires*, p. 118.
[2] Berlioz, *Memoirs* , p. 147.
[3] Théophile Gautier, *Histoire du Romantisme* (Paris, 1857), 5.

contemporaries—its influence upon mid-nineteenth-century culture was naturally multifarious. Some of the tremors in high culture were faint, for example the Gretchen-like figure of Blanche in Hugo's *Le Roi s'amuse* of 1832 (to become Gilda in Verdi's *Rigoletto*); others were more palpable. Witness the blatant imitation of Goethe by Alfred de Musset in the first act of *Manfred*, where, following Nerval's diction in the second 'cabinet d'étude' scene, the protagonist Frank utters a series of imprecations, each beginning 'Maudit soit', to accompany a toast to spiritual torment.[4] The first real French adaptations, however, emerged on a more popular level. In 1827 a three-act *Faust* by de Théaulon and de Gondelier met with success on the stage of the Théâtre des Nouveautés. No spiritual torment here: Faust is content to strike a pact with the devil in order to acquire gold that will enable him to support a wife. Rather it was the 'ingenious effects of phantasmagoria', as one reviewer described them, that drew audiences.[5] Taking its cue from that effort, the Théâtre de la Porte-Saint-Martin soon mounted its own *Faust* spectacle, according to another observer 'a feast for those who like surprises created by stage apparatus, supernatural apparitions and disappearances, sundry monsters'.[6] The same writer went on to ask: 'After all, who does not like all of those things these days?'—a question doubtless on the minds of Meyerbeer and Scribe in this period as they planned *Robert le diable*. That opera, premièred in 1831, is as much a product of contemporary taste for *diableries* as the previous Parisian *Faust*s. Indeed it has been argued with reason that adaptations of *Faust* helped to prepare the ground for the first success of Meyerbeer at the Opéra, a house that lagged considerably behind other theatres in the business of gothic horrors.[7] There is a certain irony in this as far as Gounod's opera is concerned. Meyerbeer's evil Bertram, whose road to fame at the most prestigious inferno in Paris was lined by ephemeral Méphistos and other demons from minor stages (and Caspar in Weber's *Der Freischütz*) inevitably became the model against which some early reviewers of Gounod's *Faust* measured his Méphistophélès. After the *couplets* of Siébel, 'on comes Faust, followed by his terrible Bertram', wrote Joseph d'Ortigue.[8] Albert de Lasalle wondered if Gounod possessed the necessary musical fibre 'to render the sneering of Méphisto and the howling in hell. To start with, the task

[4] On the influence of Goethe's *Faust* upon French literature in this period, see Charles Dédéyan, *Le Thème de Faust dans la littérature européenne* (Paris, 1959), ii. 278–490.
[5] Ibid. 171.
[6] Cited by Allévy, *La Mise-en-scène en France*, p. 67.
[7] Ibid. 67.
[8] Review of *Faust*, *Le Ménestrel*, 27 Mar. 1859.

must have been difficult after Meyerbeer's Bertram, who is the most successfully portrayed devil in all of music.'[9]

Enthusiasm for fashioning new works out of Goethe's *Faust* in the wake of the first French translations extended beyond the popular spoken theatre. In 1825 the painter Ary Scheffer made sketches for a canvas entitled *Marguerite implorant la Vierge*, a painting he finally completed four years later. He would continue to mine Goethe for subjects throughout his career, producing (among others) the oils *Marthe et Marguerite* (1830), *Marguerite à l'église* (1837), *Marguerite sortant de l'église* (1838), and *Faust à la coupe* (1858). The series was widely circulated in lithographs. Whereas Delacroix laid emphasis upon the fantastic and satanic in his work, Scheffer explored the character of Goethe's heroine: no fewer than eight of his eleven *Faust* paintings are depictions of Gretchen episodes in the model.

Gounod's opera, as has frequently been noted, is also centred on the Gretchen tragedy. Gounod and Scheffer were introduced to one another by Pauline Viardot in the early 1850s and soon became friends (there is even a flattering portrait by Scheffer showing the composer as defiant tribune of the avant-garde). It is impossible to estimate the extent to which Gounod's conception of a *Faust* adaptation was actually shaped by the work of the painter, although one might suppose that, if nothing else, they found kinship in an understanding of how Goethe's drama could most effectively be translated into their respective art forms. There is evidence, however, that Michel Carré, whose play *Faust et Marguerite* (1850) was the proximate source for Gounod's opera, had at least one of Scheffer's compelling images in mind. The canvas *Marguerite sortant de l'église* captures the girl, her face aglow with an air of detached *naïveté*, just before her first encounter with Faust.[10] In Goethe there is no church—the location for the meeting is simply marked as 'a street'—but in Carré's play Marguerite is indeed seen leaving church just before Faust accosts her. And, though a church did not figure in the foreground of the analogous scene at the opera's première, costume instructions in the printed *mise-en-scène* associated with those performances show some similarities to *Marguerite sortant de l'église*. They call for her to wear 'a white dress made of light wool, very simple, with a double skirt gathered on the left side . . . moneybag, plaits, no hat',[11] all features of Scheffer's depiction (contemporary reproductions of the

---

[9] Review of *Faust*, *Le Monde illustré*, 27 Mar. 1859.

[10] A reproduction of this canvas may be seen in Marthe Kolb, *Ary Scheffer et son temps* (Paris, 1937), 344.

[11] This *mise-en-scène* is part of 'Collection de Mises-en-Scène, rédigées par M. Arsène', BO B.398. The costume descriptions are given on p. 34.

Théâtre-Lyrique costumes, however, suggest that the imitation was not literal in all details).[12] It is also noteworthy that on one occasion Camille Saint-Saëns could not resist referring to both Gounod's *Faust* and Scheffer's paintings together:

The first time I saw Goethe's 'Faust' played in a German theatre I was quite astonished to behold, appearing unexpectedly on the stage during the *kermesse*, a slightly-built brunette who replied to Faust's compliments in scandalised accents: 'Je ne suis pas une demoiselle, je ne suis pas belle . . .' and then rapidly hid away in the crowd. She was anything but the ideal fair-complexioned creature with whom Ary Scheffer has familiarised us (coming out of church with angelic mien, while Faust looks on enraptured), or the fanciful creation which Gounod's music has popularised.[13]

The same *rapprochement* was doubtless made by many contemporaries. In a biography of Scheffer published in the year of the *Faust* première, Charles Lenormant even drew a parallel between Marie Miolan-Carvalho's enactment of the Marguerite role and the painter's characterization: 'with an art of mime that we did not expect of her, she has, modelling herself on one of Scheffer's paintings, created a living embodiment of the simple German girl that the poet has conceived.'[14]

French musicians also took up Goethe's *Faust* soon after the appearance of translations. A *Fausto* for the Théâtre-Italien by Louise Bertin is notable as the first operatic adaptation of Goethe's *Faust* outside Germany, but it had only a short run in 1831. Although not much more of a financial success at its première in 1846, Berlioz's *La Damnation de Faust* has become a staple of the modern repertoire. After his first reading of Part I many years before, 'the temptation grew so strong, the charm so violent' that Berlioz could not resist setting many of the musical episodes in the drama, publishing them in 1829 as his 'Œuvre 1', the *Huit scènes de Faust*.[15] He later repudiated that work as an independent composition, but used much of it for *La Damnation de Faust*.

Soon after completing the *Huit scènes*, and, in his words, 'still under the influence of Goethe's poem', Berlioz wrote the *Symphonie fantastique*, a detail which is relevant here in that it helps to clarify his understanding of *Faust* as a musical subject.[16] Whereas the popular theatres reaped shallow effects from Mephistopheles, and Scheffer (followed later by

---

[12] These lithographs are shown in Prod'homme and Dandelot, *Gounod*, i. 228, over the rubric '*Faust* au Théâtre-Lyrique (1859 et années suivantes): Principaux interprètes'. It is worth noting that the two depictions of Marguerite do not exactly match the *mise-en-scène* directives.

[13] In 'The Manuscript Libretto of *Faust*', *Musical Times*, 62 (1921), 553.

[14] Cited by Kolb, *Ary Scheffer*, p. 342.

[15] Letter from Berlioz to Goethe, 10 Apr. 1829, in Berlioz, *Correspondance générale*, i. 247.

[16] Berlioz, *Memoirs*, p. 148.

Gounod) applied himself to Gretchen, Berlioz made Faust himself the central figure of *La Damnation de Faust*. A factor behind this decision was almost certainly the composer's identification with the emotional and spiritual state of Goethe's protagonist: the artist in the Symphony, Faust the philosopher, Berlioz the man—the strands are inseparable. To step beyond charted knowledge or artistic convention was to invite isolation and *ennui* born of struggle; in both works, an awakening of sensual instincts brings another perspective, a new way to relate to the world surrounding. Only after a happy tryst with the Beloved do the artist in the Symphony and Berlioz's Faust (following Goethe) achieve a sense of unity with Nature—and a momentary reprieve from suffering. One of Berlioz's major deviations from Goethe, and from most previous renditions of the Faust legend, is a postponement of the hero's pact with the devil until very late in the work. The blissful discourse of Faust with the elements is interrupted by Méphistophélès, who informs him that Marguerite is on death row, awaiting execution for matricide; in return for saving her, Méphistophélès extracts a promise of future service from Faust. Whereas the death of Valentin and his condemnation of Marguerite constitute the tragic apex of Gounod's Marguerite-centred opera, the abrupt negation of Faust's great achievement of solidarity with Nature is the highpoint of Berlioz's drama. All that follows—the ride to Hell, the Pandemonium, the apotheosis of Marguerite—is denouement.

It is striking, of course, that the two major French composers at mid-century, Gounod and Berlioz, wrote large works on the same subject within a period of fifteen years. But even were it not for the markedly different orientation of both compositions, the ground for comparison (and possible competition) is small. Berlioz styled his work a 'légende dramatique' and did not intend it to be staged, as it sometimes is today. He wove together the most musical episodes in Goethe's drama using only three characters and very little connecting material, not enough to prepare staged set pieces by contemporaneous operatic standards. As Jacques Barzun has noted, there is ample evidence that the work would have been very different had Berlioz intended performances on the stage.[17] A possibility to enlarge *La Damnation de Faust* did briefly present itself in 1847—with Scribe as librettist. This alone suggests that the project might not have aimed as high as the original concert work. Even more significant is Berlioz's plan to make Méphistophélès the central character in an opera. That decision was not the result of profound re-evaluation of the Goethe, but rather of two more practical considerations. Since Goethe's drama was frequently staged, Berlioz

[17] Jacques Barzun, *Berlioz and the Romantic Century* (3rd edn., New York, 1969), 484.

believed that his own staged version would be more likely to invite comparisons to that source than his 'légende dramatique'. In a letter of 26 November 1847 to Scribe he argued that an enhancement of the Méphistophélès role would help to distance their new work not only from Goethe's drama but also from Spohr's *Faust* (1813), an opera not based upon Goethe at all.[18] In other words, though Berlioz developed Faust as the central character in a concert work, he felt that it would not be wise to attempt the same on the stage because of artistically important antecedents. The second, and more important, factor was the availability of the famous baritone Jan Pischek, a man with 'a devilish physique' he reported to Scribe. Berlioz thought the most direct road to success would be to make his role the largest in the work—this from the same composer who was so taken with the spirit of Goethe's *Faust* that he wrote a frankly autobiographical work, the *Symphonie fantastique*, under its spell. There is no evidence to suggest that his enthusiasm waned with the years. Yet, like Gounod after him, Berlioz seems to have been prepared to sacrifice some of that spirit to produce an effective and commercially viable Faust opera.

Carré's Faust et Marguerite

The popular theatres in Paris continued to turn out adaptations of Goethe's *Faust*: a *Faust et Marguerite* by V. Doinet in 1846, Carré's play of the same name in 1850, and Adolphe d'Ennery's *Faust* for the Théâtre de la Porte-Saint-Martin in 1858. The two latter efforts are remembered largely because of their association with Gounod's *Faust*. D'Ennery's play, it will be recalled, once threw a spanner into the composer's aspirations for a production of his opera. In the end it survived only six months, but during that time it did satisfy the voracious appetite of Parisians for spectacle. Since volcanic eruptions were popular on the boulevards, for example, d'Ennery's Méphistophélès manœuvres Faust backwards in time to Pompey in AD 79. Faust appears in one scene, perhaps to satisfy more exotic tastes, as an Indian maharajah dispensing alms to the poor. He literally rides to Méphisto's realm and the inevitable *ronde infernale* on wings of Death, represented by a giant black bird.

Gounod's opera is a weighty piece in comparison to that extravaganza, yet it was also born at a boulevard theatre. Carré's *Faust et Marguerite* had been moderately successful at the Théâtre du Gymnase-Dramatique in 1850, but he was not immediately enthused by a project

---

[18] Berlioz, *Correspondance générale*, iii. 473.

for a *Faust* opera when first told about it in 1856. Carré was much more eager to work with Meyerbeer, with whom he and Barbier had recently contracted to produce the libretto for *Le Pardon de Ploërmel*. The two librettists agreed that Carré would write the book for Meyerbeer and that Barbier alone would devote himself to *Faust*. Carré gave his partner permission to borrow whatever he needed from his earlier boulevard play.[19]

Whereas a spectacle such as concocted by d'Ennery uses a few episodes from Goethe's *Faust* merely as points of departure for a wildly fantastic, and scenically colourful, plot, Carré's *Faust et Marguerite* remains within the geographic confines suggested by Goethe. There was material aplenty in Goethe's drama for a bitter-sweet boulevard tale about the despoliation of a young woman's innocence by darker powers operating through a human surrogate; most of the scenes in Carré's play have some analogue in the Goethe, albeit distant in some cases and with a change of order. But there is one aspect of Goethe's Part I that was particularly problematic for the boulevard stage: it does not feature a complement of secondary characters to enliven the basic Mephistopheles-Faust-Gretchen dynamic. Dame Marthe, included as a foil for the innocence of Gretchen, and Faust's assistant Wagner are the only secondary figures who appear in more than one scene, and their role in the unfolding of the plot is minimal. Other minor figures—Brander, Valentin, Lieschen—appear in individual scenes to play small parts in the destinies of Faust and Gretchen, but the viewer's interest in the fate of the principals is sustained not through subsidiary complications of plot but largely through the world of ideas brought into focus by Goethe.

Carré could not hope to produce a successful boulevard play on that premiss. Plot development had to take up where philosophical substance fell short. To accomplish this, he somewhat expanded the role of Valentin and greatly enlarged that of Siébel, a minor player in Goethe's *Auerbachs Keller* episode. As preparation for Valentin's explosion of wrath in Act III (derived from Goethe, and the only episode in which Valentin appears there), Carré portrays him much earlier on, in the second scene of Act I, as the protector of his sister, Marguerite. Goethe's unseen protector, Gretchen's mother, is therefore rendered redundant and eliminated by Carré. Marguerite is *de facto* spared the crime of matricide. (To fan the flames of sentimentality in the play and opera, Marguerite even makes reference to her mother's premature death in a distant and troubled past: 'I have already wept so much', she confesses

---

[19] See Barbier's unpublished account of the genesis, cited by Prod'homme and Dandelot, *Gounod*, i. 189.

to Faust in the garden scene.) In his role as custodian of Marguerite's virtue, Valentin has the responsibility, at his very first appearance, to ensure that she is well guarded while he is away at war.

Enter Siébel. He has already been introduced in the first scene of the play both as Faust's student and as a lad who is in love with Marguerite. That scene is directly analogous to the episode between Faust and Wagner at the beginning of Goethe's drama, yet there is no clearer example of Carré's sacrifice of the original content to plot mechanics. Where Wagner's unquestioning faith in the pursuit of knowledge in the model sets Faust's greatness as a thinker in relief, Carré's Siébel drops the name of Marguerite to lay the foundation for a stock-in-trade love triangle. Valentin, for his part, is content to leave town with the knowledge that the virtuous Siébel will watch over his sister in his absence. This is a commission that Siébel takes very seriously, so seriously that he becomes an obstacle to the consummation of Faust's love for Marguerite in Act II. But he is, of course, no match for satanic powers. In the garden scene Méphistophélès puts Siébel to sleep in a tree while he himself courts Marthe, and Faust is paired off with Marguerite. Siébel awakens at nightfall. He had previously arranged to escort Marguerite to supper at his mother's house, but in the darkness he takes the hand of Marthe, who believes, in turn, that Siébel is Méphistophélès. In Goethe's rendering of the garden scene the humorous interaction between Marthe and Mephistopheles offsets the developing drama between Faust and Gretchen. Carré oversteps the tragedian's constructive use of comedy to indulge in simpleminded slapstick based upon mistaken identities.

In addition to enlarging the roles of Valentin and Siébel, Carré radically abbreviates Goethe's denouement. Death is deliberately avoided: there is no infanticide and Valentin is not mortally wounded in his duel with Faust. The *Walpurgisnacht* and the prison scene are eliminated. Instead, Carré's Faust comes upon Marguerite in the street just after Valentin has been carried off, and attempts then and there to persuade her to join him in flight. She resists long enough to ensure her celestial salvation and the play ends.

Beyond these structural changes the general tone of Carré's play is not consonant with its model. It is only semi-serious, a *divertissement* fashioned after Goethe to stir an intellectually undemanding audience with a good love story, amuse it with some diabolical comedy, and impress it with sorcery that draws upon clever stage effects. The level of discourse never rises much above brisk casual exchanges in contemporary jargon that would not have been out of place in a social comedy of the period. For example, philosopher and devil come across as two youthful pranksters as they secretly watch Marguerite descend upon the jewel box, and Méphistophélès barely manages to restrain a lovesick Faust from openly declaring his affection at that moment: 'She reminds me of Madame Eve . . . but you are too loquacious for the part of the snake,' he admonishes the philosopher. A minute before, the impatient devil shifted the heavy box from hand to hand, goading Faust to make up his mind soon simply because he could not be expected to hold the jewels forever. Carré's Méphistophélès outdoes his prototype in buffoonery, with none of the trenchant cynicism exhibited by Goethe's character.

Boulevard Play into Opera

The only extended passages that Barbier lifted verbatim from *Faust et Marguerite* for the libretto were the 'Chanson du roi de Thulé' and a set of *couplets* for Lise (one of the girls who ostracizes Marguerite in Act IV) that were cut before the première. Despite the limited number of direct citations, it is clear that the play was the model for Gounod's *Faust*. Between the start of the rehearsal period for the first performance and the Opéra production of 1869, *Faust* had a turbulent history of revisions, and the relationship of opera to play is even more evident when the libretto that Gounod first set in 1857–8 (henceforth, urlibretto) is taken into account.[20] Barbier readily accepted the enlarged roles of Valentin and Siébel as well as the general distribution of events in Carré's *Faust et Marguerite*. The first act of the play, which terminates with the first brief encounter of Faust and Marguerite, was the source for Acts I and II in the opera. The play's second act led to the opera's third, bringing events up to the nocturnal tryst in the garden. Carré's third act was the basis for the last two acts in the libretto. Many scenes in the Carré are reproduced in the same order in the urlibretto, and the general tone of the genre to which Carré's boulevard play belongs is still evident in many scenes of Gounod's final version.

Barbier's fidelity to the play is best illustrated through an examination

[20] The central documents for a discussion of the evolution of the score are the censors' libretto (AN F^{18} 736, bearing the date 17 Nov.) and the autograph full score (BN Mus. MS 17724 (1)). The former has been known to scholars for many years. In 1912 Albert Soubies and Henri de Curzon showed that the censors' libretto is much longer than the work performed on opening night by reproducing all the passages in this libretto that were cut before the première. Saint-Saëns amplified their remarks with a description of Gounod's manuscript working copy of the libretto, which contains scattered autograph musical annotations ('The Manuscript Libretto of *Faust*'). There is also an undated manuscript libretto at the Bibliothèque de l'Opéra (Liv. MS 289) that corresponds to the censors' libretto, with a few variants. This source gives every appearance of being a working copy used by the *régie* at the Théâtre-Lyrique during the first rehearsal period: there are stage and lighting directions in the margins, and pieces deleted during the rehearsals are crossed out in pencil.

of the working method he used to write a part of the urlibretto, as documented in a set of his extant working papers.[21] This material is made up largely of sheets that were used to work out the versification of individual numbers, although not all numbers in the urlibretto are represented. The only act completely drafted in the papers is the fourth, that is the set of events immediately after Marguerite's seduction, including the duel and church scene. Barbier put it together by cutting out, from the third act of a print of Carré's drama, portions that correspond to the prose *parlé* sections in the urlibretto, pasting these on to loose sheets, and filling in the interstices with versified text for the music of the numbers. The draft, on sixteen numbered pages (11–12 missing), is headed by a paste-up of the set instructions from the play followed by the scene of the young girls at the fountain written out by hand. The handwritten scene includes Lise's *couplets* (for which, strangely enough, Barbier did not use a cut out, although they are taken right from the play) and a solo number for Marguerite not found in the play. This is a prayer, 'Ô vierge sainte, mère des sept douleurs', derived from Goethe's *Zwinger* episode, instead of the spinning song 'Il ne revient plus'. This handwritten scene is followed by a paste-up of the Marguerite–Siébel dialogue; then come Valentin's *couplets*, again handwritten. The draft for the rest of the act continues in this manner, with the church tableau occurring before the duel, as in the Carré model. Barbier's verse closely reflects the content and imagery of his partner's prose. Two musical numbers not derived from Carré's play but which eventually appeared in the opera—Siébel's *romance* and Méphisto-phélès's *sérénade*—are not included. The *parlé* passages themselves were eventually modified, often in the direction of condensation, but the indebtedness to Carré, even in the libretto as actually performed in 1859, is always apparent, as the alignment of the Marthe-Siébel exchange in both play and libretto shows:

Carré (1850)
Act III, Scene iv

SIÉBEL. Elle l'aime encore!

MARTHE [*accourant et apercevant Siébel*]. Ah! Dieu soit béni! Monsieur Siébel! . . . Monsieur Siébel!

SIÉBEL. Qui m'appelle? [*Reconnaissant Marthe*] Vous! [*Il veut s'éloigner*].

Barbier/Carré (1859)
Act IV, Scene iv

SIÉBEL. Hélas . . . elle l'aime encore!

MARTHE [*entrant précipitamment*]. Ah! c'est vous, monsieur Siébel! . . . Dieu soit loué! . . .

SIÉBEL. Qu'y-a-t-il?

---

[21] These are at BO Fonds Barbier, Carton 16, MS 144.

MARTHE. Ô! Je sais bien, Monsieur Siébel, que ma vue vous déplaît . . . mais il s'agit de sauver Marguerite . . .

SIÉBEL. Hein? la sauver, dites vous? de quel danger?

MARTHE. Valentin est de retour!

SIÉBEL. Valentin!

MARTHE. Je viens de le rencontrer à deux pas d'ici—au bout de la rue . . . Ah! Dieu! que j'ai eu peur! . . .

SIÉBEL. Êtes-vous bien sûre de ce que vous dites?

MARTHE. Si j'en suis sûre! Sainte Vierge! Je l'ai bien reconnu! . . .

SIÉBEL. Oh! pauvre Marguerite! comment l'avertir . . .

MARTHE. Ne le laisser pas entrer dans la maison . . . Il serait capable de la tuer!

SIÉBEL. Il sait donc déjà? . . .

MARTHE. Il ne sait rien encore . . . mait toute la ville connaît l'histoire . . . et les voisins sont si bavards! . . .

SIÉBEL. Ô Dieu! que faire pour la sauver?

MARTHE. Il vaudrait peut-être mieux lui dire tout vous-même . . . Vous tâcherez de l'apaiser . . . Surtout ne lui parlez pas de moi . . . je vous en prie! dites-lui que j'ai quitté la ville . . . dites-lui . . . Ah! je l'entends! c'est fait de moi! Adieu, monsieur Siébel, adieu!
[*elle sort en courant*]

MARTHE. Valentin, Monsieur Siébel, Valentin! . . .

SIÉBEL. Il est de retour?

MARTHE. Je viens de l'apercevoir qui entrait dans la ville avec quelques-uns de ses compagnons! C'est qu'il est capable de tuer sa sœur, savez-vous!

SIÉBEL. Que faire? . . .

MARTHE. Si vous lui disiez tout vous-même! Une fois le premier mouvement passé . . . Surtout ne lui parlez pas de moi je vous en prie! . . . Vous savez que je n'y suis pour rien! . . . bien m'a pris de ne pas écouter l'autre . . . Dieu sait où j'en serais aujourd'hui . . .
[*Fanfares au dehors*]
Tenez! les entendez-vous? . . . Je me sauve! Surtout, monsieur Siébel ne

lui parlez pas de moi! pour Dieu! ne
lui parlez pas de moi!
[*elle sort en courant*]

SIÉBEL. Que lui dire? Je n'ose aller à sa rencontre.

SIÉBEL. Que lui dire?—Je n'ose aller à sa rencontre.
[*Il sort*]

Prose passages elsewhere in the opera also show some similarity to the corresponding Carré text; Barbier may well have produced a first draft of other acts by using the same method.

The opera, however, does not have full citizenship in Carré's boulevard world. Among the most significant changes introduced by Barbier is a return to Goethe's denouement, in short, a restoration of tragedy to the work. Valentin is actually killed by Faust, and Marguerite refers explicitly to her crime of infanticide in the prison scene, the latter only in the urlibretto, however. Merely the choice of a five-act framework for the opera bespeaks a greater seriousness of intent. Admittedly, the strands of show business and sincere emulation of Goethe in the denouement of the opera are not always easy to separate. Carvalho was hungry for a work with spectacle and the *Walpurgisnacht* episode could not be omitted for that reason alone; not surprisingly, it was lavishly staged with no less than three tableaux at the première.

In addition—and not unrelated to the last point—the mere difference of genre between opera and a boulevard spoken drama was bound to bring the former into closer orbit of Goethe's dramatic poem. The authors of an opera were naturally more attracted than a playwright to the episodes in Goethe that are designated as sung or, if not, were conventionally seen as musical, like Gretchen's soliloquy at the spinning wheel. The only musical situations that Carré reproduced are Marguerite's ballade about the King of Thulé, a chorus in the church scene, and a song for Brander in the tavern episode (though with a text not related to Goethe's). Gounod's *Faust* includes all of these and also derives from Goethe's drama the idea of introducing a chorus at the moment of Faust's suicide attempt in Act I, material from the *Vor dem Tor* ('At the City Gate') scene, both of Méphistophélès's songs—in the tavern (the 'Ronde du veau d'or') and later the *sérénade* under Marguerite's window—the spinning song 'Il ne revient plus', and a chorus for the witches in the *Walpurgisnacht* episode.

The appropriation of the original musical episodes was not literal in all cases and some of these should be considered separately. Faust's suicidal impulse in Act I of the opera is indeed quelled by the sound of singing, but, instead of an Easter chorus as in Goethe, a pastoral ditty gives him a new lease on life ('Paresseuse fille'). This change is directly linked to the weight thrown on the side of the Marguerite tragedy in Gounod's *Faust*. An Easter chorus is finally heard as her soul floats to heaven in the Apotheosis scene of the opera ('Christ est ressuscité!'), where in Goethe there is no musical number and in Berlioz there are dulcet seraphic voices that do no more than beckon her to rise. More to the point, the celebration of the resurrection—conceived by Goethe as a symbolic reference to man's power to resist destructive forces—is saved for the moment when the female lead, and not the male, overcomes death. There is no doubt about who the truly heroic figure in Gounod's work really is.

Rather than simply reproduce Carré's second tableau showing a cutaway of a tavern (from *Auerbachs Keller*) and Marguerite's church (from Scheffer), Barbier introduced a conflation of Goethe's *Auerbachs Keller* and *Vor dem Tor* scenes for Act II of the opera by conveniently situating his tavern near one of the city gates. Almost certainly the impulse here was musical. After a gloomy first act, it was eminently strategic to begin the second with a colourful mixed chorus. The carnival atmosphere of the *Vor dem Tor* episode, with its milling about of soldiers, burghers, peasants, and beggar, could be harnessed for this purpose much more effectively than the student party in *Auerbachs Keller* and its inevitable all-male chorus (as in Berlioz's setting). Though Goethe marked only two passages in *Vor dem Tor* as sung (the beggar's song and the villager's dance), the visual counterpoint among different social groups in that scene lent itself particularly well to a Meyerbeerian chorus in which each is separately introduced and then combined in a virtuosic conclusion. Gounod's famous 'Vin ou bière' chorus not only does just that but, as it was first drafted, also included Goethe's song for the beggar, rendered as counterpoint to the music for the burghers. (The beggar's music has never appeared in print but is now recoverable from the composer's autograph full score.)[22] Just as Barbier drew upon Carré's words for some of the prose passages in the libretto, he went back to Nerval's translation for some of the episodes that look beyond the Carré play to Goethe. The stanza allotted to Gounod's burghers in the 'Vin ou bière' chorus is one example:

Goethe/Nerval	Barbier/Carré
Devant la porte de la ville	Une Kermesse (Act II)
BOURGEOIS. Je ne sais rien de mieux les dimanches et fêtes, que de parler de guerres et de combats, pendant que bien loin dans la Turquie les peuples	BOURGEOIS: Aux jours de dimanche et de fête, J'aime à parler guerres et combats, Tandis que les peuples là-bas,

---

[22] The autograph full score of *Faust* was purchased by the Bibliothèque Nationale in 1977.

s'échinent entre eux. On est à la
fenêtre, on prend son petit verre, et
l'on voit la rivière se barioler de
bâtiments de toutes couleurs; le soir
on entre gaiement chez soi en
bénissant la paix et le temps de paix
dont nous jouissons.

Se cassent la tête.
Je vais m'asseoir sur les coteaux
Qui sont voisins de la rivière
Et je vois passer les bateaux
En vidant mon verre!

Another is Faust's celebrated *cavatine* 'Salut! demeure chaste et pure', based upon his monologue in Marguerite's room before Méphistophélès positions the jewels, a scene not in the Carré. Compare Goethe/Nerval 'Dans cette misère, que de plenitude, Dans ce cachot que de félicité' Barbier's 'Que de richesse en cette pauvreté, en ce réduit que de félicité'.

Following the 'Vin ou bière' chorus, the action in the opera reverts back to Carré's play, with some minor differences. Valentin bids farewell to his sister and leaves Siébel in charge ('Compte sur nous aussi!' his friends rather indelicately chime in). In Carré's play Méphistophélès and Faust then turn up together, whereas in the opera Faust coincidentally happens upon Méphistophélès only *after* the latter's brush with the revellers—an odd, unexplained wrinkle since the two are supposed to be travelling together. Carré's Faust, correctly sensing that Marguerite is in the adjacent church, does hastily dismiss himself soon after his appearance and leaves Méphistophélès to dupe the students on his own. Though the two are present throughout Goethe's otherwise eminently musical *Auerbachs Keller* episode, in the play, and especially in the opera, it would have been unseemly for the leading male to appear on stage throughout an entire scene in which he could not take an active part.

Like Goethe's Brander, Wagner in the opera attempts a song about a rat. He is cut short by the entrance of Méphistophélès, a brilliant theatrical stroke that makes a virtue out of an operatic liability. For to have gone back to Goethe's musical pieces in this episode—that is, songs for Brander and Méphistophélès—would have also been to introduce two incidental *ariettes* in succession for the low male voices (which, incidentally, Wagner-cum-Brander had to be because of a trio originally planned for Act I with tenor Faust and soprano Siébel). What better solution than to play the situation for comic effect and interrupt the first song by an appearance of the *buffo* principal. Méphistophélès's own number follows shortly. From Goethe's political parable about a flea, to a song about a beetle and assorted other subjects (at least thirteen according to Barbier), the imaginations of librettist and composer finally alighted upon the golden calf.[23] In retrospect it is difficult to understand

---

[23] According to Barbier, Carré supplied the final text of this number (see Prod'homme and Dandelot, *Gounod*, i. 189).

why there was so much indecision. The Méphistophélès of the play is disturbed merely by hearing the bells of Marguerite's church. His discomfiture is developed in the opera when he cowers before the crossed pommels of the revellers' swords during the subsequent 'Chorale des epées', and in this course of events there was a natural place for a blasphemous tribute to a false biblical idol, the golden calf. Méphistophélès's 'Ronde du veau d'or' even contains something of a musical parody of hymn style (Ex. 7.1). That Wagner and company ultimately

Ex. 7.1. *Faust*, Act II, *ronde*

get the better of the devil in the 'Choral des epées' with a bit of Christian symbolism is a slant on the scene not found in Goethe nor in the Carré play. A touch of Gounodian religiosity, of course, but it makes for successful opera. Apart from the visual impact (Meyerbeer's Benediction of the Swords lurks near) and subliminal appeal of ritualistic exorcization, the number fulfils an important structural role as a dramatically static counterpoise and conclusion to the foregoing dynamic interplay among the characters.

Carré and Gounod use Gretchen's ballade about the King of Thulé in slightly different ways. In the play, the curtain to the garden tableau opens to the ballade; this is followed by the introduction of Méphistophélès's contrivance to seduce her with jewels; then come Siébel's collection of flowers for Marguerite and her discovery of both gifts. Events in the libretto are shifted about so that Marguerite comes upon the offerings of both suitors immediately after the 'Chanson du roi de Thulé'. The change not only brought the opera closer to Goethe's work, but also permitted the incorporation of a *grand air* for the lead soprano, with the chanson as slow movement, a transitional passage in which Marguerite notices the bouquet and jewels, and a *cabalette*, the so-called 'Air des bijoux'. In the thicket of mid-century *cabalettes* that rebound from artificial changes in mood, Marguerite's shines as a response to a convincing dramatic situation.

While to acknowledge that Gounod and Barbier drew closer to Goethe's *Faust* is an alternative to the well-worn view of them as wanton plunderers of the temple, this should not be taken as a vital factor in critical assessment of the work. Many changes to Carré's original groundplan in the direction of Goethe were clearly motivated by purely operatic considerations as much as, if not more than, a desire to follow Goethe's *Faust*. And, because the starting-point was still Carré's play, Barbier and Gounod could never hope to meet Goethe on his own artistic ground. A view of Gounod's *Faust* in the context of its immediate ancestor, and beyond that of the nineteenth-century Franco-Italian operatic tradition, is a much needed corrective to the now routine derision of Gounod's opera as trivializing Goethe's drama. Any charges of that sort should also be directed against Carré's play, and both works should not be condemned for failing to reflect the range of ideas in a literary masterpiece; that was a task that neither attempted. But *Faust et Marguerite*, refurbished with elements from Goethe, did provide the raw material for highly effective music theatre: the main characters are well suited to operatic adaptation, especially Marguerite, who has a finely chiselled musical personality and is the only one of the three principals to undergo transformation.

Gounod's exquisitely tailored musical mantle for the heroine accounts more than any other feature of the work for its musico-dramatic success—and superiority to its boulevard model. The role has many highlights. Among the first of these is the 'Chanson du roi de Thulé', a piece that brilliantly conveys her awakening sensuality. It has a distinctly folklike and, by extension, simple and naïve quality: open fifths sounded by the low strings give a pastoral effect when she initially appears, and the melody of the chanson itself, syllabic and confined within an octave, has modal inflections in the manner of folksong. Her first allusion to Faust occurs in an introductory recitative that is confined to a single pitch low in her tessitura, a restrained musical utterance for unaccustomed thoughts. That she cannot keep her mind off them is projected by the structure of the ensuing chanson, for she interrupts both strophes with declaimed reminiscences about Faust—it would have been more conventional to insert such recitative between the strophes, as in Siébel's preceding *couplets*, rather than within them. Moreover, in both cases a distinctive progression within the harmonic context of the piece is reserved for that point (a tonicization of F in the first instance, of B♭ in the second). Such realism is quite foreign to the stick figures in Meyerbeerian grand opera. The *cabalette* is infused with girlish excitement by means of an effective manner of text distribution (Ex. 7.2). The first distich of six-syllable lines is set to four-bar phrases and the rhyming connection between 'voir' and 'miroir' is metrically obscured. A more breathless impression is created by subsequent three-syllable units, and the text is finally broken down even further with impatient insistence on the word 'réponds'. During Marguerite's account of her sister's death in the ensuing quartet ('Pauvre ange')—a passage imbued with simplicity and tenderness rather than a sense of tragedy—there is a naturalistic turn to two bars of recitative texture in the prevailing arioso as she unexpectedly recalls rushing to the side of the crib ('Sitôt qu'elle s'éveillait'). A similar concentration upon earthbound detail accompanied by an impulsive change of texture occurs in the love duet at the moment she breaks away from Faust to play 'he loves me, he loves me not' (Ex. 7.3). 'Il ne m'aime pas' is realistically condensed to 'pas', and the musical metaphor for her mounting excitement takes the form of an ascending melodic line accompanied by a playful orchestral motif developed in a harmonic sequence through thirds (the starting-point is F major and chords on A, C, E, G, and B are successively tonicized). While most of the temporary tonics in the sequence are made up only of notes that belong to the home key of F major, her final 'Il m'aime' is magnificently coloured by the chord of B major—a key at great distance from F major—and an

Ex. 7.2. *Faust*, Act III, *air*

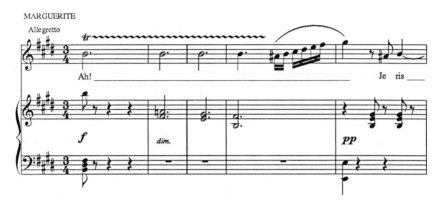

emphatic dominant–tonic leap in the voice line. Faust launches an ecstatic sequence of his own from that harmony.

Marguerite as a tragic heroine in Gounod's opera is no less effective than as a sensitive young girl, and a wealth of convincing musical ideas continues to unfold in the last two acts. Her spinning song compares very favourably to the more famous examples by Schubert and Berlioz. The number does not contain musical or textual repetition save for the recurring line 'Il ne revient pas', simply declaimed on the fifth scale degree and in most instances harmonized by a cadential progression using the Neapolitan chord, a particularly apt illustration of her desolation. Although the verse structure remains unchanged throughout, a more declaimed texture suddenly emerges four lines before the end; her imagined joy at being reunited with Faust literally breaks the gridiron of regular phrases only to sink back at the conclusion of the number to 'Il ne revient pas' and its hollow vocal cadence on the fifth degree. Nor does the church tableau, musically and visually one of the most striking scenes in the nineteenth-century French canon, follow a conventional groundplan. An organ prelude and liturgical chorus (originally set to the Latin text of Dies Irae) combine with Méphistophélès's imprecations to provide a sinister musical foil to Marguerite's attempts at prayer. Formal coherence is achieved largely by two extended periodic solos for each of the principals: Marguerite's

Ex. 7.3. *Faust*, Act III, duet

'Seigneur accueillez la prière' in C major is a counterpoise to Méphistophélès's previous 'Souviens-toi du passé' in C minor. Her steadfast prayer against all odds at 'Seigneur accueillez' is a glorious moment; Gounod arranged for the sounding of the tonic major and her highest pitch to that point in the number, as well as her first periodic music after long stretches of declamation, to converge at the beginning of the passage. This is also a rich musical event because it is referential in the wider context of the opera. The melodic shape of the first two bars is almost identical to that of Faust's earlier *cavatine*, his glorification of

Marguerite's 'chastity and purity'. And the tonality of C major projects forward to Marguerite's final redemption and apotheosis in the same key. Indeed, at the end of the opera C major is the tonal culmination of another truly heroic passage in Marguerite's role, the threefold sequence of the wide-spanned melody 'Anges purs anges radieux' that is heard successively in an ascending stepwise progression (G, A, and B major).

Shaping and Reshaping the Opera

In his *Autobiographie* Gounod maintained that during the first rehearsal period for *Faust* he had had the 'confidence of a child' in his opera and had rejected all advice to introduce changes.[24] Success evidently encouraged myth building. To Bizet he confessed on 4 January 1859, 'I really cannot tell you what my score is worth. I am so immersed that I am a very poor judge of it.'[25] There is also the matter of massive cuts introduced to the opera before opening night. Gounod's original score included several entire numbers that were excised during the rehearsals for the première: a trio in Act I for Siébel, Faust, and Wagner; a duet in Act II for Marguerite and Valentin; the second part of Faust's *air* in Act III; in Act IV three sets of *couplets* for Lise, Valentin, Siébel, and a chorus for Lise's friends; and in Act V a considerable amount of music in the *Walpurgisnacht* episode and a large strophic number for Marguerite in the prison scene.[26] Gounod tore this music out of his autograph when it was no longer needed and much of it became submerged in private collections or might even have been destroyed. But not everything has been lost. Because Siébel's *couplets* were cut relatively late in the rehearsal period, they were included in the first edition of the libretto and were even brought out by Choudens as an extract from the opera.[27] Recently three other pieces—the trio and duet as well as Valentin's

---

[24] Gounod, *Autobiographie*, p. 17.

[25] Pougin, 'Gounod écrivain' (1912), 282–83.

[26] The autograph shows that the entire libretto was set to music. Though little of this music actually survives in this score, gaps in the bifoliation of the autograph do indeed correspond to places where the cuts were made. The bifolia are arranged in succession (as opposed to gatherings) and bifoliation (numbered 1–199) runs from the beginning of the first act to the end of the fourth; it was not extended further because Gounod orchestrated the prison scene of Act V before the *Walpurgisnacht* tableaux. In the present condition of the autograph, for example, there is a gap in the bifoliation at the very spot where the censors' libretto records the Siébel, Faust, Wagner trio (bifolio 11 is succeeded by bifolio 17b).

[27] The *romance* seems to have lingered in the autograph longer than most of the other music that was cut, because the last page of the preceding recitative bears the indication 'Suit la Romance, Versez vos chagrins' (in all likelihood the recitatives to replace the *parlé* were inserted into the autograph after the première). Since the piece was reinstated at the Opéra première of 1869 (though soon dropped), Gounod's orchestration survives in the manuscript score used by the conductor at that production (BO A.622.a).

couplets—have resurfaced,[28] although the first two may only be included in productions that use the original *parlé*, since they are both preceded by expository dialogue which Gounod never converted into recitatives.[29]

Two general observations spring forth from a comparison of Gounod's *Faust* as drafted and as performed at its première. First, because it had a greater number of strophic *couplets* (and derivatives such as Méphistophélès's *ronde* and *sérénade*) than normally heard in grand opera, *Faust* originally had more in common with the *opéra comique* side of the French operatic family than simply the use of *parlé*. Second, Siébel and Valentin had larger parts to play in the initial version.

The latter point is worth considering in greater detail. Though not specifically called a *dugazon* in the first edition of the vocal score, the Siébel role belongs to that tradition because of its relative prominence but undemanding vocal writing for the soprano voice. With two solo pieces (the well-known Act III *couplets* 'Faites lui mes aveux' and the not-so-familiar *couplets* from Act IV 'Versez vos chagrins'), Siébel was admittedly conceived as a large *dugazon* part—but then *Faust* itself was larger than any *opéra comique* written before it. Performers undertaking the Siébel role today are generally allotted only one solo number, 'Faites lui mes aveux'; if they are more fortunate, a *romance* that Gounod supplied for Didiée at the Covent Garden production of 1863 'Si le bonheur', is incorporated instead of 'Versez vos chagrins'.[30]

Truth be told, the trimming of Siébel's part is not a great loss. Whereas plot development may compensate for lack of philosophical substance in the play, music should bear that burden in opera, and at no stage was Siébel an indispensable component of a strong musical situation. His trio in Act I with Faust and Wagner was largely expository in function: he is Faust's student, but love for Marguerite has turned his head away from theological tracts. His personal connection to Faust is

---

[28] Choudens published the duet and trio in piano reduction in 1980, pl. nos. AC 20.824 and AC 20.825. The autographs of these two pieces were acquired by the Bibliothèque Nationale at the same time as the main autograph full score of the opera in 1977. The Stiftelsen Musikkulturens Främjande in Stockholm owns the Act IV *couplets* for Valentin. In addition, a full score of the piece for Méphistophélès replaced by the 'Ronde du veau d'or' late in the rehearsal period, the 'Maître Scarabée' *couplets*, was offered at the sale of Gounod manuscripts at the Hôtel Drouot on 27 Nov. 1963. A fragment of another version of this piece was sold at the Hôtel Drouot on 14 Dec. 1979.

[29] An obstacle to *parlé* performances of even the current version of the opera is the absence of Gounod's orchestration for the original *mélodrames*, which he tore from his autograph when he composed the recitatives. In 1932 Henri Busser attempted a revival of *Faust* with *parlé* at the Opéra, for which he orchestrated the *mélodrames* (this material is at the BO A.622 1. Rés.), but the four performances at that time seem to have created little enthusiasm for the *parlé* version.

[30] Gounod set the *romance* to an Italian text 'Quando a te lieta'; the poet O. Pradère is responsible for the French version 'Si le bonheur'.

an ironic twist, but one that never receives musical elaboration in a set piece later in the opera, that is, after Faust himself has been smitten by the vision of Marguerite. After the trio was cut, references to Siébel as Faust's student persisted only in spoken dialogue; that these were dropped altogether in the recitative version has gone unnoticed. The misfortunes of Carré's Siébel in the later part of the garden scene, after his bouquet has been unceremoniously rejected, are also not fully developed in the opera to fulfil their true potential as comic episodes; not surprisingly, the recitative between Siébel and Marthe following the quartet was cut in every edition after the second, including that associated with the Opéra première in 1869.[31]

Valentin, on the contrary, does emerge as a strong musico–dramatic figure: the scene of his death is of cardinal importance to the Marguerite tragedy. It is a splendid number in which he is transformed by Gounod's music from a swashbuckling adventurer into a larger-than-life embodiment of irrational intolerance. The episode was bound to stimulate the appetites of lead baritones on operatic rosters. But removal of both Valentin's duet with Marguerite in Act II and his *couplets* in Act IV left the role with one magnificent scene but little else. Almost inevitably, Gounod was asked to address this problem. In 1864 he composed the familiar Act II *cavatine* 'Avant de quitter ces lieux' at the request of English baritone Charles Santley for the second run of performances (the first in the English language) at Her Majesty's Theatre in London. Santley himself noted in his reminiscences that Gounod was at first not well disposed to the idea because of his infamous business difficulties with *Faust* in England. None the less, as Santley's account goes, Gounod was so thankful that he had agreed to sing a role that had been played by a 'small man with a small voice who strutted about like a bantam' at the Théâtre-Lyrique première that he accepted his expedient suggestion to use a strain from the instrumental prelude.[32] Dramatically there is little justification for a contemplative *cavatine* in the fairground scene, and the fact that it never appeared in Choudens' French-language scores, and was given neither at the Théâtre-Lyrique nor at the Opéra in the nineteenth century, strongly supports the contention of Gounod's student, Henri Busser, that the composer had fundamental reservations

---

[31] A reliable collation of editions is supplied by Fritz Oeser in his edition of *Faust* (Kassel, 1972), 372–3.

[32] Charles Santley, *Student and Singer* (New York, 1882), 216. Osmond Raynal took the part of Valentin at the Théâtre-Lyrique première. That Gounod himself was responsible for this arrangement of the F major strain in the *introduction* to a text by his old friend Chorley 'Even the bravest heart may swell' (it was later fitted with the French text by Pradère) is confirmed by the existence of an autograph short score draft of the number at the New York Public Library (JOG 72–119).

about the use of the piece.[33] But old operatic habits die hard and it still thrives at most houses.

Substitution of Valentin's Act IV *couplets* 'Chaque jour, nouvelle affaire' for 'Avant de quitter ces lieux' as the footlight piece for the role would confront another, even more entrenched, operatic habit: the Soldiers' Chorus. According to Carvalho's anecdotal account of the *Faust* genesis, that piece owes its origins to a social gathering before the première *chez* Gounod, with himself, Édouard Dubufe, and Ingres present. As a bit of after-dinner entertainment the composer was asked to play a chorus from his ill-fated project *Ivan le terrible*. 'The effect was so considerable that, all at once, we asked him to eliminate Valentin's chanson and replace it with the chorus we had just heard.'[34] This is not to mention that Gounod had also worked a stageband into the piece, always a fetching addition to the spectacle. Carvalho's story sounds suspiciously compressed, but at least someone's intuitions were correct: the Soldiers' Chorus proved to be the most successful number at the première. A few years later, when asked by Santley to supply an *air* for the Valentin role, Gounod was not about to forgo the most popular piece in *Faust* in order to restore the *couplets*; nor is there any evidence that the possibility entered his mind. It will be seen immediately Ex. 7.4 that the *couplets* will never rank as one of the lyric gems in Gounod's œuvre. Yet today, when *Faust* is generally valued for entirely different qualities from those exhibited by the Soldiers' Chorus, there is something to be said for the alternative of the *couplets* as Valentin's solo number in place of 'Avant de quitter ces lieux'. Not only would the tattoo be set aside, but restoration of Valentin's *couplets* would better prepare his outburst against Faust and Méphistophélès by presenting him beforehand as an exploiter of his sister's reputation to inflate his own ego. Moreover, development of his musical character as a swaggering soldier seems preferable to the sentimentalization of his attachment to Marguerite in 'Avant de quitter ces lieux', since, after all, he is a fundamentally unsympathetic figure in the unfolding of her destiny.

His duet with Marguerite in Act II also had a similar sentimental quality and its removal cannot be greatly regretted. Even more important, this cut created one of the opera's theatrical coups: in the absence of the duet, Marguerite is first seen in the finale of the second act. Although an entrance aria for the *première chanteuse* was hardly a necessary convention in France, there are some important examples of it

---

[33] Henri Busser, *Gounod* (Lyons, 1961), 36. Curiously, Oeser includes Valentin's *cavatine* in the main body of his edition.

[34] Prod'homme and Dandelot, *Gounod*, i. 207.

Ex. 7.4. *Faust*, Act IV, *couplets*

mort on se pré-pa - re _____

p

in grand opera, notably large two-part *airs* for the coloratura roles of Isabelle in *Robert le diable* and Marguerite in *Les Huguenots*. The *soprano falcon* also frequently hastens to lay claim to her vocal territory early on, though often with a strophic piece rather than a two-part *air*. But coloratura roles such as Eudoxie in *La Juive*, Isabelle in *Charles VI*, and Fidès in *Le Prophète* just as often begin with a duet or a trio. They do, however, remain on stage for a prolonged period of time after their initial entries, as does Rachel in *La Juive*. This observation holds true for *chanteuses à roulades* types in *opéra comique*, where solo entries, if present, are often embedded in the multipartite introduction of the first act. To have Marguerite sing a duet upon her entry in the first version of *Faust* was not an unusual musico–dramatic decision. When the number was cut, however, the brief moment it took for her to cross the stage and deliver her modest eight-bar rejection of Faust's advances in the finale of Act II made for a first appearance as unconventional as it was effective. One would not be entirely amiss in describing Marguerite's musically understated entrance as preparation of terrain for Massenet and Puccini, who later included entirely mute stage entries for the title roles in *Esclarmonde* and *Turandot*. But it is important to bear in mind that in those operas the initial appearance of each princess is more striking visually—or at least is supposed to be, for too often Marguerite is ushered in by spotlight along a corridor that has been reverently cleared for her. The first *mise-en-scène* for *Faust*, to the contrary, calls for the dancers and choristers to go about their business without regard for the star of the evening.

A much more critical loss to the role of Marguerite than the Act II duet was her *air* at the beginning of the prison tableau, in which she reveals through her delirious ravings that she has killed her child. If the music of this is ever uncovered, it would almost certainly be a strong candidate for reintegration into the opera, allowing the *première chanteuse* a full-blown mad scene à la Lucia before she hears 'la voix du bien aimé!'[35] The removal of the prison *air* must have diminished the full gamut of her musical personality by cutting off the episode when she is at the lowest ebb of her fortunes. The motivation for the cut must be left to the realm of speculation, but in the light of Miolan-Carvalho's well-documented difficulties with the great 'Air de la Crau' near the end of *Mireille* it is reasonable to suppose that the prison *air* was too taxing for her.

The role of Faust was also not spared in the rehearsal period. Most significant of the changes, at least from the historical point of view, was the excision of a *cabalette* to 'Salut, demeure chaste et pure'. Both *Sapho* and *La Nonne sanglante* have their *grands airs* for the tenor, but, from *Faust* (as it was performed in 1859) onwards, the operas of Gounod avoid the multipartite *air* for male voices. Indeed, it is striking that a piece which became the prototype for other well-known *cavatines* in Gounod's œuvre and beyond, displaying a refined sensitivity to the text that is a harbinger of later nineteenth-century French opera, grew out of a formal procedure that had been an integral part of grand opera.

The roles of both Faust and Méphistophélès were modified by a pruning of the *Walpurgisnacht* before the première, in particular the tableau of the witches' sabbath in the Harz mountains, the first of three that constituted the entire episode. The witches' tableau did strike Berlioz as somewhat short at the première. That was a mercifully innocuous observation in view of snide remarks in other quarters about paper skeletons and 'the yelping of devilettes, straddling their broom-sticks and letting forth some *hou*, *hou*'s to the accompaniment of piccolo and cymbal'.[36] Earlier on, the tableau was much longer than that performed on opening night or currently recorded in any musical source, printed or manuscript.[37] Whether because of *mise-en-scène* headaches in the rehearsals, pangs of conscience that the title role in the opera had been short-shrifted, or a combination of both, the scene for the witches was reduced and the subsequent tableau showing Faust amidst legendary courtesans of antiquity was enlarged with a new set of *couplets bacchiques* for him ('Doux nectar'), a number that is available in early editions of the score.[38] In spite of a redistribution of weight

[35] The eight opening bars of the *air* are extant in the autograph and it is also possible that the preceding *entr'acte* contains some musical ideas used in the piece.

[36] Reyer, *Quarante ans de musique*, p. 254.

[37] One of the witches' choruses, 'Un, deux, et trois', did survive into the first edition of the vocal score, but was cut from subsequent prints.

[38] Contrary to Oeser's assertion, the *couplets bacchiques* must have been performed at the première, since they are mentioned in many reviews. A new set of *couplets* for Méphistophélès was supplied by Gounod in 1869 for insertion into the ballet music. Oeser's suggestion to use Méphistophélès's piece in place of 'Doux nectar' even when the ballet is not given is at variance with any version of the opera sanctioned by the composer.

between both tableaux, Gounod's extant music is so unterrifying that, when the ballet that replaced the *couplets* at the Opéra is not given, the episode is often completely cut. Even if the lost music does reappear and is more harrowing, it is doubtful that the *Walpurgisnacht*, essentially an elaboration of the Faust–Méphistophélès side of the opera, could be defended as anything more than a disposable distraction to the unfolding of Marguerite's fate.[39]

Adjustments continued to be made to *Faust* after the first run of performances in 1859. The addition of Valentin's *cavatine* and the ballet music are two of the most noteworthy changes. Significant variants were also introduced to the fourth act. As first drafted by Gounod, the succession of events in the act corresponds to Carré's play, with an opening tableau set in the town square, followed by the appearance of Valentin, the church scene, and a return to the square for Valentin's confrontation with Faust and Méphistophélès. The first tableau in this scheme features the curious spectacle of Marguerite seated at her spinning wheel in a public thoroughfare. As it happened, the opening scene was soon whittled down by a removal of the chorus for Marguerite's young friends, of Lise's *couplets*, and eventually of Siébel's 'Versez vos chagrins'. Upon excision of the initial chorus all justification for having the opening tableau take place out of doors was eliminated, so the spinning wheel was relocated to a more natural habitat in Marguerite's room for the performances of 1859. Another solution attempted, this one at the 1862 Théâtre-Lyrique revival, had Marguerite deliver her *air du rouet* in the street without a spinning wheel, an odd alternative in view of the quiet murmur of the wheel in the orchestra.[40]

For motives that are not entirely clear, the church tableau was transferred during the rehearsal period from its initial spot after Valentin's *couplets* (replaced by the Soldiers' Chorus) to the end of the act following the death of Valentin. It may have been felt that, with a relocation of the opening episode to Marguerite's house, a church tableau in the middle of the act would generate too many set changes (Marguerite's room—square—church—square). In addition, the critic Bénédict Jouvin hinted that Miolan-Carvalho had insisted that she bring down the curtain with the church tableau.[41] This may have been one of

[39] According to 'Bulletin théâtral', *Le Ménestrel*, 30 Oct. 1859: a 'new symphony' for the *Walpurgisnacht* that Gounod had composed specifically for the run of *Faust* in the autumn of 1859 at the Théâtre-Lyrique was warmly received at rehearsals. It seems to have been dropped before the autumn performances. Henry Chorley, writing in 1862, indicated that the original *Walpurgisnacht* music up to the bacchanalian chorus 'Que les coupes' was replaced with the 'Intermède fantastique' from *La Nonne sanglante* for some (unspecified) early performances (*Thirty Years' Musical Recollections* (New York, 1926), 306).

[40] J. Weber, 'Critique musicale', *Le Temps*, 30 Dec. 1862.

[41] Review of *Faust*, *Le Figaro*, 24 Mar. 1859.

the singer's 'ridicules éxigences' to which Bizet referred in his letter of 31 December 1858 to Hector Gruyer. At any rate, it is certain that the move of the tableau to its original location in Goethe's drama was not prompted by any belated fidelity to the German poet. By the time of the Opéra production of 1869, the church tableau had taken its definitive place in French productions before the Soldiers' Chorus, a change recorded as early as the second edition of 1860, although it cannot be assumed that productions at the Théâtre-Lyrique itself followed this order.[42] In most English performances until the present day the church scene has been placed at the end of the act, and there was flexibility on this matter in German and Italian productions of the 1860s. Gounod himself was noncommittal later in life. In a letter to a Spanish conductor he once explained that he had conceived his opera with the church scene after Valentin's death (forgetting that in the first plan the tableau was to occur in the middle of the act, immediately after Valentin's return) and that this was desirable because it is the order in Goethe's drama. But he also noted that the ensemble scene of Valentin's death is a more satisfactory conclusion to the act from a musical point of view.[43]

In view of the production circumstances surrounding *Faust*, one can only take his remark about fidelity to Goethe with a grain of salt. The fact that a removal of the church tableau from its original position after Valentin's *couplets* to the end of the act was possible at all is because, from the first, Gounod avoided a large *concertato*-type finale of the kind he had composed for *Sapho* and *La Nonne sanglante*; such a number would normally have been positioned at the curtain. Now, the scene of Valentin's death might have been developed in that manner, with several sets of parallel strophes following Valentin's repudiation of his sister: Marguerite might have sung about her shame, Siébel about his distress, Valentin about her lack of virtue, and the bystanders about Valentin's hypocrisy. But rather than spin out a crescendo with strophes that express various points of view, Gounod limits the ensemble in the number to a rebuke of Valentin for his lack of Christian compassion. He draws a clear musical line between the Christian morality of the majority and the intolerance of an individual, a highly personal adaptation of an episode in Goethe and Carré where Valentin's voice rings out unopposed by the masses.[44] Gounod's scene is successful

---

[42] That the Théâtre-Lyrique 1862 revival had the church scene appear at the end of the act is suggested by the order in which Gustave Chadeuil of *Le Siècle* listed the pieces in his review of that production on 23 Dec. 1862: 'les couplets de Marguerite, le chœur des soldats, la sérénade de Méphistophélès, la scène de l'église, et le trio final'. Because this was just a revival, reviewers were more vague about the outlines of the opera than they normally were for premières.

[43] Letter to A. Montalli, 4 Nov. 1876, in Pougin, 'Gounod écrivain' (1913), 794.

[44] In Goethe's drama only Marthe reprimands Valentin, with a single distich.

operatically because the baritone voice is not swept away by the prevailing ideological current. The situation remains fundamentally dramatic, the conflicting world views palpable, because, although there is a lack of numbers giving voice to the position that Valentin espouses, this is compensated for with real time; a large portion of the number is allotted to an elaboration of his intolerance. Nor is the exposition of differences synchronous, as it would have been in a *concertato*-type finale: Valentin's most forceful attack on his sister ('Sois maudite!') occurs after he has been urged to show clemency by his compatriots. In short, the number is dominated by his solo singing and could therefore more easily be moved to the interior of the act. Gounod's interpretation of Goethe's episode, and the attendant abandonment of the *concertato* convention, allowed an alternative placement of the church tableau.

Reference to Goethe as a model for positioning the church tableau at the act's end is only convincing if the service is conceived as a requiem for Valentin, and, more important, if the solo bass part is sung not by Méphistophélès, as it usually is, but by another (preferably unseen) singer representing Goethe's Evil Spirit, a solution attempted at the Théâtre-Lyrique revival of 1862.[45] That voice would better be understood as the reflection of Marguerite's own conscience, combining with the memory of her brother's previous curses to oppress her. On a more mundane level of plot mechanics, Marguerite does remark to Siébel in the first tableau of the act that she is on her way to church to pray for her child. Because of this, the church tableau finds its place more naturally before the Faust–Valentin duel, though it is not overly taxing to verisimilitude to suppose a second visit to church after Valentin's death.

The prison duet for Faust and Marguerite was radically shortened before the première, progressing from Faust's solo rendition of the strophe 'Oui c'est moi je t'aime' to a reprise of the Act II waltz music (but not the garden duet) and the entry of Méphistophélès with 'Alerte! alerte!' To make up for a complete excision of the *Walpurgisnacht* at either the La Scala or the London première, Gounod restored the 131 bars cut from this number, including the original *cabalette* of the duet 'Viens! viens! quittons ces lieux!' The 'Anges purs, anges radieux' music was also touched up by Gounod after the première. As first written, the final B major statement of the tune was jarringly terminated after only four bars by the headsman's drum. Modern performances, of course, give the full melody in B major, a variant introduced by Gounod for the Théâtre-Lyrique production of 1862, with Marguerite inevitably taking a high fermata b' at the cadence and a two-bar hiatus before the drum is

[45] J. Weber, 'Critique musicale', *Le Temps*, 30 Dec. 1862. The Evil Spirit actually appeared on stage in this production.

heard. The effect is of a full close, often inducing applause from the uninitiated at a place where continuity into the apotheosis seems desirable so that Marguerite's ascension does not risk appearing musically anti-climactic. Gounod's first version is dramatically far more arresting.[46]

Finally, the conversion of spoken dialogue to connecting recitatives commands attention as one of the most significant variants to the opera. Gounod did not feel at first that the version with connecting recitatives superseded the version with *parlé*. Rather, exportation of the work abroad, where recitatives were usually obligatory, seems to have been a major reason for the change. The composer was to make his opinions clear in a letter to Choudens about *Roméo et Juliette*:

It seems to me that the introduction of recitatives should be the object of a separate version as with *Faust*, and that it should in no way obstruct the existence of the first version that contains spoken dialogue—there are many reasons why I do not want a single version. First of all, there are theatres that would prefer to give the work with dialogue and, to my mind, recitative everywhere is not beneficial to *Roméo* because 1) it prolongs the performance time 2) it does not add movement.[47]

Gounod did not necessarily write recitatives because he thought that they would be an improvement and he even expressed a preference for *parlé* in the early stages of planning for *Roméo et Juliette*, a work eventually performed *with* connecting recitatives on the opening night. Although the recitatives for *Faust* were written by 1860, the norm at the Théâtre-Lyrique—the house with which Gounod was most closely associated—was performance with spoken dialogue for seven years after its première. This does not appear to have been the case elsewhere. When recitatives were included in *Faust* at the Théâtre-Lyrique for the first time in September 1866, a bulletin in *Le Ménestrel* noted that they were a novelty only for Parisians, since most other houses, *even in France* (my emphasis), were already using them. This testimony receives support from the fact that only the first edition of *Faust* gives the *parlé* version, which is musically different from the recitative version not only in the absence of those recitatives, but also because *mélodrames* and cadential phrases to bring certain numbers to a full close are included. The second edition of the piano-vocal score (brought out in 1860) and all subsequent editions give only the recitatives. Had there been a wide

---

[46] Oeser also felt that continuity is crucial at this juncture, but he concocted a variant that has no basis in any source associated with the composer. In his edition, the first snare-drum roll coincides with the vocal cadence after a complete rendition of the 'Anges purs' strophe for the third time.

[47] Letter of 28 Sept. 1866, BO Gounod l.a.s. 38.

market for the spoken dialogue, all early editions would surely have included musical options to permit performance of the *parlé*. (It was surely also in the publisher's best interest to encourage use of a single version.) Despite Gounod's observation, then, marketability of his large five-act work with spoken dialogue was not significantly enhanced by the existence of two modes of performance.

In sum, the evidence suggests that the eventual predominance of the recitatives had little to do with the authority of the composer. It had much more to do with contemporary perceptions of where *Faust* stood in relation to the opera and *opéra comique* families. A five-act frame for a work with spoken dialogue was certainly unprecedented and there was a relatively small amount of spoken dialogue by Scribean standards. Furthermore—and this must have been truly confusing to some contemporaries—the rubric 'opéra' appears on the title-page of the first edition, despite the presence of *parlé*. The composer himself also never called *Faust* an *opéra comique* in his extant correspondence and writings. One may well suppose that the poetic depth of the story, and particularly of the female protagonist, led Gounod to abandon the term *opéra comique* (despite an extended tradition of more serious examples of the genre). Performers and impresarios of the day may have been of like mind and, with a literality obviously not shared by the composer, saw spoken dialogue as inappropriate for this reason alone, especially since recitatives were available.

There is also the matter of vocal convention appropriate to each genre, especially well illuminated by a controversy that erupted at the Théâtre de la Monnaie in Brussels. That house employed two rosters of French singers, one for the *opéra comique* repertoire and the other for opera. *Faust* first proved controversial there because in the season of 1859–60 the director of the house planned to give the recitative version with his *opéra comique* roster.[48] This decision provoked such clamour among members of the opera roster that he recast the work with them, only to arouse the ire of the *opéra comique* singers initially slated for the production. In the end, the project was shelved for that year. The following season the Monnaie gave *Faust* with spoken dialogue, and in the season after that with recitatives. Both versions attracted strong partisan support, so they were alternated throughout the 1860s. It is not surprising that *Faust* proved vocally problematic. There are moments of pure *fort ténor* writing appropriate for the Opéra in the Faust role, as in the opening scene when he prepares to imbibe the poison (Ex. 7.5). Marguerite's role combines writing suitable for a *première chanteuse à roulades* in the 'Air des bijoux' with the intensely dramatic and low-lying music of the church scene. (Yet Barbot, the first Faust, was a *ténor léger*

[48] Jacques Isnardon, *Le Théâtre de la Monnaie* (Brussels, 1898), 441.

Ex. 7.5. *Faust*, Act I, *scène et chœur*

and Marie Miolan-Carvalho had established her reputation as a *chanteuse à roulades*.) And because of its wide ambitus, the role of Méphistophélès was difficult for either the Cardinal Brogni-type grand opera bass or the usual *opéra comique basse chantante*; the latter would have had difficulty with his opening scene in Act I ('Me voici'), whereas the high-lying 'Ronde du veau d'or' was a challenge to darker voices. (Casting problems persist today.) Because of the hybrid nature of the vocal writing in *Faust*, on that criterion alone the pendulum might have swung in the direction of either opera or *opéra comique*, as it did at the Théâtre de la Monnaie. It is also reasonable to assume, however, that, had it been conceived vocally more along the lines of traditional *opéra comique*, the recitative version might have encountered greater initial resistance in French houses.

There were, and still are, better musical reasons for performing the recitative version of *Faust* than with other French *opéras comiques* converted by their composers. For example, Félicien David supplied recitatives for his *La Perle de Brésil* and Meyerbeer wrote them for *L'Étoile du nord* and *Le Pardon de Ploërmel*, but the interstices between the numbers in these works are comprised almost entirely of unmeasured declamation. Gounod's are musically more substantial because they contain many passages of *parlante* and even voice-dominated lyrical writing. The connecting recitatives in *Faust* also extend the web of thematic cross-references in the work, since many of them recall or anticipate melodic material in the set pieces, like the exchange between Faust and Méphistophélès after the 'Choral des épées' where music from their Act I duet is cited along with a theme later associated with Marguerite's virtue in Siébel's *couplets*. Now the quickfire exchanges of spoken dialogue might be seen to enhance the lighter side of the work, especially in the third act, but in this respect the slower pace of the recitatives is usually compensated by sparkling *buffo* figuration in the orchestra.

8. Mireille

A Pastoral Tragedy

Today, I will report good news to you. A great epic poet has been born. Western nature no longer produces this species, but the Southern environment still does: there is virtue in the sun. A true Homeric poet in our day; a poet born, like Deucalion's sons, of a stone in the Crau; a simple poet in our age of decadence; a Greek poet in Avignon . . . a poet who strums symphonies of Mozart and Beethoven on his rustic harp.

Thus did Lamartine announce the *entrée* of the young Frédéric Mistral into the Parisian world of letters.[1] The work was *Mirèio/Mireille* and the year 1859, shortly after the sensational releases of Flaubert's *Madame Bovary* and Baudelaire's *Les Fleurs du mal*. It is perhaps not surprising that many critics contributed to the bouquet prepared by Lamartine, for in the prevailing literary atmosphere there was indeed a certain freshness to a narrative about the chaste and selfless love of a fifteen-year-old farmer's daughter for the son of a basket-weaver. Some reviewers did, however, have difficulty in perceiving more than the merely quaint in Mistral's work. Not the least of the factors that coloured certain highbrow Parisian attitudes was the language itself. Mistral had published the epic in his native Provençal with a matching French prose translation (for those highbrowed Parisians) on facing pages.

One cannot but give full recognition to a poem that contains beauties of the first rank [wrote the critic for *L'Opinion nationale*], but it is written in the language of the Midi, which we will not call a *patois* so as not to offend anyone, but simply a dead language . . . Old civilizations disappear taking with them their language. In a few years, the peasants of the Crau will more or less resemble peasants in other provinces.[2]

It was precisely to counteract such attitudes that Mistral took up his pen in the first place. No mere corruption of French, the *langue d'oc* is an independent branch on the Latinate trunk and there was a real flowering of literature to attest to the richness of that linguistic family in the mid-nineteenth century. But even in this period the *langue d'oc* remained very much just that, a family, a collection of dialects under a single

---

[1] Extract from the '40e entretien du cours familier de littérature', cited by Ch. Rostaing in the appendix of his edition of *Mirèio/Mireille* (Paris, 1978), 471.

[2] Cited ibid. 496.

umbrella with differences in finer points of grammar, spelling, and idioms. Attempts to establish common literary usage were unsuccessful, largely because of difficulties in mediating among regional preferences. Mistral was involved in such a movement in the early 1850s but soon came to the conclusion, with some of his Provençal colleagues, that there was an alternative route to a 'classical' occitan language. In 1854 he participated in the creation of the *Félibres*, a society with the express purpose of encouraging local Provençal writers and operating under the premiss that a unified practice would coalesce around a substantial body of high-quality literature in one dialect, as had happened in Italy.[3] *Mirèio/Mireille* became a landmark in that effort because of its sheer length alone, twelve books or *chants* comprising a total of 748 stanzas.

Looking beyond his linguistic crusade, Mistral saw an ever-growing network of railways spread across France in the Second Empire, a burgeoning popular illustrated Press that unfolded its tentacles from Paris to the most remote regions, in short, an increasing commercial, and attendant cultural, homogenization of the country. Early on, he sounded the alarm with expatriates in Paris, including Alphonse Daudet, whose highly charged play *L'Arlésienne*, something of a Provençal *Cavalleria rusticana*, was supplied with incidental music by Georges Bizet in 1872. The bilingual edition of *Mirèio/Mireille* was also part of a lifelong campaign to introduce northerners to a region that was as foreign to many of them as Italy or Spain. Now *Mirèio/Mireille* has none of the emotional immediacy of Daudet's play; the psychology of the characters is barely explored and the plot is remarkably simple for such a long work. The real essence of the poem lies in its *couleur locale*, Mistral's elaborate and virtuosic descriptions of regional topography, dress, and beliefs, his immortalization in verse of customs that were rapidly disappearing.

Gounod's rarefied instincts kept him clear of *paysanneries* without higher artistic pretensions. *Philémon et Baucis* had a rustic setting, but a classical one; Ovid via Lafontaine, there was the decisive factor. *Mirèio/Mireille* not only contains verse of real beauty but is also replete with allusions to Homer and Virgil. By harnessing the heavy dose of classical literature administered to him as a student, Mistral provided categories by means of which northern *literati* completely unfamiliar with Provence could evaluate his work (though, like the ancient bards, his primary goal was to appeal to the common man and woman of his *pays*); *Mirèio/Mireille* was foreign and exotic but also touched the

---

[3] On the background to *Mirèio/Mireille* in English, see Richard Aldington, *Introduction to Mistral* (London, 1956), 47–101; and Tudor Edwards, *The Lion of Arles* (New York, 1964), 37–80.

mainstream of humanistic tradition. Some have argued that Mistral laboriously drew out the denouement in order to fill out twelve books, the number in the *Aeneid*, and that he consciously mimicked that poem by filling his sixth book with Vincent's cure in the supernatural realm of the witch Taven, an obvious parallel to the descent of Aeneas into the underworld in Book VI of Virgil's epic.[4] That merely scratches the surface of Mistral's debt to antiquity. If Gounod did not notice such connections in his own reading—and it is hard to believe that he did not—there were plenty of reminders in the critical Press that welcomed *Mirèio/Mireille*. The allegiance of Mistral's poem to an epic tradition sanctified by classical roots virtually assured that in Gounod's hands it would not simply be turned into a *paysannerie* for the stage in the *opéra comique* tradition, with three acts and a happy ending, at least not at first.

Pastoral settings for *opéras comiques* were of course not infrequent. Meyerbeer's *Le Pardon de Ploërmel* (1859) had been a recent success in this area. Nor was the unsuitability of an amorous relationship because of difference in social class an uncommon situation in the repertoire. This, however, almost invariably involved at least one person of noble extraction. *Mireille* struck a new note on the operatic stage by working out this theme entirely within the hierarchy of Provençal peasant society: Vincent, the itinerant basket-weaver's son, is unsuitable for Mireille, daughter of a propertied farmer. Even the weightiest of previous peasant operas had been little more than sentimental comedies with happy endings, and the appearance of a five-act pastoral tale with tragic consequences to the forbidden love between two individuals of relatively low birth was very striking indeed. Reviewers such as Johannès Weber of *Le Temps* criticized the presence of death in a story and setting of this nature:

What was the point of having *Mireille* conclude with a catastrophe? . . . Whether the young girl arrives at the church mortally afflicted by the rays of the sun, or recovers with or without the help of a witch, is her courage less remarkable? . . . I do not think one can answer that to have concluded *Mireille* with a marriage would have been too banal; it is even more vulgar to die than to be married.[5]

Novel too was the dramatic stature attained by a peasant girl on the operatic stage. As in his portrayal of Marguerite in *Faust*, Gounod demonstrated great sensitivity in his treatment of the feminine. Mireille is the only musically three-dimensional figure in the opera. Her

---

[4] See Rostaing, p. 28; Aldington, *Introduction*, p. 94.
[5] Review of *Mireille*, *Le Temps*, 5 Apr. 1864.

characterization spans the distance from the simple candour of her first appearance and the innocence of her response to Taven's warning in Act II, to the girlish frivolity of her rejection of Ourrias, and then her seizure by divine inspiration and her ecstatic acceptance of death. The scene of her death was not the only one that struck reviewers as out of place in a pastoral setting. The slow movement of the Act II finale ('A vos pieds hélas me voilà') could not fail to remind nineteenth-century listeners of a scene that they witnessed regularly at the Opéra: Rachel's entreaty at the feet of her father in the second act finale of Halévy's *La Juive*. Albert de Lasalle complained that Mireille's anguish was blown out of perspective, that it was 'a brutal explosion of sound out of proportion to the situation'.[6] Another reviewer chastised both composer and librettist for treating the finale as the 'Last Judgement'.[7] Surely both had in mind a passage such as that shown in Ex. 8.1 (the staging of the scene at the first production is shown in plate 11). Mireille's father, Ramon, begins the

Ex. 8.1. *Mireille*, Act II, *finale*

[6] Review of *Mireille*, *Le Monde illustré*, 27 Mar. 1864.
[7] Xavier Aubreyat, review of *Mireille*, *Le Nain jaune*, 26 Mar. 1864.

finale by singing of the patriarchal role of a Provençal father. A
diminished seventh chord and change of texture and tempo ('Mais que
l'un d'eux') suggests the wrath that any sibling who defied his word may
expect—even death, he suggests. Maître Ramon attempts to carry the
music to a tonicization of D minor, but his authority is undermined
dramatically and even tonally by Mireille's interjection 'Tuez moi!' at
full volume, as the bass quite unexpectedly slips down a whole step from
A to G to another diminished seventh chord. With strident octave leaps
she wrenches the music toward the distant key of G sharp major. It was
precisely through these sorts of musical gestures that Gounod elevated a

peasant character to a position hitherto not seen on the Parisian operatic stage. There is an analogy here to Gustave Courbet's roughly contemporary painting *The Burial at Ornans*, the rallying point for the realist school of painters in the 1850s and 1860s. It also rendered monumental individuals of low birth (the denizens of the painter's native Franche Comté) with heroic postures and sheer size, thereby creating an even greater furore than Gounod's five-act canvas.

'There is nothing in the opera but Mistral,' Gounod assured the poet on 17 February 1863. The opera is indeed very faithful to its model, but Gounod's statement is slightly exaggerated, since some changes were made to accommodate the stage from the beginning. The major one is a redistribution of events as they occur in time. After having been rejected by Mireille in Mistral's epic, Ourrias strikes Vincent in a jealous rage and then is himself drowned for this act by the spirits of the Rhône. With the help of Taven's incantations, Vincent soon recovers from the wounds inflicted by his rival. It is only after he has been cured that Mistral gives the great scene in which Mireille arouses the ire of her father by telling him about her love for the young man. Her decision to undertake the hazardous journey to the shrine of the Saintes-Maries—an idea implanted in the poem by Vincent during their first encounter and not by Mireille as in the duet near the beginning of the opera—is the result of despair at being confined to the farm and at the prospect of never seeing Vincent again. In the opera, Mireille is distressed enough by the turn of events at the end of Act II when she is rebuked for letting her heart wander astray. But between this calamity and the time she sets out across the desert, Vincent is attacked by Ourrias. News of this from Vincenette, an episode not in the poem, finally drives Mireille to the shrine of the three Marys to pray for the recovery of Vincent. Carré's change produced a more urgent dramatic situation to propel Mireille into risking her life. It also entitled the opera to full membership in the ranks of theatrical *Frauenschicksals Tragödie*, for, alas, Mireille only learns that Vincent is alive and well when it is too late.

This reshuffling of events allowed incorporation of a slow–fast *concertato* finale, so conspicuously absent from *Faust*. In that finale, positioned at the end of Act II, Vincent actually witnesses Maître Ramon's rejection of him as a suitor for Mireille, unlike the situation in the literary antecedent where Mireille confronts her hostile parents alone. It would have been poor operatic dramaturgy for the lad to be represented in this finale only by his father, as in the poem; rare is the *concertato* finale in the French or Italian repertoire in which the tenor is not present. In the manner of *strettas* to finales in *Lucia di Lammermoor*, *La Favorite*, and other examples by Italian composers, the two protagonists in Gounod's *Mireille* are brought together musically in the ensemble by a melody which they emit in parallel octaves ('C'est en vain'). That they publicly clutch each other in despair one last time before separation and disaster makes for a strong operatic *tableau vivant* at the end of the second act.

But there was also a risk in placing the confrontation between Mireille and her father so early in the opera. In Mistral's epic that scene occurs in the seventh book of twelve, somewhat later in proportion to the whole but also producing an extended denouement. Whereas the poet drew out that denouement with forays into local folklore and an elaborate episode describing the appearance of 'les trois Maries lumineuses' to Mireille, the resolution of the dramatic knot established in the second act finale of the opera is protracted over the remaining acts and no new peak of confrontation caused by further complications in the plot occurs. After Vincent is wounded in Act III, the opera does not even contain a piece in which contrasting sentiments and positions are tested. The fourth act is made up largely of incidental numbers that do not push the drama forward. This state of affairs is exacerbated because a strong third character is never firmly established in the opera. Instead, a host of secondary figures spin through a revolving door opposite the soprano– tenor pair: Ourrias is eliminated in Act III; Ramon makes only brief appearances in three of the acts; Taven is a factor only in the first half of the opera; Vincenette participates marginally in the Act II finale and then suddenly emerges to sing a duet with Mireille in Act IV; and the shepherd boy, Andreloun, materializes in only one act. Early on some reviewers, such as Gustave Chadeuil of *Le Siècle*, questioned the wisdom of extracting an opera from a model so dependent upon descriptive episodes.[8] Ironically, Gounod was glad to report to Mistral that the essentials of his narrative had been retained, but it is precisely because the work did not stray from a model that was not particularly conducive to operatic treatment that the libretto is not stronger than it is; newly invented subplots might have sustained dramatic interest better. One has to wonder about how beneficial Mistral's personal involvement in the project actually was, since it is doubtful that he would have approved the massive transformations needed to produce a successful libretto.

Mireille was, none the less, a favourite at the Opéra-Comique for several decades, and justly so, since the score contains many numbers, especially in the first two acts, that are lovely in themselves. Among the most successful pieces are two duets for Mireille and Vincent. The duet in Act I ('Vincenette a votre âge') is dominated vocally by Vincent, who sings two asymmetrical strophes punctuated by an ensemble refrain. Most noteworthy is the crescendo of lyricism in his music across both

---

[8] Review of *Mireille*, *Le Siècle*, 22 Mar. 1864.

strophes: the second takes the music from B flat major to D flat major and draws upon a wider range of modulations and more rhapsodic vocal writing than the first, projecting growing intensity of feeling. Vincent confines himself, however, to a highly favourable comparison of Mireille to his own sister. There is no overt verbal declaration of love, and the music exudes elegance and grace rather than unbridled passion. Mireille is suddenly beckoned by her friends at the end of the duet but, instead of a heated vocal elaboration on mutual love (perhaps in the form of a *cabalette*), their feelings are succinctly encapsulated in a tender four-bar passage with solo cello (Ex. 8.2) after Vincent bids her 'adieu'.

Ex. 8.2. *Mireille*, Act I, duet

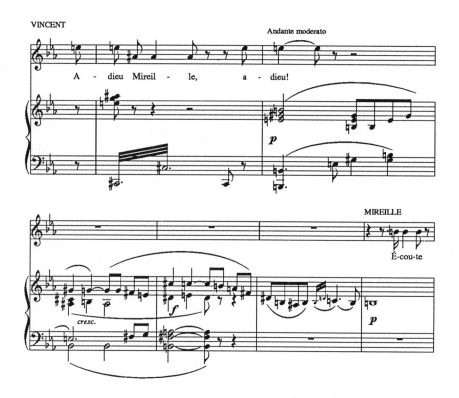

Expression of love is understated and couched in metaphor in the second duet as well, the famous 'Chanson de Magali'. Perhaps too much has been made of the strict alternation of 9/8 and 6/8 in the number. Gounod's intent may have been to produce an irregular folksong-like effect at the beginning of the piece, but rusticity gives way to artistic refinement as agogic accents soon obscure the sense of alternation between triple and duple groupings. Even the prominent oboe refrain in the number is displaced in several ways across the two metres, something seen in the score much more readily than it is heard. The entire effect is one of seamless continuity: Mireille's statements flow into Vincent's responses, which in turn melt into Mireille's new proposals, just as Mistral's original poem is built of interlocking chain links: 'VINCENT: Si tu te fais le poisson . . . je te pêcherai / MIREILLE: Si tu te fais pêcheur . . . je me ferai l'oiseau / VINCENT: Si tu te fais l'oiseau . . . je me ferai le chasseur . . .' The accompaniment consists merely of repeated chords, but each proposition is given individual character in the voice: stagnant alteration of two pitches for the somnolent field bluet, a light arpeggio for a cloud, a generous ambitus for the phrase about a sparrow. There is freshness and subtlety here, and the more bombastic passages in the opera, Mireille's 'Divine extase' in Act V for example, do not invite favourable comparison to this music.

From Five-act Tragedy to Three-act Success

The structural weaknesses in the five-act version of the opera are at least partially responsible for an extraordinarily turbulent performance history. The unsuccessful first run in the spring of 1864 was followed in July of the same year by a production at Covent Garden in which Mireille was permitted to remain alive at the final curtain. The *lieto fine* was also used at the Théâtre-Lyrique revival of December 1864. At that production *Mireille* was also shrunk into three acts, or, more to the point, the last three acts of the original were compressed into a single one, with the removal of the encounter between Ourrias and Vincent, the death of Ourrias, the 'Choeur des moissonneurs', and Mireille's large 'Air de la Crau', 'En marche'. For the next production, at the Opéra-Comique in 1874, this time in four acts, the tragic ending was restored but not all of the original music was used. In 1889 the three-act version met with success and it was given at the Opéra-Comique for a decade. A trimming of the drama after the second act finale made good theatrical sense, but it proved impossible to align the seams properly. For example, Mireille was still driven to the Saintes-Maries by news of Vincent's misfortune, despite the fact that the episode between Vincent and Ourrias was no longer staged! Not surprisingly, Gounod grumbled late in life that he had approved of the abbreviated version with great reluctance.[9] This alone ensured that there would be posthumous attempts to resurrect his initial intentions. Operatic tastes also changed rapidly. To an audience accustomed to *Carmen* and the earthiness of Italian 'verismo', the death of the peasant girl Mireille was no longer an issue at the turn of the century. In 1901 the Opéra-Comique returned to

---

[9] Prod'homme and Dandelot, *Gounod*, ii. 220.

a five-act tragic version of *Mireille*, but, because Gounod's orchestration for Mireille's 'Air de la Crau' in Act IV and for the Act V finale had been lost, these numbers were abbreviated. In 1939 Henri Busser and Reynaldo Hahn launched another revival, which purported to be as close to the version of March 1864 as the documentation available to them, including the autograph full score, would allow. Busser orchestrated the missing passages. His edition, which reflects the 1939 production, has been used for all subsequent performances at the Opéra-Comique and elsewhere.

Despite the claims of Busser and Hahn, this edition does not reflect the version of March 1864 in all details.[10] The most important point of divergence concerns the recitatives: there is no evidence that they were performed at the première instead of spoken dialogue. The question of whether recitatives or spoken dialogue were used is not as easily resolved as it normally would be because the most characteristic feature of spoken dialogue in the repertoire is absent: rather than write the *parlé* segments in prose, Carré set them in verse to reflect the lyricism of Mistral's epic. The first edition of the libretto contains longer texts between the musical numbers than those eventually set in the recitatives for the Covent Garden production. The very length of the texts in the original libretto is a function of the relatively rapid delivery of the spoken word. In addition, neither the first edition of the vocal score nor the original performing parts include the recitatives,[11] and many contemporary reviewers referred to *Mireille* as an *opéra comique*, a term used exclusively for works with spoken dialogue.[12]

Otherwise, the Busser edition is allied in some instances with the three-act version that Gounod (and Busser himself) repudiated. The finale of the second act furnishes a representative example: as first performed and published, the number was brought to a close by a homophonic choral reprise of a strophe ('Père cruel') that had been spun out earlier in *concertato* fashion. In the second edition of the vocal score,

[10] See Reynaldo Hahn, 'A propos de Mireille', in *Thèmes variés* (Paris, 1946), 103–111.

[11] Busser did not have access to the original performing parts. Fortunately they emerged in material that was transferred from the backrooms of the Opéra-Comique to the Bibliothèque de l'Opéra in 1980. The recovery of the parts permits a reconstruction of Gounod's orchestration for thirty-seven bars in the 'Air de la Crau' and for almost the entire finale of the last act.

[12] The recitatives could also not have been part of the original scheme and dropped sometime before the première. The bifolia in Gounod's autograph full score (Cary Collection, Pierpont Morgan Library) are arranged individually in succession and not in gatherings; those with recitatives are all clearly later insertions. The original sequence of music for the opera, for example, is represented by bifolia with blue crayon numeration in the upper right corners of their initial rectos. Recitatives are not included in the blue crayon bifoliation, nor are accretions that were introduced relatively late in the rehearsal period, such as Mireille's Act II *air*, or well after the first performance, such as her *valse-ariette*.

which reflects the three-act revival of December 1864, and all subsequent editions including Busser's, the homophonic rendition of 'Père cruel' is not given; in these sources an orchestral recollection of the Act II *Magali* duet follows immediately upon the end of the *strette*. The homophonic chorus was torn out of the autograph at some point, but in this case Busser did not choose to supply the orchestration, as he did with the missing sections of the 'Air de la Crau' and at the end of the opera. In so doing, he exercised an aesthetic judgement over faithfulness to the version of the first performance, albeit an easily defensible one since the homophonic chorus is somewhat anti-climactic after the *strette*.

In all fairness it must be said that the first performance of *Mireille* on 19 March 1864 was merely one event in a turbulent history that extended chronologically both forwards and backwards from that date; there is no reason why critical assessment should not supersede fidelity to the first edition. Practical performing options, however, are limited by the fact that music cut before the first edition of the vocal score was produced does not survive, even in the extant performing parts from the Théâtre-Lyrique. None the less, some of those cuts and changes were significant.

The earliest major revision was a removal of a scene set in Vincent's hut at the beginning of the opera. *Mireille* is structurally more conservative than *Faust* in that it includes both a traditional slow–fast *concertato* finale and a multipartite choral introduction to Act I. Though in all editions *Mireille* begins with the *magnanarelles* chorus and events derived from a conflation of Mistral's Books II and III, early on, in a prose scenario that Gounod sent to Mistral in 1863 and in an important working copy of the libretto, there was a tableau that must have been analogous to Mistral's first book. [13] The situation there does not seem to allow for choral participation, but affords an opportunity for Vincent to enchant Mireille with his extensive knowledge of Provençal lore, including a long exegesis on the miracle of the Saintes-Maries that was to have a decisive influence on her actions. Mistral's epic thereby better shows why Mireille is so obsessed with that holy site than do all performing versions of the opera, where she learns of the Saintes-Maries

[13] This working libretto, used as an in-house copy at the Théâtre-Lyrique to record changes, is preserved at AN AJ[13] 1157. The most concrete evidence for the one-time existence of a tableau in Vincent's hut comes in the prose scenario of the work, provided by Gounod in a letter of 17 Feb. 1863 to Mistral; for an English translation, see Tiersot, 'Gounod's Letters', p. 50. The libretto in AN AJ[13] 1157 shows evidence that the first tableau in Vincent's hut described in the scenario was worked out in full by Carré. Not only was the *magnanarelles* episode originally marked '2ième tableau' but before it are three stubs, all that remains of sliced-out pages that could only have contained that tableau. There are no physical traces of this tableau in the autograph full score.

merely from the friendly sorceress Taven after the *magnanarelles* introduction.[14] Dramatic cogency seems to have been sacrificed to a more colourful and conventional opening tableau.

One of the truly unusual features of *Mireille* is that the tenor is not heard in a solo *air* until almost the very end of the opera (the Act V *cavatine* 'Anges du paradis'). This postponement at least partly accounts for his relatively weak musico-dramatic profile as the plot unfolds. To make matters worse for poor Vincent, his moment in the spotlight occurs at a point when whatever emotions he has to express can only be of tertiary interest, since the fate of the heroine consumes so much attention in Act V; moreover, the harmonic language and melody of his *cavatine* is pallid compared to examples of the genre sung by Faust and Roméo. Better operatic sense prevailed at an early stage. The original sequence of events in Act V, as recorded in the working libretto, does not include Vincent's *cavatine*. The opening march is simply followed by a *parlé* exchange (with organ sounding in the background) between Vincent and his sister, who have just arrived breathless at the church; soon afterwards Mireille herself stumbles in. Since it is highly improbable that an opera in this repertoire could have been planned without a solo number for the tenor (even Vincent deserves a better fate), that solo must have originally occurred in the excised opening tableau of Act I, where, to judge by Mistral's Book I, Vincent must have played a prominent role.[15]

Other changes made to the opera before the rehearsal period were also not always for the better. Originally the duet for Mireille and Vincent read as in printed scores until she asks for help with her load ('Viens m'aider à poser sur mon front mon panier'). From this point the first layer of the working libretto goes on to give her *sotto voce* confession of love to the young basket-weaver:

MIREILLE. Viens m'aider à poser sur mon front mon panier.
        Ah!
VINCENT.   Qu'est-ce donc?
MIREILLE. [*fuyant vers lui*].   Une guêpe! Une abeille!
VINCENT. [*lui prenant la main*].
        Vous a-t-elle blessée?

---

[14] The libretto AN AJ[13] 1157 shows a two-stage development of this passage. In the first layer, dating from the time when the first tableau was still in place, Taven simply warns Mireille in six lines, without reference to the Saintes-Maries, that her attachment to Vincent will ultimately bring tears. It is only in a much more extended later insertion, an obvious by-product of the cut of the first tableau, that she tells Mireille to go to the shrine if matters should take a turn for the worse.

[15] Vincent's *cavatine* was later entered into libretto AN AJ[13] 1157 on a *collette*.

MIREILLE.[*effrayée*].   Elle est là! Je la vois!
        Elle bourdonne à mon oreille,
      Elle me suit! Je meurs! O Vincent défends-moi!
[*Elle se jette dans les bras de Vincent . . . long moment du silence pendant lequel on n'entend que le bourdonnement de la guêpe et le battement des deux coeurs amoureux*]
VINCENT. Pourquoi trembler encore dans mes bras, ô Mireille?
MIREILLE.[*d'une voix éteinte*].
        Vincent! Vincent! Je suis amoureuse de toi!

There is no indication after this of 'fin de l'acte' or some other concluding mark such as occurs at the end of all the other acts in this libretto, but two bits of evidence suggest that the duet could not have continued very long after this. First, the mutual confession of love occurs near the end of the corresponding episode in Mistral's epic. Second, after drafting the passage in April 1863, Gounod gave the following description of his setting in a letter to an unidentified correspondent:

I did not want to work on this ending . . . I thought that there was in Mireille's swooning and confession of love one of those singular manifestations of emotion that characterizes decisive moments in the life of the heart and of love. I abhorred the thought of capitulating at this delicate moment to the form and even the cut of conventional pieces. I have just found what I have been after, and I think that this act-end could be, in its own way, analogous to the scene of Marguerite at her window, Juliette at her balcony . . . Mireille and Vincent no longer have the strength to speak; happiness chokes them; they alternately emit fragments of sentences, feeble on the part of Mireille, inebriated and breathless on the part of Vincent, while the violins in the orchestra swell with a melody that explains why the lovers can no longer sing.[16]

The analogy to Marguerite's window scene in the third act of *Faust*, surely one of the finest passages in Gounod's operatic œuvre, can only whet the appetite for what might have been in *Mireille*. The passage is constructed of Marguerite's *parlante* above fragmentation and development (with continually changing instrumental colours) of the melody that will burst forth in complete form and 'fortissimo' at the moment she succumbs. Though it became a commonplace in Italian opera later in the century, the presentation of a grand melody in an orchestral peroration after a final vocal cadence was arresting and innovative in the 1850s. In view of the powerful effect of that passage and Gounod's desire to avoid the 'form and cut of conventional pieces' at the end of Act I in *Mireille*, it is indeed ironic that the conclusion he eventually settled upon is so

---

[16] This letter, dated 15 Apr. 1863, was probably addressed to Anna; it is partially cited by Bellaigue, *Gounod*, p. 106, but the current location of the autograph is unknown.

routine: the reprise of music from a previous number—the *magnanarelles* chorus—to bring down the curtain.[17]

That was but the first of several turns towards conventional solutions that *Mireille* was to take. Many of these were made at the behest of the Carvalhos. Saint-Saëns recalled that the biggest bone of contention between Gounod and them was the nature of Madame's *grand air* in the opera. During rehearsal she became unfavourably disposed towards the piece that Gounod had originally supplied as the vocal climax of her role, the 'Air de la Crau' in Act IV. According to Saint-Saëns, Gounod finally indulged her by removing a great deal of music from the number and by compensating for this cut with the addition of the modest *ariette* 'Heureux petit berger'.[18] But memory did not serve Saint-Saëns well in this instance. References to 'Heureux petit berger' in Gounod's letters from the spring of 1863 and its presence in the extant Théâtre-Lyrique working libretto prove that it was part of the first plans.

It is more likely that Madame Miolan-Carvalho's demands had implications for the shape of the second act. That act certainly looks very different in the working libretto from its form in later versions: at first Taven's chanson ('Voici la saison mignonne') was followed by an *ariette* for Mireille ('Comme la bergeronnette'), an extended duet for the heroine and Ourrias ('Pourquoi fuir si vite à mon approche'), and the finale.[19] Now at some point the *ariette* and duet were torn from both the autograph and the original performing parts and replaced by the definitive two-part *air* for Mireille ('Mon cœur ne peut changer') as well as by Ourrias's *couplets* ('Si les filles d'Arles sont reines').[20] There is some evidence, admittedly not conclusive, that this act of aggression against the original music in Act II was connected to the brouhaha surrounding the 'Air de la Crau'. The original duet was entered not only into the partbooks of individual singers but also into instrumental parts, which, since they were needed only for full orchestra rehearsals shortly before opening night, were likely to have been copied shortly before the

[17] It would be tempting to see a causal relationship between the excision of the tableau in Vincent's hut and the definitive conclusion of the act with the *magnanarelles* chorus. In the autograph and all printed scores, after 'Viens m'aider à poser sur mon front' Mireille proceeds to tell Vincent to seek refuge at the Saintes-Maries in the event of danger, presumably the same kind of admonition he gave her in the tableau that was cut. But the original performing parts show that Mireille's advice was added only during the rehearsals to a sequence of events that proceeded directly from 'Viens m'aider à poser sur mon front' to a reprise of the *magnanarelles* music. The addition of her exhortation made good sense as a way of explaining why Vincent rushes off to the Saintes-Maries in Act V.

[18] Saint-Saëns, *Portraits et souvenirs*, p. 92.

[19] In the censors' libretto for *Mireille* (AN F18 737), dated 25 Nov. 1863, the text of Mireille's number is changed (to 'Le bonheur est un oiseau'), but the duet with Ourrias is still in place.

[20] Music for the duet survives in three of the parts (vn. 1, desk 6; va., desk 2; vc., desk 4). Unfortunately the vocal lines do not seem to be extant.

première, that is in January or February 1864.[21] According to an anonymous report in *Le Ménestrel*, friction between the concerned parties over the 'Air de la Crau' actually occurred in the first week of February (this, too, confirms Saint-Saëns's account):

On the subject of *Mireille*, there has been much discussion this past week about the difficulties that have arisen between M. Gounod and M. Carvalho over a truly remarkable scene that is too dramatic for the voice of Madame Carvalho, who declined the honour of performing it. This kind of good sense and modesty is too rare among our singers to go unnoticed. Nevertheless, the demonstration did not move Gounod, who stood adamantly by his first idea. But upon reflection and after tempers had cooled it was remembered that similar difficulties had come up in the days of *Faust* and had been happily overcome by means of reciprocal concessions.[22]

What could Gounod's concessions have been? He obviously agreed to shorten the 'Air de la Crau' since the first run of the first edition gives the music of the piece only after 'Le ciel m'éblouit', about one-third of the way through the entire number. That still left her role without a large solo number well suited to her voice. In all likelihood Gounod also furnished Miolan-Carvalho at that time with a new *air*, 'Mon cœur ne peut changer' in Act II, that would better highlight her vocal qualities. The Mireille–Ourrias duet may have been removed to ease the pressure on Miolan-Carvalho, who would have had a large vocal part in three consecutive numbers (the *air*, the duet, and the finale) had the duet remained in place. In this scenario Ourrias's *couplets* served to compensate bass Ismaël and to round out the character of the unsuccessful suitor after the elimination of the duet (though barely, since the depiction of *machismo* was never one of Gounod's strong cards). And with all of her modesty and good sense, what was Madame Carvalho's part of the bargain? She agreed to sing at least part of the 'Air de la Crau'.

Even if there was not a relationship between the radical reduction of the 'Air de la Crau' and the addition of the *air* to the second act, one point should not be lost. As *Mireille* had been initially conceived, the soprano's *grand air* was an unusual one ('a truly remarkable scene' was the expression used by the reporter for *Le Ménestrel*) in the contemporary repertoire of French opera. No single aspect of the number was without precedent; a recent specimen of a *grand air* without vocalises,

---

[21] It does appear, however, that, when the individual orchestra parts started to be copied, Mireille's *ariette* had been dropped. The parts into which the Mireille–Ourrias duet was entered record the finale of the act as number 6 at the time of copying; had Mireille's *ariette* still been in place, the finale would have been numbered 7, as it is in the final score because of the addition of Mireille's *air* and Ourrias's *couplets*.

[22] 'Semaine théâtrale', *Le Ménestrel*, 7 Feb. 1864.

for example, had been the heroine's 'Ô nuit d'amour' in David's *Lalla-Roukh*. But the various features of the 'Air de la Crau' taken together combine to form a truly exceptional piece for its time: it is laid out in a large ternary groundplan in which the long soaring phrases of the first and last sections are in contrast with the halting breathless declamation that effectively portrays Mireille's exhaustion in the long middle episode. The duration of the declaimed middle section is greater than both outer sections combined. Instead of this, the second act *air* became the vocal highlight of the Mireille role, no doubt exactly as Miolan-Carvalho wished. And not surprisingly, with a slow movement–*cabalette* form, two statements of a *cabalette* tune driven by a single rhythmic motif, and a coda replete with *roulades*, this *air* was as conventional as the 'Air de la Crau' was unusual. The incident is also instructive about Gounod's general difficulties in the theatre. Saint-Saëns recalled how he had warned Gounod even before the rehearsals that Miolan-Carvalho would refuse to perform the 'Air de la Crau'. Making a face, Gounod is supposed to have responded 'She will definitely have to sing it.'[23] Yet Miolan-Carvalho's background was as a *chanteuse à roulades* and Gounod himself had recently added coloratura to the role of Baucis at her request. It is striking, then, that Gounod conceived a role for her without a single *roulade* and with a large *air* totally unsuited to her voice. Rather than take the nature of Miolan-Carvalho's voice into account while he composed the score, he risked almost certain confrontation in the rehearsal period. Doubtless he felt that an entirely lyrical and dramatic operatic role was true to the character of Mistral's heroine; this belief took precedence over the realities of the stage.

Unfortunately, the controversy surrounding the 'Air de la Crau' was not laid to rest at the première. Miolan-Carvalho's opening-night rendition of even the truncated version was so disastrous that it was eliminated entirely from subsequent performances. This had repercussions on neighbouring numbers in the opera. In the first run of the vocal score and the first edition of the libretto, Act IV is divided into two tableaux.[24] In this scheme of events the curtain opened to reveal a large room in the farmhouse of Maître Ramon, the setting for the 'Chœur des moissonneurs' and the Vincenette–Mireille duet. The subsequent scene was set in

---

[23] Saint-Saëns, *Portraits et souvenirs*, pp. 92–3.

[24] The title-page of the first run of the first edition reads: MIREILLE|Opéra en 5 Actes, tiré du Poème de | FRÉDÉRIC MISTAL [*sic*] | PAR | MICHEL CARRÉ | Musique de | CH. GOUNOD | Partition Chant et Piano. | A PARIS, CHOUDENS, ÉDITEUR. | Rue St. Honoré, 265, (Près de l'Assomption [)] | Propriété | pr tous Pays. Imp. V. Arouy, Paris | Angleterre, Boosey. Allemagne, Schott. The title-page of the second run is identical, except that it corrects the misspelling of Mistral's name. The last page of the first run is numbered 228, the last page of the second run 242.

the Crau desert and consisted of an orchestral introduction identical to the first twenty-four bars of the overture, Andreloun's chanson ('Le jour se lève'), Mireille's *ariette* ('Heureux petit berger'), her truncated *air*, and a considerable amount of spoken dialogue. The removal of the *air* for the second performance left 'a gaping hole in the action', according to the critic Prosper Pascal.[25] On that evening the act simply finished with the spoken exchange between Mireille and Andreloun after the *ariette*: the curtain was brought down as the two silently parted ways, Mireille ignoring the advice of the shepherd boy to seek refuge in the shade. Since this was a singularly ineffective way to conclude an act, a new solution was worked out by the third night. The Crau set was removed entirely and the first tableau transferred to a location just outside Ramon's farmhouse. After the *moissonneurs* chorus Andreloun wandered in, sang his chanson, and engaged Mireille in conversation. She then delivered her *ariette* 'Heureux petit berger'. Once Andreloun had continued on his way, Vincenette ran on to inform Mireille of what had happened to Vincent. For the remainder of the performances in April and May, and in the second run of the first edition (which relegates the 'Air de la Crau' to an appendix), the act was performed in this way. It was not until the Carré five-act revival of 1901 that the episode with Andreloun was returned to the Crau. Busser and Hahn also gave the fourth act in two tableaux, but, because they believed the second run of the first edition to be the only printed record of the performances in 1864, they positioned the chanson and the *ariette* before the Vincenette–Mireille duet and had the *air* appear by itself in the Crau scene. The result of some frantic scrambling to repair the damage caused by the complete excision of the 'Air de la Crau' thus became sanctioned as Gounod's original version. It may be added that the new arrangement of the *moissonneurs* chorus followed by the chanson and the *ariette* only re-enforced the uneventfulness of the act by presenting three dramatically stagnant pieces in succession. Gounod paid a high price for insisting that at least part of an *air* unsuited to Miolan-Carvalho's voice be retained: the middle of a first run of performances was certainly no time to consider profound structural changes to any opera.[26]

He might have counted himself fortunate had the turbulence been

[25] Pascal gave an account of the early upheavals in the score in *Le Ménestrel*, 27 Mar. 1864.

[26] In responding to a listener who seemed to remember the sequence of events for the Carré production of 1901, Hahn invoked the autograph to support what he thought was the order originally conceived by Gounod ('À propos de Mireille', p. 110). Since the autograph was the *stichvorlage* for the three-act orchestral score of the 1880s, its present layout cannot by itself support conclusions about the original state of the opera. Although the bifolia bearing the chanson and *ariette* do occur before the duet in the autograph, that they were rearranged is shown by such indications, in Gounod's hand, as '2ième tableau' beneath the title 'Heureux petit berger' or the words 'Après la scène du berger' under the title of the 'Air de la Crau'.

centred only around Miolan-Carvalho. The idea of providing Andreloun with a musical number in Act IV—not a good one from the dramaturgical point of view, since it slows the action excessively—was not in the original plan. The addition of the number probably had something to do with a change of performers. The working libretto as well as a report in *Le Ménestrel* of 25 October list a certain Madame Albrecht for the part of Andreloun and Madame Dubois-Thibaut for Taven, both minor figures on the Théâtre-Lyrique roster. By opening night both parts were taken by Madame Faure-Lefebvre, an established singer who often took lead roles herself; she may well have requested a more significant musical contribution. The back of an autographed photograph of Gounod among the Bizet papers at the Bibliothèque Nationale shows the music of the first six bars of Andreloun's chanson in Gounod's hand, but set to the text 'La plaine est vaste et le soleil géant vermeil' with the indication '(Ivan IV.) 1855' beneath. As with the Soldiers' Chorus in *Faust* and the Act I march in *La Reine de Saba*, the piece must have been broken from the unfinished torso of the lost opera.

Morini, the tenor playing the role of Vincent, also proved to be a stumbling block. Though the role is not a very demanding one, he could not get through it as written during late rehearsals and at the première. The Act V *cavatine* and Act III duet with Ourrias were among the casualties; remarkably, the *cavatine* was entirely eliminated on opening night and the duet was radically abridged. Busser did not publish the duet in its original shape because, once again, he unwittingly based his version upon the second run of the first edition. One of the features that distinguishes the first run from the second is the form of the Vincent–Ourrias duet. The groundplan of the number in the first run corresponds to what Gounod first entered into his full-score autograph. Originally the first section consisted largely of recitative for Vincent ('Où suis-je'). He is heartbroken over the turn of events at the end of the preceding act and is surprised by the sudden appearance of Ourrias ('Mort et malheur'). A parallel-strophe second section ('Au fond de ce ravin'), with an intervening middle section of declaimed dialogue, follows. In a third section, Ourrias deliberately provokes Vincent by accusing him of having used sorcery to capture Mireille's affection. Both sing of their mutual hatred in a fourth section ('Tais toi, tais toi / Tu veux donc que ma main te ploie'). At the end of the duet Ourrias strikes Vincent with his trident and flees. Taven is drawn from her cave by the ruckus and comforts Vincent.

The duet was first copied into the performing parts in this form, but, because of difficulties with Morini, it underwent extensive surgery. At one point during the rehearsals Gounod even eliminated the entire piece:

1. Portrait of Gounod by Jules-Léopold Boilly, *c.*1840 (Bibliothèque de l'Opéra)

L'ILLUSTRE COMPOSITEUR

CHARLES GOUNOD

d'après un portrait qui fut fait de lui

à l'époque de la première représentation de Faust (19 mars 1859)

2. Gounod at the time of the *Faust* première (Bibliothèque Nationale)

3. Title-page to second edition of *La Nonne sanglante* (British Library)

4. Portrait of Pauline Viardot by Ary Scheffer (Bibliothèque Nationale)

5. Marie Miolan-Carvalho in the role of Marguerite in Gounod's *Faust* (prison scene) (Bibliothèque Nationale)

6. Léon Carvalho (Bibliothèque de l'Opéra)

7. Gabrielle Krauss in the role of Pauline in Gounod's *Polyeucte* (Bibliothèque de l'Opéra; photo: S.H.)

8. The Théâtre-Lyrique, 1862 (Bibliothèque de l'Opéra)

9. The Opéra rue Le Peletier, c. 1869 (Bibliothèque de l'Opéra)

10. Gounod in the late 1880s (Bibliothèque de l'Opéra; photo: S.H.)

11. The Act II finale of *Mireille* at its first production, 1864 (Bibliothèque de l'Opéra; photo: S.H.)

12. The 'Chorale des epées', *Faust*, Act II, at the first English production of the work, Her Majesty's Theatre, 1863 (Archive of the Royal Opera House Covent Garden)

13. Autograph of the duet for Marguerite and Valentin, cut from the second act of *Faust* before its première (Bibliothèque Nationale)

an orchestral rendition of a theme associated with Vincent, to show musically that he is in the vicinity, was followed by Ourrias's shout 'Mort et malheur, c'est lui!' and then a skip over to the orchestral passage in F sharp minor (marked 'large') that in all editions appears after the duet.[27] We have it on the word of Prosper Pascal that by the première at least some of the original music had been restored: 'The duet of the dispute was removed, except for a passage that Ismaël [the singer playing the part of Ourrias] renders beautifully, "Elle t'aime . . . et moi je l'aimais." '[28] The autograph and parts do indeed show that at some point the number had assumed this shape. According to physical evidence in those documents, on opening night the duet must have included Ourrias's waltz strophe 'Tu veux donc que ma main te ploie', which contains the line cited by Pascal, preceded by a new recitative for him ('Ils s'éloignent . . . Et moi, le cœur gonflé de rage') and followed by Vincent's theme, Ourrias's 'Mort et malheur', and the orchestral epilogue in F sharp minor—a modest improvement over the cuts first considered, since at least this version allows Ourrias to expound his jealousy. Vincent did not sing and seems to have been attacked off-stage. Turgenev was in the house on opening night and described the scene in the following manner to Pauline Viardot: 'Ourrias played by Ismaël, who himself looks like a miserable provincial butcher, hurries into the wings. We hear an *ah!* and Ourrias, his hair dishevelled, re-emerges and crosses the stage. The décor changes and the so-called fantastic scene begins.'[29] All of this was more amusing than dramatic. Changes were not long in coming. Pascal noted that after the third performance the duet 'will be restored and the spectator, as well as Taven, will witness the murderer's blows'.[30] A layer of insertions in the original performing parts, however, shows that the duet was not reinstated in its original form. The new recitative for Ourrias ('Ils s'éloignent') and the waltz strophe from the original fourth section ('Tu veux donc que ma main te ploie') were retained for the beginning of the duet, and were succeeded by the original music for the second and third sections followed by a new conclusion to the piece: instead of warning Ourrias to stop his

[27] The last bifolio of the preceding set piece (*scène et chœur*: 'Voici le Val d'enfer') is numbered 81 (superimposed upon number 71) in the blue crayon bifoliation of the autograph. At one stage a bifolio numbered 82 was added to the autograph; the absence of the number 72 beneath suggests that this bifolio replaced a lost bifolio numbered 82 (superimposed upon 72) and that it was incorporated into the autograph after the Mireille–Ourrias duet had been cut. The new bifolio 82 records the skip from Ourrias's 'Mort et malheur' to the orchestral passage in F sharp minor.

[28] Review of *Mireille*, *Le Ménestrel*, 20 Mar. 1864.

[29] Letter of 29 Mar. 1864, in Turgenev, *Lettres inédites*, p. 113. This account is confirmed by J. Weber in his review of the première, *Le Temps*, 5 Apr. 1864.

[30] *Le Ménestrel*, 27 Mar. 1864.

provocations ('Tais toi, tais toi!'), Vincent delivered a strophe 'Par le ciel si tu tiens à vivre' to the completely new, and quite banal, *cabalette* tune shown in Ex. 8.3. Ourrias joined in for a middle section based loosely

Ex. 8.3. *Mireille*, Act III, duet

VINCENT

Par   le   ciel   si   tu tiens à   vi - vre   sé - pa - rons   nous ____

é - loi - gne   toi _____

upon his waltz and then both launched a boisterous reprise of Vincent's solo strain that culminated in a cadence obviously engineered to elicit applause.[31] The net result of these operations was that Gounod's original fourth section, which featured a strophe for each of the contenders and one for them together, each set to different music, was replaced for the majority of performances from March to May 1864 by a conventional tripartite *cabalette*. Virtually all reviewers of the first performance had inveighed against the incomprehensibility of the third act: 'an instrumental symphony with solo voice', 'a negation of rhythm and form', 'monotonous psalmody' were some characteristic observations.[32] Carvalho was not one to ignore the mood of public and Press, and it may well have been he who encouraged Gounod to incorporate a familiar musical procedure, even if it meant giving Morini slightly more to sing.

In the second run of the first edition, and in the Busser edition, a conflation of versions is given, in which Ourrias's recitative and waltz strophe appear at the beginning of the number, but the balance proceeds as in the first run. There is no evidence in the parts that the piece was ever performed this way on stage in 1864, neither in March nor in December. Once again, Gounod's original plan seems more effective than the one settled upon in the Busser edition. In the first run, the third section starts at the point where Ourrias's needling assumes the ugly tone that will lead to the crime—a convincing catalyst to the fourth section. The action evolves naturally from verbal sparring to physical threats. But with Ourrias's new recitative and original concluding

[31] The piece was published in this form in the *morceaux séparées* brought out by Choudens. An autograph fragment in full score of this *cabalette* is in the collection of the BO Rés. 2221.

[32] In the order cited, reviews of *Mireille* by Xavier Aubreyet, *Le Nain jaune*, 27 Mar. 1864; Albert de Lasalle, *Le Monde illustré*, 27 Mar. 1864; Arthur Pougin, *Le Théâtre*, 27 Mar. 1864.

strophe ('Tu veux donc que ma main te ploie') at the beginning of the number, the currently performed version gives his act a premeditated character that takes the edge off ensuing developments. Moreover, the emphasis on the sorrow of Vincent at the start of the number in the first scheme (recitative 'Où suis-je') enhances his stature as a sympathetic figure and renders Ourrias's act all the more offensive.

Patchwork during the first run of *Mireille* was only a foretaste of what was to come later in the same year. Changes made for the December performances at the Théâtre-Lyrique reflect many of the concerns that reviewers had expressed about the first production of the work as well as about performances at Covent Garden in the summer; Carvalho and Gounod were very sensitive to contemporary critical opinion. In the face of the universal condemnation of Act III, it was eliminated and the last two acts were combined into one. The reviewer for the *Musical Times* had complained about the gauche coda of the overture;[33] for the December revival it was changed to the *animé* section that has appeared in all subsequent editions. There was an objection from d'Ortigue of *Le Journal des débats* to the incorporation of the famous chant melody Lauda Sion (to the text 'Son âme a pris son vol vers Dieu') at the end of the opera.[34] Johannès Weber had inveighed against the tragic ending and Bénédict Jouvin of *Le Figaro* had called for a soprano–tenor duet to conclude the work.[35] A tragedy in a peasant setting had probably been seen as a calculated risk by Carvalho from the start, and, doubtless encouraged by these kinds of remarks, he persuaded Gounod to rework the ending completely. A new duet ('La foi de son flambeau divin') replaced the chorus of assembled pilgrims 'Le voile enfin s'est déchiré'. Mireille's 'Sainte ivresse! divine extase!' was removed. Further changes included the creation of a more substantial third role by combining the characters of Vincenette and Taven. It was now performed, as Taven, by one of the stars of the Théâtre-Lyrique, Delphine Ugalde. The tenor Morini was replaced by Pierre Michot, who had the stamina to perform the fifth act *cavatine*. A brilliant *valse-ariette*, 'Ô légère hirondelle', was added to Mireille's role in order to give Miolan-Carvalho an additional opportunity to shine with coloratura. It is in this three-act form that *Mireille* finally became popular, not in December 1864, but in 1889. The peasant drama that to many in March 1864 seemed too insignificant for a five-act frame found favour in a work closer to the norms of light *opéra comique*, that is, one with three acts, a *concertato*

---

[33] Review of *Mireille*, *Musical Times*, 1 Aug. 1864.

[34] Review of *Mireille*, *Le Journal des débats*, 30 Mar. 1864.

[35] J. Weber, 'Critique musicale', *Le Temps*, 30 Dec. 1862; B. Jouvin, review of *Mireille*, *Le Figaro*, 27 Mar. 1864.

finale centrally positioned at the end of Act II, a large third role, a happy ending, and a *première chanteuse à roulades*. In the process much of the faithfulness to the literary source was sacrificed. While composing the score in the spring of 1863, Gounod had secured the approval of Mistral for the project by assuring him that he would be able to translate it to the stage with a minimum of distortion. That was premature. Success was achieved with much larger concessions to the conventions of the day than he had first anticipated. Only when *Mireille* had secured a foothold in the repertoire did an Opéra-Comique director seek to proceed down the road towards Gounod's original intent; though the end of that road disappears into lost or simply inaccessible documents, there remains some distance to travel along it with currently available evidence.

9. Roméo et Juliette

The Shakespeare Play as Model

Love forbidden by family circumstance. It lay at the core of Mistral's epic, and was a well-worn theme when Shakespeare took it up in *Romeo and Juliet*, with roots that extended beyond previous Italian legends about the star-crossed lovers from Verona to ancient sources such as the Pyramus and Thisbe episode in Ovid's *Metamorphosis*. Gounod was drawn to the theme again shortly after the failure of *Mireille*, but this time the model proved better suited to contemporary French operatic convention. Unlike their librettos for *Faust* and Thomas's *Hamlet*, Barbier and Carré did not allow a popular adaptation to stand between literary masterpiece and opera in the case of *Roméo et Juliette*. The play is itself notably rich in lyrical 'set pieces', to borrow an operatic term, including Mercutio's burlesque Queen Mab speech, Friar Lawrence's sermons, Juliet's soliloquy with the vial, the sonnet of the two lovers at their first meeting, and their later dawn poem about the nightingale and the lark. Shakespeare's prologue suggested an interesting operatic experiment to enhance the traditional instrumental prelude: a summary of the plot by all the principals before the action proper begins.[1] These and other passages must have fairly leapt out at Gounod and his librettists as favourable for musical numbers. Moreover, there was a natural *entrée* for operatic spectacle in Shakespeare's masque, for comedy in the figure of the nurse, and for a choral tableau involving antagonistic factions in the street brawl. It is, then, not surprising that the Barbier–Carré libretto adheres closely to the play, borrowing from it right down to individual expressions: most of their scenes with direct parallels to the tragedy contain many metaphors drawn directly from it. (This greatly distances their work from its most prominent nineteenth-century operatic forebear, Bellini's *I Capuleti ed i Montecchi* (1830), which is only remotely connected with Shakespeare.) In the late 1860s a number of French translations were available—including those by Benjamin Laroche (1839–40), Francisque Michel (1855), and François-Victor Hugo (1860)—but no single one may be designated with

[1] Berlioz also used Shakespeare's prologue in his dramatic symphony. In his reminiscences for *Le Figaro*, 28 Oct. 1893, Carvalho took credit for persuading Gounod to modify his original concept: 'At first the prologue was sung in the wings with lowered curtain; at one of the last dress rehearsals I proposed to Gounod that the curtain be raised and that the chorus be replaced by all the soloists.'

confidence as the source for the choice of words in the opera, at least on the basis of presently available evidence. Any attempt to do so is impeded by the inevitable congruencies between them resulting from the common source and the fact that Barbier and Carré were themselves constrained by demands of versification.

Just as in Mistral's *Mireille*, much in Shakespeare's play is not about love. Also explicit in the course of events is a statement about civil disorder; Shakespeare's symmetrical arrangement of the greatly peopled scenes with the Prince at the beginning, middle, and end of the play has been pointed out often enough. In the end, even established political authority cannot escape responsibility for the tragedy ('And I, for winking at your discords too, | Have lost a brace of kinsmen', is the well-known line spoken by the Prince in V. iii). And projection of intense love in the play is matched by depictions of choleric hatred (both are fed by a common stream of irrationality and impulsive behaviour). The venom of the 'fiery Tybalt with his sword prepared' (I. i) is set in clear relief at the outset by antithesis: his first dialogue is with none other than Benvolio, who, exhibiting the attributes associated with his name, responds in conciliatory fashion to Tybalt's challenge to 'look upon thy death'.

That the Prince, Tybalt, and Benvolio are all minor players in the opera, with merely bit parts in large ensemble numbers, is the result of a one-sided approach to the literary source. Gounod's opera is sustained almost entirely by the sentimental strain of Shakespeare's tragedy. The encounters between Roméo and Juliette consume far more time in relation to the whole in the opera than they do in the play. There are no less than four duets for them in the opera and in terms of overall dramatic momentum and scope that may be at least one too many. The incorporation of so many tenor–soprano duets was by itself unprecedented in Gounod's operatic œuvre and highly unusual, if not unprecedented, in contemporary French and Italian opera.

The music for these pieces, however, is exquisite; each is a jewel individually cut and meticulously polished. For instance, the beginning of the Act I duet consists of a conventional structural procedure with a higher dramatic purpose: Roméo sings a strophe and Juliette merely repeats the same passage, music dominated by short-breathed two-bar melodic phrases with delicate violin arabesques to bridge the rests in the vocal line. It conveys at once a certain archaic spirit akin to an eighteenth-century minuet and the formality of the Shakespeare original where Romeo and Juliet first speak to one another through metaphor ('If I profane with my unworthiest hand'). To reflect the greater ease they feel in each other's company, the number continues with a *parlante* exchange; this gives way to a throbbing pedal tone in the low strings at the moment Juliette realizes that the dye has been cast ('Ah! je n'ai pu m'en défendre') and a brief concluding passage of unison singing to suggest that their fates are now joined. The delicate modesty of Juliette is played off against the heated lyricism of Roméo in the *scène et duo* of the subsequent balcony scene. In one of the finest characterizations of the opera (Ex. 9.1) she does suddenly break out of restrained declamation to confess her eternal fidelity, but just as unexpectedly reverts back to soft-spoken delivery with static accompaniment when,

Ex. 9.1. *Roméo et Juliette*, Act II, *scène*

with real feminine *pudeur*, she warns him not to misinterpret the forthrightness of her declaration as evidence of shallow emotion. The ebb and flow of passions is calculated so that Gertrude's interruption occurs in the wake of Roméo's most fervent avowal of love, the famous phrase 'Ah je te l'ai dit, je t'adore'. The tenor's music is an electrifying moment, a lyrical apogee that derives part of its great effect from a change of metre to common time (but with no change of tempo) and a shift upwards to F major after a previous cadence in D minor. The nurse's intervention is a cruel reminder of reality, and, with a final cadence marked *ppp*, the *cabalette* is a relatively restrained utterance after Roméo's outpouring.

The entire Act IV duet in Juliette's chamber brought an unprecedented degree of sensuousness to French opera. At the outset, four cellos give forth a small, but graphic, tone-poem about the night that has just passed (Verdi would later use the same scoring to begin the love duet in the first act of *Otello*): two highly chromatic phrases settle into a cadential figure (Ex. 9.2*a*), the poetic meaning of which is revealed by Roméo's later use of the same melody for his words 'reste encor en mes bras enlacés!' (Ex. 9.2*b*). The parallel-strophe slow movement 'Nuit d'hyménée' is a masterpiece of lyrical planning. At first the two lovers sing in strict parallel sixths; soon Roméo imitates each of Juliette's phrases at a bar's distance ('Ton doux regard m'enivre') and following that he provides his own melody to offset her leading strain, though still at the interval of a single measure ('Ô volupté de vivre'). The whole is a graded progression of contrapuntal freedom in Roméo's part, under-lined by a circle-of-fifths sequence after 'Ô volupté de vivre' to prepare a cadence that coincides with the registral climax of the movement ('Sous tes baisers de flamme'). Following this musical metaphor for mounting ecstasy, the two voices glide into a reprise of the opening section with parallel singing that is even softer than before. The dialogue that follows is punctuated by three appearances of the phrase 'Non, ce n'est pas le jour', by which first Juliette, and then Roméo, seek to deny the onset of light. Each time it is heard one step higher (B flat major, B major, C major), an effective variation of the technique used for 'Anges purs, anges radieux' in *Faust*, where the statements are contiguous. (In the Act

Ex. 9.2*a*. *Roméo et Juliette*, Act IV, duet

Ex. 9.2*b. Roméo et Juliette*, Act IV, duet

V duet Gounod retried another technique used in *Faust*, the musical recollection of past bliss as the two lovers stand on the brink of their destiny.) An eight-bar orchestral passage (marked 'avec délire') heard after the B major statement of 'Non, ce n'est pas le jour' is the point of articulation between a situation in which Juliette resists Roméo's plea to accept reality and an episode where it is Roméo who prolongs the encounter. Rather than merely decorate action on-stage, as such orchestral interpolations conventionally do in the mid-century French repertoire, it is meant to portray the emotional state of the lovers as they embrace.

In short, the duets in *Roméo et Juliette*, along with certain numbers in *Faust*, are as close to greatness as Gounod comes as a composer. Now since the appearance of *Faust*, if there was one piece in his operatic œuvre that even his detractors acknowledged as a masterpiece, it was the Marguerite–Faust duet. As early as 1862 an anonymous Belgian reviewer of *La Reine de Saba* had even asked, 'When will you give us that *Roméo et Juliette* that seems made for you and that only you can give to the French stage?'[2] Put most bluntly, Gounod drew upon widely

[2] Review of *La Reine de Saba*, *Le Guide musical*, 18 Dec. 1862.

acknowledged strengths in *Roméo et Juliette*: he fell back to what he did well. After three operatic failures in succession, he can hardly be blamed for that. Indeed, this suggests a degree of pragmatism wanting at other times in his career. The prospect of writing a string of intimate duets may well have been a factor in Gounod's decision to turn to the Shakespeare play as a subject in the first place; even if it was not, he had the good sense to stick with the project in the face of an attractive offer from his friend Ernest Legouvé to adapt the comedy *Les Contes de la Reine de Navarre*. 'One cannot trifle with love', the composer wrote. 'In vain did I leaf through both plays—Juliette has entwined me with the famous silk thread meant to capture Roméo'[3]—Juliette and, surely, the lure of a much-needed success.

The adjustment of emphasis as well as the musical requirements of the operatic stage brought inevitable changes to the play. Unlike some of Gounod's previous operas, such as *La Reine de Saba*, *Roméo et Juliette* contains very effective instances of operatic compression. For example, the masque is the last of five scenes in Act I of the model; before this the spectator has been introduced to Paris's attraction to Juliet in scene ii and the heroine's innocent disinterest in marriage in scene iii. Mercutio's passage about Queen Mab follows in scene iv. In the opera, the masque occupies far more time in proportion to the whole and serves as the setting for the entire act and the essential elements exposed in scenes ii, iii, and iv of the Shakespeare. Not only is this a reflection of Gounod's sentimental programme—from that perspective the masque is one of the capital scenes in the play because it gives rise to the impossible love—but it also provides a conventional operatic introduction containing static mood-setting choruses and small set pieces for soloists. As with *Mireille*, Gounod elected to round off the first act with a reprise of music heard earlier on, the chorus 'Nargue les buveurs' and an instrumental mazurka; the first act of the play, on the other hand, concludes on a sombre note with Juliet's discovery of Romeo's family name ('My only love sprung from my only hate! | Too early seen unknown, and known too late!'). Shakespeare's solution, immeasurably more dramatic, gave way in the opera to pure musical formalism, the tying together of the whole with a reprise. The act-ending also appealed to Gounod because of its musical contrast with subsequent acts. In a letter to Choudens, sounding much more like one describing the different character of movements in a symphony than in a stage work, he expressed satisfaction that the first act finished in 'brilliant' fashion, the second 'tender and dream-like', the third 'animated and grand', the fourth 'dramatic', and the fifth 'tragic'. The second act of the opera is, indeed,

[3] Letter to E. Legouvé, 2 May 1865, private collection.

intimate and quiet, and Gounod's impulse to bring the first act to a rousing finish was the same as that of a symphonist who provides an animated conclusion to a first movement before a placid second.

Purely musical motivation must lie behind the invented episode in the second act in which Grégorio and other Capulet retainers stumble through the garden after the mischievous Montaigu page Stéphano; there is no direct connection with the Shakespeare here, though their good-humoured suggestion to nurse Gertrude that she had arranged a secret assignation with the page ('Est-ce pour vos beaux yeux que le traître est venu!') is in keeping with the fun that Mercutio enjoys at her expense in the play (II. iv). These events were almost certainly included to provide animated contrast to the elegiac tone that predominates in the balcony scene. Another major change between opera and play concerns the marriage scene. Shakespeare's second-act curtain falls as Friar Lawrence prepares to unite the two in matrimony; in the opera the marriage ceremony itself actually takes place on the stage. In view of Gounod's past creative patterns, this spirituality is perhaps not unexpected. Mireille and Marguerite are motivated by love so pure that it earns them divine protection. Roméo and Juliette make a plea for salvation at the end of the opera, an element also not in the Shakespeare. From a literal Catholic perspective, the actual enactment of their union before God earlier on strengthens the force of that entreaty; their unison 'Seigneur pardonnez-nous!' at the final curtain is even textually reminiscent of their fourfold unison supplications in the marriage scene ('Seigneur! nous promettons d'obéir à ta loi', 'Seigneur, sois mon appui, sois mon espoir', etc.).

In the play truculent Tybalt ignites the great brawl in Act III by spontaneously taunting Mercutio and Roméo in the street. Any sharp definition of Tybalt as the personification of hatred in the opera is undermined in this instance by the page boy Stéphano, the *dugazon* role in the opera. It is he who causes the mêlée by boldly appearing in front of the Capulet house (after having trespassed the night before) to sing a song alluding to the forbidden love of Juliette and Roméo. The change in the opera provides dramatic continuity with the new episode in the previous act and, more important, an occasion to insert the obligatory *ariette* for the *dugazon*. Shakespeare *aficionados* will also note that, unlike his counterpart in the play, Gounod's Roméo remains on stage for that entire scene, surely because it would have been uncharacteristic operatic dramaturgy for the tenor protagonist to leave suddenly in the middle of the grand finale and not be present to demonstrate his reaction to the duke's sentence.

A quest for theatrical effect must also have been behind the decision to overstep Shakespeare and have Juliette succumb to Frère Laurent's potion in front of masses assembled for her wedding at the end of Act IV—this after a nuptial cortège with stage band as well as a *chœur dansé*. This episode was not in Gounod's original draft, where the act ended with Juliette administering the brew to herself. Second thoughts in the summer of 1866 evidently led to the conclusion that the opera would have to deviate from the play in order to satisfy the voracious appetite of Parisian audiences for spectacle. Gounod even found himself cast in the (for him) unusual role of defending a decision taken merely to create 'an extra effect' to Choudens.[4] Undoubtedly drawing upon the experience of *Mireille*, Gounod resigned himself before the rehearsals to make at least some major concessions to the parterre at the expense of fidelity to the model. But, ironically, that did not necessarily lead to a more successful operatic solution than the frantic shuffling and rewriting of numbers in the days after the *Mireille* première. As so often before, Gounod did not incorporate a concession to popular taste convincingly into the dramatic fabric of his opera. After the bombast of the ceremony itself, Juliette's sudden collapse only spawns the words 'Juste Dieu' and eight bars of music, an act ending that is disconcertingly abrupt, especially in view of the amount of time allotted to pure *divertissement* in this tableau.

Of course the most conspicuous sentimentalization of Shakespeare is Gounod's conclusion. As in Bellini's opera and David Garrick's version of the play that made such a deep impression upon Berlioz in 1827, Gounod's Juliette awakens before Roméo dies to allow for a final duet that provides musical and dramatic recapitulation of past events. Some of the musical reprises are mechanistic, but others are handled with great subtlety and sincerity, particularly in the final bars of the work. For example, the 'avec délire' orchestral interruption of the Act IV duet, in D major on its first appearance, is recapitulated in the same key as Juliette awakens near the beginning of the final duet; it is also heard again after her suicide, but this time set in the warm glow of G flat major, a magnificent tonal change that enhances the tender pathos of Juliette's 'Va! ce moment est doux!' Gounod saves the furthest flatward movement in the entire opera for just this moment. Juliette's soft 'je t'aime' then ushers in a new tonality, E flat major, with which the opera closes. This too is referential, for E flat major is the very key of Roméo's first promise of eternal allegiance directly to Juliette in the balcony scene. There she bids Roméo to declare his love: 'Chèr Roméo! dis-moi

---

[4] In a letter of 3 Aug. 1866: 'In addition I have on stage for the appearance of the cortège, an extra wind band of eight instruments . . . it would be worth considering this: first of all it is necessary and, in addition, it is an extra effect.' (BO Gounod l.a.s. 37).

Ex. 9.3*a*. *Roméo et Juliette*, Act II, *scène*

Ex. 9.3*b*. *Roméo et Juliette*, Act V, duet

loyalement: je t'aime! | Et je te crois!', analogous to Shakespeare's 'Dost thou love me? I know thou wilt say "Ay"; | And I will take thy word' (Ex. 9.3*a*). Before the final curtain Juliette sings the same descending fourth to express her own affection (Ex. 9.3*b*): whereas in the balcony scene she seeks merely to place 'je t'aime' into Roméo's mouth, she utters it herself before death envelops them. These musical cross currents ring with dramatic truth, for in the end Juliette matches the intensity of the commitment she elicited from Roméo at the beginning. The very conclusion of the opera, a twelve-bar orchestral postlogue, is also a conflation of previous musical ideas. The first four bars are developed from the symphonic passage that depicts Juliette's temporary sleep (the salient musical motifs are a descent of a fourth that figures prominently in that orchestral interlude and a quaver motif from the fourth bar of the passage) and the remaining bars recall the quaver turn in the famous cello strain that evokes their night of intimacy at the beginning of Act IV: the suggestion is that, though, for the eyes of man, Roméo and Juliette have passed away (as Juliette appeared to do earlier in the eyes of her kinsmen), their love will transcend death.

Old Problems Rekindled

The internal history of *Roméo et Juliette* is only slightly less eventful than that of *Mireille* and *Faust*. Many of the same issues flared up: *parlé* versus recitative, Madame Miolon-Carvalho, the large internal finale. Solutions to the first two were negotiated before the première, the last smouldered through a number of revivals.

There is no doubt that at one point Gounod was prepared to defend *Roméo et Juliette* tooth and nail against the encroachment of recitatives. From a turn in Gounod's phrasing in a letter of 28 September 1866 to Choudens it appears that at that time he was pressured to write them by his publisher, whose interest lay in producing a single version exportable to all houses: 'I do not recognize [the methodical precision of the way you operate] in your delay in going to print. It seems to me that recitatives should result in a separate version as with *Faust*.' The composer summed up his preference for *parlé* by urging Choudens to proceed with engraving the first act and by maintaining that

in this act I will certainly not set to music the scene between Juliette and the nurse, which says nothing to me . . . In addition, I do not see a need to transform the scene between the young people before Queen Mab into recitative. Let us not strain the musical attention of the public with filler sounds . . . give it instead resting points and breaks, except when pathetic accent would be enhanced.[5]

Presumably on the basis of this letter, Gounod's biographers Prod'homme and Dandelot maintained that *Roméo et Juliette* was given as an *opéra comique* during its first run of performances. In truth, this was another battle that Gounod lost. The extant primary sources connected to the première (including the censors' libretto, corrected proofs of the first edition, and the first edition of the vocal score itself) contain every recitative composed for the opera—including the dialogue between Juliette and her nurse and the exchange before the Queen Mab ballade.[6] The text of the *parlé* has yet to surface, if it ever will, to allow modern audiences to judge the merits of both versions. Gounod's composition draft at least shows which passages were originally intended to be spoken, since it does not contain the music for them.[7] Continuing the trend of *Mireille*, there were relatively few episodes of *parlé*. Gounod's commitment to the principle of 'resting points' and 'breaks' in the music softened further over the years: a decade later he planned only four short passages of spoken dialogue for *Cinq-Mars*, his only work written for the Opéra-Comique.

Disagreements over the character of the solo piece for Juliette were less publicized this time than they had been during the preparation period of *Mireille*. But revisions before the première show that the Carvalhos were not happy with what Gounod had composed. The celebrated *valse-ariette* 'Je veux vivre' in Act I, a reincarnation of 'Ô légère hirondelle' from *Mireille*, does not appear in any extant source for the opera until the corrected proofs for the first edition. Mistakes in the sequence of page numbers in that document suggest that it was a

---

[5] BO Gounod l.a.s. 38.

[6] The censors' libretto is at AN F[18] 738 and the corrected proofs of the first edition at BN Mus. Rés. 1976 (formerly part of the Malherbe collection). In the first edition, and all subsequent ones, some of the recitatives are individually numbered: 1bis, 2bis, 3bis, 10bis, and 20bis. The 'bis' postscript as well as the fact that they are not listed in the *catalogue des morceaux* suggest that Choudens went ahead with engraving without the recitatives and that they were added to the print only after it had been assembled.

[7] In addition to the dialogue before the Queen Mab ballade and the encounter between Juliette and her nurse, they were as follows: the banter between Roméo and his friends immediately after the ballade; the scene in which Grégorio leads Gertrude away to leave the stage bare for the first love duet; Roméo and Juliette's discovery of each other's names (from the beginning of the finale to 'sa mort est certaine' in printed scores); the words before Roméo's Act II *cavatine*; the passage between Juliette and Gertrude following immediately upon the 'Bonne nuit' chorus in the same act (this was intended for execution as *mélodrame*, with the orchestra part as it is given in all editions); the episode between Frère Laurent, Roméo, and later Juliette before 'Témoins de vos promesses' in the marriage scene; Stéphano's taunting of the Capulets before his chanson; the dialogue for Gertrude and Juliette before Capulet's entry in Act IV, and the exchange between Frère Laurent and Frère Jean in the last tableau.

relatively late accretion to it.[8] This time, rather than wait until after an unsuccessful première to shore up the work with a *valse-ariette*, the Carvalhos successfully pressed Gounod to provide a vehicle for Madame's *roulade* technique in the weeks before opening night.

These developments should be seen in the light of Juliette's *grand air* in Act IV. As first drafted, that number was much longer than the version in all available vocal scores. In these, an initial recitative is followed immediately by what was first conceived as a *cabalette* ('Amour ranime mon courage') to a much longer, multipartite piece. Gounod's draft shows a slow tripartite section after the first recitative ('Viens ô liqueur mystérieuse'), followed by a transitional passage to the *cabalette*. Although Gounod had composed, and then readily cut, an *air* with slow section and *cabalette* in *La Reine de Saba*, and had only added such a piece to *Mireille* and *Philémon et Baucis* in order to satisfy the Carvalhos, the source material for *Roméo et Juliette* shows that he still embraced the convention of the *grand air* several years after *Faust*, his last opera for which such a piece appeared in his early plans and was maintained into performance. In the end, not even the printed portion of Juliette's *air* was performed on the opening night.[9] This is not surprising, since it makes similar demands upon the voice as the 'Air de la Crau' in *Mireille*: it includes an extended section of dramatic recitative inspired by a vision (this time of Tybalt's ghost) and the triadic sweep at the beginning of the main strain harks back to its forebear in *Mireille* (both *airs* are marked at roughly the same tempo, 'allegro moderato' in *Mireille* and 'moderato ben risoluto' in *Roméo*). Triplet flourishes at the end of Juliette's phrases even give her piece a distinct Meyerbeerian flavour (Ex. 9.4). Gounod's tenacity verges on the incredible: even after the experience of the 'Air de la Crau', he once again wrote a piece of similar character for a role he knew was to be performed by Miolan-Carvalho. And, as before, the dramatic *air* gave way to a musically inferior *valse-ariette*.

Unfortunately, though Gounod's orchestration for Juliette's dramatic *air* is available, it is rarely given today. Yet a viable performing alternative would be to open the role to singers whose voices are not suited to the *valse-ariette* by substituting for it the Act IV *air* as the solo

---

[8] Two layers of events from different pre-publication runs are represented in the extant proof pages for Act I. Until p. 56, the sequence of music is identical to that of all printed editions until this point and includes the *valse-ariette*. Immediately after this the pagination drops back to 49 in a sequence of events from an earlier run, which skips from Gertrude's exclamation 'J'étais mariée à votre âge' to Roméo's question 'Le nom de cette belle enfant?' that appears *after* the *valse-ariette* in all editions. In other words, two sets of pages in the proofs are labelled 49–56, with the first set (bearing the *ariette*) representing a late addition.

[9] Of over a dozen reviews of the première consulted, many of which give a number-by-number description of the opera, not one mentions the piece as having been performed.

Ex. 9.4. *Roméo et Juliette*, Act IV, *air*

JULIETTE

Moderato ben risoluto

A - mour _____ ra-ni - me mon cou-

ra - ge, Et de mon cœur chas - se l'ef-

froi! _____ Hé - si - ter, c'est _____ te faire ou-

highlight of the role. Further changes from current practice are possible in this act. In the composition draft, the Act IV quartet for Juliette, Gertrude, Capulet, and Frère Laurent extends beyond Capulet's proposal of Paris as a husband to Juliette in a pair of solo stanzas ('Que l'hymne nuptiale'), to a section of dialogue in which Juliette declares outright (as in Shakespeare) that she does not intend to marry Paris and her father angrily threatens to evict her from the household. It continues with a brief concluding ensemble to allow those assembled to give vent to their reactions. Like the subsequent *air*, the quartet was conceived in conventional four-part form with an extended transition between slow section (Capulet's strophes) and *cabalette*, but appears only with its slow section in the censors' libretto and all editions. Fortunately, an orchestral autograph of most of the unpublished music for the quartet has been preserved; small lacunae in it may be readily filled from the composition draft.[10] It may be argued that *Roméo et Juliette* is already long enough without the conclusion of the quartet. But one performing possibility would be to eliminate the entire wedding tableau (a weak addition made for 'effect') as well as the *valse-ariette* and to include instead the full quartet as well as the dramatic *air* 'Amour ranime mon

[10] It is currently at the Stiftelsen Musikkulturens Främjande in Stockholm.

courage'. Juliette's role would gain greatly by this, because (for the only time in the opera) she would be brought into a situation of conflict that is developed musically—one that is, moreover, generally recognized as among the finest scenes in the play. And compelling drama would surely prevail until the end of the act, for her confrontation with conventions of society would be followed by internal struggle with almost overwhelming fear in the *grand air*. This solution seems all the more appropriate because, in the next act, Roméo's suicide receives much more extensive musical preparation than that of Juliette, including extended *parlante* over the cello strain from the Act IV duet and his voice-dominated music 'Ah! je te contemple sans crainte'. Hers is prepared only by a short passage of declamation; in fact, she has no voice-dominated, lyrical music of her own in the entire final duet. That compositional decision is explained by her fatalism throughout the opera (and play), her premonition even following her first encounter with Roméo that death lay close at hand. Her suicide is of necessity quick and musically understated, the mere enactment of an eventuality she had come to accept long before. As it is customarily performed, then, musical interest at the end of the work is weighted heavily in Roméo's favour, whereas Juliette's musical profile after the Act IV bedroom duet is decidedly lack-lustre. Yet her fortitude as the plot unwinds is no less remarkable and also deserves elaboration; it may be projected through restoration of the complete quartet and her *grand air* at the end of Act IV.

In *Roméo et Juliette* the structure of the large internal finale, rather than its position in the opera, gave rise to revisions. From the time he started sketching the opera in April 1865, Gounod complained about the formidable task of setting a succession of on-stage duels (there are no less than four) at the end of Act III. As first entered into the composition draft, the number is considerably different from that performed on opening night and, not surprisingly, the music that actually accompanies the duels was considerably reworked at later stages. For example, the 'Quelle rage' chorus with canonic underpinning that accompanies the Stéphano–Grégorio engagement is much shorter in the draft than in later sources. Perhaps only once the stage rehearsals had begun was it realized that more music was needed here. The orchestral background of the Mercutio–Tybalt duel was also first realized with counterpoint (a venerable operatic technique), and Gounod may have recast the passage into running sixteenth notes above tremolo because he used imitative polyphony for duel music just a few bars before.

Beyond his struggles with those passages, the character of the finale was turned inside out during the first rehearsals. In the draft, a noisy ensemble in which partisans of the rival families give voice to their mutual hatred ('Capulets! Montaigus!') occurs before Mercutio is wounded by Tybalt, and is restated after Roméo hurls his own challenge ('Il n'est ici d'autre lâche que toi!'). Following Tybalt's death (CAPULET: 'Reviens à toi!'), the draft continues with a C minor choral lament 'Ô jour de deuil!', the duke's sudden appearance on the scene to restore order, and his pronouncement of a sentence of exile for Roméo, which spawns the tenor's anguished 'Ô désespoir . . . mais je veux la revoir!'. A musical reprise of the lament 'Ô jour de deuil!' brings down the curtain. By the time the first edition was engraved, however, the entry and departure of the duke were accompanied by a bombastic march executed by a stage band, and both statements of the lament were eliminated. The rendition of 'Ô jour de deuil!' at the curtain was replaced by an expanded second reprise of the fast ensemble 'Capulets! Montaigus!', leading to a brief peroration in slow tempo 'Que la justice d'un Dieu vengeur sur vous s'appesentera'.[11] Following the addition of the stage-band march to the wedding tableau in the summer of 1866, the rehearsal decision also to use a stage band in the preceding act can only be described as a serious miscalculation, not to mention that it was preposterously out of place in the dramatic context. In an important letter of 1872 to Bizet concerning the revival of *Roméo et Juliette* at the Opéra-Comique, Gounod did not mention the march, but admitted that the second reprise of the 'Capulets! Montaigus!' ensemble was inappropriate. 'WITHOUT ANY HESITATION finish with "Non, je mourrai mais je veux la revoir!" The reprise of the ensemble "Capulets! Montaigus!" does not have a shade of justification: it is a reprise motivated by the sole desire of producing even more noise in the hope of creating . . . EFFECT!'[12] Surely Gounod would have privately voiced the same opinion five years before, but once more, against his better artistic judgement, he succumbed to a contrivance that had not been well prepared dramatically. The usual practice in *opéra comique* and grand opera was to bring down at least one curtain with a boisterous ensemble in fast tempo, usually the *strette* of a *concertato* finale. Although a reprise of the lament 'Ô jour de deuil!' at the curtain was apposite after the death of Tybalt and the exile of Roméo, a more artificial, but conventional, procedure took precedence at one time.

Fortunately, the situation at the end of the third act was salvaged

---

[11] The proof pages for the first edition show an intermediate stage which includes the second reprise of the 'Capulets! Montaigus!' ensemble and the peroration as well as the march music for the duke's departure, but shows no trace of the longer first statement of the march. Four pages after Capulet's 'Reviens à toi' are torn from the proof; they probably contained the first statement of the lament.

[12] Letter of 15 Oct. 1872, BN MSS n.a.f. 14346.

because the opera was deemed too long during the last rehearsals. This is not to say that all of the cut music in the work was of equal merit: a *cavatine* for Frère Laurent in the third act[13] and a fine funeral march to accompany Juliette to the Capulet tomb at the beginning of Act V were among the casualties.[14] But it is hard to imagine that Gounod was disturbed by the removal of the stage band or of the second reprise of the 'Capulets! Montaigus!' ensemble. During the first run in 1867, the act finished with Roméo's 'Mais je veux la revoir!' and no restatement of 'Ô jour de deuil!'. [15] That solution, however, was somewhat abrupt, inducing a remark from one reviewer that 'the finale is too short . . . it doesn't conclude but rather breaks off at the moment one least expects'.[16] Gounod addressed the problem at revivals. At one point during the long run of *Roméo et Juliette* at the Opéra-Comique from 1873 to 1887 (recorded in the third edition of the vocal score), Gounod restored 'Ô jour de deuil!' after the death of Tybalt but went on to conclude with a reprise of music that accompanied the previous duel between Roméo and Tybalt and a general on-stage brawl (the role of the duke having been completely excised).

Ducal authority was restored to the finale in the fourth edition, which reflects the Opéra production of 1888. He orders the families not to break the law again and the act is brought to a close by a new chorus to the words 'Ô jour de deuil!' (the text is expanded into alexandrines but significant expressions from the first 'Ô jour de deuil!' lament are kept). After Carvalho's attempt to enhance the finale with a stage band and contrived repeats of the fast 'Capulets! Montaigus!' ensemble, over the years the finale reacquired features of the groundplan that Gounod had first entered into his composition draft: at some of the Opéra-Comique performances the first 'Ô jour de deuil!' chorus was reinstated and that

[13] The *cavatine* appears in abbreviated form in the first edition; the draft is the only extant musical source to contain the entire piece, initially planned in three parts with a contrasting middle section.

[14] A copy of the first edition of the vocal score that once belonged to Bizet (Library of Congress, shelf mark ML96/G67 Case) contains the piece, though the proof pages at the Bibliothèque Nationale do not. Hopefully Gounod's orchestration will surface one day.

[15] A tabular comparison of the printed vocal scores is provided by Joël-Marie Fauquet in 'Quatre versions de Roméo et Juliette', *L'Avant scène*, 41 (1982), 66–9. It is claimed there that the first edition reflects the work as it was given at the Théâtre-Lyrique in 1867, that the second and third editions were published immediately preceding the Opéra-Comique production of 1873, and that the fourth reflects the Opéra revival of 1888. A careful survey of contemporary reviews shows that the variants between the first and second editions were all introduced as early as the opening night in 1867.

[16] Review of *Roméo et Juliette*, *Le Ménestrel*, 12 May 1867. Reviewers did not mention a stage band in Act III, whereas many of them noted its use at the end of Act IV. Moreover, the solo piano arrangement of the opera, issued at the same time as the first edition of the vocal score, does not contain the duke's march nor the second reprise of the 'Capulets! Montaigus!' ensemble (nor, for that matter, Frère Laurent's Act III *cavatine* and Juliette's Act IV *air*).

lament, set to one of the most imposing phrases that Gounod ever penned, was repeated at the curtain at the Opéra production of 1888. Now, in the year after the Opéra première of *Roméo et Juliette*, the Opéra-Comique, under the stewardship of Carvalho, gave successful performances of the three-act version of *Mireille*. In view of Gounod's repudiation of *Mireille* in this form, there was some justice in that he lived to witness the ultimate triumph of his original intent over the shallow demands of the Carvalhos in another opera.

10. *The Short* Opéras comiques

STRUCTURALLY speaking, Gounod's Le Médecin malgré lui is an unusual *opéra compique* for the period. Its distinctive shape is conditioned by fidelity to the famous three-act play of the same name by Molière, the prose of which is duplicated exactly in all spoen passages of the *opéra comique* (notwithstanding cuts to compensate for the lengthening of certain scenes by music) and is also the scaffolding for the verse of the set pieces. That play is problematic as a source for a close operatic adaptation because it consists of two separate dramatic threads that are developed in succession rather than simultaneously. The first half is occupied with the marital strife between Martine and the woodcutter Sganarelle, as well as the playing out of her ruse to have him recruited as a doctor to cure Lucinde, daughter of the wealthy Géronte. The amorous intrigue only becomes clear in the second half of the play. Lucinde is in love with Léandre and merely feigns dumbness to avoid marrying the man whom Géronte has chosen for her. Léandre, the prospective tenor lover, does not appear until the last scene of Act II and Lucinde is silent until the last act.

That Gounod and his librettists were sensitive to this problem is clear from their decision to depart from the model by supplying Léandre with a *sérénade* at the beginning of Act II—a disquisition on the sweet pain of love that does not fall naturally into the sequence of events but serves to bring on the tenor in the first half of the work. The dramatic purpose of the *sérénade*, and even the identity of the character in whose mouth it is placed, remain a mystery for most of the act, but Gounod achieves a measure of coherence by recapitulating this music in a melodrama that accompanies the reunion of Léandre with Lucinde in Act III: while Sganarelle attempts to distract Géronte by babbling on (in spoken prose) about the refinements of the medical profession, the orchestra communicates the essence of a simultaneous, and largely unheard, tête-à-tête between the two lovers. The play also presented another problem to the composer in that the end of its second act did not lend itself well to a large multisectional finale. Now the great consultation scene, in which the mock doctor tends to Lucinde's loss of speech and dazzles Géronte's household with his rudimentary Latin, might have been enlisted for this purpose, and does give rise to the largest ensemble number in the score.

But it falls in the middle, not the end, of Act II. The remaining events—
Sganarelle's further diagnosis and receipt of payment, and Léandre's
explanation of the real reason for the impediment to Lucinde's tongue—
seem not to have been strongly suggestive of a musical setting to
Gounod. His librettists added new action to close out the second act:
Sganarelle persuades Géronte that Lucinde's spirit may be improved
with a *divertissement* that has no basis in the play. Though this chorus
of mock doctors and the *fabliau* about unrequited love sung by Léandre
were concocted to fill the stage and provide a musical number at the
second act curtain, the finale to Act II is unconventional in as much as it
has no real dramatic purpose.

The two newly invented musical pieces for Léandre are the only
sentimental moments in an *opéra comique* that, following its literary
model, glosses over matters of the heart. The expression of emotion is
even depersonalized in Léandre's pieces. In the first instance Léandre
moralizes, in the second he makes his point with a parable. Moreover,
the *sérénade* is cast as a minuet in the manner of Lully, complete with
walking bass and *agréments* applied to musical repetitions (Ex. 10.1),
archaic touches that further objectify his feelings. Indeed archaicism of

Ex. 10.1. *Le Médecin malgré lui*, Act II, *sérénade*

this kind proves to be a fitting handmaiden to the comic muse in many
other parts of the work, often lending an air of mock-seriousness to the
machinations of the mock doctor himself. In Act II, for example, the
chorus of doctors is once again suggestive of Lully; Sganarelle's
bombastic entry in the earlier consultation scene looks back to the
genuine grandeur of Mozart's Haffner Symphony; and Géronte's over-
anxious enquiries in the same episode are underpinned with a facsimile
of baroque prelude style ('Mais dites-nous d'où vient ce mal qui nous
désole').

The score demonstrates a real gift for objective, farcical comedy that
extends beyond skilful manipulations of idioms from previous periods
to writing that is full of verve and sparkle throughout. The episode in
which Lucinde recovers her speech is representative of dozens of musical
delights in the work. Naturally, since she is only too loquacious at that
moment, she emits a patter song in the form of *couplets* with an
ensemble refrain. The usual strophic structure, however, is slightly
modified for comic effect: in the second stanza she unexpectedly
abandons her frantic pace of delivery, draws in her breath, and declares
in a melodramatic sweep through the interval of a twelfth that, if she
does not get her way, she will be convent-bound (Ex. 10.2). To find a
French *opéra comique* from this period that uses sophisticated harmonic

Ex. 10.2. *Le Médecin malgré lui,* Act III, *couplets et ensemble*

language is also refreshing; in this respect Gounod's work stands head and shoulders above contemporary efforts by Auber and Adam. Not only do the myriad of chromatic scales that crackle on the surface of the texture in almost every number impart a truly piquant flavour to the bustling about on stage, but the composer's impressive arsenal of witticisms also includes colouristic harmonic progressions. What better way to show that Sganarelle's world is blurred after his drinking song than to modify the final cadence of that piece by an alteration of the dominant chord with the interval of an augmented fifth (Ex. 10.3*a*)? This skewed progression emerges in other passages directly associated with the mock doctor, notably the first ensemble of the consultation scene (Ex. 10.3*b*) and the chorus of peasants who pester Sganarelle for his services in Act III (Ex. 10.3*c*).

Gounod's two other *opéras comiques*, *Philémon et Baucis* and *La Colombe*, are cast in a much more sentimental vein, and, it must be acknowledged, are not as engaging as *Le Médecin malgré lui*. In both, Barbier and Carré were left to their own wits to fill out a rather thin premiss supplied by a La Fontaine fable.

The ancient legend of the virtuous elderly couple who, of a thousand inhabitants visited by Jupiter and Mercury incognito, were the only ones to offer food and lodging to the gods had served La Fontaine in his own *Philémon et Baucis* as a vehicle to celebrate the magnificence of his friend and benefactor, the duc de Vendôme. This ulterior motive notwithstanding, La Fontaine followed closely the rendition of the story in Ovid's *Metamorphosis*. In La Fontaine's poem the rejuvenated

Ex. 10.3*a*. *Le Médecin malgré lui*, Act I, *couplets*

Ex. 10.3*b*. *Le Médecin malgré lui*, Act II, sextet

Ex. 10.3*c*. *Le Médecin malgré lui*, Act III, *scène et chœur*

Philémon and Baucis watch as the dwellings of their decadent neighbours are swept away in a cataclysmic flood unleashed by Jupiter. Their own small cabin is transformed into a temple which they are permitted to guard for the remainder of their lives. After these wondrous events, the couple beseech Jupiter not to permit one to die without the other. The god accedes, and many years later, at the moment of Baucis's last breath, she and Philémon suddenly sprout branches and leaves to continue their existence together eternally in the shadow of the temple.

To flesh out the sparse story-line for a three-act *opéra comique*, Barbier and Carré show Jupiter in a metamorphosis of his own on stage. The dignified god of Act I who, impressed by their repudiation of materialism and dedication to one another, restores youth to Philémon and Baucis, becomes a lecherous womanizer intent upon seducing the comely young Baucis by Act III. Not all contemporary critics took well to the change. Joseph d'Ortigue felt that the authors 'were mistaken in transforming Jupiter into a disreputable subject after he had been established as a virtuous figure',[1] and Paul Scudo dismissed the entire seduction scene as a debasement of La Fontaine 'worthy only of vaudeville'.[2] Scudo might well have substituted the Bouffes-Parisiens in his analogy. *Orphée aux enfers* had recently completed its phenomenally successful first run, and, as is well known, the Jupiter in that work also lustily amuses himself in a dalliance with a mortal. Another instance of the effect that Offenbach's brand of irreverence might have had on *Philémon et Baucis* was the decision to replace Ovid's and La Fontaine's Mercury, the god who usually accompanied Jupiter on terrestrial visits, with Vulcain. A limp, feisty good humour, and constant preoccupation with the extra-marital meanderings of his wife Venus, made the god of fire a better character for a light-hearted *opéra comique* on marital fidelity than the more serious Mercury. Though both works present the spectacle of Olympian gods whose outer dignity and pomp are thin camouflage for much baser behaviour, they are not similar in all respects. With gods spouting boulevard argot and romping about in a torrid bacchanale, Crémieux and Offenbach did push their mockery of the ancients a step or two further, not to mention the satirical element in *Orphée aux enfers* that is totally absent from *Philémon et Baucis*. With a conclusion in which Baucis outwits Jupiter and willingly abandons youth out of devotion to her spouse, Gounod's *opéra comique* ultimately shows its true colours as a moralizing sentimental comedy. This is altogether different from Offenbach's solution, which has Eurydice happily joining Jupiter's retinue to be forever rid of her

---

[1] Review of *Philémon et Baucis*, *Le Ménestrel*, 26 Feb. 1860.
[2] Review of *Philémon et Baucis*, *La Revue des deux mondes*, 21 (1860), 507.

husband Orphée; he, in turn, is only too glad to run off with his lover Chloé.

'It is difficult to understand the motive that induced two writers, a composer, and a director to bring to the theatre a purely descriptive subject that is, because of its very nature, totally devoid of action and passion,' was Jouvin's assessment of Gounod's work after the première, one that accurately reflects the views of many of his colleagues as well. Carvalho's idea to enlarge the work from two to three acts—with only minimal elaboration of plot—was clearly detrimental to its success. Three acts were the norm for *opéra comique* and did make for a work that would provide an evening's entertainment on its own. But it also resulted in an unusual disposition of performing forces: the two outer acts are occupied solely by the four soloists (except for the brief 'Filles d'Athor' chorus in Act I), whereas the middle act consists only of choral numbers in which the two principal characters do not even participate. The action of the second act, which shows orgiastic celebrations in Jupiter's temple, is only tangentially related to the tale of Philémon and Baucis. Carvalho may well have hoped to compensate for the relatively static plot with scenic spectacle—the middle tableau was nearly an exact reproduction of Couture's famous painting *Les Romains de la décadence* and was lavishly staged—but in the final analysis this touch of grand opera was wholly artificial in a work of fundamentally intimate scope.

Philémon et Baucis was enlarged before its first performance, not only by the implantation of another act but also by the addition of set pieces to the outer acts. As first conceived in Barbier's working papers (for the Baden summer theatre, it will be recalled), the first act contained six musical numbers, the second four; by opening night these figures had risen to eight and seven.[3] Unfortunately new events were not added to the plot to prepare these additional pieces. For example, in Act I there are no dramatic developments between the appearance of Jupiter and Vulcain (trio: 'Étrangers sur ces bords') and the scene in which Jupiter puts Philémon and Baucis to sleep (finale: 'Allons triste buveur'). In Barbier's outline this space is filled by no less than three numbers: *couplets* for Vulcain, a sentimental *romance* for Baucis in which she wistfully recalls her days of youth, and a short ensemble followed by a recounting of the fable of the town mouse and the country mouse.[4] Surely it was unwise to augment this succession of dramatically stagnant

[3] Barbier's working papers for *Philémon et Baucis* have the shelf mark Fonds Barbier, MS 37, at the Bibliothèque de l'Opéra. Barbier's first operation was to list the anticipated scenes and plot the locations for musical numbers.

[4] The fable appears in the first edition of the piano vocal score (Choudens, plate no. AC 703, last page numbered 175) but was eliminated from subsequent editions.

numbers with another set piece, yet this is precisely what was done during the rehearsal period by the addition of an *ariette* for Jupiter ('Hé quoi') that pokes fun at Vulcain.[5]

The role for Miolan-Carvalho began its existence without coloratura and predictably it was turned into one suitable for a *première chanteuse à roulades*. Baucis's two-part *grand air* ('Il a perdu ma trace') was not in Barbier's original outline and was clearly inserted into the autograph full score after it had been assembled—with no greater dramatic preparation than that for Jupiter's *ariette*. Most unusually for Gounod, *roulades* appear not only in the *cabalette* of this piece, but also in the slow movement, where, in the manner of Jeanette's famous *'Air du rossignol'* (in Massé's *Les Noces de Jeannette*), flute and voice engage in an ornate dialogue. Nor did *roulades* cease their infiltration at that point. As the score was first drafted, the final curtain was brought down after a strictly homorhythmic, syllabic ensemble; by the first edition of the piano–vocal score Baucis gave voice to her delight at being reunited with Philémon in coloratura passagework ('Ô félicité ravie').[6]

La Colombe is a marginally more animated and witty work than *Philémon et Baucis*, though, curiously, it has not been performed as often. La Fontaine's *Le Faucon* is the model for this piece about the attempt of an impoverished nobleman named Frédéric to win the heart of a wealthy countess, Clitie. In the poem Frédéric has but one companion in life, a nameless falcon who unfortunately has struck the fancy of the countess's young son. Soon after the death of his father, the lad falls sick and malevolently resists all attempts to amuse and bribe him back to good health. He declares that the falcon is the only gift which will assure his recovery. Reluctantly, the countess goes to her good-willed admirer in order to procure his prized possession, but it happens that her visit occurs on a day when his larder is bare. In desperation to provide Clitie with supper, Frédéric kills the bird. Her son soon expires anyway, the victim of his own capriciousness, but so impressed is she with Frédéric's sacrifice that her grief is soon superseded by new-found love.

In the two-act *opéra comique*, Clitie is turned into the character Sylvie, Frédéric into Horace, and the falcon into a dove. The latter transformation bespeaks an effort to sentimentalize La Fontaine's

[5] The full-score autograph of the opera, at the Stiftelsen Musikkulturens Främjande in Stockholm, shows two versions of the piece, one in which Jupiter sings it entirely alone, and another that is musically identical except for Vulcain's participation in the refrain.

[6] The ending of the finale was modified yet another time for the 1876 production and its matching vocal score (Choudens, plate no. AC 703, last page numbered 178), where the 'Ô félicité ravie' strophe is compressed into eight bars for Baucis and a reprise of the *cabalette* of the Act I duet, stands at the conclusion of the opera.

somewhat sardonic and morbid tale, as does a change in the course of the plot: Sylvie's attempt to own the dove is induced, not by the tyranny of an over-indulged brat, but out of rivalry with another Florentine lady who owns a loquacious parakeet that receives an inordinate amount of local attention. Death is even spared Horace's dove, since, in the major *coup de théâtre* manufactured for the *opéra comique* the bird served at the end is none other than the obnoxious parakeet, captured by marvellous coincidence at the moment Horace's pet is to be roasted.

Horace is a two-dimensional pining tenor throughout. Since the overture is dominated by a solo cello rendition of his Act I *romance* about the little dove, the sentimental aura is clear from the outset, and even the most humorous scene of the work takes a slightly saccharine turn: in the course of racing frantically though the house with his valet to prepare for Sylvie's visit in Act II, Horace finds time for a lament about his poverty ('Ô pauvreté funeste'). The La Fontaine poem is also embellished by the *dugazon* trouser role of Mazet, who serves as valet to Horace, and by a *basse chantante* in the part of Sylvie's majordomo, Maître Jean. They have little bearing on the action—by the second act there is little left for Maître Jean to do than to sing a light-hearted *air* on the art of cooking—but musically speaking they are the true comic figures in the piece. Particularly effective are the Act I *couplets* for Mazet added for the production at the Opéra-Comique in 1866: he gives voice to a misogynic streak in a refrain with pattering declamation above chromatic scales in the orchestra ('Ah! les femmes!'), an obvious contrast to his evocation of an isolated existence in the more sedate—and diatonic—changing section of each stanza. Both *Philémon et Baucis* and *La Colombe* will almost certainly never be revived by major companies, but as small chamber operas (*Philémon* in its two-act form) they are well suited to small professional or student productions.

11. *Early Works for the Opera*

GOUNOD's opera *Sapho* was not the first appearance of the celebrated Greek poet Sappho on the lyric stage. In the late eighteenth century Niccolò Piccini and Simone Mayr were among those who supplied operas on this subject, and his immediate predecessors included Anton Reicha and Giovanni Pacini; the latter's *Saffo* was the only work based on the story to achieve any kind of success. The skeleton for all these operas was furnished by the famous legend associated with the poet after her death. It tells of Sapho's unrequited love for the handsome Phaon, his falling in love with a rival, her long journey in his train and stop at the Isle of Leucas, where, in a final act of desperation, she hurled herself into the sea from its henceforth famous cliffs.

Little more plot was needed for a libretto that could sustain an evening's entertainment during the Empire and early Restoration. In the Empis and Cournol book for Reicha, performed without success at the Opéra in 1822, the legend is only slightly embellished by a Phaon who does eventually succumb to the amorous advances of Sapho but changes his mind by the end; it is enhanced scenically by a large nuptial tableau and an apotheosis after the suicide. To enliven the basic love triangle of the legend for the Pacini opera of 1838, Salvatore Cammarano invented high priest Alcandre, who falls in love with Saffo only to discover at a most inopportune moment that she is his daughter. In his libretto for Gounod, Emile Augier complicated the issue by another means. He added the feckless figure of Pythéas and a conspiracy led by Alcée and Phaon to provide instruments for the revenge brought upon Sapho by Glycère (the third corner in the triangle) and thereby an explanation for Phaon's ultimate rejection of the poet.[1]

---

[1] Contrary to Théophile Gautier's suggestion in his review of the opera (*La Presse*, 22 Apr. 1851), the conspiracy idea was not entirely of Augier's invention. Beyond the certifiably mythological, one of the few incidents associated with Sappho's life was her connection with the poet Alcaeus. Although she rejected him as a suitor, Sappho is believed to have been involved in an unsuccessful attempt led by him to overthrow Pittacus, the tyrant of Lesbos, and to have been banished to Sicily because of her participation. In the opera, myth is intertwined with fact as Phaon becomes the figure who enlists in Alcée's faction and is forced into exile. With the transplantation of the legendary cliffs to the Isle of Lesbos, the geographical displacement of Sappho for her suicide was conveniently eliminated. On Sappho as a figure in legend and history, see David M. Robinson, *Sappho and her Influence* (Boston, 1924), and Arthur Weigall, *Sappho of Lesbos, her Life and Times* (New York, 1932).

Whereas Italian composers in the 1830s and 1840s still occasionally worked with subjects drawn from classical antiquity, these had fallen completely out of favour at the Opéra after the 1820s. The grand opera libretto of the July monarchy took its cue from Romantic innovations by drawing its themes from late-medieval to early modern history and by providing spectacle that centred on the interaction of powerful historical contingencies with human passions. Not only was *Sapho* the first libretto for the Opéra in two decades to feature a Greek subject, but its dynamics also departed from the model of Scribe. 'M. Augier speaks well, but he speaks too much: he should provide more action,' said one critic, echoing the reaction of most to a libretto which, by then current standards, was uneventful.[2] In spite of Augier's additions to the legend, the plot of the opera focuses on a single issue to a degree that is against the nature of grand opera. In the works of Scribe, Saint-Georges, and the Delavigne brothers, the drama inevitably unfolds on several conflicting fronts, normally including political intrigue and love interest. The course of love is often determined by politics: Protestant in love with Catholic, Jew with Christian, Christian with Muslim, forced marriages to cement political alliances, nuptials forestalled by rebellion, princes cast into prison by unscrupulous usurpers. Love in grand opera almost inevitably flounders on the rocks of racial, religious, or nationalistic antagonisms. In *Sapho* neither the social class nor the beliefs of the players in the triangle are an issue in their interrelationship, and political turbulence gives way to jealousy to obstruct the course of love. So subordinate is the political aspect that Pittacus, the tyrant against whom the conspiracy is directed, never even makes an appearance to state his case and to repel, or gain the sympathy of, the listener. The conspiracy is introduced not as a pervasive element of conflict between two camps but merely to provide a vulnerable spot in the background of Phaon that can be exploited by the devious Glycère. In the second act of Halévy's *La Reine de Chypre*, Catarina is drawn through the same ordeal as Sapho when she is forced to declare to her lover Gérard that she cannot flee with him—this in order to save him from assassination (unbeknownst to him). But politics is the real moving force here, as the design of the Venetian council to wed Catarina to the King of Cyprus requires the liaison with Gérard to be terminated.

Because the amount of pertinent family or political business is so minimal, the dramatic problem is put in place far more rapidly in *Sapho* than is usually possible in the kaleidoscopic grand opera. By the ensemble of the quartet midway through the first act, the chief concerns and characteristics of the main players are already abundantly clear:

[2] P. Mercier, review of *Sapho*, *Le Théâtre*, 19 Apr. 1851.

Glycère warns that she will not be conveniently swept aside; Sapho expresses confidence that the heart of Phaon is hers; Pythéas wallows in self-pity; and Phaon, shaken by Glycère's interruption of his tête-à-tête with Sapho, falls back into the indecisive vein of his previous *romance*.[3] In contrast to Scribe's *drang nach dem Finale*, the maximum point of dramatic tension in the first act occurs at this quartet, with the remainder allotted to a static competition among poets and celebration of Sapho's victory. The hymn of praise in the finale is suitably grand, but is not infused with the dramatic clashes that are introduced in the more powerful ceremonial finales of *Le Prophète* or *Charles VI*. A Scribe libretto on the *Sapho* scenario might well have made a great deal more of Glycère's fury with a strophe of unconcealed threats parallel to Phaon's public proclamation of devotion to Sapho. Instead, Glycère sums up her reaction in a single line ('Tombe sur eux mon anathème') with ineffective music lost in the little *scène* before the finale proper. In this way, an act in which very little happens, and which has an early climax, is provided with an ending lacking discord and suspense.

The motor of many grand operas is fuelled by mistaken identity, unexpected revelation, and extraordinary coincidence. For the first time in years Opéra audiences heard a work not propelled by these devices. The playwright Ernest Legouvé once wrote that such dramatic preparation as Scribe usually provides is only explicit enough to foster a certain self-congratulatory response from the listener in retrospect:

The effective framework requires that all in the theatre be well set up and unexpected at the same time. If the audience is completely taken aback . . . then it is shocked; if an event is too well forecast, then it is bored. We should, to satisfy the audience, treat it as a confidant and as a fool, that is let a key word drop haphazardly and unnoticed in some corner of the play to enter the ears without drawing attention, and which, at the moment that the *coup de théâtre* erupts, draws an exclamation of pleasure, that ah! which means 'How true, he has already announced this!'[4]

At the end of the second act of *La Juive*, the rejection of Rachel by her Christian lover Léopold because he does not want to forsake his faith is a real surprise when it happens. But Léopold's covert disposal of the bread blessed by Rachel's father, an event at the beginning of the act that receives little musical emphasis, did serve as a subtle foreshadowing of

---

[3] The ensemble of this quartet that appears in the printed piano–vocal score (brought out by Choudens in 1860) was written for the 1858 two-act revival to replace an earlier ensemble. In the Opéra copyists' score for the work, shelf mark A537a, the new music for the quartet appears on the same paper type used for changes that can only be associated with the 1858 revival, for example a compression of events at the beginning of Act II. The original version of the quartet ensemble is still extant in A537a.

[4] Ernest Legouvé, *Eugène Scribe* (Paris, 1874), 19–20.

this drastic decision in the finale. Each event in the second act of *Sapho*, on the other hand, grows inexorably out of the preceding one. Rather than erratically changing course, the figures run steadily along the tracks set up for them in the parallel strophes of the quartet ensemble. Even Phaon's rejection of Sapho in the trio finale of Act II does not have much dramatic impact. In *La Juive* it is precisely because so much weight has been allotted to the love interest (duets in Acts I and II) that the holy bread incident does not initially impress. Phaon and Sapho never join in a love duet; his love for her is not given enough emphasis, especially after his vacillations in the *romance* and quartet, for subsequent developments to be truly arresting. The trio finale does indeed contain the expression of conflicting emotions in slow movement and *stretta* that was characteristic of this kind of piece, but the symmetrical strophes are not ignited by a jarring *coup de théâtre*.

The last act was widely acclaimed by the Press as the strongest and it too departed from contemporary norms. The point of highest tension between the characters in grand opera, and often the weight of the spectacle also, is placed in the fourth and fifth acts; the most successful moments occur when the two are combined, as in the coronation scene of *Le Prophète* or the execution scene of *Vêpres*. In *Sapho* tension and spectacle are divorced and occur before the third act, a point which did not go unheeded by one reviewer who noted that 'one of the most annoying aspects of the libretto is that the accumulation of choral sound and massed effects happens in the first act, whereas the third, containing only a few bars, consists entirely of a succession of solos'.[5] Indeed, there are no confrontation pieces at all in the static final act. Pauline Viardot herself admitted that an ending on a strictly personal note, unaccompanied by the usual 'tambours et trompettes', was a considerable risk.[6] Equally noteworthy, and highly successful from the musico-dramatic point of view, was the pastoral episode immediately before Sapho's outpouring of pathos and her suicide. Here rustic *couleur locale* does more than supply the context for the drama, as in the opening of *Le Prophète*; it provides a real enhancement of tragedy with a contrasting foil of pastoral *naïveté, a device that Gounod drew upon again in Mireille* and Puccini was to use to great effect in the third act of *Tosca*. The piece is no less remarkable from a musical point of view, since *couleur locale* informs its very structure. The effect is of a written-down improvisation, with a vocal line that does not fall into regular phrases and is constructed by a stringing together of ever-changing melodic cells, save for a recapitulation of the first five measures.

[5] M. Bourges, review of *Sapho, La Revue et gazette musicale de Paris*, 20 Apr. 1851.

[6] Letter to George Sand, 22 Apr. 1851, cited partially in Thérèse Marix-Spire, 'Gounod and his First Interpreter', *Musical Quarterly*, 31 (1945), 209.

The reappearance of the ancients on the stage of the Opéra after a prolonged absence was preceded by similar ventures in the spoken theatre by François Ponsard and Emile Augier himself. But literary critics have often pointed out that Ponsard did not turn back the clock in all respects to pre-Romantic days in his benchmark play *Lucrèce* (1843). René Canat sums up the prevailing view about that work in his important study *L'Hellénisme des romantiques*:

The aim was, quite justifiably, to reduce somewhat the dignity and solemnity of the classical tragedy; to admit into the gamut of emotions and style certain familiar traits; and, without completely rejecting the old ideas, to show greater proximity in the realities of daily existence, morals, and characterization to the natural course of things and to historical reality.[7]

These observations are relevant to Gounod's first opera: Augier's book is the most complete manifestation of this neoclassicism in the sphere of the opera libretto. In its slow progress of events the plot is closer to Empire works such as *La Vestale* than anything Scribe wrote, but it also contains distinctly unclassical characters in the figures of Phaon and Pythéas.

Even by standards of weak tenor heroes in grand opera, Phaon cuts a very unsympathetic figure, as some critics of the time pointed out.[8] Tenor hero vacillation is a potent device to generate suspense in the finales of *Les Huguenots* (Act IV), *Le Prophète* (Act II), and *Vêpres* (Act IV), and, regardless of the poor reputation that their behaviour earned for them among commentators, Raoul, Jean, and Henri are, to their credit, genuinely torn between duty and instinct.[9] But when the moment of choice is upon Phaon, *devoir* and *honneur* play no role. After Sapho tells him that she must remain on Lesbos, he is still mainly concerned with self-preservation. When rejected outright by the poet, he rapidly switches allegiance to Glycère, and he caps his most dishonourable behaviour by roundly condemning Sapho before his departure in Act III ('Sois trois fois maudite'). In his wavering between two women and his reaction according to baser instincts at the fork in his destiny, Phaon strikes a note in tune with the Romantic spoken theatre.

Phaon's co-conspirator Pythéas, on the other hand, is prone to play the buffoon and this aspect of his character was even more pronounced

---

[7] René Canat, *L'Hellénisme des romantiques* (Paris, 1955), iii, 184. See also Marvin Carleson, *The French Stage in the Nineteenth Century* (Metuchen, 1972), 82–93; and W. D. Howarth, *The Sublime and the Grotesque: A Study of French Romantic Drama* (London, 1975), 334–67.

[8] See reviews by P. A. Fiorentino, *Les Grands Guignols* (Paris, 1870), 338, and Gautier, *La Presse*, 22 Apr. 1851.

[9] See, for example, William Crosten, *French Grand Opera: An Art and a Business* (New York, 1948), 47.

in the score as first drafted by Gounod. Cuts made to the opera during the rehearsal period somewhat attenuated his comic streak. For example, the theme of conspiracy, vested with the highest degree of solemnity in grand operas such as *Guillaume Tell*, *Gustave III*, and *Les Huguenots*, was given a light-hearted twist in the uncut score; during Act I Pythéas admitted frankly that he had nothing against tyrants and was drunk when he joined the conspiracy.[10] Spouting lines that resonate with the fatuity of an *opéra comique basse bouffe*, he later recklessly tried to win Glycère's esteem by boasting that he was no less than the ringleader of the plot.[11] Contemporary critics such as Pol Mercier took note of Pythéas's use of 'familiar tone' instead of 'formal language', and perceived that he was a new type of ancient, one who engaged in banter alien to characters in the works of Spontini and Reicha.[12] Here was a figure who truly (in Canat's words) 'reduced the dignity and solemnity of classical tragedy', and even in the score as performed and printed the music associated with him has a strong *buffo* flavour.

Gounod and Augier, then, departed from the beaten path; it was especially bold to do so in a first opera and of course this drew attention to the composer in the Parisian musical establishment. The reasons that *Sapho* never gained a foothold in the repertoire are clear enough: the characters do not spring to life and the course of the drama is often long-winded. This is evident not only towards the end of the first act but also in the second, particularly in two long duets (Glycère–Pythéas, Glycère–Sapho) followed by a trio (Glycère–Sapho–Phaon) where very extended declamatory passages are not balanced by ensembles that effectively project each situation. For example, triple soliloquy in the central parallel strophes of the trio does not convince because the preceding drama and music do not reach a sufficient degree of intensity adequately to prepare a long passage of static introspection. Such conventional frozen moments do not well support protagonists whose emotions run only skin deep: who can take Phaon's 'Ô douleur qui m'oppresse' seriously, with its initial poignant flat-sixth melodic inflection of the dominant, when he is so ready to abandon his lover after the ensemble ('Adieu donc, je vous rends votre foi décevante')? Contemporary critics certainly did not. The preceding duet for Glycère and Sapho also has

---

[10] The music for this passage, which occurs immediately after Alcée's ode in Act I, has been lost; the text is preserved in the first edition of the libretto.

[11] The vocal lines for this passage are in partbooks used by soloists for the first production (Bibliothèque de l'Opéra, *Sapho matériel*). Unfortunately the autograph for the three-act version of *Sapho* is currently inaccessible. The 1884 version of the opera was dismembered and portions of it are currently preserved at the Bibliothèque de l'Opéra, the Stiftelsen Musikkulturens Främjande in Stockholm, and the New York Public Library.

[12] Review of *Sapho*, *Le Ménestrel*, 20 Apr. 1851.

two sets of parallel strophes, but the length of this number does not seem warranted by the events: Sapho capitulates to her rival before the *first* set. Following this ensemble, Sapho has second thoughts about her decision, which Glycère quickly suppresses; in short, the dramatic situation that prepares the second ensemble is no different from that of the first.

But many numbers commanded attention (and still do) as the work of a very promising young composer. At least some of Gounod's contemporaries, including Berlioz, savoured his evocation of classical spirit, achieved both through stylistic archaicism, as in the Handelian Introduction and March in Act I, and the restraint and sobriety of Sapho's numbers (the first section of her Act I *ode*, her Act II *cantilène*, and her Act III *stances*) as well as the shepherd's song. The first part of the *ode* was an adaptation of 'Le Soir', a previous *mélodie* to poetry by Lamartine; a piece with origins in the drawing-room made for an unusually intimate first *air* of the title role on the Opéra stage (see Ex. 11.1). The setting is primarily syllabic and stepwise motion predominates beneath a monochromatic accompaniment of high string

Ex. 11.1. *Sapho*, Act I, ode

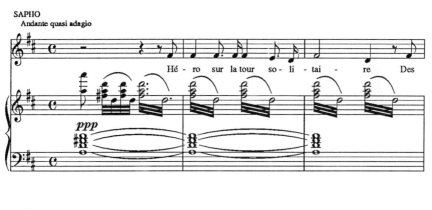

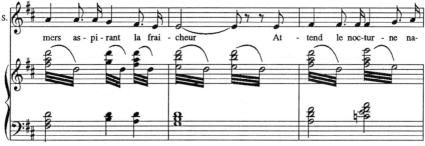

tremolo. The ambitus of each phrase is regulated according to the text, and prosody is carefully observed. After a first quatrain centred between the lower tonic and dominant, the melody shifts slightly upwards at 'Brillante à la voûte des cieux' only to sink again at 'Tout dort sur la terre embaumée'; the entire passage is none the less confined within an octave. The registral climax (prepared by a gentle expansion of ambitus to a tenth) and most lyrical phrase of the movement unfolds at the final line of text, the only explicit reference to the 'cœur de la bien aimée'. But the *cabalette*, attached to the adapted *mélodie* after the entire score had been drafted, is as heavy-handed as the slow section is refined and understated, a total capitulation to popular taste for vocal pyrotechnics.

Juxtaposition of the banal and the truly sensitive plagued even Gounod's greatest successes on the stage.

There is little that is sensitive in Gounod's next opera, *La Nonne sanglante*. Scribe's libretto is drawn froman episode in *The Monk*, a novel by Matthew Gregory Lewis. That it is founded upon a literary source is an exception to his usual procedure for five-act operas in which the plot is freely invented within a more or less accurately constructed framework of real historical events. Lewis's gothic novel was immensely popular with French readers after its first appearance in translation in 1799, and in 1835 a play by Anicet Bourgeois and J. Maillion entitled *La Nonne sanglante* was given with some success at the Théâtre de la Porte-Saint-Martin. This, in turn, became the source for Salvatore Cammarano's libretto *Maria de Rudenz*, set by Donizetti in 1837. A ghost who seeks revenge for having been murdered by her lover does wander into the play, but this figure, along with another lady who is locked up in a convent by a venomous Mother Superior, is the only element drawn directly from the novel. In short, the plot woven by Bourgeois and Mallion around the nun's regular nocturnal appearances is almost entirely new, and Cammarano managed to follow it quite closely without ever bringing in the figure of the Bleeding Nun. Scribe's libretto is closer to the novel, with the result that, though both operas are derived from the same source, they have virtually nothing in common.

Scribe built his work up from an episode where Lewis's ghoulish nun foils the elopement plans of Agnès and Rodolphe (Raymond in the novel). Rodolphe is the victim of both his own scepticism and his family's past. In the novel, his unfortunate tryst is with the ghost of a woman who was killed by a distant relative; to be relieved of her midnight visits he must perform the relatively innocuous task of transferring her bones to the family tomb. To fill out the later acts, Scribe invented a more complicated solution in which Rodolphe's own father is revealed to him as the culprit and he is faced with the prospect of patricide in order to secure release from the nun. Rodolphe secretly learns of his fate at the moment of his marriage to Agnès and, to the stupefaction of all, he cannot go through with the ceremony. A prime consideration in the remoulding of the plot, then, was the creation of a grand ceremonial finale, a wedding tableau complete with march music, ballet, over-populated stage, *coup de théâtre*, and individualized drama; Gounod's musical response was distinctly Italianate, including a slow *concertato* in compound metre capped by a twofold crescendo. Other adjustments were made to the Lewis novel to render it appropriate for the genre of grand opera. The family feud between the Ludorfs and Moldaws is a fresh element in the libretto; it creates the requisite political background but is rather improbably interwoven with the pre-existent supernatural story. In the novel, a jealous aunt obstructs the course of love, thereby inducing the initial elopement attempt, whereas Scribe made a marriage alliance between two families the obstacle. Rodolphe's refusal to conclude the marriage treaty in Act IV breaks open the old feud, and the rage of the rival Moldaw family combined with the repentance of Rodolphe's father are mechanisms through which the nun is avenged. There is even a contrived connection to real history: the pact in Act I is arranged by Peter the Hermit in the course of a campaign to organize the First Crusade. That character was probably suggested by Gounod himself, since Scribe's early drafts for Berlioz do not include Peter, and Gounod had completed a short cantata entitled *Pierre l'ermite* shortly before he began to work on *La Nonne sanglante*.[13] Even a libretto as patently sensationalistic as this one (its flavour is well communicated by the title-page of the Choudens edition, see plate 3) was not immune from the spiritual side of Gounod's temperament; Pierre is given pride of place at the outset with a large double aria that includes a hymn-like *cabalette* with a booming repetition by unison chorus of 'C'est Dieu qui nous appelle!'

Several ingredients in the libretto must have had a distinctly familiar ring to audiences of the time. A marriage alliance was, after all, formulated and shattered many times annually on the stage of the Opéra in *Les Huguenots*. A night-crier episode sends people home in this work as well as in Halévy's *Le Juif errant*, and a scene in which a youth confesses to a monk that he is tormented by worldly love opens Donizetti's *La Favorite*. The fifth act of *Le Juif errant* also features a march for the dead; the first act a recounting of a sombre legend; and the Bleeding Nun herself (without wound) might easily have waltzed out of the ballet in *Robert le diable*. It was the blend of the big historico-political opera with the occult in both *Le Juif errant* and *La Nonne sanglante* that was somewhat unusual, and not a popular success in both cases. As in *Faust*, Gounod's music for the supernatural sequences is pale: an *intermède fantastique* in Act II, for example, is comprised almost entirely of surface chromatic sighs and scales set off against a single chord.

The impressive dramatic knots in operas such as *Les Huguenots* or *La Juive* were formed and resolved by strictly human foibles. It is true that *Robert le diable* was a perennial favourite, but then this was a

[13] Scribe's working papers for the libretto are at BN MSS n.a.f. 22506. On the Berlioz work, see A. E. F. Dickinson, 'Berlioz' "Bleeding Nun" ', *Musical Times*, 102 (1961), 584–8. Berlioz drafted much of the first act in a version somewhat different from the one set by Gounod.

conspicuously apolitical libretto, one that stood astride grand opera and *opéra comique*. The main issue of whether good is destined to predominate over evil remains untouched by the antagonism of rival factions, and the supernatural operates within a less pretentious framework than that of *bona fide* historical grand opera. In presenting Rodolphe of *La Nonne sanglante* with the unenviable choice between killing his father or being eternally haunted by a ghost, Scribe gave the stock grand opera situation of filial devotion versus a compelling political force a bizarre twist that verges on the ridiculous. At the beginning of Act V there is a heartfelt *air* for Ludorf in which he expresses a desire to see his son again; at the final cadence Gounod takes the listener twice through the line 'Revoir mon fils, l'embrasser sans rougir', the second time with poignant chromatic embellishment of the cadential progression. In another context this might have been very effective, but the sudden emergence of Ludorf as the key player in the tragedy at the very end of the opera was seen by contemporary critics exactly for what it is: merely an expeditious way to tie up the plot. Whereas in the great majority of his five-act grand operas Scribe controlled all threads from the start, he was less successful at integrating a freshly invented denouement with pre-existent material. It seems unlikely that any composer could have rescued this concatenation.

12. La Reine de Saba

THE source for this Barbier-Carré libretto is the interpretation of the
biblical meeting between King Solomon and the Queen of Sheba in
Gérard de Nerval's *Les Nuits du Ramazan*, part of his compendium of
experiences and tales from the Near East entitled *Le Voyage en Orient*.
Nerval was, in the words of his friend Théophile Gautier, the 'apodal
swallow' of the group of young writers who rallied to defend Hugo's
Hernani in 1830. Like all good French Romantics of the 1820s, Nerval
read Byron and Scott and immersed himself in the fantastic stories of
Hoffman and Novalis. He also developed an interest in the mystic
writings of Emmanuel Swedenborg and the even more ethereal realms of
Orphism, Rosicrucianism, Gnosticism, and various other Middle
Eastern cults. The legend of Balkis, Queen of Sheba, which has an
extensive Arab tradition, attracted Nerval long before he actually
travelled east. In 1834 he became spellbound by the singer–actress Jenny
Colon, a passion that exerted a lasting influence on Nerval's creative life
and outlived both her marriage to another and her premature death less
than a decade later. In the euphoria of his initial infatuation, Nerval
invested inherited money in a short-lived weekly newspaper on Parisian
theatrical life, the real purpose of which was to provide a vehicle to
trumpet the accomplishments of Jenny. Convinced that the proper frame
for her talent was the Opéra, Nerval set about to write a libretto in
which she would play the illustrious Queen of Sheba. Balkis became a
double obsession: the bejewelled, radiant, and exotic woman who tested
the wisdom of Solomon with enigmatic riddles hovered seductively
between the bedposts at night, and her incarnation tormented him
during his waking hours. The success of *Robert le diable* in 1831 had
established Meyerbeer as the pre-eminent opera composer in Paris, and
Nerval would not settle for second best. He submitted a detailed
scenario and a complete act to Meyerbeer.[1] According to Gautier,
Meyerbeer was interested enough to keep it for several years, but
ultimately these plans did not bear fruit.[2] On a trip to the Near East in

[1] Nerval recounts his plans to write an opera for Jenny Colon in 'Petits châteaux de Bohème',
Poésies et souvenirs (Paris, 1974), 90–1. On the life of Nerval, see Bettina Knapp, *Gérard de
Nerval: The Mystic's Dilemma* (University, Alabama, 1980).

[2] Théophile Gautier, *Portraits et souvenirs littéraires* (Paris, 1892), 18–21. There is no trace
of this project in Giacomo Meyerbeer, *Briefwechsel und Tagebücher*, ed. Heinz Becker, ii
(Berlin, 1970).

1843, Nerval enriched his knowledge of Arab lore associated with Balkis and incorporated the story in *Le Voyage en Orient* by putting it into the mouth of a professional *raconteur* in a smoke-filled Turkish café.

Nerval's scenario and libretto, if they were ever completed, have since disappeared, but his telling of the legend described a full circle when it came back to the Opéra signed by Gounod, Barbier, and Carré. The libretto is very faithful to the essentials of Nerval's story, which led one scholar to propose that Barbier and Carré had somehow appropriated Nerval's verse from the archives of the Opéra and presented it as their own.[3] This hypothesis is hardly plausible: the two librettists often stayed close to their models and the genetic material for the libretto in Barbier's extant papers leaves no doubt that the work is theirs.

Of all the librettos that Barbier and Carré produced for Gounod, this one furnishes the most complete case study of how they fashioned an opera from a literary model. The papers show a four-stage process from earliest plans to final text. The first step was to extract an outline of the principal episodes in the story, with only a few slight changes of order. The most significant modification was a repositioning of the initial appearance of the three malcontents Amrou, Phanor, and Méthousaël. Nerval introduces them immediately before the cataclysmic eruption of the furnace, in a report to Soliman about sabotage planned by three workers dissatisfied with the regime of the king's master architect (and the opera's tenor protagonist), Adoniram. To avoid censure as a mere 'effect without cause', the most spectacular scenic effect in the opera required far more substantial preparation. Barbier's outline has Amrou, Phanor, and Méthousaël appear much earlier, in a quartet near the beginning of the opera where they expose their grievances to Adoniram.

These events were distributed into acts and scenes in the second stage, and additional changes were introduced at that point. Since grand opera rarely admitted death before the last act, Benoni, Adoniram's faithful apprentice, does not die just before the ill-fated casting, as he does in the model. In the third act the librettists evidently could not resist a dash of operatic melodrama: a protagonist at the lowest ebb of his fortunes when he confesses love to the queen. Nerval's Adoniram oversees the mending of the furnace over a period of three days, after having learnt the secret of how to do this from Tubalkaïn himself at the centre of the earth, but before his love scene with Balkis, the Queen of Sheba; when he meets her at the washing pool, Adoniram is once again in an

[3] André Lebois, 'La Reine de Saba ou amour et franc-maçonnerie', *Littératures*, 15 (1968), 18–36. Joseph-Marie Bailbé has already discounted the theory of Lebois in 'Autour de la Reine de Saba: Nerval et Gounod', in *Regards sur l'Opéra* (Paris, 1976), 113–26.

optimistic frame of mind after the brief setback of the explosion. In the act–scene outline, and the opera as performed and printed, it is only after their mutual declaration of love that Adoniram and Balkis find out that the vessel has been miraculously repaired. There are other melodramatic streaks discernible only in the opera. In a brief scene after the explosion, Adoniram searches through the smoke to check whether Balkis is safe.[4] In the final tableau he dies in her arms, and this after the orchestra has recalled the fine melody from their previous love duet 'Ah ne parlez pas, laissez-moi le doute', resplendent in A major after having been heard earlier in E flat.[5]

The skeletons of the first two stages were filled in the next step. Rather than provide their own detailed prose résumé after having extracted from the story the events that would be used in the opera, the librettists simply went through the Nerval book and jotted down verbatim a great many of its key words and phrases in order of their appearance. In the fourth stage they merely fashioned this prose condensation into verse. Because of the exigencies of rhyme, not to mention the addition of dialogue to animate the drama on stage, much of Nerval's imagery could not be retained. The number of the author's expressions that were incorporated is none the less striking, as exemplified by the opening lines of the libretto, spoken by Adoniram:

Nerval	Prose condensation
Une fête! que m'importe? le repos … je ne l'ai jamais connu, moi. Ce qui m'abat c'est l'oisiveté! Quelle œuvre faisons-nous? un temple d'orfèvrerie, un palais pour l'orgueil et la volupté des joyaux qu'un tison réduirait en cendres. Ils appellent cela créer pour l'éternité …	une fête que m'importe! le repos, je ne l'ai jamais connu moi!
	Quelle œuvre faisons-nous? un temple d'or, un palais pour l'orgueil et la volupté.
	Ils appellent cela créer pour l'éternité—

Libretto

Faiblesse de la race humaine!
Quelle œuvre faisons-nous? Tâche impuissante et vaine!
Un palais pour la volupté;

[4] This passage appears only in the first edition of the vocal score (Choudens, plate no. AC 880, last page numbered 298), where the entire tableau, however, is relegated to an appendix.

[5] In the second edition of the vocal score (Choudens, plate no. AC 880, last page numbered 254) the original prolonged death scene was cut short by an apotheosis in which Adoniram is accepted into the realm of Tubalkaïn—a pale imitation of the conclusion to *Faust*. Information about appearances of *La Reine de Saba* in Germany and Belgium in the season of 1862–3 that Choudens supplies in a letter of 12 Jan. 1863 to Opéra director Emile Perrin (AN AJ[13] 502) makes clear that the second edition is a reflection of those performances.

> Un temple pour l'orgueil, digne à peine d'un homme!
> Toute grandeur absente. Et c'est là ce qu'on nomme
> Créer pour l'éternité!

As in works such as *Mireille* and *Roméo et Juliette*, this represented substantially greater adherence to a model than generally demonstrated by French librettists of the preceding generation. And, as with *Mireille*, though for different reasons, Nerval's story did not lend itself well to operatic adaptation without more changes (especially of the melodramatic sort) than Gounod and his librettists were willing to introduce. It was also a particularly problematic antecedent, in as much as the delineation of the racial origin and ideological imperatives for the marriage of Balkis and Adoniram, and the consequent unsuitability of Soliman as a mate for the queen, were difficult to illustrate on the stage, especially given the mentality of Parisian opera audiences.

Barbier and Carré did allude to the predestined nature of the liaison between master architect and the Queen of Sheba, but, though they followed its external events closely, they did not fully explain the complex background in the model. Gounod also attempted to communicate the premiss of Nerval's story through purely musical means. Both Adoniram and Balkis are descendants of the divine race of Tubalkaïn. The *cornet à pistons* and trombone figure heard at the outset of the prelude (Ex. 12.1) becomes associated throughout the opera with

Ex. 12.1. *La Reine de Saba*, Act I, prelude

the power that Adoniram derives from his origins. It is spun out in the opening *air* as Adoniram invokes the help of his forefathers, and, in turn, the tonality and melodic cut of that strain are taken up by Adoniram and his workers when they solicit the protection of Tubalkaïn before the casting. The Tubalkaïn motif itself appears in several other episodes, including the *scène* during which Adoniram reveals his distinguished origins to Balkis at the end of Act III, and the Act IV encounter with Soliman where Adoniram states in no uncertain terms that he will set the conditions for his departure ('Adoniram dicte sa loi'). When Adoniram meets Balkis for the first time in the Act I finale, her voice immediately suggests to him that they share a common back-ground ('Ô douce voix, écho d'un souvenir lointain!'), producing a melody (unrelated to the Tubalkaïn motif) that comes to signify the deep-rooted bond between them (Ex. 12.1*a*). Balkis, for her part, is attracted to Adoniram even though she does not know anything about him. In the connecting recitative before her *cavatine* in Act III, the clarinet gives a variant of the 'souvenir lointain' phrase, and the main strain of the *cavatine* itself is derived from this variant; as Balkis sings of the stranger who appears to be far greater than Soliman himself, the music expresses her intuitive realization that Adoniram is part of her

Ex. 12.2*a*. *La Reine de Saba*, Act I, finale

Ex. 12.2*b. La Reine de Saba*, Act V, *scène*

own royal past. The 'souvenir lointain' phrase is used again when the predestined union finally takes place at the end of the opera: here it appears expressively transformed as Balkis slips a ring on her dead lover's finger (Ex. 12.2*b*).

But these musical signs do not fully project the motivations of Nerval's protagonists, in large part because they are not supported by a sufficient amount of text narrative to make their significance clear and because they are thinly grafted upon a conventional number opera that readily invites assessment as a simple love triangle. The recurring material went unnoticed by reviewers on the look out for powerful musico–dramatic situations derived from the triangle; what they saw was a piece in which the jilted lover, Soliman, weak-spined as he was, seemed undeserving of his fate. Paul Smith voiced an objection frequently encountered in contemporary assessments of the opera when he wondered why 'Balkis, instead of devoting herself in spirit and heart to the Prince [Soliman], asks to see a worker, an artist employed by the king, and conceives a sudden and violent love for him, one of those passions which does not stop short of crime and dishonour to be satiated'.[6] Beyond the disconcerting affiliation between queen and artisan, many critics summed up the opera's shortcomings with the observation that none of the characters inspires real sympathy—and for this they cannot be blamed. 'What interest can there be in a libretto in which the six principal players are foolish and ridiculous if they are not cowards, villains, cheats, or repulsive,' bemoaned Johannès Weber of *Le Temps*.[7]

Adoniram was subject to particularly harsh censure as a vain and haughty individual who, even at the lowest ebb of his fortunes, cannot inspire compassion. His counterparts in other works are faced with impressive obstacles in love and politics at the outset, as the title role in

[6] Review of *La Reine de Saba*, *La Revue et gazette musicale de Paris*, 2 Mar. 1862.
[7] Review of *La Reine de Saba*, 14 Mar. 1862.

Robert le diable or the Dauphin in *Charles VI*, or are individuals of humble background, as Jean in *Le Prophète*. Adoniram, to the contrary, starts the opera from a position of strength. The curtain opens to the artist's elaboration of his credo, in an *air* which projects an almost superhuman quality by its predominantly triadic phrases set very high in the tenor voice (a vocally more challenging *sortite* than even 'Celeste Aida' or 'Esultate').[8] He proceeds confidently to reject the petition of the three workers and to express nothing short of irritation at being invited by the high priest to an audience with the king. Even the explosion of the furnace does not inspire real sympathy for the tenor. The first time he is seen after this calamity, there is no soul-searching, no humanity; instead, at the beginning of his duet with Balkis his musical characterization is all impetuosity and fire as he rebukes her for having fallen in love with Soliman ('Qu'importe ma gloire effacée'). On opening night Adoniram actually cast away the necklace given to him previously by the queen, a shocking degree of *lèse-majesté* for many reviewers, including Lucien Morel, who wrote: 'Instead of returning the necklace to the queen with respect, Adoniram throws it far away, forcing Balkis to pick it up herself a few minutes later. One has to be in Jerusalem to see a sovereign treated with such carelessness.'[9] By the end of the third act the damage to the furnace has been miraculously repaired and the stage set for the architect's complete humiliation of Soliman in the next act. Small wonder that contemporary critics were unmoved by Adoniram's death.

It was most uncharacteristic of the classic grand opera libretto for the love between tenor and soprano to encounter no obstacles to fulfilment until the death of one of the protagonists. Soliman appears so feckless *vis-à-vis* the usurper of the queen's affections that he neither engenders sympathy nor is effective as an antagonist. The real antagonists are the three rebel workers, yet even they cannot convince Soliman of Adoniram's perfidy. In this, the opera displays a disjunction of elements that departs from Scribe's practice where various sub-plots affect each other directly from the beginning. In *La Reine de Saba* Adoniram's high artistic principles become a central issue when he rejects the petition of Amrou, Phanor, and Méthousaël; but his ideology only affects his relationship with Balkis when he dies for these principles at the end of the opera. In the course of the work Adoniram is not actually confronted

---

[8] In the third and fourth Choudens editions of the work (Choudens fils, plate no. AC 880, third edn., last page numbered 254; fourth edn., last page numbered 230), which may be dated after 1888 from internal evidence, Adoniram's *air* appears at the beginning of the second act. There is no evidence to suggest that this variant, as well as other changes in these editions such as the elimination of the Balkis-Soliman duet in Act IV and large cuts in the Fonte tableau, were sanctioned by the composer.

[9] Review of *La Reine de Saba*, *Le Théâtre*, 2 Mar. 1862.

with that choice between ideology and love that would surely have been stressed by the librettist for *La Juive* and *Les Huguenots*. As the dispossessed lover in the triangle, Soliman does not harness Adoniram's commitment to his art and the ire of the three workers to win Balkis back. Yet such is the raw material for strong musical situations in nineteenth-century voice-dominated number opera. And the few events that might have proved effective on the stage are not well developed musically. There is, for example, no musically gripping confrontation between bass and tenor, despite the obvious potential for such a number in the fourth act. The sequence of events there begins well: Soliman sings of his love for Balkis in a stirring *cavatine* with many fine touches, including a natural flow between lyrical and more declaimed phrases and a descending chromatic sequence above a pedal that effectively projects the extent to which his heart has melted (at 'Soliman, ô folie' in the return). In the next number, suspicions about a nocturnal meeting between Adoniram and Balkis are planted in Soliman's mind by Amrou, Phanor, and Méthousaël. Adoniram himself soon appears. That he is escorted into the king's hall on a triumphal chariot to the strains of an extended march and celebratory chorus serves unfortunately to diffuse the dramatic potential of the situation immediately. The subsequent encounter between Adoniram and the king, in which the architect informs Soliman that he will be leaving his service, is largely declaimed, with changing figuration in the orchestra that is tapered to individual expressions but does not vividly capture the drama of the situation. When Soliman attempts to crown Adoniram, yet another solemn chorus is heard. After Adoniram finally rejects Soliman's offer, a brief ensemble brings the number to a close (Ô sacrilège audace'), but Soliman's part is barely distinct from that of the chorus in a lyrical section that seems to demand a realization where the tenor and bass voices are played off against one another.

The only number in which all three principals are brought together, the finale to Act I, is no more cogent. The beginning of the piece is mainstream grand opera as the curtain opens to reveal a large crowd that has gathered to witness the first appearance of Soliman with the Queen of Sheba; an impressive vista of Jerusalem is seen in the background. The brilliant royal procession is accompanied by a long instrumental march in the tradition of marches that accompany the appearance of the Emperor in the first act finale of *La Juive* and the entry of Jean into the Münster cathedral in the fourth act of *Le Prophete*. But, in spite of the presence of multitudes on stage, the rest of the finale is given over almost entirely to interplay between Balkis, Adoniram, and Soliman: Balkis reluctantly gives her ring to Soliman; Adoniram appears and recognizes Balkis; and, much to the surprise of Soliman, the queen asks Adoniram to assemble his workers. There is no ensemble singing for the principals and the dialogue is conducted to a succession of different textures, with recitative predominating. Neither the voices nor the orchestra have recurring thematic material. The dialogue culminates in a *jeu scénique* by which Adoniram directs the masses with a mystic hand signal. Most unusually for the first act finale of a grand opera, the occurrence that raises the most questions about the future course of events receives little musical elaboration: Soliman stands silently by, as, to acknowledge Adoniram's charismatic power, Balkis removes her necklace and places it around his neck. This action would surely have been milked musically by a Meyerbeer or a Verdi, with contrasting expressions of bewilderment, rejoicing, and amorous anticipation in parallel strophes sung by the soloists and assembled masses. In Gounod's setting it sparks only a brief ceremonial choral Hosannah above a reprise of the opening march. As so often, Gounod puts his best foot forward with effective characterizations on the local level. For example, Soliman's sudden change of disposition in the face of Adoniram's feat is underlined by a contrast of the jocular figures accompanying his expression of disbelief before the hand signal episode ('Eh! comment rassembler, répandus dans la plaine') with a rising chromatic line over the Tubalkaïn motif to evoke his subsequent panic ('De quelle puissance invisible'). But in this context intimate dialogue with continually changing textures has little impact and goes on for too long; Gounod did not make effective use of the choral forces available.

Not all of the problems in *La Reine de Saba* originated on the work table of the composer and his librettists. A large number of cuts were made to the score that Gounod brought to rehearsals. The original performing parts at the Opéra contain a *récit du songe* in Act III for Sarahil, Balkis's confidante, where she recounts a recent dream in which Tubalkaïn designates a mysterious individual as the only man worthy of the queen. The mystery is not sustained very long: at the end of the act, after the miraculous salvaging of the great bronze vessel, Sarahil interrupts Balkis's enquiry about whether Adoniram is the beneficiary of divine protection ('Est-il vrai que les Djinns vous protègent?') by exclaiming, to a restatement of the dream music, that he was the figure whom Tubalkaïn had favoured in her dream. Whereas this cut obfuscated the legendary background to the work, a removal from the previous act of an entire tableau set in Soliman's banquet hall buried the more unsympathetic aspects of the king's character. In the Nerval story and the opera's second act as first drafted, Balkis had good reason to be disenchanted with him. In the eliminated passage she reveals to Sarahil that the king confronted her with a seemingly harmless challenge during the banquet: she must not leave the palace with anything of his, or else accept his hand in marriage. Balkis expresses some anxiety in an *air*, for evil does seem to lurk in the magnificent surroundings, but this mood fades into an insubstantial *cabalette* in which she abandons herself to more optimistic thoughts. She also abandons her vigilance, for, overcome by thirst following her *roulades*, she drinks from a nearby fountain. The water is Soliman's and he promptly appears to claim his prize.[10]

One of the unusual features of the work as it was performed on opening night, and as it appears in the printed editions, is the absence of a *grand air* with slow movement and *cabalette* for the leading lady, which, right into the 1860s, had been a fixture of grand opera. The presence of such a piece in the parts shows that at first Gounod had not meant to suppress the convention. Since many reviewers concurred with Lucien Morel that 'the score of *La Reine de Saba* upsets conventions generally adopted',[11] a conventional *cabalette* with *roulades* would undoubtedly have helped Gounod's cause.

The most glaring hole left by the elimination of the entire tableau was the matter of Balkis's betrothal to the king, since it is taken up as a *fait accompli* in Acts III and IV; Gounod quickly supplied a new passage to the Act I finale, where Soliman slips a ring on to Balkis's finger.[12] She now seems to consent to the marriage without any sort of coercion. To contemporary reviewers, the queen's involvement with Adoniram and administration of a narcotic to the king in Act IV gave her the appearance of a wanton adventuress, altogether different from the original plan in which she is a wronged woman who, by the end of Act IV, deservedly triumphs over Soliman with a ruse of her own.

The second tableau of Act II, with its aborted casting of the great

---

[10] The original numbers in the first tableau of Act II were a recitative and duet for Sarahil and Balkis, a recitative and *air* for Balkis, a recitative and duet for Balkis and Soliman, and a recitative for Balkis, Soliman, and Sadoc. Only the vocal lines and bass are extant in partbooks used by Gueymard (soprano) and Belval (bass) during the rehearsals. There are a number of additional cuts elsewhere in the opera which may be fully reconstructed from singer partbooks and instrumental parts. These include the *récit du songe* for Sarahil, an entirely different finale to Act V from the one eventually performed and printed, and internal cuts within printed numbers, such as the Act III duet for Adoniram and Balkis and the Act V quartet for Adoniram and his three workers. The original finale took the form of an oath by Balkis and Adoniram's followers to wreak vengeance upon the king. This attack on royal authority, especially upon a king who had done nothing conspicuously malicious, must have disturbed the censors, or perhaps was seen as something of an overreaction by the authors themselves. Unfortunately, a *procès-verbal* for this opera does not survive at the Archives Nationales.

[11] Lucien Morel, review of *La Reine de Saba*, *Le Théâtre*, 2 Mar. 1862.

[12] The new passage consists of forty-four bars between the end of the march and the queen's exclamation of wonder at Adoniram's achievements, 'Le monde a retenti du bruit de ces merveilles.'

bronze vessel, was also cut before the first performance; to inform listeners of this calamatous event Balkis's recitative before her *cavatine* in the next act was enlarged, hardly a fitting substitute for the visual effect of a stage inundated with red hot molten metal.[13] Conflicting testimony exists about the reasons for the cut. The Opéra *Journal de la régie* records that the Minister of State Walewski was present at the rehearsal of 13 February 1862, and this is corroborated by a brief report in *La France musicale* three days later. The newspaper bulletin goes on to explain that, because the explosion of the furnace at the end of this tableau entailed an undue risk of fire, it was decided to eliminate it altogether after the rehearsal.[14] Choudens proffered another reason for the elimination of this tableau in the appendix of the first edition: he claimed that it had been dropped because of the inordinate length of the dance music that Gounod had been asked to provide. Now many reviewers did ultimately complain that the ballet was much too long. The instrumental parts show no attempts to reduce the length of the ballet during the rehearsal period, and rumour had it that the famous choreographer Petipa had vehemently responded 'Jamais on ne me coupe rien' to a suggestion from Barbier that some of the ballet be eliminated.[15] If Choudens's explanation for the removal of the 'Mer d'airain' tableau is true, it would certainly point up the prominence given to the ballet in French grand opera during this period, suggesting that, in order to reduce the total playing time of the work so that it would finish around midnight, the elimination of an entire act and spectacular scenic effect was preferred to the shortening of the ballet.[16] There may be some truth to the explanations of both Choudens and *La France musicale*, though the documents do not support anything more than speculation. The run through of the opera on 13 February finished at 1.30 a.m. Major cuts were obviously necessary. The Opéra's administration and the authors may have decided, with encouragement from Walewski, that, since there was even a slight risk of fire in the execution of the 'Mer d'airain' tableau, it should go.

The genesis of *La Reine de Saba* is instructive about the variegated

[13] In the first edition of the vocal score the 'Mer d'airain' tableau is relegated to an appendix and Balkis recalls the explosion in the passage before her *cavatine* that begins 'Ô reine! à quelle rêverie s'abandonne votre âme?' In the second edition the tableau was restored to its place in the second act.

[14] In a letter written many years later in association with a proposed production of *La Reine de Saba* at the Eden-Théâtre, Barbier supported the restoration of this tableau, suggesting that it was a minister (undoubtedly Walewski) who requested that the scene be dropped. See letter to M. Porel, 13 Nov. 1893, cited by Arthur Pougin in his review of the production of *La Reine de Saba* at the Théâtre-Populaire, *Le Ménestrel*, 2 Dec. 1900.

[15] 'Le Petit Figaro', *Le Figaro*, 23 Feb. 1862.

[16] In the second edition the ballet was reduced from twelve *entrées* to five.

pressures put on new works for the Opéra in this period. The sense left by the documentary landscape is of an unsuccessful marriage between fidelity to the progress of events in a literary source and the conventions of grand opera. There was simply not enough time in a single evening to combine a complete exposition of all the essential moments in the story with a ballet, spectacular tableau, grand ceremonial tableau, and obligatory solo numbers for soprano, tenor, and bass; in the opera each of these elements inevitably took more time in relation to the whole than the incident from the story on which it is based. Hence, some of the plot's coherence—as well as the conventional *grand air* for soprano and the spectacular tableau—were sacrificed in the rehearsal period, and the gaping holes were hastily patched up. Such radical reshaping during rehearsals was common in France (witness other Gounod examples and the operas of Meyerbeer and Verdi), where composers undoubtedly wrote too much music in the expectation that it would be trimmed during the weeks before the performance. The very length of the rehearsal period at houses such as the Théâtre-Lyrique and the Opéra, especially compared to the usual situation in Italy at mid-century, invited this working method. To be sure it enabled composers actually to see the effect of what they had written and to make pre-performance adjustments based upon this; but in cases such as *La Reine de Saba* decisions about effective operatic compression might have been more profitably made in sober moments of fashioning the libretto and the score than under pressure of production. In any case, though the changes were prejudicial to artistic success, it would be extreme to suggest that the reinstatement of some passages might by itself breath new life into Gounod's work.

13. *The Late Works*

SIR Walter Scott's historical novels were enormously popular in France during the 1820s and left a mark upon writers of various stripes. Scribe, for example, drew material for several *opéras comiques* from them; characters such as Scott's Waverly were imposing precedents for grand opera heroes caught in the winds of conflicting political forces.[1] By writing the historical novel *Cinq-Mars* in 1826, Alfred de Vigny, a figure much closer to the heart of French Romanticism than Scribe, ventured early on into the very genre with which Scott achieved fame. Vigny is better remembered today as a poet than as a novelist, but fourteen editions in the author's own lifetime bear witness to the former popularity of *Cinq-Mars*. Scott himself is said to have waxed enthusiastic about this recreation of one of the more sombre moments in *ancien-régime* political history: the unsuccessful attempt by the Marquis de Cinq-Mars to usurp the office of Cardinal Richelieu, prime minister to Louis XIII, by enlisting help from the Spanish army. Meyerbeer even considered the subject for a grand opera, one that would have been set just fifty years after *Les Huguenots* and would also have included a conspiracy.[2] With its episodes of spectacle well integrated into the plot, struggle of rival factions for power, and love interest inflected with political overtones, Vigny's novel was particularly well suited for a reworking at the Opéra.

It is a measure of how thin the line between French operatic genres could be in the second half of the nineteenth century that an adaptation of Vigny's novel eventually appeared on the stage of the Opéra-Comique. The libretto by Poirson and Gallet that Gounod set in 1877 is faithful in its broad outlines to the events in the latter part of the novel, that is after Cinq-Mars has become a favourite of the king, but with an adjustment in the role that the love of Cinq-Mars for Marie de Gonzague plays in the unfolding of the plot. One might well imagine that Scribe himself might have introduced a similar change had he set the subject as a grand opera: whereas Vigny's Cinq-Mars agrees to lead the conspiracy because he is fired by a desire to become the social equal of

---

[1] For a discussion of Scribe's adaptations of Scott, see Karin Pendle, *Eugène Scribe and French Opera of the Nineteenth Century* (Ann Arbor, 1979), 251–78.

[2] On this project, see Meyerbeer, *Briefwechsel und Tagebücher*, iii, (Berlin, 1975), 670.

Princess Marie, in Gounod's opera he takes up arms when Richelieu seeks to cut him off from his beloved by arranging a marriage for Marie to the King of Poland. Just as in *Gustave III* and *Le Prophète*, a disruption on the romantic front pushes the tenor protagonist into political action against the instigator of his unhappiness.

The problem of genre vexed some contemporary critics. 'The result is a poem which is not simple *opéra comique* without being grand opera either,' wrote the reviewer for *La Revue et gazette musicale*.[3] Moreno of *Le Ménestrel* elaborated upon this point: 'On the one hand, in effect, *Cinq-Mars* has neither the high goals nor the unremitting ambitions of grand opera; on the other, it descends only periodically to the familiar style, to the tone of *conversation musicale*, of which the ever-so-French genre of the Salle Favart is the model and incarnation.'[4] A good deal more than the character of the plot may be added to the grand opera side of the ledger. The second act includes a ballet, and spoken dialogue is limited to only four scenes in the whole work. Moreover, the role of Cinq-Mars is specifically designated for a 'premier ténor d'opéra' (that is, the *fort ténor* type) and that of Marie for a *chanteuse falcon*. Nevertheless the work could not be mistaken for unalloyed grand opera. With only four short entrées, the balletic *divertissement* was much too small by Opéra standards. *Cinq-Mars* contains no spectacular scenic coup nor an enactment of ritual, either sacred or secular, despite several obvious occasions for this, especially in the two episodes involving the king. The small role of the courtesan Marion Delorme was taken by a *première chanteuse légère*, a seemingly perfunctory nod in the direction of *opéra-comique* convention, since she is completely superfluous to the unfolding of the plot. Though the political dimension to the love interest in the work springs from the world of grand opera, it is difficult to believe that Meyerbeer or Halévy would have permitted Cinq-Mars and Marie to appear together in four intimate scenes reminiscent of *Roméo et Juliette* (duets in Acts I and IV, Cinq-Mars's *cavatine* in Act II, and the trio in Act III where they are joined, just before their marriage, by de Thou). Finally, the opera contains more light-hearted musical numbers than was customary in grand opera, including the solo pieces for Fontrailles, Marion, and the shepherd, and several of the choruses.

It is doubtful whether the hybrid nature of the work accounted for its failure as much as the dramatic flaccidity of the music. As usual with Gounod, there are many beautiful moments. The *divertissement* shows the composer's ability at pastiche of eighteenth-century style in as favourable a light as the better-known examples in *Le Médecin malgré*

[3] Paul Bernard, review of *Cinq-Mars*, *La Revue et gazette musicale de Paris*, 8 Apr. 1877.
[4] Review of *Cinq-Mars*, *Le Ménestrel*, 8 Apr. 1877.

lui; Marie's Act I *cantilène*, recalling the perfumed atmosphere of the Act IV duet in *Roméo et Juliette*, and the two *cavatines* for Cinq-Mars deserve to be heard in the concert hall. But the two *cavatines* in particular furnish examples of Gounod's musico-dramatic short-comings: Cinq-Mars sings the first to Marie in Act II upon their blissful reunion after a long absence, and the second while on death row recalling his former happiness with her but now believing that she has abandoned him. For Gounod the genre of the tenor *cavatine* seems to have transcended the boundaries of context: the music of the second *cavatine* could serve very well for the earlier scene. The Cinq-Mars of Act IV might just as well be a lovesick Roméo or Vincent and they might all readily assume Faust's place in Marguerite's garden.

The Italian publisher Lucca, who arranged the performances of *Cinq-Mars* at La Scala, once communicated his concerns about the score to Gounod.[5] Some of these had to do with differing vocal conventions between the two countries. For example, the parts of Marion and Fontrailles, with one aria each, were too large for *comprimarii* and too small for first-string stars on Italian stages. Utility roles included mainly for purposes of *divertissement* might work on French stages, he argued, but in Italy their dramatic profile would have to be enhanced. Likewise, the opera needed a larger baritone role (in response Gounod furnished a *cantabile* for de Thou in Act III).[6] Lucca also observed that in Gounod's setting of a central episode in the work, the conspiracy scene at the end of Act II, he had written not one, but two, reprises of the ensemble 'Oui le sang repandu' 'in the same key and with the same disposition of voices and orchestra'. A threefold statement of a homorhythmic ensemble at such a crucial juncture was bound to be tedious. The Italian publisher could certainly have groused about the excessive reliance upon homorhythmic ensembles throughout *Cinq-Mars*. Another case in point occurs in Act II when Marie and Cinq-Mars learn from Père Joseph that Richelieu has forbidden their marriage. Marie launches an ensemble alone and, when it is taken up again after additional dialogue, Cinq-Mars and Père Joseph join her to bring the number to a sonorous but empty conclusion (Ex. 13.1). This musical solution is aggravated by the dull rhythmic cut of melody and accompaniment, where an unconvincing

---

[5] Undated letter in the Gounod file at the Bibliothèque de la SACD.

[6] The opera was published by Léon Grus; the first French edition bears the plate no. LG 3381 with the last page numbered 287. Curiously, the Italian edition brought out by Grus (plate no. LG 3384, last page numbered 293) does not show the recitatives to replace the passages of spoken dialogue. These only appear—along with de Thou's *cantabile*, and an enlargement both of the overture and the finale to Act III—in the second French edition (LG 3381; last page numbered 317).

Ex. 13.1. *Cinq-Mars*, Act II, trio

unconvincing figure in the orchestra must bear the whole burden of supplying agitato character to the episode.

Gounod's next opera, *Polyeucte* to a Carré and Barbier libretto, also fared badly with contemporary critics and posterity. Corneille's *tragédie chrétienne* of the same name was an unpromising operatic model, with main characters altogether too highminded for a genre that had evolved to become so obviously dependent upon human weaknesses to create strong musical situations. Polyeucte and Pauline in the play unflinch-ingly embrace *devoir* over *amour*, he infused by Christian ideals to the detriment of her happiness and she, despite all, committed to a marital bond with him. Sévère, the powerful Roman envoy and Pauline's erstwhile lover, is the perfect embodiment of selflessness and magnanim-ity when he learns that he has no chance of bending Pauline's tough moral fibre with reawakened love. Better-honed musico–dramatic instincts than those of Gounod were even drawn to this unusual operatic premiss. Donizetti turned to the play forty years before, possibly at the suggestion of the tenor Adolphe Nourrit and almost certainly with the intention of writing a work that would be appropriate both for Italian stages and for an impressive début at the Opéra.[7] Unadulterated virtue, however, would not do for an Italian setting of the subject. Donizetti and his librettist Cammarano introduced into *Poliuto* that most un-Corneillian of emotions, jealousy, by presenting a protagonist who is temporarily distracted from his higher Christian mission after secretly witnessing Severo's declaration of love to Paolina. That wrinkle was dropped from *Les Martyrs*, the French version written in collaboration with Scribe, and does not figure in Gounod's adaptation either (but, of the three, *Poliuto* has proven the most successful!). Predictably, the libretto by Barbier and Carré is generally closer to the sequence of scenes in the play than Scribe's book and, as so often in their previous work for Gounod, incorporates a large number of direct borrowings from the model, including Polyeucte's well-known *stances*, large portions of an Act III duet for Polyeucte and Néarque, and a final duet for Pauline and Polyeucte. Despite Gounod's high goal in writing the opera—his wish to portray 'the unknown and irresistible powers that Christianity has spread among humanity'—critics even as late as 1878 inevitably measured his work against the less-lofty formula of grand opera: the setting is historical and involves two conflicting politico-religious parties, and even by Opéra standards the work contains an enormous number of scenic tableaux, derived from episodes mentioned but not enacted in Corneille's classical three-unity play. Stated most succinctly, like *La Reine de Saba* the work exhibits an unhappy blend of grand opera extravagance and a sincere attempt to project the spiritual essence of an unoperatic literary model. Polyeucte the man is cut from the same cloth as Adoniram; the failure of that character to excite the sympathies of Opéra audiences should have served as ample warning to steer clear of a tenor protagonist who is obsessed with his own destiny, and that of mankind in a general way, at the expense of exhibiting more vibrant

[7] On the genesis of Donizetti's *Poliuto* and *Les Martyrs*, see William Ashbrook, *Donizetti and his Operas* (New York, 1982), 131–3.

human attributes. Given the theme of religious intolerance in *Polyeucte*, an unfavourable comparison with *Les Huguenots* was obvious to many contemporary reviewers. Raoul does decide to join his co-religionaries in Act IV of that opera, but there is never any doubt that 'he is hopelessly enamoured of Valentine', noted Victor Wilder for *Le Ménestrel* after expressing genuine doubt about whether Gounod's Polyeucte is actually in love with Pauline.[8] And the critic for *La Comédie* found Pauline herself much too cold: 'We know that with her there will be no re-enactment of the duet from *Les Huguenots*, for, as much as she is in love with Sévère, she is too great a mistress over her own emotions to forget herself with him as Valentine does with Raoul.'[9]

The family resemblances notwithstanding, these observations by Gounod's contemporaries suggest something of a gap between *Polyeucte* and vintage grand opera, one readily apparent by a comparison of the work to *Les Martyrs*. The version by Donizetti and Scribe gains a great deal by its eminently operatic reformulation of Corneille's scenes and, above all, by a redefinition of the characters so that they become ensnared by internal struggle and, for all their grandeur, occasionally display wrenching emotion. The difference is most noticeable in the figure of Pauline. In the first act of *Les Martyrs* she tearfully implores her mother's spirit for strength to quell her lingering passion for Sévère even before she knows that he will return, a scene with no analogue in the versions by Corneille and Gounod. Later, in their Act III duet, Pauline actually confesses her love directly to him. In Gounod's opera she is not as forthright in his presence and can only bring herself to allude vaguely to her misdirected affections in a private prayer to Vesta in Act II (also not in the play), a musical passage more churchly than troubled. Ideological programme supersedes emotional immediacy: far more than capturing Pauline's inner anguish, the Vesta episode serves to establish a strong visual connection of the heroine to a pagan deity and thereby to set her ultimate conversion to Christianity in relief.

The first tableau in *Les Martyrs*, the setting for Pauline's invocation to her mother, is a fine example of the effective co-ordination of ritual with personal drama that characterizes some of the most successful scenes in grand opera. As she sings, Polyeucte is baptized in the catacombs below. A Christian prayer becomes audible following her final cadence and Polyeucte soon emerges with his brethren; as the Christians continue to pray in the 'finale', Pauline angrily rebukes her husband for his decision to convert. In short, the twin crux of Pauline's dilemma in the opera, her

---

[8] Review of *Polyeucte*, *Le Ménestrel*, 13 Oct. 1878.
[9] Review of *Polyeucte*, *La Comédie* 70 (no date), 4–5.

continuing love of Sévère and her distress at the course Polyeucte's beliefs have taken, are vividly presented near the beginning against a backdrop of ritual. Now Polyeucte's baptism was bound to attract Gounod as one of the capital spiritual actions implied in the play. Instead of Donizetti's off-stage rendition at the outset of the opera, Gounod moved the baptismal scene to centre stage—and away from its position in Corneille's play to the centre of the work, the end of Act II. It is a very long episode, complete with march, prayer, and ecstatic rambling from Polyeucte—ritual and nothing more. A possible outlet for truly dramatic music does momentarily present itself as Sévère emerges from the rocks to witness the event, but, oddly enough, the potential nemesis sings not a note in the whole number. Small wonder that contemporary critics down to the last man roundly condemned the scene. Another strong card of grand opera at its best was the display of raw individual emotions before large public throngs. Where Donizetti's Pauline boldly attempts to intercede on her husband's behalf in the well-populated scene where he breaks the idols, running frantically between the high priest and her father just before the *strette*, in the Gounod opera she manages only a 'Ciel! mon époux!' apart from the concluding ensemble. In both operas the assault on the idols is premeditated, but how much more effective in *Les Martyrs* to have Polyeucte suddenly appear well after the beginning of the finale to intercede on behalf of his friend and fellow Christian Néarque. In the Gounod (and the Corneille) he is motivated to action entirely by ideology; in the Donizetti his heart also directs him towards the pagan temple to save a friend.

Gounod once remarked that the failure of *Polyeucte* was 'the sorrow of his life' and in this instance his commitment to the morally edifying potential of opera cannot be questioned. Just as *La Nonne sanglante* was an abrupt volte face from the artistic direction implied in *Sapho*, so too was *Le Tribut de Zamora* erected upon a radically different premiss from *Polyeucte*. It is ironic that the last opera of a composer who, throughout his career, for better or worse, aimed to create faithful adaptations of literary antecedents was the only one since his stage début not modelled upon a pre-existent source. The plot invented by d'Ennery and Brésil does, however, have a connection to real history. The setting is Moorish Spain in the tenth century; the political backdrop to the work is a treaty between Ramiros II, king of the Christian territories of Leon, Castille, and Asturia, and the Caliph Abderrahman following the bloody battle of Zamora in 939, where both Christian defenders and the ultimately victorious Muslim attackers suffered heavy losses. There is some confusion about the historical testimony here, since medieval chroniclers report that the city reverted back to Christian rule by the time the treaty was concluded in 944, whereas the narrative in the opera suggests that Zamora remained under Arab domination for many years.[10] In the absence of any record about the conditions of the treaty, the librettists concocted a tribute of one hundred virgins payable annually by the Christians and named after the site of the Pyrrhic victory.

And so it goes in a plot about the separation of two Spanish lovers by the odious pact. Whereas destinies of characters in *Polyeucte*, as in many previous Gounod operas, unfold along predictable paths—Pauline's dream at the beginning, for example, foreshadows the course of the drama—the figures in *Le Tribut de Zamora* are rocked by bizarre and unexpected twists of fate: conveniently, the brother of the tenor protagonist's rival in love is a man whom he once saved in the heat of battle, and the revered mad woman of the Caliph's palace is none other than the mother of the female character in the tenor–soprano pair. In contradistinction to some better-known operatic heroines, she progresses from folly to reason, but the opportunity for a mad scene is none the less not lost. Most contemporary critics commented on the effectiveness of that part of the opera, which is made up largely of Hermosa's exit aria. Along with her later duet with Xaïma, it was the most favourably received number, taking full advantage of Krauss's large tessitura and powerful declamatory abilities. (Gounod's success there can only contribute to regret about the disappearance of Marguerite's mad scene in *Faust*.) The story of *Le Tribut de Zamora* has all the melodrama, violence, and dramatic contrivances of *Il trovatore* or *La forza del destino*. Within a short span of Act III, for example, the tenor Manoël risks his life by wishing death upon his rival if his fiancée is not returned, soprano Xaïma threatens to hurl herself down a well if Manoël is harmed, and Hermosa realizes that she is Xaïma's mother. Such traffic could only survive on the operatic stage when set to music infused with virility, energy, and dramatic chiaroscuro. The passage that accompanies Manoël's appearance (Ex. 13.2)—delicate violin filigree of the sort that serves so often as connecting tissue in Gounod's operas—hardly sets the tone for the events to follow. Nor is there much else in the ensuing music that is truly gripping. In sum, Gounod's style was singularly inappropriate for a libretto with far greater musico–dramatic potential (albeit crude) than most he set, especially in view of recent Italian successes with *spagnuolismo*.

[10] See C. Paquis, *Histoire de l'Espagne* (Paris, 1844), v. 426–32.

Ex. 13.2. *Le Tribut de Zamora*, Act II, trio

PART THREE

Style

14. *Melody*

'YOUNG musicians today can imagine only with difficulty what the state of music was in France at the moment of Gounod's appearance,' wrote Saint-Saëns near the turn of the century, in a fine review of the composer's career.[1] In certain quarters the downward slide of Gounod's reputation had begun to affect even his best-known compositions— Arthur Hervey noted in 1903 that 'his work is spoken of by some with the familiarity that is often the precursor of contempt'[2]—and Saint-Saëns undoubtedly set pen to paper with the intention of rehabilitating his mentor's contribution. There were many things wrong with French musical culture when Gounod's star emerged, according to Saint-Saëns: the horizon of taste for most listeners did not extend beyond opera, the Viennese classics were appreciated by only a few, Italians were overrated, and so too were French composers such as Auber and Adam. It was an era when 'a cult of melody' reigned supreme, melody where 'the motif implanted itself effortlessly in the memory [and was] easy to grasp at first hearing'; the norm among composers was first to conceive a vocal line according to purely musical or dramatic criteria and only then to think about adapting the words to it. For Saint-Saëns one of Gounod's greatest achievements was to disrupt that cult.

Saint-Saëns was disturbed in particular by an Italianization of French verse and, by extension, of French melody. Because the pattern of accentuation from line to line is constant in many Italian verse types, poetry in that language is well suited both to the unfolding of one or two rhythmic motifs across an entire melody and to the creation of melodies in which identically placed syllables in different lines of text have the same metrical position in the music. To be sure, primary prosodic accents in successive lines of French poetry also occur in fixed positions: on the sixth and twelfth syllables in the alexandrine (the twelve-syllable line) to mark two six-syllable hemistichs, on the fourth and tenth syllables in ten-syllable lines, and on the last syllable of shorter lines. The essence of French poetry, however, is a fluid placement of secondary prosodic accents from line to line, as well as a wide range in the

[1] Saint-Saëns, *Portraits et souvenirs*, p. 50.
[2] Arthur Hervey, 'Gounod and his Influence', in *French Music in the Nineteenth Century* (London, 1903), 111.

possibilities for oratorical emphasis within lines because of a relatively weak sense of tonic accent in the language. Yet many attempted to negate that very flexibility. Giacomo Meyerbeer, for example, badgered French librettists throughout his career to produce verse where the prosodic accents fell in the same place in each line of a strophe.[3] 'Because music is essentially regular in its progression, it is vital that the poetry should not be an obstacle to this,' wrote the critic Fétis in 1829.[4] As late as 1858 Castil-Blaze codified his lifelong conviction that the exact sequence of longs and shorts in the first line of a stanza should be reproduced in all subsequent lines; he dismissed most French librettos as rhymed prose.[5]

The scores of grand opera and *opéra comique* are replete with illustrations of these preoccupations. Halévy's music in Ex. 14.1 adheres carefully to the prosody of a quatrain containing three lines of eight syllables and one of ten:

> Si la rigueur et la vengeance
> Leur font haïr ta sainte loi,
> Que le pardon que la clémence
> Mon Dieu les ramène en ce jour vers toi!

The composer emphasizes the secondary accent in each eight-syllable line, that is the fourth syllable is emphasized with a down-beat. Now, as Scribe had first drafted Cardinal Brogni's *cavatine*, the second line read 'Leur font détestēr notre loi' instead of 'Leur font haïr ta sainte loi'.[6] The reason a change was made to the text in the musical setting seems clear enough: Halévy preferred to maintain the integrity of his main rhythmic motif (repeated no less than six times) rather than make an adjustment for a line with a secondary accent on the fifth rather than the fourth syllable. Furthermore, his setting has prominent durational and metrical emphasis on the first and fifth syllable in each eight-syllable line. The impulse for this seems to have been musical rather than rhetorical. There are several options in any expressive reading of this text viva voce: for example, either or both of the words 'si' and 'et' in the first line might be glossed over. In short, the potential for shaping each half-line with a slightly different rhythmic configuration is not fully realized here.

Meyerbeer's no-less-famous *air*, given in Ex. 14.2, shows that Scribe did not always adhere to the composer's directives about regular patterns of accentuation. The main secondary accent in the first and

[3] For further information on this point, see Steven Huebner, 'Italianate Duets in Meyerbeer's Grand Operas', *Journal for Musicological Research*, 8 (1989), 203–58.
[4] 'Sur la coupe des vers lyriques', *La Revue musicale*, 4 (1829), 173.
[5] Castil-Blaze, *L'Art des vers lyriques* (Paris, 1858), 60.
[6] This version is recorded in all printed versions of the libretto.

Ex. 14.1. *La Juive*, Act I, *cavatine*

second lines of the poetry falls on the fourth syllable, whereas in the third line it is on the third syllable 'Doux ruisseāu':

> O beau pays de la Touraine
> Riants jardins, verte fontaine
> Doux ruisseau qui murmure à peine
> Que sur tes bords j'aime à rêver

Ex. 14.2. *Les Huguenots*, Act II, *air*

mu - re, qui mur- mu - re à

pei - ne, que sur tes bords j'ai - me à rê -

ver, oui,_____ que sur tes

bords _____ j'aime à rê - ver!

The up-beat figure in the musical setting is only slightly modified to accommodate the new prosodic situation of the third line, with no major change in surface rhythms and a slightly awkward upward melisma on the word 'doux'; even more ungainly is the previous treatment of the word 'verte'. Meyerbeer chose to set the third line with four bars of music rather than two. Although there can be no objection to the stress on 'murmure'—it is the first time a sixth syllable is accented in the piece—the subsequent repetition of the words 'qui murmure' before the entire line has been heard betrays more of a filler function to accommodate an independent musical plan than a truly expressive purpose. Throughout the entire melody, sensitive projection of text seems secondary to vocal mellifluousness.

The kind of melodic writing seen in both of these examples does appear on occasion in the operas of Gounod. For example, there are pieces, particularly those with short lines such as the concluding section of the Faust–Méphistophélès duet ('A moi les plaisirs') or the *cabalette* of Mireille's *air* ('A toi mon âme'), where a single sharply profiled rhythmic cell is spun out many times. Sometimes that sort of approach stands adjacent to more progressive passages, as in the *cabalette* of the duet from *Polyeucte* cited in Ex. 14.4 below. But at his best moments Gounod approached melody from a different perspective from French composers of the preceding generation. There is no more better evidence of this than his attempt to abandon poetry for prose in the unfinished *opéra comique, George Dandin,* an experiment that would have been inconceivable to a Meyerbeer or a Halévy. Though the score is currently inaccessible, fortunately Gounod published a short essay that he had initially intended as an explanatory preface to the work. In it he draws a stark contrast between the effects of verse and those of prose upon melody:

Verse with its symmetry offers the musician a much simpler canvas, often even a dangerously simple one, in the sense that, once having succumbed to the rhythm that the first line of many has sparked in his spirit or ear, he becomes something of a slave to the dialogue rather than its master, and abandons himself to the purely rhythmic consequences of his first impression. . . . In effect, the infinite variety of periods in prose opens a new horizon for the musician that releases him from monotony and uniformity. [In the setting of prose to music] independence and freedom of musical shapes may be reconciled with the great laws that regulate periodic measure and the thousand nuances of prosody. In such settings, each syllable may have its own length, its exact and finely calculated weight to reflect the expression of truth and the exactitude of the language. The longs and shorts are not subjected to cruel concessions, those barbarous sacrifices before which, one has to admit, composers and singers have shown themselves to be less than scrupulous.[7]

Though Gounod did not attempt to set prose in any other work, this passage is instructive about his orientation towards verse librettos as well. Beyond a rigorous attention to prosody, the melodic style in his operas is often shaped by rhythms that are carefully moulded around the expressive nuances of the verse. Two corollaries flow from these observations in Gounod's case. His melodies are largely syllabic—the Meyerbeer phrase cited above, for example, is more melismatic than a typical first phrase by Gounod. And the surface figuration in Gounod's melodies is usually quite plain from a strictly musical point of view and not conceived for purely vocal display, again unlike the Meyerbeer excerpt.

Certainly among the worst of the 'barbarous sacrifices' that had so often crippled the expressive potential of operatic set pieces (and to which Gounod himself sometimes succumbed) were the twin evils of obsession with a single rhythmic motif and adherence to a regular succession of strongly articulated down-beats. Notwithstanding his diatribe against predictable formulae, Gounod also declared in the *George Dandin* preface that composers were subject to the 'great laws of periodic measure', by which he seems to have meant, to judge from his musical style, 'regular' four-square phrases. In short, Gounod the composer confronted the task of reconciling two fundamentally opposing impulses. He did not attempt to achieve expressive impact, a greater degree of 'truth', through phrases of varying lengths or the abandonment of stereotypical tonal cadential formulae. Rather, he wrote melodies that evolve in a fluid and unpredictable manner within regularly spaced pillars of four-square phraseology, creating music with a marked tendency to obscure metre through durational accents on weak beats.[8]

[7] Gounod, 'Préface à George Dandin', *Autobiographie*, pp. 88–90. The original reads: 'Le vers, par sa symétrie offre au musicien un canevas beaucoup plus facile, souvent même dangereusement facile, en ce sens qu'une fois entrainé par le rythme que le premier vers d'un série fait jaillir dans l'ésprit ou dans l'oreille du musicien, celui-ci devient en quelque sorte l'ésclave du dialogue, au lieu d'en rester le maître, et s'abandonne, sans plus de contrôle, aux conséquences purement rythmiques de sa première impression. . . . En effet, la variété indéfinie des périodes, en prose, ouvre devant le musicien un horizon tout neuf qui le délivre de la monotonie et de l'uniformité. Là, l'indépendance et la liberté d'allure peuvent se concilier avec l'observance des grandes lois qui régissent la mésure périodique et les milles nuances de la prosodie. Là, chaque syllabe peut avoir sa quantité, son poids exact et rigoreux dans la vérité de l'expression et la justesse du langage. Les longues et les brèves ne sont exposées à s'y fair ces concessions cruelles, ces sacrifices barbares devant lesquels, il faut bien l'avouer, les compositeurs et les chanteurs se montrent trop souvent si peu scrupuleux.'

[8] Gounod's syncopated style has already drawn the attention of Frits Noske in *French Song from Berlioz to Duparc*, trans. Rita Benton (New York, 1970), 163–6.

The essential features of Gounod's progressive style may be illustrated by a close examination of two examples with different metre and tempo (Exx. 14.3 and 14.4). It is worth considering certain textual matters before musical ones. Both are lyrical and voice-dominated settings of complete strophes. The mixture of lines of differing lengths within the same strophe is characteristic of the verse that Gounod's librettists provided (despite Meyerbeer's interdiction, such mixtures surface occasionally in set pieces written by Scribe as well). Faust's first alexandrine in Ex. 14.3 shows well certain subtleties of the French language:

> Laisse-moi, laisse-moi, contempler ton visage
> Sous la pâle clarté
> Dont l'astre de la nuit, comme dans un nuage,
> Caresse ta beauté! . . .

Prosodic accents fall on every third syllable ('Laisse-mōi, laisse-mōi, contemplēr ton visāge'). In an inexpressive, declaimed rendition such as

Ex. 14.3. *Faust*, Act III, duet

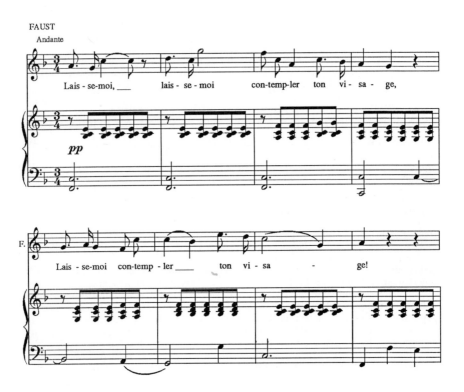

Sous la pâ - le clar-té Dont l'as - tre de la nuit___

comme dans un nu - a - ge Ca - res - se ca - resse ta beau - té

that practised in French classical theatre, the rhythmic framework supplied by these prosodic accents would be unambiguous and clearly audible. In a more expressive interpretation, of the kind especially in vogue during the nineteenth century, the prosodic accents may compete for attention with expressive emphases or oratorical accents (when of course these accents occur on syllables other than those that receive prosodic accents).[9] The oratorical accents will vary from speaker to speaker and, of course, from composer to composer. In any given line of poetry they may be applied to some syllables (usually tonic accents that are also not prosodic accents), but not to others. For example, in Faust's initial alexandrine the first syllable of 'laisse' and the pronoun 'ton' may receive oratorical accent, but the mute 'e' in 'laisse' and in 'visage' (the last is, properly speaking, not counted as a syllable) as well as the first two syllables in 'contempler' and the first syllable of 'visage' are not suited to expressive emphasis. (Were 'contempler', however, to have been followed by a monosyllabic word at the end of a poetic line, say 'Je veux la contempler tôt', two additional solutions would have been

---

[9] On this point, see Jean Cohen, *Structure du langage poétique* (Paris, 1966), 87–91. Readers seeking additional information on French versification should consult Louis-Marie Quicherat, *Traité de versification française* (Paris, 1850), or L. E. Kastner, *A History of French Versification* (Oxford, 1903).

possible: either no emphasis at all in the word or a stress on its second syllable; the word 'appartient' at the end of Ex. 14.4 is analogous and there the second syllable receives slight oratorical emphasis.)

In the first two bars of Gounod's setting there is a subtle dynamic between prosodic and oratorical accent, or, to use the composer's own terms of reference, between 'the exactitude of language' and 'the expression of truth'. The first three prosodic accents ('moi', 'moi', 'contempler') receive durational emphasis on weak beats; at the same time the option for oratorical stress on the first syllable of each occurrence of 'laisse' is realized through both metrical accent and a rhythmic figure of a dotted quaver followed by a semi-quaver. The initial syllable of 'contempler' also occurs on a down-beat, but, since it cannot be enlisted for expressive effect, it is rapidly passed over in favour of durational emphasis on the last syllable. How different would the result have been had the composer chosen to maintain the rhythmic figure associated with 'laisse' on the first beat of the third bar! As it stands, the down-beat is greatly overshadowed by durational emphasis on a weak beat; instead of alternation between prosodic and oratorical accent, the two seem to coincide on the last syllable of 'contempler'. The first line of text is immediately repeated with a different metrical interpretation. This time the last syllable of 'contempler' receives durational, metrical, and even melodic emphasis. The stress on the second syllable of 'visage' is also intensified, giving the impression that Faust sings with greater insistence the second time through. The next four-bar phrase ('Sous la plâe clarté | Dont l'astre de la nuit') offers more examples of Gounod's propensity to bestow durational rather than metrical emphasis upon prosodic text accents and there is also an expressive down-beat emphasis on the monosyllable 'dont'. Finally, in the last phrase ('Comme dans un nuage, | Caresse ta beauté') the verb 'caresse' is singled out for special attention by the composer, an expressive gesture that is also quite functional from the semantic point of view, since 'caresse' is the predicate of the last three lines of poetry.

Ex. 14.4, drawn from Pauline's encounter with her former lover in *Polyeucte*, is one of the many Gounodian jewels buried in largely unsuccessful operas. The melody adheres to a binary prototype favoured by Gounod in different kinds of solo numbers (including slow sections and *cabalettes* in multipartite *airs*, the A section of ABA *cavatines*, and music before the refrain in strophic pieces) as well as in extended solos within duets and larger ensembles. Normally the end of the first part is marked by a cadence in another key or at least by a tonicization of a scale degree other than the tonic. The second part does not contain a phrase previously heard; it is unstable at the outset or, if it plunges

Ex. 14.4. *Polyeucte*, Act II, duet

Que vous promettez - vous _____ de ces vœux su-per-

flus? _____ Ves - ta _____ con-naît mon â - - me! elle

cre - - - scen -

a sé - ché mes lar - mes! Pour - quoi ve -

- do   *f*   *dim.*

nir _____ par de per - fi - des ar - mes Trou -

cresc.

immediately back to a tonic chord, soon moves to tonicizations of scale degrees other than the tonic or dominant; the music, however, always works its way back to a complete cadence in the tonic by the end. Gounod rarely writes melodic periods with thematic or even tonal reprise in the manner of the ternary lyric prototype favoured by Italian opera composers at mid-century, an AABA' model in which the exposition of new text continues during the A' melodic reprise.[10] His sensitive orientation towards each new line of text is singularly incompatible with that sort of melodic closure on the local level, though large-scale ternary forms where melodic reprise coincides with text reprise are common in his operas. A high degree of responsiveness to subtle inflections in the poetry is more conducive to a continual unfolding of new melodic and rhythmic motifs, which Gounod usually accomplishes within four-square phrases that combine to make a larger binary form, as in Ex. 14.4. The medial point there, a rather weak articulation of the subsidiary tonic D minor, occurs at the word 'larmes' and is followed by tonal motion away from that key; F major is only restored at the conclusion, but the expected final tonic chord is replaced by a diminished seventh harmony in order to produce tonal continuity with the next section of this duet. At the beginning of the passage Gounod applies his elegant syncopated style, this time to binary metre and fast tempo: a weak-beat emphasis on the last syllable of 'passé' (adjusted on the repeat of the line) and further weak-beat accents in a threefold melodic sequence ('Que vous promettez-vous'). But, instead of following through with the rhythmic pattern of the sequence until the medial point at 'larmes', he abandons it in order to adjust to a new prosodic situation—it is the first time in the strophe that a prosodic accent falls upon the fourth syllable of a hemistich ('elle a séch̄e mes larmes')—as well as to lend oratorical emphasis to the auxiliary of the verb ('elle ā séché'); the effect is of an expressive broadening to underline Pauline's faith in the healing powers of the pagan goddess Vesta. Thereafter, since the lines are shortened to ten syllables (grouped four plus six), the rhythmic character of the melody changes once again. As he does so often, Gounod brings the melody to a close with a rhythmic reinterpretation of previously exposed text before the final tonic has been heard: on second hearing the last syllable of 'pourquoi' is much less prominent than before and the second syllable of 'appartient' is highlighted. But for all of Gounod's invective against formula, punctuation for this passage is as conventional as its overall formal design; the framework of the final cadence is a $\hat{6}$–$\hat{5}$–$\hat{7}$–$\hat{1}$ melodic figure, the same

[10] On Italian lyric form, see Scott L. Balthazar, 'Rossini and the Development of Mid-century Lyric Form', *Journal of the American Musicological Society*, 41 (1988), 102–5.

one heard at the end of Ex. 14.3 and dozens of other tunes in the œuvre of Gounod and his contemporaries.

The setting of different words to the same melody was, of course, unavoidable in the strophic forms, but in such pieces Gounod usually adjusted the musical rhythms to suit the new prosodic accents of the second strophe. In Ex. 14.5, the beginning of both strophes in Benoni's *romance* from *La Reine de Saba* are superimposed to show the small changes that Gounod introduced to accommodate a new text. He did not avoid a metrical emphasis upon the second syllable of 'une' in the second strophe (marked with an arrow in the example), but the effect of this is mitigated by a regular succession of quavers. The entire piece is a particularly good example of Gounod's tendency to avoid elaborate surface rhythms in favour of a supple text-oriented flow of relatively

Ex. 14.5. *La Reine de Saba*, Act I, *romance*

undifferentiated note values. The poetic lines are of different lengths, do not have a regular succession of prosodic accents, and are run into one another in a musical setting comprised of four-bar phrases that contain little internal articulation of separate rhythmic motifs. In the first strophe the rhyming connection between 'aurore' and 'encore' is overshadowed by a durational accent on the word 'azur'; later, by not providing a pitch for the mute 'e' of 'brulante', Gounod introduces an *enjambement* between two poetic lines. It is easy to understand how one who could write such a passage might develop an interest in setting prose to music.

An even more pronounced example of a flexible approach to operatic verse by Gounod and his librettists is furnished by Faust's *cavatine*; the first part of the binary main section is shown in example Ex. 14.6. The initial alexandrine is syntactically unusual, since the grammatical articulation at the caesura which serves as a point of division between its two hemistichs, that is after the word 'chaste', is far less important than the one that occurs after the ninth syllable, 'pure':

> Salut! demeure chaste et pure, où se devine
> La présence d'une âme innocente et divine!

As for the musical setting, the primary prosodic accents at the end of each hemistich are not marked by a down-beat. Nor does the end of the first alexandrine coincide with the end of the first four-bar phrase; instead, the last three syllables of the first alexandrine are heard only after the first crotchet rest, in accordance with the sense of the text and the syntactical organization of the verse. The rhyming connection between 'devine' and 'divine' is thereby completely obscured.

It must be admitted that this is a rare example in Gounod's œuvre; his

Ex. 14.6. *Faust*, Act III, *cavatine*

music does normally exhibit greater congruity between poetic line and musical phrase in voice-dominated, lyrical passages. More often, however, the pace at which the verse unfolds varies from line to line, again in response to the text. A fine instance of this is the setting of the following three lines at the beginning of the middle section in the same celebrated *cavatine* (Ex. 14.7):

Ô nature, c'est là que tu la fis si belle,
C'est là que cette enfant a dormi sous ton aile,
A grandi sous tes yeux.

Ex. 14.7. *Faust*, Act III, *cavatine*

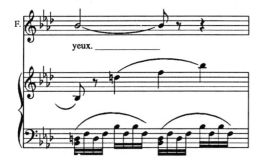

The first four syllables of the first alexandrine are set off from the remainder of the line by a rest; the entire alexandrine is spread over four bars. The second alexandrine is compressed into three bars with a solitary six-syllable line bringing the conclusion of the phrase. Whereas the first hemistich of the second line ('C'est là que cette enfant') crosses two down-beats, the remaining two hemistichs receive only one down-beat each. The oratorical effect is carefully calculated so that musical parallelisms reflect parallelisms in the poetry, which in turn seem to transcend the grid of hemistichs. The expression 'c'est là' is set in a similar way each time—hence the protracted delivery of the first hemistich in the second poetic line to mirror the first utterance of 'c'est là'—as are the two structurally analogous clauses 'a dormi sous ton aile' and 'A grandi sous tes yeux'. The subtle acceleration in the presentation of the text also creates a melodic flowering at the cadence that is one of the hallmarks of the Gounod sound.

That the first encounter of Faust with Marguerite (Ex. 14.8) is one of the most memorable, and historically significant, moments in the canon of nineteenth-century French opera is due mainly to a naturalistic unfolding of the text:

> F. Ne permettrez-vous pas, ma belle demoiselle
> Qu'on vous offre le bras pour faire le chemin?

> M. Non monsieur! je ne suis demoiselle, ni belle
> Et je n'ai pas besoin qu'on me donne la main!

Faust's first two alexandrines are handled conventionally enough: they each occupy four bars with articulation of hemistichs on the down-beat of every second bar. Marguerite's response, also a distich of alexandrines, is musically asymmetrical to this, a function of the characterization that the composer and his librettists wished to impart. The most important syntactical break in her first alexandrine occurs after only

Ex. 14.8. *Faust*, Act II, *valse et chœur*

FAUST (abordant Marguerite)

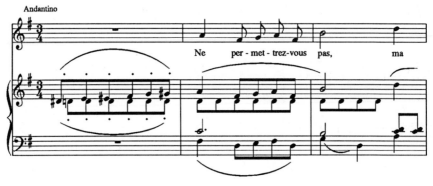

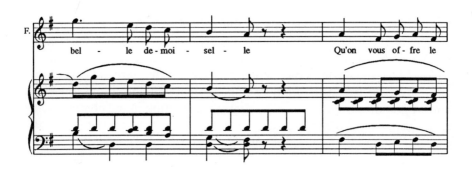

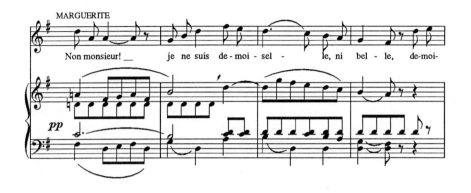

MARGUERITE

Non monsieur! __ je ne suis de - moi - sel - le, ni bel - le, de - moi-

pp

M.

sel - le ni bel - le Et je n'ai pas be - soin qu'on me don - ne la

M.

main! __

three syllables to underline her instinctive withdrawal from Faust's offer. But the orchestral accompaniment to her first alexandrine is the first four bars of Faust's phrase; at the point of metrical emphasis on the primary prosodic accent in his first hemistich ('Ne permettrez-vous pas'), Marguerite sings short syllables and small note values that move through a durational emphasis on 'suis' to later down-beat stresses on 'demoiselle' and 'belle'. In effect, an alexandrine subdivided into a three-syllable group followed by a nine-syllable one is superimposed upon music that had previously served for two regular six-syllable hemistichs. Dropping the counterpoint from Faust's previous music altogether, she goes on to repeat the last hemistich of her first line ('demoiselle ni belle') to a two-bar modulating phrase extension, as if reflecting in wonder that these words have been applied to her. Regular periodicity is abandoned when, unwilling to linger, she hastily adds that she does not need assistance; her last alexandrine is compressed into the space of three bars with simple chordal accompaniment.

These and many similar examples in Gounod's operas represent the cutting edge of developments in French vocal music during the third quarter of the nineteenth century. Another aspect of style where Gounod sought to innovate was the relationship between vocal melody and instrumental accompaniment, an issue which he also addressed in the *George Dandin* preface:[11]

Beyond the undeniable advantages pertaining to truthful diction, music associated with prose must inevitably lead the composer to use accompaniments that are more concerted, more symphonic; this would lend greater interest to these accompaniments, a much greater impression of variegated and truthful conversation than the stereotypical formulae of which dramatic music furnishes so many examples. The orchestra in the theatre is often given too secondary a role, the poverty of which is the result of the *exclusive* importance that composers give to the vocal part.[11]

The tenor of his argument is that, just as composers had all too often settled for facile solutions in letting themselves be seduced by rhythmic patterns inherent in verse, by the same token they had adopted an insouciant attitude in their choice of accompaniment. According to Gounod, the voice must be assisted by the orchestra in its mission to

---

[11] Gounod, *Autobiographie*, p. 89. The original reads: 'Outre ces avantages incontestables quant à la vérité de la diction, la musique associée à la prose doit fatalement amener le compositeur à des formes d'accompagnement plus concertantes, plus symphoniques, qui donnent aux accompagnements de l'orchestre un intérêt plus soutenu, une conversation plus variée et plus vraie que les formules stéréotypées dont les accompagnements de la musique dramatique fournissent de si nombreux exemples. L'orchestre, au théâtre, est souvent chargé d'un rôle par trop secondaire, dont la pauvreté résulte de l'importance *exclusive* que beaucoup de compositeurs donnent à la partie vocale.'

communicate 'truth'. The implication is that an intolerable disjunction would arise if mechanical, nondescript accompaniments were applied to truly expressive vocal writing.

Just as Gounod's prescriptions about the character of the vocal line as expressed in the *George Dandin* preface are illustrated in the extant operas, so the operas show seeds of the preoccupations expressed in the preface about the role of the orchestra. In considering the nature of his innovations in this area it is important to distinguish between two types of texture: *parlante* and voice-dominated. The former is a texture mentioned prominently by the nineteenth-century Italian critic Abramo Basevi in a study of Verdi's operas and arises when the voice is made to fit a melody or, at least, a phrase structure supplied by the orchestra. *Parlante* abounds in both Italian and French opera in the generation before Gounod, in set pieces rather than in connecting recitatives, so his own use of the texture is not new *per se*. Gounod, however, almost never wrote the kind of *parlante* that surfaces in Italian opera—as well as in the works of Meyerbeer, Halévy, and, especially, Auber—in which dialogue is conducted above a single motif spun out in regular phrases; in the few instances of this—the beginning of the Act IV quartet in *La Reine de Saba* or the beginning of the Act III finale in *Roméo et Juliette*—it is not extended beyond eight bars. He almost invariably colours long stretches of dialogue with a rapid turnover of motifs. But Gounod did make more extensive use than previous French composers of another kind of *parlante*, in which the orchestra emits a slow lyrical melody and the vocal line alternates declamation in speech rhythms with snatches that double the instrumental strain. This appears for the first time in Gounod's œuvre in *Faust*. In the central slow section of the garden duet ('O nuit d'amour!'), for example, Faust sings eight bars of voice-dominated music, Marguerite follows with eight voice-dominated bars of her own, and the section is brought to a close with *parlante* texture in which the orchestra leads with Marguerite's melody. The orchestra is truly an active participant in the lyrical effusion of this duet, and the building of a tonally closed section of an ensemble piece out of both voice-dominated music and this type of *parlante* was unusual in French opera at this time. Often the leading strain in Gounod's orchestra is a recollection of music heard elsewhere in the work. After Roméo first sees Juliette in the Capulet tomb, for example, a complete orchestral rendition of the twenty-bar cello strain from the Act IV *entr'acte* provides a foil for his declamation. That melody is never sung in complete form, a point of some historical interest, for, although there is a considerable amount of motivic and even thematic recall in operas such as *Le Prophète* and *La Reine de Chypre*, there is no precedent in the six major grand operas by Meyerbeer and Halévy for *parlante* above a recurring period that is never actually given to the voice. Nor is the music at the beginning of the tomb scene in *Roméo et Juliette* an isolated instance of this in Gounod's operas. Other occurrences include the setting of 'Je veux ayant sur vous les droits' in the first Cinq-Mars–de Thou duet, Frère Laurent's declamation above the *sommeil de Juliette* music in Act IV of *Roméo et Juliette*, the recollection of the Act IV 'avec délire' instrumental interlude during the Act V duet in the same opera, and the music of Marguerite's window scene; parts of the *entr'acte* to Act V in *Faust* are repeated by the orchestra in *parlante* texture as the act unfolds.

Gounod also enhanced the role of the orchestra in voice-dominated texture—and it is to this that his remarks in the *George Dandin* preface seem most pertinent. His orchestra in this texture is rarely restricted to simple chordal accompaniment or instrumental doubling of a vocal part at pitch or at the third or sixth. Instead, it usually gives an independent contrapuntal line against the melody, one that serves especially to bridge rests in the voice but also goes well beyond that. The examples of Gounod's melodies already cited show the application of this technique to varying degrees. The expressive impact of such contrapuntal elaborations is not always very profound, as they frequently sound decorative, like the result of a reflex action rather than a genuinely evocative response to the words. But at Gounod's best moments, voice and instrumental strain enter into a symbiotic relationship where each is given nearly equal importance in the lyrical whole, where the boundary between *parlante* and voice-dominated texture is, in the final analysis, very thin. The middle section of Roméo's ternary *cavatine* 'Ah! lève-toi soleil' is one such moment (Ex. 14.9). The violin takes the lead during the first eight bars, providing a sense of articulation into two four-bar phrases; only after this does the voice sound on the down-beat of a four-bar phrase for the first time ('Qui vient caresser sa joue') and emerge as truly predominant. This passage also elucidates Gounod's view in the *George Dandin* essay that truthful attention to the words must inevitably result in a 'more symphonic' orchestral accompaniment. In composing this *cavatine* he was obviously concerned with adhering to the true sense of the first distich. Hence, though 'Elle rêve! elle dénoue' forms one line of poetry, 'Elle rêve' is considerably set off from 'elle dénoue', which in turn flows naturally into its grammatical object 'Une boucle de cheveux'. The phrase structure of the orchestra is used here for oratorical effect: 'Elle rêve' sounds during the first four-bar phrase, whereas the remainder of the poetic line is heard during the second. Moreover, the rhetorical pause in the voice is thoroughly lyrical and is

Ex. 14.9. *Roméo et Juliette*, Act II, *cavatine*

not merely filled with a 'stereotypical formula', a repeated chord pattern
for example, much disparaged by Gounod in the preface. But it could
have been. The lesson that Gounod the writer and critic sought to
impart is that empty orchestral figuration could nullify expressive vocal
gestures such as irregular rhetorical caesurae.

In a review of *Mireille* the critic Albert de Lasalle declared that 'the
principles which M. Gounod espouses mean the death of melody'—and
this over a decade before the publication of the *George Dandin*
preface![12] One of the principal objections to Gounod's work, at least
during the Second Empire, was that he could not write a melody; as
surprising as this criticism may appear today, it surfaces over and over
again in contemporary reviews of the operas, from *Faust* to *Roméo et
Juliette*. But seen in the context of the kind of melodies that his
contemporaries were writing, it is not hard to understand how
Gounod's approach of letting the melody 'grow naturally out of the
declamation',[13] to cite Saint-Saëns once again, met with incomprehension in some quarters. For those who were mystified by Gounod's
melodic style, the other side of the coin was that his orchestral writing
was too overbearing, that he was essentially a symphonist lost in the
theatre. 'Gounod's error is that he has placed his effects in the
instruments rather than in the voices' was a characteristic assessment of
one critic after *Faust*.[14] Unmelodiousness and an overly active orchestra
together spelled *wagnérisme* for conservative French music critics of the
1860s and beyond. This, of course, was hardly an accurate assessment:
Gounod does not sound remotely like Wagner, as the more perspic-
acious critics of his day also quickly realized.

In the *George Dandin* preface, however, Gounod does assume the
stance of an operatic reformer, proselytizing about a new kind of opera

[12] *Le Monde illustré*, 27 Mar. 1864.
[13] Saint-Saëns, *Portraits et souvenirs*, p. 123.
[14] Léon Escudier, *La France musicale*, 27 Mar. 1859.

where preoccupation with 'truth' would supersede enslavement to formula, where composers would make brave attempts to steer clear of easy solutions. He developed these points in other essays as well; indeed the subsidiary title of the entire *Autobiographie* is *articles sur la routine en matière d'art*, and the introduction to the volume seethes with impatience about the state of music:

> *Routine* is a chronic illness, the most acute manifestation of which is *prejudice*. Among the numerous obstacles that hinder the forward march of the human spirit and slow the progress of enlightenment, one of the most deadly is certainly routine, that mental paralysis that accepts or rejects a proposition without having previously submitted it to the control of reflection. Nothing is more detrimental to the development and vigour of the mind than those ready-made formulae which education or experience casts into the spirit, and which, instead of exercising it with gymnastics of thought that alone can put it in the possession of *ideas*, lets the spirit fall little by little into a state of cadaverous rigidity which one calls routine.

In an article written a few years later which served as a preface to an annual review of Parisian theatre life, Gounod took aim at a close relative of *la routine*, *l'ésprit du système*, declaring that the authority of beauty and truth transcends particular methods, staid convention, and fashionable procedures—including the 'system' of Wagnerian leit-motifs.[15] Gounod's book on *Don Giovanni* (which contains its share of jabs in the direction of 'the system of leitmotifs') is written from that perspective; it is short on analysis of formal or dramatic 'types' and of historical context, and long on local-level description of Mozart's 'ideas' and 'truthful responses' to each shading of word or character.

These preoccupations were not foreign to some of Gounod's colleagues on the other side of the Rhine. In *Opera and Drama* Wagner has no kind words for metrical, rhyming verse—those 'five-footed monsters' masquerading as iambic verse in German poetry. Moreover, true melody can only be built from a succession of significant, original ideas; horizontal events based upon stereotypes are inexpressive and unmelodic. As Carl Dahlhaus has cogently summarized that composer's position: 'A melody is "narrow" if the truly melodic is forever breaking off, as in Italian opera, to be replaced by "unmelodic" filling-out.'[16] In short, each tone in Wagner's conception of 'endless melody' must be meaningful, as vital as all other tones. And Brahms was not the polar opposite of Wagner that nineteenth-century polemicists held him up to

---

[15] Preface to A. Mortier, *Les Soirées parisiennes de 1883* (Paris, 1884).
[16] Carl Dahlhaus, 'Issues in Composition', in *Between Romanticism and Modernism*, trans. Mary Whittall (Berkeley, 1980), 51. On Wagner's *Opera and Drama*, see also Jack M. Stein, *Richard Wagner: The Synthesis of the Arts* (Detroit, 1960), 67–79.

be. He was, however, much less verbose than Wagner, and it was left to Arnold Schoenberg later succinctly to describe Brahmsian developing variation technique as one also based upon a continual unfolding of genuine ideas without padding and empty repetitions.

It seems to have hitherto gone unnoticed that the same compositional concerns about melody were expressed in a non-Teutonic culture by a composer who had written a most non-Teutonic *Faust*. There were, of course, some profound differences: as we have seen, Gounod obviously did not ascribe to the Wagnerian tenet that truly expressive melody could only be achieved by the abandonment of quadratic phrase structure and cadential formulae. Where and how did Gounod develop the militant attitudes expressed in the *George Dandin* preface and at least partially worked out in his music? The question is worth a separate, independent study. Suffice it to say that documents presently available offer no evidence that Wagner himself was an influence. Rather, the best place to start looking seems to be Gounod's own humanistic roots, not the least important branch of which was his early experience as a *Prix de Rome* winner.

15. *Harmony*

CONTEMPORARY critics spilled much ink over the degree of melodiousness in Gounod's work, but harmony was a matter they rarely touched upon. This was undoubtedly because few reviewers had formal training in music; moreover, technical discussion about harmonic procedures could not have been of interest to the vast majority of their readers. The composer/critic Ernest Reyer did once provide a rare assessment of Gounod's harmonic language when he noted in a review of *La Nonne sanglante* that 'on each page of his score there are learned harmonies, new modulations, and cadences which depart from the beaten path'.[1] Gounod was clearly not the innovator in the realm of harmony and tonality that he was in melody writing, but, though his harmonic language appears conservative against the larger context of developments in European music, seen in the narrower perspective of French opera and *opéra comique* it does give off a faintly modern glow.

Certain techniques became an integral part of Gounod's sound. The most notorious of these is the rosalia, a stepwise ascent of a melodic idea harmonized by successive tonicizations; it is not used in *Sapho* nor in *La Nonne sanglante* but makes regular appearances in *Faust* and the remaining operas. The procedure in itself is hardly revolutionary, but in the Marguerite–Faust garden duet Gounod gave it an up-to-date sheen with a chromatically rising voice part harmonized by diminished-seventh chords that proceed with stepwise motion to each new tonal level (Ex. 15.1a). Variations of this chromatic progression appear on a large number of occasions in Gounod's work. In the Act V prison duet for Marguerite and Faust a chromatic ascent in the voice is set to diminished-seventh chords resolving to triads in second inversion ('Au milieu de vos éclats'); to prepare the *cabalette* of the Balkis–Adoniram duet in *La Reine de Saba* ('Balkis, l'avez-vous dit?') the same sort of vocal line is harmonized by parallel diminished-seventh chords above a pedal; similar instances may be found in the first Mireille–Vincent duet ('Oui adieu!'), the Act I duet for Marie and Cinq-Mars ('Aimé! Marie!'), and the Act II duet for Juliette and Roméo ('Écoute moi!'). The resemblance of these passages to one another is highlighted by the fact that they all occur in love duets. And when music virtually identical to

[1] Review of *La Nonne sanglante*, *L'Athenaeum français*, 28 Oct. 1854, 1014.

Ex. 15.1*a* surfaced in the last act of *Roméo et Juliette* (Ex. 15.1*b*)—
including even the pedal tone in the bass—Gounod fell easy prey to
critics who accused him of constantly repeating himself; Adolphe
Jullien, for one, remarked that 'there is hardly a piece in *Roméo* where
the refined ear does not detect some reminiscence of the older work [i.e.
Faust]'.[2]

Ex. 15.1*a*. *Faust*, Act III, duet

² Adolphe Jullien, *Musiciens d'aujourd'hui* (Paris, 1892), 132.

Ex. 15.1b. *Roméo et Juliette*, Act V, duet

Roméo et Juliette also contains several examples of more classical rosalias where each successive tonal level is strongly articulated by a root-position triad, not only within modulatory kinetic passages of declamation or dialogue, where one most expects to find them, but also within lyrical voice-dominated sections (a threefold sequence twice repeated in both the *cabalette* of the Act II duet and the ensemble of the marriage scene). That was more than contemporary critical opinion could tolerate; Gustave Bertrand was not the only one to object to what he called 'the lazy rosalia' patterns in that opera.[3] A more striking effect than these local-level sequences is Gounod's elevation of the rosalia to real structural significance by the repetition of much longer passages in ascending fashion. The most famous example is, of course, the chain of 'Anges purs! anges radieux!' phrases at the end of *Faust*—it is easy to forget just how truly electrifying an operatic ending this must have seemed to French audiences in 1859. Gounod modified the technique in the fourth act duet of *Roméo et Juliette* by separating each tonal level of the thrice-repeated melody 'Non! ce n'est pas le jour' with additional music—just as Wagner had done before him between each rendition of Tannhäuser's ever-rising 'Dir töne Lob'. The structural function of Gounod's rising passage in the *Roméo et Juliette* duet lies in its long-range tonal preparation for the *cabalette*: the melody progresses from B flat major to B major to C major, which, in turn, is the dominant key of the F major *cabalette* ('Il faut partir, hélas'). Instances of sequences of even longer passages in Gounod's œuvre, twofold in each case, include the *cabalette* of the Faust–Méphistophélès duet (heard first in G major, then in A flat), the ensemble of the Act V quartet in *La Reine de Saba* (heard first in E flat major, then in E—but only in the first edition), and the Pauline–Sévère duet, where Pauline sings her hymn to Vesta, 'Chaste déesse', a semitone higher than it was heard before the number. The temporal distance between statements could be very large indeed: in the first edition of *Roméo et Juliette* the ensemble of the marriage scene is a semitone higher in the fifth act than it is in the third! Though there was at least one French precedent for a semitonal rise between statements of an ensemble (in the Gérard–Lusignan duet of Halévy's *La Reine de Chypre*), as parallel-strophe ensembles without tonal closure the *cabalette* from *Faust* and the *strette* from *La Reine de Saba* were patently forward-looking. Bizet would use effectively the same procedure for Don José's resolute 'Dût-il m'en coûter la vie' in the finale to the third act of *Carmen*; moreover, the curtain of that act is brought down to an F major rendition of the Toréador song, music heard in F sharp major at the end of the opera to underline the victory of machismo in the work.

[3] Review of *Roméo et Juliette*, *Le Ménestrel*, 12 May 1867.

Among the colours that give Gounod's harmonic palette a slightly wider range than that of many French contemporaries is a penchant to emphasize the major triad built upon the mediant (III). To be sure, he prefers the dominant as the main subsidiary key in closed lyric sections; the principal internal point of articulation in most examples of his binary lyric form, for example, is a cadence in that key. But occasion is also often found to highlight the mediant as well; there is scarcely an act in the operas that does not contain many examples with different structural functions. It may, for example, be integrated into the binary form on the local level in a number of ways. To cite only passages from *Faust*: in the *cabalette* of the Faust–Méphistophélès duet the tonal movement of the two phrases that constitute the first part is I–III and I–V; the returning section of Valentin's *cavatine* contains a shift to the mediant immediately after a central cadence on the dominant; in Faust's *cavatine* the final cadential progression in the second part of the binary form is decorated with a fermata on the mediant. The mediant is also often a more extended key area in multisectional numbers, such as the waltz finale of Act II, where Méphistophélès attempts to revive Faust's spirit in B major ('Allons! à tes amours') after the latter has been rebuffed by Marguerite in G major. Marguerite's *grand air* shows the use of the mediant in an important pivotal role. The slow section is in A minor and the *cabalette* in its dominant, E major; the first part of the declamatory transition between these sections hovers about C major (III of A) and a strong cadence in that key is actually heard just before the dominant preparation for E (Ex. 15.2). The key of the *cabalette*, then, is the mediant of the key established by the cadence immediately preceding it. Following the cadence, a C major chord with an added augmented sixth is made to function as a predominant German sixth chord of the new key. The modulation up a third by a reinterpretation of old tonic as the flattened submediant of the new key is one of the thumbprints of Gounod's harmonic style. Ex. 15.3 is an illustration from a voice-dominated, four-square passage in the first act trio of *Philémon et Baucis*: the modulation from G major to B major is once again effected by the addition of a seventh to the old tonic, which then functions as a predominant augmented sixth chord. On occasion Gounod developed this technique beyond a single modulation. One noteworthy example of mediant modulations occurs in the choral prelude to *Roméo et Juliette* where a symmetrical division of the octave is produced through major thirds: the declamation starts in D minor, but when there is reference to the love of the two protagonists it moves to F sharp major ('Comme un rayon vermeil'). This new tonic is subsequently reinterpreted as the flattened submediant of B flat major, which is the flattened submediant of the final tonic, D major.

Ex. 15.2. *Faust*, Act III, *air*

Ex. 15.3. *Philémon et Baucis*, Act I, trio

In the nineteenth century, predilection for the mediant is usually
mirrored by frequent modulations to the major third below the tonic as
well, that is, to the flattened submediant. One glorious example in
Gounod's œuvre is the Marguerite–Faust garden duet, where the first
section is in F major and the slow central section ('O nuit d'amour') is in
D flat major. Following Marguerite's flower game and Faust's ensuing
sequence ('Oui crois en cette fleur') the music actually hovers between
the two key areas, beginning with a dominant preparation for D flat
major which opens into F major and finally settles back into D flat. Even
the least objective of critics must admit, however, that the technique of
third relations is sometimes thoroughly abused in Gounod's music. The
scène for Frère Laurent and Roméo preceding the *trio et quatuor* in the
third act of *Roméo et Juliette* shows the extent to which these can
govern the succession of harmonies in Gounod's open-ended declamatory passages. In the first bit of dialogue the music moves from F major to
D flat. The tenor's subsequent arioso, 'L'œil des élus', is accompanied by
hovering between the flattened submediant and I^6_4 in B flat major and
finally settles on a G flat major chord. At the textual contrast of Juliette
to Rosaline, the music then bends to bright A major, a chord that is soon
reinterpreted as the flattened submediant of C sharp major, in turn the
flattened submediant of the next key, F major. And all of this within
only thirty bars of music!

The succession of chords at the beginning of Marguerite's window
scene in *Faust* is B flat major, D major, and G flat major (Ex. 15.4)—a
twofold rise through major thirds; each tonal level is not prepared by a
cadential progression but is simply the result of chromatic movement of
the voices against pedal tones. This method of voice leading creates that
'plague of smoothness' (to cite Shaw) which to modern ears seems one of
the chief characteristics of Gounod's music. But the technique can also
be undeniably evocative. The beginning of the instrumental prelude to
Faust springs readily to mind, as does the chromatic descent against a
tonic pedal to depict the fading-star metaphor that Roméo describes at
the beginning of his *cavatine* (Ex. 15.5). Gounod produced his tonally most
adventurous music through the enharmonic reinterpretation of common
pitches, as in the supernatural Rhône scene of *Mireille* (Ex. 15.6). The
progression from the opening B major chord to a G sharp minor chord
(VI of B major) at 'quels accents' is effected by a chromatic voice leading
(F sharp–G–G sharp) against the two common tones B and D sharp. The
next chord, E flat major at 'S'exhalent', is the enharmonic dominant of
G sharp minor (as well as the mediant of B major), and the original tonic
chord is reinstated by chromatic shifting around the tone common to the

Ex. 15.4. *Faust*, Act III, duet

B major and E flat major triads, E flat (= D sharp); the next two phrases
unfold in this manner and movement between E flat major and B major
continues to be prominent. But even in this chromatic setting Gounod
does not avoid the maudlin touch of a rosalia when the subject of divine
power is alluded to in the next phrases (at 'Le ciel est bleu') and the end
of this subsection is marked by an authentic cadence in B major (as is the
entire number). In short, suave chromaticism never flows on very long in
Gounod's music before strong functional progressions intervene; small
wonder that, whereas Reyer saw 'learned harmonies and new modulations' in 1854, by the last quarter of the century Gounod's procedures
were seen as rather timid audacities by French composers and critics
who had more fully embraced developments on the other side of the
Rhine.

Ex. 15.5. *Roméo et Juliette*, Act II, *cavatine*

Ex. 15.6. *Mireille*, Act III, *scène et chœur*

quels ac-cents fu -nè - bres   S'ex - ha -lent   dans les airs. ___

Quels fan -tô - mes   er - rants ___

p dim.   *p*   dim.

16. *Form*

'[IN this work] you will not find *airs*, duets, trios, ensembles, and finales', wrote one reviewer about *La Reine de Saba* in 1862.[1] In contrast, after the Théâtre-Populaire revival of that opera in 1901, Edmond Stoullig noted that 'Gounod's score is clearly conceived in the old manner of opera—the numbers, the ritornellos, the ensembles, the *cavatines*, the *couplets* are cut in accordance with the system prevalent thirty years ago'.[2] As in the area of harmony, rapid developments in the last part of the century account for such different perspectives. But both opinions are overstated for, generally speaking, form in Gounod's operas is neither as revolutionary as claimed by one nor as pedestrian as implied by the other.

One of the birthmarks of *opéra comique* was the strophic number with refrain, and the prevalence of this type in *opéra comique* of the nineteenth century continued to be an important characteristic of the genre.[3] True to the tradition in which he worked, Gounod filled his small two- and three-act *opéras comiques* with a greater number of strophic pieces than his works for the Opéra: whereas *Le Médecin malgré lui* has five and *Philémon et Baucis* and *La Colombe* have no less than six each, no opera intended for performance with recitatives from the start has more than three strophic pieces—and this out of a much larger number of set pieces in each case than in the *opéras comiques*. As for the works whose genetic histories straddle both the realms of *parlé* and recitative, *Faust* has a relatively larger number of strophic pieces (four in the first edition but several more at other stages in its history),[4] but both *Mireille* and *Roméo et Juliette* have only one each.

The two most common strophic types in the nineteenth-century French repertoire are the *romance* and *couplets*. The latter is usually a very light piece in quick tempo, usually in the major mode and with poetic lines of eight syllables or less. It was rarely heard at the Opéra: of the major grand opera successes by Meyerbeer and Halévy, only

[1] G. Hequet, *L'Illustration*, 8 Mar. 1862.
[2] Edmond Stoullig, *Les Annales du théâtre, 1900* (Paris, 1901), 379.
[3] Karin Pendle has tabulated the frequency of independent strophic pieces in the operas and *opéras comiques* of Scribe in *Eugène Scribe*, App. A, 570–84; App. C, 587–96.
[4] See above, Ch. 7. Siébel's famous *couplets* are unusual in that there is no refrain in the number.

Robert le diable and *Le Prophète* contain examples, and *La Nonne sanglante* is the only one of Gounod's five Opéra pieces with *couplets*. The more sentimental *romance* took somewhat better hold after having been transplanted from its native habitat of *opéra comique* to opera in the first third of the nineteenth century. It was, however, adapted to the new territory. Castil-Blaze's description of the *romance*, formulated in 1821, as a piece 'written in a simple and antique style . . . [with] no ornaments, no mannerisms, and a sweet, natural bucolic or knightly melody' is applicable to the great majority of these pieces written for *opéras comiques* between 1830 and 1870 but is less generally apposite for Opéra *romances* in this period. Examples such as Raoul's 'Plus blanche que la blanche hermine' and Valentine's 'Parmi mes pleurs' in *Les Huguenots* are filled with vocal artifice. Although a piece such as Odette's 'Ah! qu'un ciel sans nuage' in *Charles VI* comes closer to the prototype described by Castil-Blaze than any of Meyerbeer's operatic *romances*, Halévy could also write a highly dramatic number containing sudden changes of texture and agitato passages such as Rachel's 'Il va venir' in *La Juive* and call it a *romance*. Gounod, on the other hand, took care not to transgress the traditional borders of the *romance* in both opera and *opéra comique*. His are always sedate pieces with limited vocal ambitus and a largely diatonic melody.[5]

There is some room for structural inventiveness within strophic forms, and composers of French opera and *opéra comique* often explored these possibilities—particularly after 1840, and Meyerbeer and Halévy more than Adam and Auber. Gounod's strophic numbers run the gamut from the strictly orthodox to the reformed, with a distinct preference for the latter. On the one side stand Sylvie's *romance* 'Que de rêves charmants' in *La Colombe* and Méphistophélès's 'Ronde du veau d'or', where the vocal line as well as accompaniment for the second strophe remain largely unchanged and (in Sylvie's piece) the same orchestral phrase is used to introduce each strophe and bring the number to a close, a classical device of structural articulation. Gounod usually modifies somewhat this most conventional of frameworks. The options that he brings into play include a mere change of accompaniment from strophe to strophe (Benoni's *romance*, Méphistophélès's *sérénade*) as well as a real change of musical substance for a portion of the second strophe (Baucis's *romance* and Jupiter's *couplets* in *Philémon et Baucis*); in Jupiter's *couplets* only the music of the refrain is repeated.

[5] The *romance* for Ben-Saïd in the third act of *Le Tribut de Zamora* ('Ô Xaïma') does not adhere to any of the characteristics of the genre as exemplified by Gounod's previous work. It is a rather dramatic piece in ternary, rather than strophic, form—in short, it is much more like a *cavatine* and should have been called that in the published piano–vocal score.

Another variation, also used by Meyerbeer in both of Corentin's strophic numbers in *Le Pardon de Ploërmel*, is the threefold sounding of the refrain, at the beginning, instead of its usual spot at the end, of each strophe as well as at the conclusion of the number (Sganarelle's and Jacqueline's *couplets* in *Le Médecin malgré lui*, Mazet's *couplets* in *La Colombe*); the result is a miniature rondo design. The greatest degree of structural variation possible before all sense of strophic construction is lost is represented in Gounod's work by Sganarelle's *air* 'Vive la médecine': both strophes are set to different music and the refrain is heard three times, in effect a conflation of the miniature rondo principle and the technique used in Jupiter's *couplets*.

The joining of ensembles to strophic forms conventionally did not go beyond homophonic choral refrains, and, like Meyerbeer and Halévy before him, Gounod sought to extend the possibilities in that direction as well. One avenue, best left for later discussion, is the incorporation of solo strophes within larger multisectional numbers. Another is the elaboration of self-contained strophic numbers with ensemble writing, exemplified in a piece such as Lucinde's *couplets* near the conclusion of *Le Médecin malgré lui*. She breathlessly sings of her determination to marry Léandre, while her father Géronte attempts in vain to interpolate his objections. In the refrain, the garrulous bystanders enter individually with the same phrase to offer advice to Géronte ('Eh vite, donnez-lui Léandre' chimes in Léandre himself last of all), and he responds to each in turn. It is the kind of ensemble writing that would have more typically appeared in a multisectional finale than in the refrain of *couplets*. The first act of *Philémon et Baucis* ends with an imaginative combination of strophic piece and ensemble. Jupiter sings two *romance*-like strophes ('Que les songes heureux'), each of which is answered by a short homophonic passage sung by Baucis, Philémon, and Vulcain. The slow descent into slumber of Philémon and Baucis is delineated by continuity between both ensemble responses: the first traces a chromatic line from tonic to dominant—they are still half-awake for Jupiter's second strophe—and the second picks up the dominant at the same pitch level for a continued chromatic descent to the lower tonic and total somnolence. Another method by means of which a strophic piece could be combined with ensemble singing is through division of the music for the changing part of each strophe between two or more singers, as in the *romance à deux voix* in Meyerbeer's *Le Prophète* where Fidès echoes snatches from Berthe's predominating line in each strophe and both combine in the refrain. The material is divided differently in the *terzetto* of *La Colombe*: one strophe is sung by Horace, the other by Sylvie, and the third voice, that of Mazet, participates only during the ensemble refrain.

A distinction between subsection and complete set piece must also be made in any consideration of ternary form in the nineteenth-century French repertoire. Gounod's preferred self-contained ternary number is the slow *cavatine*. The French *cavatine* is not exactly analogous to its mid-nineteenth-century Italian cognate *cavatina*, generally a non-ternary exit aria. In mid-century Italian examples, a *cabaletta* usually follows the *cavatina* as part of the same set piece and on occasion composers for French stages also append a *cabalette* to their own ternary *cavatines* (examples include Fidès's 'Ô toi qui m'abandonnes' in *Le Prophète*, and Carlo's 'Reviens ma noble protectrice' in Auber's *La Part du diable*). But, unlike their Italian counterparts, French *cavatines* insinuate themselves into other kinds of numbers as well, particularly large patchwork introductions and finales.

Though Gounod's most famous example of this number type, Faust's 'Salut demeure chaste et pure', began its existence as the slow section of a *grand air*, he never considered integrating a *cavatine* into a larger set piece after *Faust*. His *cavatines* have a distinctly personal (and, as an unsympathetic critic might remark, predictable) profile that sets them apart from those of his immediate predecessors and contemporaries. For one, Gounod associates this type with genre more than was customary: whereas the three small *opéras comiques* do not contain a single *cavatine*, every one of his large serious works for the stage, save *Sapho*, has an example. He also almost always presses the *cavatine* into service on behalf of the principal love interest in the work, for the explicit expression of affection or to allow one lover to wonder or worry about the other (the only exceptions among the thirteen examples are Frère Laurent's homily at the beginning of *Roméo et Juliette* Act III, dropped from every edition after the first and never performed, as well as Valentin's petition on behalf of his sister, added belatedly to *Faust* and never fully sanctioned by the composer).[6] In *Le Tribut de Zamora* both male lovers in the triangle sing their own *cavatines* about the same woman! As befits their amatory character, the *cavatines* generally draw upon a much more chromatic idiom than Gounod's own strophic *romances* and *couplets*. In eleven of them, binary form in the outer sections takes the place of classical period construction (two balanced phrases, the first ending on the dominant, the second on the tonic) preferred by other *cavatine* composers.[7] Gounod's middle area is slightly faster than the principal section and always brings in new orchestral figuration; most often the orchestra doubles the voice at the

[6] Only the manuscript continuity draft of *Roméo et Juliette* shows a ternary piece for Frère Laurent; by the time of the first edition the number had been reduced to only its main section.

[7] The exceptions are Rodolphe's *cavatine* in *La Nonne sanglante* and the first *cavatine* for the title role in Act II of *Cinq-Mars*.

return, a change from its previous role in the first section as the provider of accompaniment or a contrapuntal foil.

The middle sections are also usually longer than the returning section and the sheer size of some of them is out of all proportion to what was customary in the first half of the century; this not only in the *cavatines* but also in other self-contained ternary numbers such as those in a more heroic mould that earned the designation *air* (for example, the set pieces for Adoniram in his workshop and Mireille in the desert 'En marche'). Balkis's *cavatine* in the third act of *La Reine de Saba* is a fine illustration of Gounod's temporal extension of the self-contained ternary number. Rather than freeze a fixed mood like the middle sections in more conventional *cavatines* from the period, that portion of Balkis's *cavatine* moves through many contrasting musical ideas to trace every inflection in her thoughts: *parlante* for the sudden and painful recollection that she is betrothed to Soliman, a voice-dominated lyrical period to portray her resolve to forget Adoniram, an animated strophe for the realization that, alas, she cannot forget him, and a transition to the return in which she revives the sentiments experienced during the aborted casting of the bronze vessel. It is a succession of varied textures that at the time would have more conventionally constituted a dramatic transition between slow movement and *cabalette* in a multisectional number than the middle section of a *cavatine*. With a total of forty-seven bars, compared to twelve in the first statement and sixteen in the return, that section is large even by Gounod's standards. A piece with similar proportions and variety of textures is Mireille's 'Air de la Crau': the middle section there contains a long passage of *parlante* above a complete orchestral rendition of the 'Divine extase' music that Mireille herself will sing at the end of the opera.

Of the major multisectional types used in French opera and especially in *opéra comique*, the one least well represented in Gounod's operas is the compound introduction, a number at the outset of the work in which one or more soloists are highlighted against a choral background. The solo music in such a set piece may range from recitative and a few small measured passages (*La Juive*, *Les Huguenots*) to complete strophic or ternary sections (Auber's *Le Cheval de bronze*) and, apart from the oft-encountered technique of framing the number with the same chorus at the start and conclusion (Auber's *La Fiancée*, *Le Premier jour de bonheur*, Adam's *Si j'étais roi*), there is little in common from one piece to another. The works of Gounod where one most expects to find the compound introduction, that is the smaller *opéras comiques*, do not contain one—but that is very much a factor of circumstances other than aversion to this type. *La Colombe* was conceived for the Baden opera as a small-scale work without chorus; so too was *Philémon et Baucis* before it was rather artificially enlarged for the Théâtre-Lyrique; and *Le Médecin malgré lui* is an *opéra comique* replica of the Molière play, which has only two figures on stage at the beginning. Two of Gounod's operas, *Mireille* and *Roméo et Juliette*, do indeed begin with a conventional compound introduction and both use the framing technique. The solo contributions by Taven, Clémence, and Mireille in the former are all through-composed interpolations. Usually even the more weighty *opéras comiques* avoid the lugubrious, and that *Mireille* is a full-blown tragedy is signalled almost immediately by the unexpected gloom cast by Taven's metaphorical prediction in G minor ('Écoutez les chanter et rire'). The introduction to *Roméo et Juliette* steers clear of prefiguring later tragic developments and contains a complete ternary number for a minor character, Capulet's piece 'Allons jeunes gens'; though insignificant in the long run, it does provide a foil for the youthful ebullience that Juliette displays in the number. The extended musical preparation for her (a crescendo over a pedal and the chorus 'Ah! qu'elle est belle') cannot be further from the spirit of Shakespeare's corresponding scene. In contrast to the subdued first appearances of Marguerite and Mireille, Juliette's is a grand entry for the *première chanteuse* that could only have met with a favourable reaction from Madame Miolan-Carvalho.

More than a third of Scribe's operas and *opéras comiques* do not begin with a compound introduction; in these the usual method of getting started is the self-contained choral number, generally to set the tone or locale, and the solo *air*.[8] And so it is in Gounod's works other than *Mireille*, *Roméo et Juliette*, and the three small *opéras comiques*. His most unconventional operatic introduction is that of *Faust*. In place of a lyrical solo number, Faust's solo musings are largely conducted in non-periodic declamation, a bold opening scene for its time. Nevertheless, the scaffolding of a conventional *grand air* with slow section and *cabalette* is still faintly visible, since on two occasions Faust does start a passage that appears to be the beginning of a complete periodic section. The first ('J'ai langui triste et solitaire') has the earmarks of a lyrical slow section, but after only eight bars a modulation to the mediant and a change of texture is effected. The second beginning ('Salut! ô mon dernier matin') has the cut of a martial *cabalette* and it is also interrupted, this time by young people outside. That chorus functions merely as an external intervention rather than the core of the number against which events occur.

Any survey of other multisectional types—duets, finales, and some

---

[8] Pendle, *Eugène Scribe*, p. 91.

solo numbers—must take Italian forms into account. Since many composers of French opera had a distinctly Italianate approach to text setting, it is reasonable to posit an Italian influence upon larger structural levels as well, particularly in the case of Rossini and Meyerbeer, who both had significant Italian careers before writing for Parisian houses. As the two most highly regarded composers in France during the second quarter of the nineteenth century, their influence upon others was considerable. When planning *Les Huguenots*, Meyerbeer made a distinction between duets *à l'italienne* and those *à la française*; in the former, the words of the parallel-strophe 'middle ensemble' are different from those for the final one, whereas in the latter they are the same.[9] (As it turned out, the three duets in *Les Huguenots* were composed *à l'italienne*.) Abramo Basevi once distinguished four sections in the typical Verdian duet ('tempo d'attacco', 'adagio', 'tempo di mezzo', 'cabaletta') and it is clear from his description that Meyerbeer's 'middle ensemble' *à l'italienne* may be equated with the tonally closed central 'adagio', and his 'final ensemble' (which Meyerbeer himself frequently called *cabalette* or *strette*) with the 'cabaletta'.[10] A change of words for the final ensemble also entails some evolution of dramatic positions pertaining during the slow middle ensemble and that adjustment is made to a variety of textures (recitative, *parlante*, voice dominated) in the tonally open-ended area between the ensembles (Basevi's 'tempo di mezzo'). In many works by Rossini and Donizetti the section before the slow middle ensemble begins with parallel strophes as well—a lyrical response to dramatic tensions built up during the previous connecting recitative—followed by more rapid dialogue and a modulation to prepare the central strophes. By Verdi's time, however, the 'tempo d'attacco' itself is usually made up entirely of dialogue, albeit in lyric rhyming verse set to measured music, that culminates in the 'adagio'. Multisectional solo arias and finales adhere to the same outline (following Italian usage it is best to reserve the term *strette* for concluding sections of numbers involving more than two people); in arias, however, the 'tempo d'attacco' is generally dispensed with and the set piece begins immediately with one or two lyrical strophes in slow tempo.

[9] 'Remarques générales' on the prose scenario of *Les Huguenots*, BN MSS n.a.f. 22502, fo. 65.

[10] On Italian formal conventions, see discussions of individual operas in Ashbrook, *Donizetti and his Operas*, and Budden, *The Operas of Verdi*; see also Philip Gossett, 'Verdi, Ghislanzoni, and Aida: The Uses of Convention', *Critical Inquiry*, 1 (1974), 291–324, and *Anna Bolena and the Artistic Maturity of Gaetano Donizetti* (Oxford, 1985), as well as Robert Moreen, 'Integration of Text Forms and Musical Forms in Verdi's Early Operas', Ph.D. thesis (Princeton, 1975). Abramo Basevi's *Studio sulle opere di Giuseppe Verdi* (Florence, 1859) is summarized in Moreen, fos. 27–37. On the appearance of these conventions in Meyerbeer's grand operas, see Huebner, 'Italianate duets', pp. 203–58.

These are merely rough outlines of an extraordinarily rich set of formal conventions. Whereas this prototype has been greatly developed as a historical and analytical tool in relation to the Italian repertoire, French manifestations have hardly received attention. Yet no less than ten of the sixteen duets in Meyerbeer's grand operas may be related to the Italian prototype, and a good many of the arias and finales as well. For example, at the beginning of their duet in the third act of *Les Huguenots*, Valentine and Marcel sing a set of almost-parallel strophes while stumbling around in the dark unaware of each other's identity; in the ensuing dialogue Marcel reveals who he is and Valentine warns him about a plot to assassinate his master Raoul; this gives rise to the slow 'middle ensemble'; in the dramatic transition between middle ensemble and *cabalette* it is Valentine who reveals her true identity to Marcel. Sometimes a more significant *coup-de-théâtre* occurs between the ensembles, as in the grand 'finale' of the previous act, where Raoul's hot-headed refusal to conclude a marriage pact with the rival Catholic faction occurs at just that juncture. There are many examples of the prototype in the grand operas of Halévy and Auber as well. To the most famous tune in Halévy's 'œuvre' ('Rachel quand du Seigneur'), Eléazar of *La Juive* regrets that his adopted daughter must die; he considers saving Rachel in a passage of *parlante* and recitative after this, but upon hearing the screams of the Christian mob for Jewish blood he abandons that sympathetic stance and voices his resolve in the *cabalette* ('Dieu m'éclaire'). The duet for Eudoxie and Rachel earlier in *La Juive* also follows closely the Italian prototype, as does the finale to Act III.

Many Italianate numbers in French grand opera share one structural feature that sets them apart from the norm in the work of Rossini, Donizetti, and Verdi. Donizetti himself, in a letter written during the preparation of *Les Martyrs* for the Opéra in 1839, noted that

French music and theatrical poetry have a cachet all their own, to which every composer must accommodate himself . . . for example away with crescendi etc. etc., away with the usual cadences *felicità, felicità, felicità*; then, between one and the other statement of the *cabaletta* theme there is always some poetry which carries forward the action without the typical repetition of verses which our poets use.[11]

He might well have enlarged the scope of his observation: there is a marked tendency in French grand opera not only to expand the tonally closed *cabalette* into ternary form, but the central slow section as well. The middle area between statement and reprise frequently features not just new verse, but a change of texture as well. This fact alone shows

[11] Letter to Simone Mayr, 8 Apr. 1839, cited and translated by Philip Gossett in the introduction to Donizetti, *Les Martyrs* in the Garland Reprint Series 'Early Romantic Opera' (New York, 1982).

Meyerbeer's Italianate and French forms to be rather close relatives. For, on the basis of Meyerbeer's definition, it is sometimes difficult to categorize a number containing a central ensemble duplicated at the end as a piece *à la française* or as one *à l'italienne* that is merely missing a movement. As we have seen, production pressures at the Opéra frequently forced composers such as Meyerbeer and Gounod to make huge cuts at the eleventh hour. The entire slow section of the third act finale was removed from *Les Huguenots* before the first performance, leaving a number with an opening declamatory passage followed by a section originally conceived as a *strette* (though not a ternary one).[12] In the case of the Sélika–Vasco duet in the second act of *L'Africaine*, Meyerbeer decided in his own workshop to remove the transitional third section and *cabalette* following the large ternary slow section that he had composed.[13] The number appears in all scores as cut *à la française*, but it was really conceived *à l'italienne*. Though not as numerous as ensembles with more than one set of strophes, there are many examples in grand opera of numbers with a central set of parallel strophes that is recapitulated at the end. These include the Act III finale of Auber's *Gustave III*, where the discovery that Ankastrom seems to have had a nocturnal tryst with his own wife prepares the parallel strophes; before they are restated, however, he sets up an appointment with the conspirators. At the outset of the Act I finale of *La Reine de Chypre* by Halévy, Andrea unexpectedly announces that the wedding between his daughter Catarina and Gérard must be aborted, and, in the interstice between the blocks of parallel strophes, Catarina presses her father to explain his decision. That nothing in the available sources connects these two numbers to a larger piece *à l'italienne* does not significantly widen the gap between the two structural types.

Though Meyerbeer's *coupe italienne* and *coupe française* made inroads into the *opéra-comique* repertoire as well, the arrangement of parallel strophes and more open-ended sections of dialogue in that genre is subject to more variation than in opera. The most fertile ground for Italianate structural conventions is the solo *air*: the great majority of *opéras comiques* contain at least one solo number, often called *grand air*, with a slow section and a *cabalette* separated in most (though far from all) instances by a transition. Usually one or both of these lyrical sections are cast in ternary form. Italianate finales with chorus also surface in *opéra comique* (the conclusions to the second act of Auber's *Fra Diavolo*, Hérold's *Zampa* and *Le Pré aux clercs*, and Adam's

[12] Sieghard Döhring, 'Die Autographen der vier Hauptopern Meyerbeers: Ein erster Quellenbericht', *Archiv für Musikwissenschaft*, 39 (1982), 45–6.

[13] Huebner, 'Italianate Duets', p. 216.

Giralda), though a more prominent finale type in the genre involves a patchwork of one or two solo numbers, or simply a long passage of rapid-fire dialogue, that culminates with parallel strophes in fast tempo. The layout of duets is highly variable. The Marie–Edmond duet in the first act of *Le Serment* is perhaps closest to the Italianate prototype in Auber's *opéras comiques* before 1840. It contains a central slow section followed by dialogue and concluding strophes, though even in this example (as in the occasional Italian duet) there is no change of tempo between the transition and the *cabalette*. Other duets may proceed from parallel strophes in slow tempo to quick parallel strophes without an intervening section (Léocadie–Carlo in Auber's *Léocadie*), from fast strophes cast in ternary form to dialogue and new stanzas in fast tempo (Angela–Léonie in his *Actéon*), or from stanzas for one of the characters to dialogue and a concluding ensemble (Lucette–Le Comte in *La Bergère châtelaine*). In the final analysis, the existence of prototypes in nineteenth-century *opéra comique* other than Meyerbeer's Italian and French cuts will only become clear when that very large repertoire benefits from more scholarly attention than it has received to date.

What of multisectional numbers in Gounod's works for the stage? As with opera and *opéra comique* generally at mid-century, the slow section–transition–*cabalette* design had the most staying power in connection with Gounod's *airs*, though this is clear only when the documentary histories of the works are taken into account. At one time or another all but two of his operas and *opéras comiques* written before 1870 (the exceptions are *Le Médecin malgré lui* and *La Colombe*) contained at least one example. And though not present in *Cinq-Mars* and *Polyeucte*, the prototype is actually linked to the entrance aria principle in Hermosa's second act *air* from *Le Tribut de Zamora*, a particularly conservative solution at a time when even Italian composers had abandoned the *cavatine–cabaletta* first appearance. In some works (*Sapho*, *Philémon et Baucis*, and *Mireille*) the design was not a part of Gounod's first draft and was doubtless added to accommodate conventional tastes. In others (*Faust* and *Roméo et Juliette*) Gounod intended to use the prototype from the start of his own earliest deliberations and only later made a substantial cut that eliminated a connection to the multisectional design. The two latter *airs* illustrate particularly well the extent to which the ternary principle may contribute to the temporal expansion of individual sections in French multisectional pieces. Like some of Gounod's own self-contained ternary numbers, the middle part of Juliette's *cabalette*, for example, is as long as the outer ones combined. Since the drama and musical architecture could be well enough developed within a single section for it to stand alone as a separate number, that very expansion may have contributed in this case, as in the Selika–Vasco duet cited above, to the abbreviation and effective abandonment of the slow section–transition–*cabalette* design.

Gounod did not rigorously apply the groundplans *à l'italienne* or *à la française* to any of his finales. Those of the third act of *Roméo et Juliette* and the fourth act of *La Nonne sanglante* genetically have the most in common with the latter prototype, but in printed versions of these operas that is not so apparent. As first entered into the performing parts, the Bleeding Nun's unwelcome appearance to Rodolphe just as his marriage to Agnès is to be enacted at the end of Act IV provided the impetus for a first set of strophes marked 'allegro' ('Qu'a-t-il donc?'). His declaration that he could not conclude the pact furnished dramatic impetus for a complete reprise. That shape was obscured late in the rehearsal period by the insertion of a parallel-strophe slow section ('Ah! sans retour') between the exposition and reprise, resulting in the curious hybrid between the *coupe italienne* and the *coupe française* that appears in editions of the score. With compound metre, a long solo for the protagonist Rodolphe that is then sung by his bride, contrapuntal embellishment from additional soloists and chorus, and a twofold crescendo passage in the manner of, say, the slow section in the first act finale of Verdi's *Attila*, the accretion is in itself one of the most Italianate passages in Gounod's œuvre.

In the third act finale of *Roméo et Juliette* as first drafted, both words and music of the central lament 'Ô jour de deuil' were taken up again at the end of the number. This groundplan, however, is only superficially related to the French type, since the lament is constructed of a single text sung by all characters rather than of different strophes, giving more the effect of a ritualistic response to a tragic event than an individualized reaction from all parties. By opening night Gounod had changed his original plan completely. Multiple parallel strophes ('Capulets! Montaigus!') also appear in the draft as well as in the definitive version of this finale for the Opéra, but in both they occupy only a small part of the whole (twenty-six bars marked 'allegro'), perhaps inevitably so in a number that contains a large amount of stage action, including four duels, the death of Tybalt, the entrance of the duke, and the sentencing of Roméo. Nor does the 'Capulets! Montaigus!' ensemble function dramatically as parallel-strophe ensembles normally do in both the *coupe italienne* and the *coupe française*, that is, as a relatively static reaction to previous events; instead it is merely a brief preparation for the ensuing duel between Mercutio and Tybalt.

The only one of Gounod's finales with chorus related to the Italian prototype is that of the second act of *Mireille*. This number too is something of a hybrid, not between Italian and French types like the Act IV finale of *La Nonne sanglante*, but between the Italian form and the *opéra-comique* patchwork finale consisting of solo numbers followed by a *strette*. The central slow section is a solo piece for Mireille in ternary form with contrasting middle section ('A vos pieds hélas'). Ensemble participation from the assembled principals is confined only to the reprise, where Mireille's line still leads. That section is not preceded by recitative texture, *parlante*, or a celebratory chorus, but rather by a miniature *air* for Ramon that falls within the body of the finale. The *air* is itself cast in a slow-section ('Le chef de famille')–transition–*cabalette* ('Brave la honte') design, and the major *coup-de-théâtre* of the finale— Mireille's revelation to her father of her love for Vincent—actually occurs in the transition between Ramon's lyrical sections. Whereas in most Italianate finales the *coup-de-théâtre* leads directly into the concertato slow section, in this piece Ramon's *cabalette* and a new passage of recitative texture intervene. Following the slow section, Ramon turns upon Vincent's father, accusing him of having engineered the liaison to improve his son's social standing. In the ensuing parallel-strophe *strette* he continues to rail against Vincent and Ambroise, Ambroise responds, Mireille and Vincent express their commitment to one another, and various onlookers voice their opinions about what has happened.

Though it is not present in all of his works and never follows strictly the conventional groundplan, Gounod did not completely shake off the large *concertato* finale, that is, a tableau in which soloists and assembled masses react to a sudden turn of events with more or less independent contrapuntal lines. In the Act I finale to *Polyeucte*, for example, a ceremonial march frames both a kinetic section of dialogue where Sévère is met with the completely unexpected news that Pauline is married to another and a large non-ternary ensemble response to that event. That ensemble would not have been out of place in a finale by a contemporary Italian composer; and, like the slow section in the Act IV finale of *La Nonne sanglante*, the conduct of the parts is undeniably Italianate. At the outset Sévère, Polyeucte, and Félix each sing the same halting melodic strain in succession, a pseudo-canon à la Rossini; the texture gradually thickens around these entries with additional voices until the chorus is finally heard; after the pseudo-canon has spent its course, the soprano line of Pauline takes the lead, guiding those assembled along the path of a long crescendo.

Another example of a *concertato* finale is associated with *Cinq-Mars*. Now, as first performed in April 1877, there was nothing approaching a *concertato* movement in the internal finale ensembles of that work: the end of Act II was laid out as a rondo design, with the homophonic ensemble 'Oui le sang répandu' as refrain, and a hunting chorus 'Hallali, Hallali' framed the events in the finale of the third act. When performances of *Cinq-Mars* at La Scala were planned, the publisher Lucca urged Gounod to take Italian taste into consideration:

Regardless of whether Italians like crescendi because of their musical nature, or for some other reason, it is certain that theatrical effect, especially at the end of an act, would be greatly enhanced in reprises by some elevation in tonality, as well as by some new disposition of the voices and orchestra which slowly leads to one of those terrifying explosions that hit the public like an electric shock and of which you incontestably possess the marvellous secret. With the force of the vocal masses that we have at La Scala such a crescendo would produce an irresistible effect.[14]

Lucca seems to have advocated a conflation of the *concertato* with impressive crescendo and ascending sequence in the manner of 'Anges purs, anges radieux'. That is certainly how Gounod responded to his suggestions in a revision of the third act finale. Like the characters in the first act finale of *Polyeucte*, Père Joseph, the King, and the Polish ambassador sing a pseudo-canon; in this instance, however, the strain is heard a minor third higher at each occurrence, first in G flat major, then in A and C. The climactic point of the ensuing crescendo is made to coincide with the first cadence in the original key of G flat major (spelled as F sharp major).

Many of Gounod's multisectional duets, trios, and quartets bear some family resemblance to the Italian groundplan. This is particularly true of those in the early works: the two duets and trio in the second act of *Sapho*, for example, each contain two different sets of parallel strophes prepared and separated by dialogue in a variety of textures. Two first act duets in *La Nonne sanglante* (Pierre l'ermite–Rodolphe, Agnès–Rodolphe) are also related to Italianate form, but, as with all of Gounod's later duets (and many duets in Italian opera from this period, it should be added), that model stands in the background behind a variety of foreground formal solutions. The slow section of the number for Pierre l'ermite and Rodolphe ('Agnès ma douce idole') consists merely of two strophes for Rodolphe instead of parallel strophes for both (it is even called a *romance* in the first edition of the libretto), a procedure with a venerable lineage back to the famous solo slow section of the Valentine–Raoul duet in *Les Huguenots* and one which Gounod was to use again in the Mireille–Vincenette duet as well as the Balkis–Adoniram duet of *La Reine de Saba*. In the first section of a more

---

[14] Letter from Lucca to Gounod, no date, Bibliothèque de la SACD, Paris.

conventional duet Rodolphe might have admitted his love for Agnès, and Pierre might have responded with advice to forget her; this would have prepared a parallel-strophe second section in which Rodolphe might have sung of his inextinguishable love (as he actually does in the opera), with Pierre offering words of consolation. In Gounod's score Pierre saves his advice for the transition, one followed in Scribe's first plans by a ternary *cabalette* ('Dieu nous commande l'espérance') consisting of a solo strophe for Pierre, a declamatory middle part, and an *a due* reprise of Pierre's music. By the time the parts were copied, both the middle area and the reprise of the *cabalette* had fallen off, leaving a duet where one character sings the slow section and the other the *cabalette*. There are strophes for both Agnès and Rodolphe in the slow section of the subsequent duet ('Avant minuit'), but, despite this, the two never combine in ensemble singing. The slow section was conceived not as a lyrical contemplation upon previous events, but rather as a means to advance the drama (as was the slow section in many Italian duets also): in her strophe Agnès tells the legend of the nun, in the middle area of dialogue Rodolphe suggests that the legend may be useful to them, and in his solo strophe, sung to Agnès's previous music, he explains the ruse they will attempt. One might argue, holding forth local-level verisimilitude as the prime criterion, that an ensemble does not occur because it is inappropriate in this dramatic plan. But the real reason there is no ensemble singing in this section is undoubtedly connected more to an unconventional previous layout, where such considerations of verisimilitude were not an issue. As first planned by Scribe and Gounod, the slow section was interrupted by an *a due* reprise of a lyrical strophe about the intransigence of the two rival families that had been sung separately by both singers in the first section;[15] a mere cut of that passage produced the version that appears in printed editions.

The only Gounod duet after *Sapho* with a slow section containing ensemble singing is the number for the two protagonists in the fourth act of *Roméo et Juliette*, which, along with the Marguerite–Faust garden duet, follows the conventional scheme more closely than any of the other operatic duets after *Sapho*. But even these may hardly be held up as classical models. In the slow section of the duet for Juliette and Roméo ('Nuit d'hyménée'), Gounod eschews a separate delivery for each singer in favour of a main strain sung in parallel sixths, a procedure with French antecedents in the Gérard–Catarina duet in Halévy's *La Reine de Chypre* and the Zora–Lorenz duet in David's *La Perle de Brésil*. With almost as many bars as both lyrical sections combined, the transition between both sets of parallel strophes in that duet is much longer than usual. And the structure of the *cabalette* ('Il faut partir hélas') is

[15] The first edn. of the libretto contains this version.

abbreviated, since it proceeds directly from a main strain sung by Juliette alone to ensemble singing; it is followed by a short section of *parlante* for Juliette, as the orchestra recalls the cello melody heard before the duet, a direct dramatic and visual analogue to the end of the Act II duet, where it is Roméo who is left alone while the orchestra sounds the previously heard *entr'acte*.

Neither does the *cabalette* of the Marguerite–Faust duet ('Partez, partez') ring that famous piece to a close; instead it gives way to lyrical *parlante* for Faust, above a viola–cello rendition of his earlier *cavatine*, in which he persuades Marguerite to agree to another rendezvous. Once again the Valentine–Raoul duet in *Les Huguenots* is the most important French forebear, though there are other examples of the usurpation of the *cabalette*'s function as a concluding section, including the Charles–Odette encounter in *Charles VI* and, in Italian opera, the Violetta–Germont duet in *La traviata*. But the end of the Marguerite–Faust garden duet is far more extended than all of these examples, allowing Marguerite to leave, Méphistophélès to appear, and then her to sing from the window—fully 102 bars of additional music after the *cabalette*. The entry of a third character might even suggest that a duet is no longer operative as a structural category after the *cabalette*, that this music is a large *scène* with a variety of textures. Gounod, however, steers back to F major, the tonic of the *cabalette*. Moreover, though Méphistophélès is not physically present in the duet, he certainly lurks near in spirit throughout. It is he, after all, who is seen immediately before Faust launches the first section with 'Laisse-moi, laisse-moi'. After the duet Méphistophélès does not assume the function of a new character who suddenly appears to urge the drama forward; rather at that point he merely supplies a *buffo* sideshow to the ongoing drama between Faust and Marguerite. Méphistophélès's role points up the larger musical and dramatic context for the duet. That set piece is a greatly prolonged episode in a dramatic movement initiated during the previous quartet: the continual appearance and disappearance of Faust and Marguerite on the one hand, and Méphistophélès (together with Marthe at first) on the other. The front end of the duet is deftly grafted to preceding music: the motif associated with 'Laisse-moi' sounds as Méphistophélès reaches for the daisies and it has even been heard before, when Faust and Marguerite were last seen at the end of the quartet, he running off-stage in desperation after the frightened girl (Ex. 16.1). The conventional Italianate shape, then, forms part of a much longer complex, one that extends back to the quartet and forward beyond the *cabalette* to the scene of Marguerite at her window. That shape is articulated clearly enough, though not without an individualized profile. The opening of two parallel strophes set to the same music

Ex. 16.1. *Faust*, Act III, quartet

is structurally a most conservative one at a time when Italian composers
had long abandoned that sort of *tempo d'attacco*. It is certainly unique
in Gounod's œuvre. The central section of the duet ('Ô nuit d'amour') is
marked at the same tempo ('andante'). It contains only twenty-five bars
of music, without ensemble singing: Marguerite's strain is given twice,
once in voice-dominated fashion and the other in *parlanto*, a texture
normally associated with the first and third sections. These unusual
features must be related to the pre-history of the duet. The slow section
is an exact transcription (save transposition from E flat major to D flat)
of a nocturne for piano four hands that Gounod wrote in 1849 and that
may well have served as the point of departure for the entire duet.[16]
Fidelity to previously composed music accounts for the shape of the
central slow section and also probably prompted Gounod to supply each
singer with a more extended lyrical solo in the same tempo at the outset
of the number to compensate for the brevity of the borrowed material.

Many of Gounod's duets and other ensemble numbers have merely
one set of strophes after dialogue in a variety of textures. For example,
the Faust–Méphistophélès duet is largely taken up with the latter's
comic posturing until the strophes 'A moi les plaisirs'. That section has a
ternary design with a long middle area that introduces new textures and
important developments in the plot, namely Faust's signing of the pact
once he has savoured a glimpse of Marguerite. The motor rhythms
of the setting to 'A moi les plaisirs' have a particularly Italianate
quality. A fast tempo marking suggests that it is a *cabalette* and that the
entire number may best be understood as Italianate without a slow
section, but once again Meyerbeer's *coupe française* is also an
appropriate conceptual tool for this music, as it is for most of Gounod's
other single-strophe ensemble numbers. Regardless of how one may
want to classify these pieces, it is most important to recognize that
Gounod maintained allegiance to ternary organization within such
multisectional numbers throughout his career. This is particularly clear
in a set of instructions he supplied to Georges Bizet for the revival of
Roméo et Juliette at the Opéra-Comique in 1872. Both the duet for
Juliette and Roméo in Act II and the *trio et quatuor* in Act III contain a
single set of parallel strophes developed into ternary form. He insisted
that these numbers be kept intact: 'I ask that the ensemble "De cet
adieu" (in the duet) be given TWICE. Without this, the expression in this
period [read section] of the duet does not have force, and the whole
piece does not have form.'[17] And, upon hearing that only one statement

---

[16] A facsimile of the nocturne is given by Marc Pincherle in *Musiciens peints par eux-mêmes*
(Paris, 1939), 140.
[17] Letter of 15 Oct. 1872, cited in Fauquet, 'Quatre versions de Roméo et Juliette', p. 71.

of the strophes in the marriage scene would be given out of deference to
the stamina of the singers, he wrote: 'I profoundly regret that the final
phrase is being given only once—it is morally complete only with the
reprise. Let them do what they want, but I am sure that the piece will
suffer.'[18]

The final duet in *Roméo et Juliette* stands in contrast to this impulse
to produce ternary forms: it is Gounod's least conventional ensemble
piece, organized into three large sections with no parallel strophes
(except in reminiscences of previous music) and no reiteration of any
of the new material it does introduce. The three sections are defined
by dramatic events. The first is occupied by Roméo alone and culminates
in his taking the poison. *Parlante* texture predominates. Roméo
declaims first over a clarinet melody derived from the impassioned
'avec délire' orchestral strain in the Act IV duet and then over a complete
rendition of the fourth act *entr'acte*. At the moment the vial is emptied,
harp and tremolo strings bring in the *sommeil de Juliette* music and the
second section: the orchestra first gives the descending fourth motif
that is prominent in that melody and then spins out motifs derived from
the 'avec délire' theme until the entire melody is reproduced beneath
Juliette's 'Dieu, quelle est cette voix', a musical analogue to her gradual
awakening. From here the two launch a passage that culminates in a
vocal rendition of the 'Sois béni' rosalia from the marriage scene,
recalling the happiest moments in their relationship and the inviolable
sacred trust between them. Except for the last four bars before the
orchestral postlude to the number, this is the only ensemble singing in
the duet. The ecstatic atmosphere is abruptly broken, and the third part
of the duet initiated, by the sounding of the same diminished chord to
which Roméo had earlier swallowed the poison. He reveals to Juliette
what he has done and attempts to comfort her with a new sixteen-bar
period of voice-dominated music ('Console-toi'); but most of the third
part is declaimed to punctuating chords and tremolo, save for a final
turn to the 'avec délire' theme. In short, all the new music in the number
is given to Roméo; of 304 bars only 45 are taken up by voice-dominated
periodic music. The duet relies for its musical coherence on recollections
of significant material in the orchestra, presented with *parlante* singing
by the voices; indeed it is doubtful that Gounod would have ever
attempted such an unconventionally organized number if a large degree
of thematic recollection from previous acts—that is, melodic reprise at
the largest temporal level—were not involved. This was not the first
time he produced an operatic ending that recapitulates previous music;

---

[18] Letter of 29 Oct. 1872, cited in ibid. 71.

the two lovers in *Faust* also ruminate upon their past bliss in a duet near the conclusion of that opera. But one difference between the two duets eloquently underlines the innovative character of the later piece: in the *Faust* duet the *parlante* recollections occur between two different sets of parallel strophes, the first of which ('Oui, c'est toi je t'aime') is developed into ternary form.

Epilogue

IN his preface to Arnold Mortier's *Les Soirées parisiennes* of 1883 Gounod identified one of the most dangerous tendencies in artistic endeavour as a 'quest for effect', adding that 'the preoccupation with effect is nothing but a lack of faith in the Truth ... when you see an artist who is concerned with the effect that his work will produce, be sure that what he loves is not his art but his person: he is vain'.[1] Admittedly, Gounod penned these words after he had written his last opera, at a time when he was notorious as a pontificator on matters concerning art, but they do illustrate a lifelong suspicion of facile operatic entertainment. Even at the height of his career Gounod was only slightly more ambivalent about this point; describing a passage in Meyerbeer's *L'Africaine* shortly after he heard the work for the first time in 1865, he noted: 'The great unison of the fifth act seems more filled with effect than with true emotion, but on this point I must yield to the storm of public enthusiasm. I think, none the less, that the achievement of effect is only half the battle.'[2] As questionable as it may have been from the artistic point of view, then, the impact of 'effect' upon audiences could sometimes not be entirely ignored. At other times Gounod expressed greater faith in the public, even bestowing a major role in the creative process upon it in his *Mémoires* by acknowledging that the audience 'brings to the judgement of a work a competence and authority of its own'. He went on to explain that:

The theatre public ... does not need to know the value of a work from the point of view of taste; it only assesses the power of passions and degree of emotion—that is, the essence of a dramatic work, a reflection of the individual and collective soul. The result is that the public and the composer are reciprocally called upon to educate one another: the public provides the author with the criterion and sanction of Truth; the author initiates the public to the elements and conditions of Beauty.[3]

Beyond mere effect, then, lay dramatic truth. One can hardly imagine such words from a Meyerbeer or a Verdi—composers for whom dramatic truth and scenic or melodramatic 'effects' were intertwined,

---

[1] In Mortier, *Les Soirées parisiennes de 1883*, p. 2.
[2] Letter to Ernest Legouvé, 8 June 1865, private collection.
[3] Gounod, *Mémoires*, p. 149.

and who recognized that their audiences came not only to be moved, but also to be entertained. That was a notion with which Gounod was uncomfortable: the word 'effect' for him had a distinctly pejorative edge, one that implied an unhealthy dose of empty exaggeration and sensationalism in order to appeal to the lowest common denominator of taste within audiences. But since the line between dramatic truth and theatrical effect in mid-nineteenth French and Italian opera was thin, a reluctance to embrace the latter could not fail to make itself felt upon the former. It is hard to deny that a great many of Gounod's operatic acts fall flat in their direct appeal to gut emotion. He often maintains aristocratic poise at the expense of flesh-and-blood vitality. When he adopts a more popular cut, as in the Soldiers' Chorus of *Faust*, or attempts to write in an expansive manner to fill the cadre of the Opéra, as in the baptismal scene of *Polyeucte*, the result is frequently unconvincing.

A predilection for restraint is perhaps not surprising from one who admired the amalgam of 'expressive force and economy of means' in *Don Giovanni*[4] and whose book on that opera is an extended paean to the virtues of 'balance', 'moderation', and 'harmony' (apropos is the portrait of Gounod clutching the score of *Don Giovanni* to his breast with eyes staring fixedly ahead into the distant reaches of *le Beau*; plate 10). Gounod attains his own 'expressive force with economy of means' through careful attention to the prosody of the text and finely wrought details of characterization—at his best moments the doctrine of 'most with least' is eminently satisfying. Gounod also looked to Mozart to justify conservatism in operatic form: in his view, the twofold rendition of the ensemble 'Hai sposo, hai padre' in the Act I Donna Anna–Don Ottavio duet produced greater 'intensity of expression' than a single statement.[5] In short, for Gounod dramatic truth in the highest sense is served by structural reprise; hence his observation that the marriage scene in *Roméo et Juliette* was 'morally complete' only with two statements of the ensemble.[6]

There is real artistic conviction in the positions that Gounod adopted. Though to many in the twentieth century he seems little more than a shallow popularizer, Gounod's contemporaries, especially during the Second Empire, never regarded his work as facile or superficial. Adolphe Jullien once felt obliged to remind his readers that Gounod was a fine example of the vast distance separating talent from genius, for in some

---

[4] In reference to the Act I quartet, in Charles Gounod, *Le Don Juan de Mozart* (Paris, 1890), 66.

[5] Ibid. 28.

[6] Cf. p. 279 above.

quarters he had attained that status.[7] Nevertheless, within the limits of an extraordinary talent that we may justly say today fell short of genius, Gounod did forge a personal sound and approached some contemporary conventions with considerable freedom. He was an enormous influence upon the subsequent generation of French opera composers, establishing a high standard for text setting, giving greater expressive weight to the orchestra, and providing a model for a kind of opera in which love between the two protagonists fills virtually the entire frame. As works with four love duets, for example, Massenet's *Manon* and *Werther* have an antecedent in Gounod's *Roméo et Juliette*; the musical recollection of past bliss between the two lovers before the final curtain in *Faust* and *Roméo et Juliette* finds later manifestation in *Le Roi de Lahore* and *Manon*. Gounod took the substance of his models very seriously and sincerely aimed to communicate some of the emotions and ideas they embraced, sometimes at the expense of the practical realities of the stage. Unfortunately what gave the appearance of 'depth' in the Second Empire no longer did so by 1900. But this should not detract from what was surely one of Gounod's greatest achievements: the restoration of a higher sense of artistic purpose to the French stage.

[7] In a review of *Roméo et Juliette*, repr. in Jullien, *Musiciens d'aujourd'hui*, p. 134.

APPENDIX: PLOT SUMMARIES

Each of these plot summaries follows the first edition of the vocal score.

Sapho (first performed Opéra, 16 April 1851)

Cast: Phaon (tenor, Gueymard); Alcée (baritone, Marié); Pythéas (bass, Brémond); Cratès (tenor, ***); Cygénire (bass, ***); Sapho (mezzo-soprano, Viardot); Glycère (soprano, Poinsot)

Setting: Olympus and Lesbos, 6th century BC

Act I. *The games at Olympus.* After an introductory procession, Phaon and Pythéas are left alone on-stage. Pythéas openly wonders about the reason for the low spirits of his friend. He suspects that Phaon is not so much concerned about the oppressive rule by the tyrant Pittacus in Lesbos as torn between the love of two women, the courtesan Glycère and the poet Sapho. Pythéas has a stake in the matter, for he himself is enamoured of Glycère. Phaon succumbs to his needling by admitting that Pythéas's suspicions are well founded (*romance*: 'Puis-je oublier'). Sapho, who is preparing to compete in a contest of poetic recitation, happens upon the two. Much to Pythéas's glee, Phaon and Sapho start to express their mutual love. Their encounter is abruptly interrupted by Glycère, who was unaware that she had a rival for the affection of Phaon (*quatuor*: 'Quel entretien si doux'). The imbroglio is cut short by the entry of the poet Alcée, Sapho's main competitor. He draws Pythéas and Phaon aside and tells them that he will test the mood of the populace for political change with his poetic offering. The contest begins. Alcée sings of liberty and justice (*ode*: 'Ô liberté, déesse austère') and both he and Phaon are satisfied that those responded well to his call. Sapho follows with a recitation of the story of Hero and Leander (*ode*: 'Héro sur la tour solitaire'). The people react even more favourably to Sapho's poetry by proclaiming her victory over Alcée. The act concludes with her hymn of gratitude (*final*: 'Merci Vénus'), Phaon's pledge that his heart is now hers, and general shouts of praise and thanksgiving.

Act II. *Phaon's villa on the Isle of Lesbos.* A group has gathered for a banquet. The festivities, however, are a cover for a plot to oust Pittacus (*serment*: 'Oui, jurons tous'). Pythéas is unexcited by the plan, but is given the written oath so that his slaves may make copies of it to post around the island at the appointed hour. After all except Pythéas leave, Glycère enters and questions him about the gathering. Seizing an opportunity for intimacy with her, he agrees to provide her with proof of the covert operation if she will visit him at home later that night (*duo*: 'Il m'aurait plu'). Having extracted the truth from Pythéas for this price, Glycère quickly writes to Pittacus to reveal the conspiracy. She instructs an attendant to deliver the note to him at once. Glycère then confronts Sapho, who has just entered the villa to see Phaon, with the proposition that she will tell the tyrant about the conspiracy unless Sapho agrees to persuade Phaon to leave Lesbos without her (*duo*: 'Phaon pour vous est magnifique'). Sapho accedes to these demands. Phaon himself arrives, expecting a rendezvous with Sapho. Glycère falsely informs him that Pythéas has gone to Pittacus with news of the conspiracy (*trio*: 'Je viens sauver ta tête'). Phaon asks Sapho to follow him into exile, but she insists that she will stay behind. Phaon reproaches Sapho for her lack of fidelity and quickly agrees to take Glycère with him.

Act III. *A windswept beach*. Phaon awaits the other conspirators so that they may escape together. He sings of his misfortunes in life and love (*air*: 'Ô jours heureux'). The conspirators and Glycère arrive one by one (*chœur*: 'Adieu patrie'). Sapho is also present and Glycère, to be sure of Phaon's fidelity, asks him if he still loves the poet. Phaon responds by condemning Sapho to the infernal gods. As the conspirators leave, Sapho rises above bitterness to give Phaon her blessing. Drained by his rejection, she faints. A shepherd passes (*chanson*: 'Broutez le thym'). Upon recovery, Sapho assumes the only course open to her; after singing a set of *stances* ('Ô ma lyre immortelle'), she casts herself into the sea.

La Nonne sanglante (first performed Opéra, 18 October 1854)

Cast: Count Ludorf (bass, Merly); Baron Moldaw (bass, Guignot); Pierre l'ermite (bass, Depassio); Rodolphe (tenor, Gueymard); Agnès (soprano, Poinsot); Agnès, la nonne sanglante (mezzo-soprano, Wertheimber); Arthur (soprano, Dussy)
Setting: Bohemia, 11th century

Act I. *The castle of the Baron Moldaw*. The curtain opens to a pitched battle between the vassals of the Baron Moldaw and those of Count Ludorf. Suddenly, Pierre l'ermite appears to enlist support from both sides for a crusade against the Infidel (*air*: 'Dieu puissant'). He urges the two families to stop their internecine feud and proposes an alliance whereby Moldaw will give the hand of his daughter Agnès in marriage to the eldest of Ludorf's sons, Théobald. Moldaw and Ludorf agree and the pact is sealed. Moldaw invites Ludorf and his followers into his castle. When all but Pierre have entered, Ludorf's youngest son, Rodolphe, appears; he is stunned to learn that Agnès, with whom he is in love, is to be given to his brother Théobald (*duo*: 'En vain la discorde inhumaine'). After trying unsuccessfully to console Rodolphe, Pierre leaves. Agnès runs out to meet Rodolphe, distressed at the prospect of marrying a man whom she does not love (*duo*: 'Mon père d'un ton inflexible'). Rodolphe proposes that they meet at the northern ramparts at midnight in order to elope. Agnès is reluctant because this is the very night when the legendary ghost of the Bleeding Nun is to appear at the castle. All the gates will be left open for her and she is not to be disturbed on her rounds. Rodolphe dismisses the legend as fantasy and suggests that they may use it to their advantage: Agnès will disguise herself as the Bleeding Nun, so that she may walk unhindered through the gates at midnight. She is horrified by the scheme. Ludorf, Moldaw, and their vassals suddenly come upon the two (*final*: 'Que vois-je'). Rodolphe refuses outright to renounce his love for Agnès and is expelled from his father's household. As all assembled express indignation at this turn of events, Agnès whispers her agreement to Rodolphe.

Act II. *A road leading to the main gates of the Moldaw castle.* A convivial gathering of peasants disperses for the night. Rodolphe's page Arthur makes light of the Bleeding Nun legend and sings of his master's *galant* rendezvous with a noble lady (*couplets:* 'L'espoir et l'amour'). Rodolphe sends Arthur away to make sure all is ready for a quick departure and waits for midnight to sound. At the stroke of twelve, Rodolphe loses his composure. When the figure whom he believes to be Agnès descends an outer staircase of the building, he frantically swears eternal allegiance to her. Unfortunately for Rodolphe, it is not Agnès who has appeared, but the Bleeding Nun herself. *The ruins of a gothic castle.* Rodolphe has led the Bleeding Nun to his ancestral home. The dilapidated castle is suddenly transformed to its original grandeur; the ancient candelabras are magically set ablaze and a banquet table heaped with food materializes at centre stage. The muffled sound of a march is heard. The ghosts of Rodolphe's ancestors appear at every door and glide to their places at the table. The Bleeding Nun finally reveals her identity to Rodolphe and explains that his ancestors have come to witness their marriage. As the ghosts withdraw, the Nun gloats that Rodolphe will be hers forever.

Act III. *A large room in a farmhouse.* After a peasant waltz, Arthur enters in search of his master. The peasants tell him that Rodolphe has been staying with them for several months. After being reunited with him, the page informs Rodolphe that his older brother has been killed in battle and that he is now free to marry Agnès. In response, Rodolphe reveals his predicament to Arthur (*duo:* 'Au milieu de l'orage'): every night the Bleeding Nun appears at his bedside to remind him of their marriage vows. Arthur attempts to lift his spirits. Calm descends upon Rodolphe (*air:* 'Un jour plus pur'), but true to her custom the Nun appears at midnight (*duo:* 'Me voici!'). In desperation he begs her to break the pact that unites them. She explains that there is only one way that this can be done: he must kill the man who murdered her while she was a mortal. She refuses to reveal his identity to Rodolphe, but he hastily agrees to perform the task in order to be free of her.

Act IV. *The gardens of Ludorf.* Rodolphe and Agnès are about to be married. Ludorf exhorts all his guests to eat and drink (*couplets:* 'Bons chevaliers'). A ballet is performed to entertain them. Following the dance music, the clock strikes midnight. The Nun appears, visible only to Rodolphe, and points to his own father, Ludorf, as the assassin. Horrorstruck, Rodolphe is unable to continue with the marriage ceremony. The old hatred between the families flares up once again.

Act V. *A barren spot near the Moldaw Castle. The grave of the Bleeding Nun and the chapel of Pierre l'ermite in the background.* Ludorf is repentant (*air:* 'Mon fils me fuit'). His son has been avoiding all contact with him, and Ludorf is now willing to accept punishment for his crime, if only to see Rodolphe once again. He hides and overhears passing members of the Moldaw family discuss their plans to ambush his son at Pierre's chapel. Rodolphe appears, with Agnès trailing (*duo*: 'Toi Rodolphe, perjure et traître'). He tells her about the curse of the Bleeding Nun. Because he cannot kill his own father, Rodolphe resolves to seek refuge in a distant land. Marriage is impossible for him because of the Nun's nocturnal appearances. Moved by his son's turmoil, Ludorf rushes into the chapel knowing that he will be mistaken for Rodolphe. He is mortally wounded by Moldaw's men and drags himself to the grave of the Bleeding Nun, where he dies in his son's arms. Avenged at last, the nun ascends into the clouds to seek divine clemency for Ludorf and herself.

Le Médecin malgré lui (first performed Théâtre-Lyrique, 15 January 1858)

Cast: Géronte (bass, Lesage); Lucinde (soprano, Caye); Léandre (tenor, Fromont); Sganarelle (baritone, Meillet); Martine (mezzo-soprano, Faivre); Mr Robert (*trial*, Leroy); Valère (bass, Wartel); Lucas (tenor, Girardot); Jacqueline (mezzo-soprano, Girard)
Setting: Rural France, 17th century

Act I. *A forest.* The woodcutter Sganarelle and his wife Martine complain vociferously to one another about their marriage, and their argument ends by Sganarelle striking his spouse with a stick (*duo*: 'Non je te dis que je n'en veux rien faire'). After the intervention of a neighbour, Mr Robert, the two agree to call a truce, though Martine still vows to obtain revenge. Valère and Lucas, two servants of the wealthy Géronte, appear on the scene and inform Martine that their master has sent them in search of a doctor to cure the dumbness that has afflicted his daughter Lucinde. Martine sees her opportunity for vengeance and suggests that Sganarelle is the man they seek. She warns Valère and Lucas that at first Sganarelle will deny he is a doctor but that they may easily extract a true confession by beating him. Sganarelle appears, singing a drinking song (*couplets*: 'Qu'ils sont doux'), following which Valère and Lucas spring to action (*trio*: 'Monsieur n'est-ce pas vous qui vous appelez Sganarelle?'). At first Sganarelle protests that he is a mere woodcutter, but is soon more than happy to admit anything after receiving a thorough drubbing from Valère and Lucas. A chorus of woodcutters (*chœur des fagotiers*: 'Nous fesons tous') brings down the curtain.

Act II. *A room in the house of Géronte.* After Léandre, Lucinde's lover, is heard in a brief serenade about how vain it is to resist the power of love (*sérénade*: 'Est-on sage dans le bel âge?'), the action of the story continues. Géronte complains to Lucinde's nurse Jacqueline that Léandre is too poor to marry Lucinde and that her hand is destined for another; Jacqueline in turn warns that riches do not make love (*couplets*: 'D'un bout du monde à l'autre bout'). Sganarelle makes a grand appearance in doctor's robes and sets about to diagnose Lucinde (*sextuor*: 'Eh! bien charmante demoiselle'). When the mock doctor spews a series of nonsense syllables, all those assembled express wonder at his learning; he suggests a remedy of bread dipped in wine. Following the consultation scene, Sganarelle meets Léandre, who explains that Lucinde has merely feigned dumbness in order to avoid an undesirable marriage. Sganarelle proposes a *divertissement* to Léandre to lift his spirits (*final*: 'Sans nous, tous les hommes deviendraient malsains').

Act III. *Near the house of Géronte.* Sganarelle has agreed to make Léandre his apothecary so that the latter may effect entry into Géronte's house to see Lucinde. Sganarelle admits that he is not a real doctor, but that he will continue to practise the profession, since it brings lucrative rewards, even if patients are not cured (*air*: 'Vive la médecine'). A chorus of peasants attempts to extract professional advice from Sganarelle (*scène et chœur*: 'Sarviteur, Monsieur le Docteur'). The scene shifts back to a room in Géronte's house, where Sganarelle is seen flirting with Jacqueline. Géronte reports that Lucinde's condition has deteriorated, so the mock doctor and his apothecary begin another consultation. Soon after seeing her lover, however, Lucinde bursts into speech and declares that she will only marry Léandre (*couplets et ensemble*: 'Rien n'est capable mon Père'). Géronte begs Sganarelle to make her dumb again; while Sganarelle takes him aside, Lucinde and Léandre manage to escape together. Sganarelle is blamed for the elopement. Géronte calls for the police commissioner and threatens to have Sganarelle hanged, a turn of events that Martine finds none too distressing when she happens upon the scene. Finally, Léandre and Lucinde appear. Léandre explains that he has just received a large inheritance from a deceased uncle and would rather be given the hand of Lucinde by her father. Géronte agrees. The work closes with the chorus of woodcutters that was heard at the end of Act I.

Faust (first performed Théâtre-Lyrique, 19 March 1859)

Cast: Faust (tenor, Barbot); Méphistophélès (bass, Balanqué); Valentin (baritone, Raynal); Wagner (baritone, Cibot); Marguerite (soprano, Miolan-Carvalho); Siébel (soprano, Faivre); Marthe (soprano, Duclos)
Setting: Germany, 16th century

Act I. *Faust's study.* The philosopher Faust is deeply depressed by his inability to reach fulfilment through knowledge, and contemplates suicide. He fills a cup with a vial of poison, but is stopped short of drinking the deadly liquid by the sound of a pastoral chorus. He condemns happiness, science, and faith, and calls upon Satan for guidance. Méphistophélès appears (*duo*: 'Me voici!'). Faust confesses to him that he seeks youth above wealth, glory, and power. Méphistophélès agrees to provide the philosopher with what he wants, in return for eventual service in the nether regions. When Faust hesitates to agree to that condition, Méphistophélès conjures up a vision of Marguerite at her spinning wheel. Faust then signs the document and is transformed into a young nobleman.

Act II. *Fairgrounds at the town gates. A tavern is seen on the left.* The curtain opens to a festive chorus of students, soldiers, burghers, young girls, and matrons (*chœur*: 'Vin ou bière'). Valentin appears, clutching a medallion given to him by his sister Marguerite; he is about to leave for battle and instructs his friends, including Wagner and Siébel, to look after her. They sit down for a final drink. Méphistophélès suddenly materializes and entertains them with a song about the golden calf (*ronde*: 'Le veau d'or'). Valentin is incited to anger when Méphistophélès takes the name of his sister lightly, but his sword breaks in mid-air before reaching its target. Confronted with a sinister supernatural power, Valentin and his companions brandish the crossed pommels of their swords before the devil (*chœur*: 'De l'enfer'). Méphistophélès is left alone on stage, but is soon joined by Faust and a group of waltzing villagers (*valse et chœur*: 'Ainsi que la brise légère'). When Marguerite appears among them, Faust offers his arm to her; she modestly rejects his advance and quickly departs.

Act III. *Marguerite's garden.* Siébel is enamoured of Marguerite and leaves a bouquet for her (*couplets*: 'Faites-lui mes aveux'). Faust and Méphistophélès enter the garden; while the devil busies himself with procuring a gift for Marguerite, Faust apostrophizes her home and the protective embrace of nature (*cavatine*: 'Salut demeure chaste et pure'). Méphistophélès returns and positions a jewel box for the young girl. Marguerite enters, wondering about the young gentleman who approached her earlier. She sings a ballade about the King of Thulé, discovers both the bouquet and the jewel box, and excitedly tries on earrings and a necklace (*scène et air*: 'Il était un Roi de Thulé'). Dame Marthe, Marguerite's guardian, tells her that the jewels must be a gift from an admirer. Méphistophélès and Faust join the two women; the former attempts to seduce Marthe and Faust converses with Marguerite, who still remains somewhat reluctant (*quatuor*: 'Prenez mon bras'). While Faust and Marguerite temporarily disappear from view, Méphistophélès casts a spell over the daisies in the garden. The two return and Marguerite allows herself to be embraced by Faust (*duo*: 'Laisse-moi, laisse-moi contempler ton visage'); she suddenly breaks away, however, and asks him to leave. Convinced that his efforts have been futile, Faust resolves to abandon the entire project. He is held back by Méphistophélès, who bids him to listen to what Marguerite has to say at her window. Upon hearing her wish for his quick return, Faust makes his presence known and seizes her hand; as she lets her head fall upon his shoulder, Méphistophélès cannot restrain his laughter.

Act IV. *Marguerite's room.* Marguerite has given birth to Faust's child and is ostracized by young girls in the street. Saddened that Faust has abandoned her, she sits down to spin (*air*: 'Il ne revient pas'). Siébel, ever faithful, attempts to encourage her. *A public square.* The return of Valentin is heralded by a Soldiers' March and it becomes clear that matters will take a turn for the worse. After receiving evasive replies from Siébel to enquiries about his sister, Valentin furiously charges into the house. While he is inside, Méphistophélès satirically plays a lover delivering a serenade beneath Marguerite's window (*sérénade*: 'Vous qui faites l'endormie'). Valentin reappears and demands to know who is responsible for Marguerite's fall from innocence. Faust draws his sword; in the ensuing duel Valentin is mortally wounded. As he dies, he lays the blame upon Marguerite and damns her for eternity. *A Cathedral.* Marguerite is seen attempting to pray but is at first prevented from doing so by the voice of Méphistophélès and a chorus of demons. She eventually succeeds in completing her prayer but faints when Méphistophélès unleashes a final imprecation.

Act V. *The Harz Mountains. Walpurgisnacht.* A chorus of will-o'-the-wisps is heard as Méphistophélès and Faust appear. They are soon surrounded by a group of witches (*chœur*: 'Un, deux, et trois'). Faust wishes to flee but Méphistophélès hastens to carry him off. *A decorated cavern peopled with queens and courtesans of antiquity.* In the midst of a sumptuous banquet Faust sees an image of Marguerite and demands to be taken to her. As Méphistophélès and Faust depart, the mountain closes and the witches return. *The interior of a prison.* Marguerite has been incarcerated for infanticide, but, through the offices of Méphistophélès, Faust has obtained keys to her cell. Marguerite awakens to the sound of Faust's voice; they sing a love duet (*duo*: 'Oui c'est toi je t'aime') and Faust begs her to flee. Méphistophélès appears and urges Faust and Marguerite to follow him. Marguerite resists and calls for divine protection. Faust looks on with despair and falls to his knees in prayer as her soul rises to heaven (*apothéose*: 'Christ est ressuscité!').

Philémon et Baucis (first performed Théâtre-Lyrique, 18 February 1860)

Cast: Philémon (tenor, Froment); Baucis (soprano, Miolan-Carvalho); Jupiter (bass, Battaille); Vulcain (bass, Balanqué); a Bacchante (soprano, Sax).
Setting: Mythological Phrygia

Act I. *The hut of Philémon and Baucis.* Philémon and his wife sing of their enduring love despite advanced age (*duo*: 'Du repos voici l'heure'). Hearing the blaspheming of their neighbours (*chœur*: 'Filles d'Athor'), Philémon decries those who dare offend the gods. A storm wells up and there is a knock on the door. Jupiter and Vulcain appear in disguise and ask for shelter, explaining that they have been turned away by all the neighbours. Philémon receives them graciously. Jupiter is pleased that at least one mortal has demonstrated hospitality, but Vulcain expresses displeasure at the whole adventure and wishes he were back at his smith's hearth in Mount Etna (*couplets*: 'Au bruit des lourds marteaux'). Jupiter teases Vulcain for having lost the beautiful Vénus to Mercure (*ariette*: 'Hé! Quoi!'). Baucis brings goat's milk to the two guests. When Jupiter expresses surprise that she seems so content in humble surroundings, Baucis tells him that her happiness is the result of love for Philémon. Her only regret is that youth cannot be restored to enable her to start her life with him again (*romance*: 'Ah! si je redevenais belle'). Philémon brings in more food and Baucis entertains the guests with the fable of the town mouse and the country mouse. Much to the astonishment of the couple, Jupiter is able to fill the empty water pitcher with wine. Jupiter accounts for this by explaining that he and Vulcain are messengers from the gods, who have come to punish the evil neighbours of Philémon and Baucis. He puts the couple to sleep, promising that a blissful future awaits them upon their awakening (*final*: 'Allons triste buveur').

Act II. *A temple.* The decadent neighbours of Philémon and Baucis are using the temple for orgiastic celebrations. At the outset they are seen in a half-awakened state, having succumbed to the effects of their festivities (*chœur de l'ivresse*: 'Dans l'ombre de la nuit'). A Bacchante urges them to rise and partake of the pleasures of wine. They resume their merry-making (*chœur des bacchantes*: 'Filles d'Athor'). Vulcain suddenly appears to warn them that they are invoking the wrath of the gods by their disrespectful behaviour. The townspeople laugh him away, shouting that they cannot be frightened into submission. They declare that man is master of the world (*chœur des blasphèmes*: 'Nous chantons aux lueurs'). Jupiter himself finally eradicates the entire blasphemous group by engulfing the temple in fire (*final*: 'Jupiter!').

Act III. *The hut has been converted into a palace.* Philémon and Baucis are seen asleep. Baucis awakens and quickly realizes that she and Philémon have had youth restored to them (*ariette*: 'Philémon m'aimerait encore'). She awakens her mate but is annoyed when he does not recognize her at first; she playfully resists his ardent advances and runs off. Vulcain and Jupiter appear set to return to Olympus, but when the latter catches a glimpse of the beautiful rejuvenated Baucis he decides to stay (*couplets*: 'Vénus même n'est pas plus belle'). Jupiter instructs Vulcain to distract Philémon while he attempts to seduce his wife. Baucis sings of the joys of youth (*air*: 'Ô riante nature'). Jupiter appears, reveals his true identity, and confesses love to her (*duo*: 'Relevez-vous jeune mortelle'). Unable to resist the attentions of a god, she succumbs to his advances and grants him a kiss. At that moment Philémon happens upon them. He curses the seducer of Baucis but is made aware of who he is only after Jupiter angrily leaves. Much to the amusement of Vulcain, the couple quarrels (*trio*: 'Qu'est-ce-donc?'). Baucis is finally overcome by regret at having betrayed Philémon and devises a plan to make Jupiter lose interest in her. She promises to be Jupiter's forever in return for a single request. Jupiter lustily agrees to the bargain. He realizes that he has been duped when Baucis reveals that she wishes to have old age restored to them (*romance et final*: 'Sous le poids de l'âge'). Philémon and Baucis gladly return to the tranquil existence that they had enjoyed at the outset of the first act.

La Colombe (first performed at the Théâtre de Bade, 6 August 1860)

Cast: Sylvie (*première chanteuse légère*, Miolan-Carvalho); Mazet (*première dugazon*, Faivre); Horace (*premier ténor léger*, Roger); Maître Jean (*première basse d'Opéra-Comique*, Balanqué)
Setting: Near Florence

Act I. *A small cottage.* Mazet, manservant to the impoverished Horace, sings to his master's dove while feeding it (*romance*: 'Apaisez blanche colombe'). Maître Jean, the majordomo of the Countess Sylvie, arrives with the intention of purchasing the bird for her. Mazet explains that the dove does indeed have remarkable prowess as a messenger and that he will try to persuade his master to sell it. Despite his dire straits—and much to the astonishment of Maître Jean—Horace cannot part with his pet (*romance et trio*: 'Qu'il garde son argent'). Maître Jean learns, however, that Horace is enamoured of Sylvie and hastens to report this to her. He suggests that Sylvie herself attempt to purchase the dove; she hesitates at first, but, upon reflecting jealously about the splendid parrot of her society rival Amynte, she agrees to Maître Jean's idea. Alone, Sylvie expresses confidence that the power of love will make Horace surrender his pet (*air*: 'Je veux interroger ce jeune homme'). Horace is overjoyed to receive Sylvie, and she promptly announces that she will stay for dinner (*quatuor*: 'Ô douce joie').

Act II. *Same set*. Maître Jean has volunteered to help prepare the meal and sings about the art of cooking (*air*: 'Le grand art de cuisine'). Mazet returns from a shopping expedition empty handed because merchants will not extend Horace's line of credit. After lengthy discussion with Maître Jean about the best way to serve various dishes which are clearly impossible to prepare under the circumstances, Horace and Mazet set the table and resolve to kill the dove in order to offer a meal (*duo*: 'Il faut d'abord dresser la table!'). In the interim, Sylvie is overcome with tender thoughts for Horace (*romance*: 'Que de rêves charmants'). They sit down to eat, and just as Sylvie is about to ask Horace for his dove, he tells her that it has been killed. Mazet appears with a roasted bird; to the relief of all, however, it is not the dove but rather the parrot of Amynte that had escaped earlier. Sylvie expresses her happiness that Horace's dove is still alive, for it will forever remind her of his love.

La Reine de Saba (first performed Opéra, 28 February 1862)

Cast: Adoniram (*fort ténor*, Gueymard); Soliman (*première basse de grand opéra*, Belval); Amrou (*second ténor*, Grisy); Phanor (baritone, Marié); Méthousaël (*première basse d'opéra comique*, Coulon); Sadoc (*deuxième ou troisième basse*); Balkis (*chanteuse falcon*, Gueymard); Benoni (*dugazon*, Hamackers); Sarahil (*duègne*, Tarby)
Setting: The biblical kingdom of Soliman

Act I. *Adoniram's workshop*. Adoniram is troubled by his own mortal limitations as an artist and calls upon his divine forefather, Tubalkaïn, to help him with his latest project: the casting of a monumental bronze vessel (*air*: 'Inspirez-moi, race divine'). His reflections are interrupted by the appearance of his young apprentice, Benoni, who tells him that the illustrious Balkis, Queen of Sheba, will be arriving in Jerusalem shortly to visit Soliman. Benoni sings of her legendary beauty (*romance*: 'Comme la naissante aurore'). Adoniram then receives three of his workers—Amrou, Phanor, and Méthousaël; they ask for a better salary and the secret password which only master craftsmen may know. Adoniram rejects their petition, and, after high priest Sadoc makes a brief appearance to escort Adoniram to an audience with the king and his radiant guest, the three vow to take revenge (*quatuor et trio*: 'Il nous repousse'). *Before the temple*. A long instrumental march heralds the arrival of Soliman and Balkis (*cortège et final*). The assembled masses, many of them Adoniram's workers, greet the royal couple with joyous acclaim. When the din of the welcome has subsided, Soliman expresses his love for Balkis and asks for a ring that she has promised him as a symbol of their betrothal. Balkis reluctantly gives it to him. She marvels at the magnificence of the temple and asks to see its builder. When Adoniram appears, Balkis praises him for the splendour of his work; her voice awakens in him a mysterious echo of his own ancestral background.

Responding to a request from the queen, Adoniram calls the assembled masses to attention with a mysterious hand signal: when they see it members of the various trades group themselves together and march by Soliman and Balkis in perfect order. Soliman is horrified by Adoniram's control over such a large segment of population. Balkis, however, is so impressed that she removes her necklace and places it around Adoniram's neck.

Act II. *The plain of Sion. A large furnace is seen at the back of the stage.* Adoniram's workers tell him that all is ready for the casting of the great bronze vessel, but he is momentarily preoccupied with the memory of his meeting with Balkis. He soon regains composure and announces to his disciples that a decisive moment is upon them. Soliman and Balkis arrive to witness the casting. At the moment the molten metal is released from the furnace, Benoni rushes to Soliman with the news that three traitorous workers have sabotaged the project. Soliman declares that it is too late to take action. The three culprits—Amrou, Phanor, and Méthousaël—gloat when a torrent of molten metal flows uncontrollably from the furnace to destroy the mould. All quickly take cover. As Adoniram looks on, the furnace explodes.

Act III. *A clearing in a wood of cedars and palms; the washing pool for the retinue of Balkis.* After two choruses and ballet for the queen's serving girls and their counterparts from Soliman's court, Balkis sings of the feelings that Adoniram has stirred within her (*cavatine*: 'Plus grand dans son obscurité'). The artist himself unexpectedly appears. He is despondent because the casting of the vessel has failed and, claiming that he is unworthy of the queen, tears off the necklace she gave to him (*duo*: 'Qu'importe ma gloire effacée!'). When she admits that she does not love Soliman, he is more willing to reveal his own attraction to her. Balkis ends the duet by declaring outright that she is in love with Adoniram. Their encounter is suddenly interrupted by Benoni, who informs them that the Djinns (spirits from the underworld realm of Tubalkaïn) have repaired the mould and the completed bronze vessel is now in place. In response to Balkis's query about this remarkable turn of events, Adoniram admits that he is protected by the Djinns and that he is related by blood to the queen through their common forefather, Nemrod the hunter. Adoniram, Balkis, her confidante Sarahil, and Benoni sing a prayer of thanks to Tubalkaïn, while Amrou, Phanor, and Méthousaël slide by stealthily in the background, muttering that they will inform Soliman of what they have just witnessed (*septuor*: 'Ô Tubalkaïn mon père').

Act IV. *A hall in Soliman's palace.* An opening ceremonial chorus (*chœur*: 'Soliman notre roi') belies the king's dejected state of mind. Balkis has not appeared for four days to conclude the marriage pact, causing Soliman to ruminate about the futility of being so taken with her (*récit et cavatine*: 'Sous les pieds d'une femme'). Sadoc announces that Amrou, Phanor, and Méthousaël are waiting for an audience. They have come to tell Soliman about the nocturnal tryst of Adoniram and Balkis, and to urge him to take action (*quatuor*: 'Hâtez-vous de parler'). Remembering that they are the three who disrupted the casting of the great vessel, Soliman does not believe them. Doubts enter the king's mind, however, when Adoniram comes to be relieved of his duties. Soliman tries to dissuade Adoniram by offering to share power equally with him. The artist haughtily rejects the proposal and stalks off. Abandoning Adoniram to 'eternal justice', Soliman prepares to receive the queen. Alone with the king, Balkis asks for another day before their marriage, mollifying him with a promise of an hour of her time at present (duo: 'Elle est en mon pouvoir'). He admits that he has been told of the illicit nocturnal rendezvous and, in his inebriated state, alternately threatens the queen and sings of his love for her. When he attempts to force Balkis into an embrace, Sarahil slips in from behind a curtain and pours a strong narcotic into the king's cup. The sleeping potion quickly takes effect, and, as the king falls into unconsciousness, he curses Balkis. She seizes the moment to snatch the ring from Soliman's inert hand.

Act V. *An isolated ravine. Stormy weather.* Adoniram waits anxiously for the queen so that they may flee together. He is surprised by the sudden appearance of Amrou, Phanor, and Méthousaël. The three press him to give in to their demands, but Adoniram responds only with contemptuous remarks (*quatuor*: 'Tes yeux ont su me reconnaître'). They stab him and flee. Balkis comes upon the mortally wounded artist and, after a final embrace, slips the ring she has recovered from Soliman on to his finger. The queen's slaves and followers rush on to witness her brief eulogy over the corpse (*final*: 'Emportons dans la nuit').

Mireille (first performed Théâtre-Lyrique, 19 March 1864)

Cast: Mireille (soprano, Miolan-Carvalho), Vincent (tenor, Morini); Ourrias (baritone, Ismaël); Maître Ramon (*première basse*, Petit); Taven-Andreloux (contralto, Faure-Lefèvre); Vincenette (*première dugazon*, Reboux); Maître Ambroise/Un Passeur (*deuxième basse*, Wartel); Clémence (*deuxième dugazon*, Albrecht)
Setting: Provence, 19th century

Act I. *A mulberry orchard.* A group of peasant girls is seen gathering mulberry leaves (*introduction*: 'Chantez Magnanarelles'). The good sorceress Taven sadly notes that the girls will one day experience sorrow in love. Clémence, one of the gatherers, retorts that this will not happen because she will be taken from Provence by a handsome prince to live in a splendid castle in a far-off land. Another of the girls, Mireille, quietly says that she would be satisfied simply if a young lad confessed love to her in complete sincerity. Her comrades are not surprised that she has such modest expectations because she has been seen lately in the company of Vincent, son of the poor basket-weaver Ambroise. They playfully mock her for being in love with one of such humble birth. After her friends leave, Mireille tells Taven that the rumour is true. Taven warns her that wealth and poverty are ill matched but assures Mireille that she will help her at any moment of distress. Vincent himself passes by and Mireille engages him in conversation. He describes his family, telling Mireille that she is even more attractive than his sister (*duo*: 'Vincenette a votre age'). Mireille is flattered by the comparison. She would like to linger but is called away by her friends. Before they part company they agree that, if misfortune should befall either of them, the other will make a pilgrimage to the shrine of the Saintes-Maries to pray for assistance.

Act II. *At the entry to the arena at Arles.* A number of peasants have gathered to sing and dance a Provençal farandole. Mireille enters with her friends. When Vincent also comes upon the festivities, a few bystanders suggest that the two sing a love song together. Mireille and Vincent oblige with a traditional Provençal song (*Chanson de Magali*: 'La brise est douce et parfumée'). After this, the assembled revellers take up the farandole again and go into the arena. Mireille stays behind and is called aside by Taven, who warns her that this is the time of year that she will be courted (*chanson*: 'Voici la saison mignonne'). The young girl innocently believes that this has little to do with her, as her heart is already taken. She sings of her love for Vincent (*air*: 'Trahir Vincent'). In accordance with Taven's prediction, the bull-tamer Ourrias has set his eyes upon Mireille. He greets her with the promise that, as his wife, she will be treated like a queen; he confesses his love to her (*couplets*: 'Si les filles'). Because he is much too insistent for her taste, she leaves hastily. Mireille's father Ramon steps out of the arena and Ourrias complains to him that Mireille has not been receptive. At that moment Vincent and his father, Ambroise, also walk into the square. Ambroise informs Ramon that Vincent is enamoured of a girl from a higher social class and asks him how he would handle the situation. Ramon answers that Vincent should forget about her immediately. If he resists, Ramon suggests use of the iron fist that all fathers must wield to make members of the family see reason (*final*: 'Un père parle en père'). Ramon goes on to say that, in his own household, no one would dare to defy him. Mireille reappears and reveals that it is she who is the object of Vincent's love and that the feeling is mutual. Ramon immediately disowns her. He is about to strike Mireille when she falls on her knees to beg for clemency and understanding. Ramon angrily curses Vincent and his father, and vows that he will not let Mireille see the lad again. Mireille and Vincent sing that the attempt to separate them is in vain; Ambroise returns Ramon's verbal abuse; the assembled crowd deplores Ramon's cruelty.

Act III. *The Val d'enfer. Near the cave of Taven.* Ourrias and his friends are returning home together. They advise him to forget about Mireille. He tells them to go on without him for he is still distressed by her rejection and has made up his mind to take revenge upon Vincent (*duo*: 'Ils s'éloignent'). Vincent enters, also distraught by the turn of events at the end of the previous act. He is surprised by Ourrias, who accuses him of using sorcery to obtain Mireille's affection. Vincent is angered by the accusation, but Ourrias ignominiously strikes the unarmed lad with his trident. Hearing the moans of the wounded Vincent, Taven rushes from her cave and curses Ourrias. *On the banks of the Rhône. The waters are lit by a full moon.* Ourrias is plagued by remorse and fear (*scène et chœur*: 'Ah! que j'ai fait!'). He calls upon the ferryman to transport him to the opposite bank. Suddenly, white ghosts emerge from the depths of the river. A distant bell sounds midnight. The phantoms float on the surface of the water and disappear into the fog. Ourrias, terrified, renews his call to the ferryman. He jumps on to the boat when it finally appears. As it sets off, the waters become very agitated. The ferryman reminds Ourrias of Vincent. The boat sinks; Ourrias drowns.

Act IV. *The interior courtyard of Ramon's farm. Saint John's Eve. Bonfires light the scene.* Ramon and his farm hands celebrate the harvest (*chœur*: 'Après la moisson finie'). Mireille is despondent and enters the house. After the hands leave, Ramon bemoans the fact that the laws of nature have made his daughter unhappy. Mireille opens her window and dreamily remembers the *Chanson de Magali.* Day begins to break and a shepherd boy appears playing his pipes. After singing a brief song about the new day (*chanson*: 'Le jour se lève'), he leaves. Mireille envies him for the blissful existence he must lead (*ariette*: 'Heureux petit berger'). Vincenette unexpectedly rushes on to tell Mireille about what has happened to Vincent (*duo*: 'Ah! parle encore'). Despite Vincenette's assurances that Taven is looking after Vincent and that he will recover, Mireille resolves to undertake the perilous pilgrimage across the Crau desert to the Saintes-Maries. She gathers all her jewels as an offering and the two girls pray for Vincent's recovery. *The Crau desert. A vast rocky and arid plain. Midday.* Mireille is exhausted and disoriented (*air*: 'En marche'). She sees a mirage of a splendid city on the edge of a lake. She collapses in despair when it disappears. The shepherd's pipes in the distance revive her and she pushes on to her destination.

Act V. *Outside the chapel of the Saintes-Maries.* The faithful cross the stage and enter the chapel, invoking divine protection (*chœur*: 'Ô vous qui du haut du ciel'). Vincent appears and looks for Mireille; he prays for her safety (*cavatine*: 'Anges du paradis'). Mireille stumbles in, delirious and on the brink of death. She is ecstatic at being reunited with Vincent and has a vision of the sky opening to receive her (*final*: 'Grand Dieu!'). Ramon and others rush on. Mireille dies of sunstroke, but her soul is beckoned to an eternally blissful existence in heaven by a celestial voice.

Roméo et Juliette (first performed Théâtre-Lyrique, 27 April 1867)

Cast: Juliette (soprano, Miolan-Carvalho); Stéphano (soprano, Daram); Gertrude (mezzo-soprano, Duclos); Roméo (tenor, Michot); Tybalt (tenor, Puget); Benvolio (tenor, Laurent); Mercutio (baritone, Barré); Paris (baritone, Laveissière); Grégorio (baritone, Troy jeune); Capulet (*basse chantante*, Troy); Frère Laurent (bass, Cazaux); Le Duc (bass, Wartel); Frère Jean (bass, Neveu). Setting: Renaissance Verona

After a tempestuous orchestral introduction depicting the animosity between the rival Capulet and Montaigu houses, the curtain opens for a declaimed choral prologue that summarizes the tragedy.

Act I. *A masked ball at the Cpulet residence.* The assembled guests sing of the pleasures that await them that evening (*introduction*: 'L'heure s'envole'). The young nobleman Paris marvels at the magnificence of the ball, but Tybalt, nephew to Lady Capulet, assures him that he will become oblivious to the splendour when he sees the beautiful Juliette, daughter of Capulet. When Capulet escorts his daughter into the hall, she does indeed become the centre of attention. Capulet jovially invites the guests to dance in adjoining rooms and is more than happy to allow Paris to escort Juliette. When the stage is clear, the masked Roméo Montaigu and his friends, Mercutio and Benvolio, come out of hiding. Because of their disguises, they have been able to enter the rival Capulet house unnoticed. Roméo has developed reservations about their prank and wishes to leave. He explains that he has recently had a dream that has filled him with foreboding about the adventure. Mercutio lightly dismisses his premonitions as the work of the fairy queen Mab (*Ballade de la reine Mab*: 'Mab, la reine des mensonges'). Roméo derives little comfort from the ballade but then suddenly catches a glimpse of Juliette through an open door. He falls in love instantly. Spellbound, Roméo is dragged away by his friends just as Juliette and her nurse Gertrude enter. Gertrude speaks to her in glowing terms about Paris as a future husband. Juliette for her part protests that she is not interested in marriage (*ariette*: 'Je veux vivre'). The nurse leaves and, just as Juliette herself is about to return to the dance, Roméo steps out from a corner. After a few words, the two realize that their destinies are linked (*madrigal*: 'Ange adorable!'). In the ensuing exchange, Roméo realizes that he has fallen in love with a Capulet. Despite the fact that Roméo has replaced his mask, Tybalt is able to identify him. After Roméo rushes out, Tybalt reveals to Juliette that she has been speaking with a hated Montaigu. The guests return to centre stage: Roméo and his friends are among them. Mercutio suspects that they have been noticed, so the Montaigus bid a hasty retreat. Capulet does not allow Tybalt to follow them and encourages his guests to continue their merry-making.

Act II. *The Capulet garden. To the left, Juliette's window and balcony. Night.* Roméo has separated himself from his friends and has stealthily made his way into the Capulet garden. He apostrophizes Juliette as the morning sun (*cavatine*: 'Ah! lève-toi soleil'). Shortly after she appears on her balcony, Roméo reveals his presence. She asks for a declaration of love and fidelity and he enthusiastically gives it. Their tender words are momentarily interrupted by Grégorio and other Capulet servants, who run through the garden in search of a Montaigu page boy seen on the grounds (*scène et chœur*: 'Personne! le page aura fuit'). When all is still again, Roméo re-emerges from hiding (*duo*: 'O nuit divine'). Juliette confirms that she will be ready to marry him at any time and Roméo renews his pledge. Once again they are interrupted, this time by Gertrude, who calls Juliette into the house. The two lovers part reluctantly.

Act III. *The cell of Frère Laurent. Daybreak.* An off-stage chorus of monks is heard. Frère Laurent enters with a basketful of plants and flowers which he will use to make secret potions. He sings of nature's wonders (*chœur et cavatine*: 'Berceau de tous les êtres'). Roméo rushes on and reveals his love for Juliette Capulet. Juliette soon follows with Gertrude. The two lovers ask Laurent to marry them. Convinced of the strength of their attachment, he performs the ceremony (*trio et quatuor*: 'Dieu qui fis l'homme à ton image'). *The street in front of the Capulet house*. Roméo's page, Stéphano, taunts the Capulets with a song about a turtledove held prisoner in a nest of vultures (*chanson*: 'Que fais-tu, blanche tourterelle'). This draws Grégorio and other Capulet servants out of the house (*final*: 'Ah! voici nos gens!'). Stéphano immediately repeats the refrain of his song in their presence and challenges Grégorio to a duel. Mercutio is indignant over the fact that Grégorio is duelling with a mere child. Tybalt warns Mercutio to mind his words and the two engage in a duel themselves. When Roméo rushes on, Tybalt turns immediately to confront him. The latter retains his composure and asks Tybalt to forget the days of hatred between the two families. It is Mercutio who takes it upon himself to defend Roméo's honour. He resumes his duel with Tybalt and is wounded when Roméo throws himself between the two combatants. Suddenly angered by this development, Roméo seeks revenge; he duels with Tybalt and inflicts a mortal blow. A fanfare and march herald the arrival of the duke. The partisans of both houses clamour for justice and, after acquainting himself with what has happened, the duke exiles Roméo from Verona. Before the curtain falls, the members of the two households renew their words of hatred.

Act IV. *Juliette's room. Daybreak*. Juliette pardons Roméo for having killed one of her relatives (*duet*: 'Va! je t'ai pardonné'). The two sing of their love on their wedding night. Roméo suddenly breaks from the embrace when he hears the morning lark. Juliette at first refuses to believe him but then comes to grips with reality. The two realize that they must part company before they are discovered together. Shortly after Roméo leaves, Capulet, Gertrude, and Frère Laurent enter the room (*quatuor*: 'Juliette! Ah! le ciel soit loué'). Capulet informs his daughter that Tybalt's last wish was for Juliette to marry Paris and that the wedding has already been arranged. Juliette is in despair. When her father leaves, she tells Frère Laurent that she would rather die than marry Paris. He suggests a ruse by means of which she and Roméo may escape. She is to drink a potion that will make her appear dead. The Capulets will transport her body to the family tomb, where Roméo will meet her. Juliette agrees to the plan. She summons her courage (*air*: 'Dieu quel frisson court dans mes veines'). She hesitates when she sees a vision of the bleeding Tybalt but finally empties the vial. *A magnificent hall in the house of Capulet*. Juliette is led on with a wedding march (*cortège nuptial*). The guests offer their best wishes and present her with gifts, but, as Capulet takes her by the arm into the chapel, she collapses. Much to the horror of all, Capulet cries out that she is dead.

Act V. *The underground crypt of the Capulets. Juliette lies outstretched on a tomb*. Frère Laurent learns from another monk, Frère Jean, that Roméo has not received the letter explaining the ruse because his page has been attacked. Frère Laurent instructs Jean to find another messenger. After an instrumental interlude meant to depict Juliette's state, Roméo appears. Believing Juliette dead, he drinks the poison he has been carrying with him. At that moment, she awakens and the two sing of their love. Roméo tells her that he has just imbibed fatal poison. As he weakens, Juliette uncovers a sword hidden in her clothes and stabs herself. With a final monumental effort, Roméo and Juliette ask for divine clemency before they die.

Cinq-Mars (first performed Opéra-Comique, 5 April 1877)

Cast: Le Marquis de Cinq-Mars (*premier ténor d'opéra*, Dereims); Le Conseiller de Thou (*premier baryton*, Stéphanne); Père Joseph (*première basse*, Giraudet); Le Vicomte de Fontrailles (*premier baryton d'opéra comique*, Barré); Le Roi (*basse chantante*, Maris); The Chancellor (bass, Bernard); De Montmort (tenor, Lefèvre); De Montrésor (bass, Teste); De Brienne (baritone, Collin); De Monglat (tenor, Chenevière); De Château-Giron (baritone, Villars); Eustache (bass, Davoust); Princesse Marie de Gonzague (*première chanteuse falcon*, Chevrier); Marion Delorme (*première chanteuse légère*, Franck-Duvernoy); Ninon de l'Enclos (soprano, Périer)
Setting: 17th century France, last years of the reign of Louis XIII

Act I. *The chateau of the Marquis de Cinq-Mars.* A chorus of local nobles celebrates the imminent rise in prominence of Cinq-Mars (*chœur et scène*: 'A la cour vous allez paraître'); some suggest that his ultimate debt of allegiance is to Cardinal Richelieu, others to the king. For his part, Cinq-Mars is not preoccupied by political matters: alone with his closest friend de Thou, he confesses that he loves the Princess Marie de Gonzague (*duo*: 'Henri! vous nous parliez'). Both intuitively recognize that this liaison will not end well. The guests reappear. Among them this time are Père Joseph, a *porte-parole* for Cardinal Richelieu, and the Princess Marie. The former announces that Cinq-Mars has been called to the royal court and also that a political marriage has been arranged between the Princess Marie and the king of Poland. Cinq-Mars and Marie agree to meet later that evening. After the guests depart Marie yearns for her heart to be overcome by nocturnal peace and gentleness (*récit et cantilène*: 'Nuit resplendissante'). Cinq-Mars enters and confesses his love to Marie; before he leaves she reciprocates his declaration (*duo*: 'Ah! vous m'avez pardonné ma folie').

Act II. *The apartments of the King.* After an opening chorus extolling the beauty of the courtesan Marion Delorme, Fontrailles, Montrésor, Montmort, De Brienne, Monglat, and other courtiers discuss the rise in the influence of Cinq-Mars with the king. The courtiers are dissatisfied with the inordinate power that Cardinal Richelieu has wrested for himself and wonder whether Cinq-Mars will eventually join their cause. Marion reports that the Cardinal has been threatening to exile her; Fontrailles is surprised and is sure that Paris would become quite dull without her elegant salons (*chanson*: 'On ne verra plus dans Paris'). The courtesan announces that she will throw a ball the next day which will provide an occasion to lay the groundwork for a plot to oust the Cardinal. Cinq-Mars appears and is greeted by the courtiers (*chœur*: 'Ah! monsieur le grand Écuyer'). Marie has just arrived at court and the two lovers are reunited (*cavatine*: 'Quand vous m'avez dit un jour'). Just after that blissful moment, however, Père Joseph appears with news that, despite approval in principle from the king for the marriage of Cinq-Mars and Marie, the Cardinal has refused to sanction the union, preferring instead to follow the original plan of having Marie marry the king of Poland. *At the house of Marion Delorme.* The evening opens with a reading of Madeleine de Scudéry's latest novel *Clélie*, followed by an extended balletic pastoral *divertissement* including a sonnet rendered by a shepherd (*sonnet*: 'De vos traits mon âme est navrée'). The more serious business is reserved for later (*La Conjuration*: 'Viendra-t-il?'). Font-railles assures everyone that Cinq-Mars will join the conspiracy and, as predicted, he does soon appear. Cinq-Mars declares that the king is no longer in full command of the land and that the mission to remove the Cardinal is a just one; civil war is anticipated and he assures his co-conspirators that he has arranged a treaty with Spain which commits its armies to intervene on their side. De Thou suddenly breaks in with a warning to Cinq-Mars not to open French soil to a foreign power, but the Marquis remains resolute.

Act III. *The next day. Exterior of a chapel.* A meeting for the conspirators is about to take place; Marie unexpectedly appears and she and Cinq-Mars agree to exchange marriage vows immediately (*trio*: 'Madame c'est le lieu du rendez-vous'). After they leave, Père Joseph and Eustache emerge from hiding: the latter has been a spy and gives a complete report of the plot to Père Joseph. Père Joseph savours the power he yields over the fate of Cinq-Mars (*air*: 'Tu t'en vas'). He confronts Marie with the news that the Marquis will be hanged as a traitor for dealing independently with a foreign power; the Polish ambassador will return shortly from a hunting expedition with the king and he advises her that, if she responds favourably to him, Cinq-Mars will be spared. When the royal party does arrive, Marie reluctantly capitulates (*chœur*: 'Hallali! chasse superbe').

Act IV. *A prison.* As he awaits execution, Cinq-Mars bemoans the fact that Marie has abandoned him; none the less he summons her image for consolation in his final hour (*cavatine*: 'Ô chère et vivante image'). Marie enters, explains the ruse of Père Joseph, and admits her continuing love for Cinq-Mars (*duo*: 'Ah! qu'ai-je dit!'). De Thou outlines plans that have been prepared to allow Cinq-Mars to escape the next day. When the Chancellor and Père Joseph appear with the news that the Marquis is to die before dawn, it is clear that these plans will not be put into effect (*final*: 'Messieurs, appelez à vous votre courage'). Before Cinq-Mars is led to the gallows, he and de Thou intone a final prayer.

Polyeucte (first performed Opéra, 7 October 1878)

Cast: Polyeucte (*fort ténor*, Salomon); Sévère (*premier baryton*, Lassalle); Félix (*première basse*, Bérardi); Néarque (baritone, Auguez); Albin (*première basse*, Menu); Siméon (*deuxième basse*, Bataille); Sextus (*premier ténor léger*, Bosquin); Un Centurion (*troisième basse*, Gaspard); Pauline (*soprano dramatique*, Krauss); Stratonice (mezzo-soprano, Caldéron)
Setting: Melitène, capital of Armenia, 3rd century AD

Act I. *Pauline's chambers*. Pauline's attendants are seen preparing her quarters for the night (*chœur et scène*: 'Déjà dans l'azur des cieux'). She confesses to her confidante Stratonice that she has been troubled by a dream in which her husband, the Armenian aristocrat Polyeucte, receives baptismal waters and is immediately struck down by Jupiter. Polyeucte himself soon appears, troubled by a new sacrifice of Christians that will be offered the next day to the pagan gods (*duo*: 'Quelle morne douleur'). Pauline is horrified to learn that her husband is indeed sympathetic to their cause. Polyeucte also tells her that the day of the sacrifice has been advanced in order to coincide with the visit of an Imperial general named Sévère to celebrate a recent victory. Pauline needs no introduction to Sévère: she tells her husband that Sévère had formerly confessed love to her and, were it not for the intervention of her father, she would today be married to him. *A public square with a triumphal arch*. The Imperial party, followed by the retinue of Félix, governor of Armenia and father of Pauline, is led on to the strains of a triumphal march and chorus. Sévère soon recognizes Félix and Pauline; they introduce Polyeucte to him as Pauline's husband. Since he is still in love with her, Sévère is dismayed to learn that Pauline has married (*quatuor avec chœur*: 'Je frémis'). The curtain is brought down to a reprise of the march and chorus.

Act II. *A garden with a small Vestal temple*. The sounds of celebration are heard in the distance. Sévère, however, cannot partake of the festivities since he suffers from the knowledge that Pauline is married to another (*récit et cavatine*: 'Ô dieux, ô puissances célestes'). He draws aside as Pauline enters with her attendants. She deposits an offering at the temple of Vesta. Sévère makes his presence known and recalls their time together (*duo*: 'Pauline! . . . Dieux!'). Pauline begs him to forget the past since her duty is now to her husband; she asks him not to attempt to see her again. Pauline returns to the temple and Sévère takes cover when he sees Polyeucte and his friend Néarque approaching. They speak in vague terms about Polyeucte's impending conversion to Christianity. *A wild site. Moonlight*. Sextus, a young Roman patrician, sings a barcarolle in the distance as a small boat carrying various young people in leisurely postures glides by. Siméon, a Christian elder, decries the decadence of the pagans and ushers in a group of his Christian brethren. After a long prayer, Néarque introduces Polyeucte to the assembled worshippers while Sévère is seen to assume a place of hiding. Polyeucte is baptized in an extended ceremony.

Act III. *A room in the palace of Félix*. The pagan high priest Albin tells Félix, Polyeucte, and Sévère that he has had reports of a nocturnal meeting of Christians and vows that Jupiter will wreak vengeance upon them. Sévère is reluctant to express such unequivocal hatred for Christians; he indicates that he witnessed the gathering and, without revealing a name, that a person of considerable social distinction was baptized. After Félix and Albin leave, Polyeucte thanks Sévère for his generosity but adds that he would gladly die for his beliefs. Before he leaves, Sévère expresses surprise that Polyeucte could so easily put faith above Pauline (*récit et cantilène*: 'Quoi! c'est peu de perdre Pauline!'). The sacrifice of Christians at the temple is imminent and Polyeucte informs his friend Néarque that he intends to smash the pagan idols (*duo*: 'Où pensez-vous aller?'). Néarque agrees to join him. *A public square with the temple of Jupiter in the background.* Following a long sacred procession to lead on the Christian victims as well as a pagan balletic *divertissement*, Polyeucte bursts on to the scene declaring that he is Christian and launches an imprecation against the false gods of Rome. Pauline attempts unsuccessfully to restrain him from carrying out his project of destroying the idols. The assembled crowd cries out for vengeance.

Act IV. *A prison.* Polyeucte's thoughts are only for the hereafter and the vacuity of temporal existence (*stances*: 'Source délicieuse'). Pauline implores him to save himself and their marriage by renouncing his conversion, but her husband is deaf to her pleas (*duo*: 'Polyeucte! il en est temps encore'). He turns for comfort and solace to a recitation of the principal events in the life of Christ. Pauline declares that she is willing to die on Polyeucte's behalf. Polyeucte attempts to persuade his wife to embrace Christianity so that they may be united after death. Sévère suddenly appears and offers Polyeucte an avenue for escape (*trio*: 'Sévère! vous ici!'). Pauline urges him to seize the opportunity, but Polyeucte remains determined to meet his fate. In vain, Félix offers him a final chance to live by asking Polyeucte to render homage to the pagan gods.

Act V. *A public square with an arena in the background.* The crowd calls for the blood of Christians. Polyeucte is led on and intones a Christian Credo. Pauline runs to join him, declaring that she has embraced the Christian faith. Both sing the Credo as they are led into the arena to their death.

Le Tribut de Zamora (first performed Opéra, 1 April 1881)

Cast: Xaïma (soprano, Daram); Hermosa (soprano, Krauss); Iglésia (soprano, Janvier); Manoël (tenor, Sellier); Ben-Saïd (baritone, Lassalle); Hadjar (bass, Melchissédec); the King (bass, Giraudet)
Setting: Asturias, Northern Spain, 10th century

Act I. *A public square in Oviedo.* After a chorus to introduce Manoël and Xaïma, two lovers who are to be joined in wedlock that day, they share a strophic dawn song (*aubade*: 'Ô blanc bouquet de l'épousée'). A fanfare sounds the arrival of an Arab delegation representing the Caliph Abderrahmman led by Ben-Saïd. He has come to Christian territories to claim the annual tribute of one hundred virgins stipulated by a treaty following the defeat of the Christians in battle at Zamora many years before. Xaïma recalls details from the battle, including how the defenders sang a national hymn as they went down to defeat. Ben-Saïd is struck by her beauty and character, and admits his love to her. Manoël intervenes, warning that he and Xaïma will be married within an hour. Ben-Saïd advises him not to be so confident, but the lovers sing a duet about their future bliss (*duo*: 'Pourquoi ce langage odieux?'). The king appears bearing news that the town of Oviedo must give up twenty virgins that very day as its part of the annual tribute. The names of the young girls are drawn by lot and among them are Iglésia and Xaïma (*final*: 'Vous osez proférer'). As they are dragged away, Manoël leads his compatriots in a rendition of their national hymn.

Act II. *Picturesque site on the banks of the Oued-el-Kédir near Cordoba*. It is the anniversary of the victory at Zamora and a celebration is in progress. The mad woman Hermosa, captured at the battle, joins the festivities. She is ridiculed, but Hadjar, brother of Ben-Saïd, orders her to be left in peace, citing an aphorism from the Koran: 'Hold fools as holy or be damned.' Hermosa likens herself to a swallow that has flown to heaven (*scène et air*: 'Pitié car je ne suis qu'une pauvre hirondelle'). The one hundred virgins are led in with an elaborate cortège. Manoël, disguised as an African soldier, has made the trip as well. Hadjar immediately recognizes him as the Spanish soldier who, in the heat of battle, saved his life by dressing a wound. Hadjar offers to help Manoël in any way he can. Manoël tells him that the virgins are to be auctioned that very day and that he hopes to buy Xaïma's freedom. Before the auction, Hermosa sees Xaïma and claims vaguely to recognize her; her remarks are quickly dismissed. Hadjar supplies Manoël with a large sum of money but he is, none the less, outbid by Ben-Saïd (*final*: 'A cent dinars d'or').

Act III. *A large room in the palace of Ben-Saïd*. Xaïma has become part of Ben-Saïd's household. He attempts to cheer her by hosting an elaborate balletic spectacle, following which he begs her to accept his love (*romance*: 'O Xaïma'). Hadjar enters with Manoël and announces that he is the Spanish soldier who once saved him. Ben-Saïd feels duty bound to offer Manoël any of his possessions. It is not material goods that Manoël desires but Xaïma, and Ben-Saïd is so outraged by the request that he orders his soldiers to take him away. Xaïma interrupts by threatening to commit suicide and Manoël is released. Ben-Saïd warns Xaïma that his love for her may turn to blind hatred. Hermosa wanders in and begins to question Xaïma about her background (*duo*: 'De sa mort qui donc parle ici?'). They learn that each was present at the battle of Zamora; Hermosa sings the national hymn and regains her reason; soon both realize that they are mother and daughter.

Act IV. *Gardens in the palace of Ben-Saïd*. Manoël has returned to Ben-Saïd's palace, risking his life in the hope of seeing Xaïma once again (*cavatine*: 'Que puis-je à présent regretter'). She does appear and they resolve to commit suicide together (*duo*: 'Manoël, sans moi tu veux mourir?'). Hermosa intervenes and reproaches Xaïma for wishing to leave her so soon after being reunited (*romance*: 'Tu trouves donc'). Manoël and Xaïma beg her for forgiveness. Ben-Saïd makes another attempt to win over Xaïma's heart and, when she does not respond, tries to force himself upon her (*duo*: 'Lui! Manoël, encore'). Hermosa reappears and attempts to persuade Ben-Saïd to let her daughter go free. Faced with his persistent refusals, she stabs him. Hadjar and a group of soldiers run on, but, as they draw their swords around Hermosa, Hadjar reminds them of the aphorism from the Koran. Hermosa, Manoël, and Xaïma are permitted to leave unscathed.

SELECTED BIBLIOGRAPHY

THIS bibliography lists only books and journal articles that are cited in the text. It does not include manuscript documents, printed musical scores and librettos, auction and dealer catalogues, or reviews and bulletins in nineteenth-century daily or weekly newspapers.

ALCANTARA, COMTESSE D', *Marcello: Sa vie, son œuvre, sa pensée, et ses amis* (Geneva, 1961).

ALDINGTON, RICHARD, *Introduction to Mistral* (London, 1956).

ALLÉVY, MARIE-ANTIONETTE, *La Mise-en-scène en France dans la première moitié du dix-neuvième siècle* (Paris, 1938).

ASHBROOK, WILLIAM, *Donizetti and his Operas* (New York, 1982).

BAILBÉ, JOSEPH-MARIE, 'Autour de la Reine de Saba: Nerval et Gounod', in *Regards sur l'Opéra* (Paris, 1976), 113–26.

BALTHAZAR, SCOTT L., 'Rossini and the Development of Mid-Century Lyric Form', *Journal of the American Musicological Society*, 41 (1988), 102–25.

BARBIER, JULES, Preface to Édouard Noel and Edmond Stoullig (eds.), *Les Annales du théatre et de la musique*, 12 (1886), pp. i–xxii.

BARBIER, PATRICK, *La Vie quotidienne à l'Opéra au temps de Rossini et de Balzac* (Paris, 1987).

BARZUN, JACQUES, *Berlioz and the Romantic Century* (3rd edn., New York, 1969).

BELLAIGUE, CAMILLE, *Gounod* (Paris, 1910).

BERLIOZ, HECTOR, *Le Chef d'orchestre: Théorie de son art* (Paris, 1856).

—— *Correspondance inédite de Hector Berlioz, 1819–1868,* ed. D. Bernard (Paris, 1879).

—— *New Letters of Berlioz, 1830–1868,* trans. and ed. Jacques Barzun (New York, 1954).

—— *Correspondance générale,* ed. Pierre Citron (vols. 2–3; Paris, 1975–8).

—— *Les Grotesques de la musique,* ed. Léon Guichard (Paris, 1969).

—— *The Memoirs of Hector Berlioz, 1830–1868,* trans. and ed. David Cairns (London, 1970).

BIZET, GEORGES, *Lettres: Impressions de Rome, 1857–60,* ed. Louis Ganderax (Paris, 1907).

BUDDEN, JULIAN, *The Operas of Verdi* (3 vols.; New York, 1973–81).

BUSCH, HANS, *Verdi's Aida: The History of the Opera in Letters and Documents* (Minneapolis, 1978).

BUSSER, HENRI, *Gounod* (Lyons, 1961).

CANAT, RENÉ, *L'Hellénisme des romantiques* (3 vols.; Paris, 1955).

CARLESON, MARVIN, *The French Stage in the Nineteenth Century* (Metuchen, 1972).

Castil-Blaze, *Théâtres lyriques de Paris: L'Académie Impériale de Musique de 1645 à 1855* (Paris, 1855).

—— *L'Art des vers lyriques* (Paris, 1858).

CHINN, GENEVIÈVE, 'The Académie Impériale de Musique: A Study of its Administration and Repertory from 1862 to 1870', Ph.D. thesis (Columbia, 1969).

CHORLEY, HENRY, *Thirty Years' Musical Recollections* (New York, 1926).

COHEN, JEAN, *Structure du langage poétique* (Paris, 1966).

CONATI, MARCELLO, *Interviews and Encounters with Verdi* (London, 1984).

CROSTEN, WILLIAM, *French Grand Opera: An Art and a Business* (New York, 1948).

CURTISS, MINA, 'Gounod before Faust', *Musical Quarterly*, 38 (1952), 48–67.

—— *Bizet and his World* (New York, 1958).

DAHLHAUS, CARL, *Between Romanticism and Modernism*, trans. Mary Whittall (Berkeley, 1980).

DAVISON, HENRY (ed.), *From Mendelssohn to Wagner, Being the Memoirs of J. W. Davison* (London, 1912).

DEAN, WINTON, 'Bizet's Ivan IV', in Herbert van Thal (ed.), *Fanfare for Ernest Newman* (London, 1955), 58–85.

DEBILLEMONT, J. J., 'Charles Gounod: Étude', *Nouvelle Revue de Paris*, 2 (1864), 559–68.

DÉDÉYAN, CHARLES, *Le Thème de Faust dans la littérature européenne* (2 vols.; Paris, 1959).

DESARBRES, NÉRÉE, *Sept ans à l'Opéra* (Paris, 1864).

DICKINSON, A. E. F., 'Berlioz' "Bleeding Nun" ', *Musical Times*, 102 (1961), 584–8.

EDWARDS, TUDOR, *The Lion of Arles* (New York, 1964).

FARIS, ALEXANDER, *Jacques Offenbach* (New York, 1981).

FAUQUET, JOËL-MARIE, 'Quatre versions de Roméo et Juliette', *L'Avant-scène*, 41 (1982), 66–71.

FIORENTINO, P. A., *Comédies et comédiens* (2 vols.; Paris, 1866).

—— *Les Grands Guignols* (Paris, 1870).

FITZLYON, APRIL, *The Price of Genius: A Life of Pauline Viardot* (London, 1964).

FULCHER, JANE, *The Nation's Image: French Grand Opera as Politics and Politicized Art* (Cambridge, 1987).

GAGNON, P. A., *France since 1789* (New York, 1964).

GAUTIER, THÉOPHILE, *Histoire du Romantisme* (Paris, 1857).

—— *Portraits et souvenirs littéraires* (Paris, 1892).

GENEST, EMILE, *L'Opéra-Comique connu et inconnu* (Paris, 1925).

GOSSETT, PHILIP, 'Verdi, Ghislanzoni, and Aida: The Uses of Convention', *Critical Inquiry*, 1 (1974), 291–324.

—— *Anna Bolena and the Artistic Maturity of Gaetano Donizetti* (Oxford, 1985).

GOUNOD, CHARLES, *Autobiographie de Charles Gounod et articles sur la routine en matière d'art,* ed. Georgina Weldon (London, 1875).

—— 'Considérations sur le thèâtre contemporain', in Édouard Noel and Edmond Stoullig, *Les Annales du théâtre et de la musique*, 11 (1885), pp. i–xxii.

GOUNOD, CHARLES, *Le Don Juan de Mozart* (Paris, 1890).

—— *Mémoires d'un artiste* (Paris, 1896).

—— 'Lettres à Bizet', *Revue de Paris*, 6 (1899), 677–703.

—— 'Lettres à Madame Augé de Lassus', *La Revue musicale*, 7 (1907), 312–16.

—— 'Lettres à Richomme', *Revue hebdomadaire*, 26 Dec. 1908, 151–69; 2 Jan. 1909, 23–42.

—— 'Six lettres inédites', *Revue politique et littéraire*, 57 (1919), 347–50.

—— 'Lettres de Gounod au Baron de Vendeuvre', *La Revue musicale*, 16 (1935), 110–15.

GOURRET, JEAN, *Ces hommes qui ont fait l'Opéra* (Paris, 1984).

GÜNTHER, URSULA, 'La Genèse de Don Carlos de Giuseppe Verdi', *Revue de musicologie*, 60 (1974), 87–158.

HAHN, REYNALDO, 'A propos de Mireille', in *Thèmes variés* (Paris, 1946).

HALÉVY, LUDOVIC, *Carnets* (Paris, 1935).

HARDING, JAMES, *Gounod* (London, 1973).

HEMMINGS, F. W. J., *Culture and Society in France, 1848–91* (London, 1971).

HENSEL, SEBASTIEN, *Die Familie Mendelssohn* (Berlin, 1880).

HÉRITTE DE LA TOUR, LOUIS, *Mémoires de Louise Héritte–Viardot* (Paris 1922).

HERVEY, ARTHUR, 'Gounod and his Influence', *French Music in the Nineteenth Century* (London, 1903).

HILLEMACHER, P. L., *Gounod* (Paris, 1906).

HOWARTH, W. D., *The Sublime and the Grotesque: A Study of French Romantic Drama* (London, 1975).

HUEBNER, STEVEN, 'Paris Opera Audiences, 1830–1870', *Music and Letters*, 70 (1989), 203–56.

—— 'Italianate Duets in Meyerbeer's Grand Operas', *Journal for Musicological Research*, 8 (1989), 203–58.

ISNARDON, JACQUES, *Le Théâtre de la Monnaie* (Brussels, 1898).

JULLIEN, ADOLPHE, *Musiciens d'aujourd'hui* (Paris, 1892).

KASTNER, L. E., *A History of French Versification* (Oxford, 1903).

KOLB, MARTHE, *Ary Scheffer et son temps* (Paris, 1937).

KNAPP, BETTINA, *Gérard de Nerval: The Mystic's Dilemma* (University, Alabama, 1980).

LANDORMY, PAUL, *Faust de Gounod* (Paris, 1922).

LANGEVIN, KENNETH, ' "Au silence des belles nuits": The Earlier Songs of Charles Gounod', Ph.D. thesis (Cornell, 1978).

LASSUS SAINT-GENIÈS, JACQUES AND JEAN DE, *Gounod et son temps* (Paris, 1963).

LEBOIS, ANDRÉ, 'La Reine de Saba ou amour et franc-maçonnerie', *Littératures*, 15 (1968), 18–67.

LEGOUVÉ, ERNEST, *Eugène Scribe* (Paris, 1874).

LIEBRECHT, HENRI, *Théâtre de la Monnaie, 250ᵉ anniversaire* (Brussels, 1949).

LONGYEAR, RALPH, 'The Opéras–Comiques of D. F. E. Auber', Ph.D. thesis (Cornell, 1957).

MACHIN, HOWARD, 'The Prefects and Political Repression, February 1848–December 1851', in Roger Price (ed.), *Revolution and Reaction in 1848 and the Second French Republic* (London, 1975), 286–302.

MAPLESON, JAMES, *The Mapleson Memoirs, 1848–1888* (London, 1888).

MARIX-SPIRE, THÉRÈSE, 'Gounod and his First Interpreter', *Musical Quarterly*, 31 (1945), 193–211, 299–317.

MERRIMAN, JOHN M., *The Agony of the Republic: The Repression of the Left in Revolutionary France, 1848–1851* (New Haven, 1978).

MEYERBEER, GIACOMO, *Briefwechsel und Tagebücher*, ed. Heinz Becker (4 vols. to date; Berlin, 1960–   ).

MISTRAL, FRÉDÉRIC, *Correspondance de Frédéric Mistral à Paul Meyer et Gaston Paris*, ed. Jean Boutière (Paris, 1978).

—— *Mirèio/Mireille*, ed. Charles Rostaing (Paris, 1978).

MOREEN, ROBERT, 'Integration of Text Forms and Musical Forms in Verdi's Early Operas', Ph.D. thesis (Princeton, 1975).

MORTIER, A., *Les Soirées parisiennes de 1883* (Paris, 1884).

NERVAL, GÉRARD DE, 'Petits châteaux de Bohème', *Poésies et souvenirs* (Paris, 1974).

NEWMAN, ERNEST, 'Faust in Music', in *Musical Studies* (London, 1905).

NICOLAISON, JAY, *Italian Opera in Transition, 1871–1893* (Ann Arbor, 1980).

NOEL, ÉDOUARD, and EDMOND STOULLIG (eds.), *Les Annales du Théâtre et de la Musique* (1875–1916).

NOSKE, FRITS, *French Song from Berlioz to Duparc*, trans. Rita Benton (New York, 1970).

PAGNERRE, LOUIS, *Charles Gounod: Sa vie et ses œuvres* (Paris, 1890).

PAQUIS, C., *Histoire de l'Espagne* (Paris, 1844).

PENDLE, KARIN, *Eugène Scribe and French Opera of the Nineteenth Century* (Ann Arbor, 1979).

PIERROT, ROGER, 'Le Don Marcelle Maupoil à la Bibliothèque Nationale', in *Cahiers Ivan Tourguenev, Pauline Viardot, Maria Malibran*, 4 (1980), 32–4.

PINCHERLE, MARC, *Musiciens peints par eux–mêmes* (Paris, 1939).

PLESSIS, ALAIN, *De la fête impériale au mur des fédérés, 1852–1871* (Paris, 1979).

POUGIN, ARTHUR, 'Gounod écrivain', *Rivista musicale italiana*, 19 (1912), 239–85, 637–95; 20 (1913), 453–86.

POUPET, MICHEL, 'Gounod et Bizet', *L'Avant-scène*, 41 (1982), 106–17.

PROD'HOMME, J. G., 'Miscellaneous Letters by Charles Gounod', *Musical Quarterly*, 4 (1918), 618–53.

—— and A. Dandelot, *Gounod: Sa vie et ses œuvres* (2 vols.; Paris, 1911).

QUICHERAT, LOUIS-MARIE, *Traité de versification française* (Paris, 1850).

RÉMOND, RENÉ, *Les Droites en France* (3rd edn., Paris, 1982).

REYER, ERNEST, *Quarante ans de musique* (Paris, n.d.).

RIDLEY, JASPER, *Napoléon III and Eugénie* (New York, 1979).

ROBINSON, DAVID M., *Sappho and her Influence* (Boston, 1924).

ROQUEPLAN, NESTOR, *Regain: La Vie parisienne* (Paris, 1853).

ROYER, ALPHONSE, *Histoire de l'Opéra* (Paris, 1875).

SAINT-SAËNS, CAMILLE, 'The Manuscript Libretto of *Faust*', *Musical Times*, 62 (1921), 553–7.

—— *Portraits et souvenirs* (Paris, 1899).

SAND, GEORGE, *Lettres inédites de George Sand et de Pauline Viardot, 1839–1849*, ed. Thérèse Marix-Spire (Paris, 1959).

—— *George Sand: Correspondance*, ed. Georges Lubin (vols. ix–x; Paris, 1972).

SANTLEY, CHARLES, *Student and Singer* (New York, 1882).

SCHAPIRO, LEONARD, *Turgenev: His Life and Times* (Oxford, 1978).

SHAW, GEORGE BERNARD, *The Great Composers: Reviews and Bombardments*, ed. Louis Crompton (Berkeley, 1878).

SOULIÉ, FRÉDÉRIC, *Deux séjours: Province et Paris* (Brussels, 1836).

SOUBIES, A., and H. D. Curzon, *Documents inédits sur le Faust de Gounod* (Paris, 1912).

STEIN, JACK M., *Richard Wagner: The Synthesis of the Arts* (Detroit, 1960).

STOULLIG, EDMOND, *Les Annales du Théâtre, 1900* (Paris, 1901).

TENÉO, MARTIAL, 'Le Centenaire de Charles Gounod', *La Grande Revue*, 96 (1918), 589–607.

THURNER, A., *Les Transformations de l'Opéra-Comique* (Paris, 1865).

TIERSOT, JULIEN, 'Gounod's Letters', *Musical Quarterly*, 5 (1919), 40–61.

TURGENEV, IVAN, *Lettres inédites de Turgenev à Pauline Viardot et à sa famille*, ed. Henri Grandjard and Alexandre Zviguilsky (Lausanne, 1972).

—— *Nouvelle correspondance inédite*, ed. Alexandre Zviguilsky (2 vols.; Paris, 1971–2).

VIARDOT, P., *Souvenirs d'un artiste* (Paris, 1910).

VIEL CASTEL, COMTE HORACE DE, *Mémoires du Comte Horace de Viel Castel sur le règne de Napoléon III* (Paris, 1883).

WADDINGTON, PATRICK, 'Courtavenel: The History of an Artists' Nest and its Role in the Life of Turgenev', Ph.D. thesis (Cambridge, 1972).

WALKER, FRANK, *The Man Verdi* (London, 1962).

WALSH, T. J., *Second Empire Opera: The Théâtre-Lyrique, 1851–1870* (London, 1981).

WEIGALL, ARTHUR, *Sappho of Lesbos, her life and times* (New York, 1932).

WELDON, GEORGINA, *Mon Orphelinat et Gounod en Angleterre* (3 vols.; London, 1875).

—— *My Orphanage and Gounod in England* (3 vols., London, 1882).

WRIGHT, LESLIE, 'Bizet before Carmen', Ph.D. thesis (Princeton, 1981).

ZELDON, THEODORE, *France 1848–1945: Taste and Corruption* (Oxford, 1980).

INDEX

Index compiled by Peva Keane